AF473991

Deng Guoyuan

Impressum / Colophon
Dieser Katalog erscheint anlässlich der Ausstellung / This catalogue is published on the occasion of the exhibition
Deng Guoyuan.
Butterflies Conquer the Dinosaurs' Garden
Ludwig Museum im Deutschherrenhaus, Koblenz
12. Mai – 09. Juni 2019 / May 12 – June 9, 2019

Herausgeber / Editor
Beate Reifenscheid, Ludwig Museum, Koblenz

Redaktion und Organisation / Editing and organization
Suzana Leu, Ludwig Museum, Koblenz

Autoren / Authors
Wang Duanting, Research Fellow, Supervisor of Doctorate Candidate, Institute of Fine Arts, Chinese National Academy of Arts
Lao Zhu
Liang Kegang
Robert C. Morgan
Beate Reifenscheid, Director Ludwig Museum, Koblenz

Verwaltung / Administration
Thomas Rinck, Ludwig Museum, Koblenz

Sekretariat / Office
Barbara Leers, Ludwig Museum, Koblenz

Aufbauteam / Construction team
Holger Schumacher, Marcus Mose, Slawek Wisniewski Ludwig Museum, Koblenz
Cai Feng, Mason Hollway, Li Hongyu, Zhu Jiabiao, Yuan Song, Liu Tianxu

Abbildungen / Images
Alle Kunstwerke Deng Guoyuan / All artworks by Deng Guoyuan

Foto- und Bildnachweis / Photo credits
© Deng Guoyuan Atelier / studio für die Seiten / pages: 8, 10, 11, 12, 13, 14, 15, 16, 17, 18, 19, 20, 21, 26, 29, 30, 31, 36, 39, 42, 43, 44, 45, 49, 50, 51, 52, 53, 54, 55, 56, 57, 58, 59, 217

© Liu Tianxu für die Seiten / pages: 79, 82, 83, 84, 85, 90, 129, 133, 147, 151, 222

© Liu Gaofeng für die Seiten / pages: 86-220

© Simon de Myle „Noah's ark on the Mount Ararat", Öl auf Leinwand / oil on panel, 1570, 114 x 142 cm © Sotheby's Paris 2011, für das Werk auf Seite / for the work on page 18

Umschlagabbildung / Cover illustration
© Deng Guoyuan, 2019, Fotografie / Photograph Lin Gaofeng, 2019

Für alle Werkabbildungen / For all the works' pictures: Liu Gaofeng; für alle Aufnahmen bei Eröffnungen / for all the pictures at the opening of Deng Guoyuan Studio

Übersetzungen / Translations
Chinesisch zu Englisch: Li Jin für den Text von Lao Zhu / Chinese to English: Li Jin for the text by Lao Zhu
Kathrin Fuchs und / and Madeleine Brook für / for NTL, Firenze

ISBN 9788836643691

Bibliografische Information der Deutschen Nationalbibliothek / Bibliographic information of the German National Library

Deng Guoyuan

Butterflies Conquer the Dinosaurs’ Garden

SilvanaEditoriale

Vorwort

Beate Reifenscheid

Die Welt befindet sich in einem radikalen Umbruch: Traditionen werden auf den Prüfstand gestellt, oder leichtfertig „über Bord geworfen". Der Trend, immer das Neueste, das Schnellste, das (vermeintlich) Avantgardistischste betreiben und besitzen zu wollen, beflügelt zahlreiche Kulturen der sogenannten zivilisierten Welt.

Auf der Strecke bleibt viel, vor allem das Bewusstsein, dass dieser Planet endlich ist und es nicht Refugien für Glückselige gibt. Letztlich wird die Menschheit gezwungen sein, sich auf eine gemeinsame Linie des Daseins zu verständigen, wenn sie sich nicht selbst abschaffen will.

Deng Guoyuan, seit Jahrzehnten erfolgreicher Künstler in China und zudem bis Ende 2018 Präsident der renommierten Tianjin Academy of Fine Arts, die im Ranking an dritter Stelle der acht staatlichen Kunstakademien firmiert, befasst sich geradezu exzessiv mit der Frage nach dem Dasein in einer Welt, in der die Natur nicht nur gezähmt, sondern durch die massiven Eingriffe der Menschen bedroht ist. In einer langen, überaus logischen Abfolge von zahlreichen neuen Schöpfungen hat er einen Weg beschritten, der aus der chinesischen Tradition der Tuschezeichnung, zu abstrakten Ölgemälden herausführte. Bereits hier zeigte sich die Fragmentierung einzelner Bildmotive, die gerade noch Reminiszenzen an Natur erkennen ließen, die zu artifiziellen Installationen führt, in denen die gebändigte Natur nur noch aus der Retorte denkbar und schließlich als Relikt konserviert wird. Ein weiterer Schritt war dann seine Erfindung von *Noahs Garten*, jenem im Alten Testament verbrieften Diener Gottes, Noah, der von der Sintflut verschont wurde und mit seiner Arche neues Leben in eine neue Welt zu retten vermochte. *Noahs Garten* ist in Dengs Vorstellung jedoch ein künstlicher Bezirk, der ganz und gar in einer artifiziellen Weltvorstellung einmündet. In einem Spiegellabyrinth gefangen, entfalten sich hier neue Spezies und Kreaturen.

Foreword

Beate Reifenscheid

The world is undergoing a radical change: traditions are put to the test or "thrown overboard" without thought. The trend of always wanting to pursue and own whatever is the latest, fastest, (supposedly) most avant-garde is the inspiration for numerous cultures of the so-called civilized world.

Much is left behind, in particular the awareness that this planet is finite and that there are no refuges for fortunate individuals. Ultimately, humanity will be forced to agree on a common line of existence if it does not wish to condemn itself to extinction.

Deng Guoyuan has been a successful artist in China for decades. He is also President of the renowned Tianjin Academy of Fine Arts, which ranks third among China's eight state art academies. Deng deals almost excessively with the question of existence in a world in which nature has not only been tamed but is threatened by massive human intervention. In a long, extremely logical sequence of numerous new creations, he has taken a path that has led from the Chinese tradition of ink drawing to abstract oil painting, to the fragmentation of individual pictorial motifs in which it is just about possible to recognise reminiscences of nature, to artificial installations in which it is only possible to conceive tamed nature in term of retort and is finally preserved as a relic. Another step on this path was his invention of *Noah's Garden*, a title that uses the figure of the Old Testament servant of God who was spared by the Flood and was able to save new life for a new world with his ark. In Deng's imagination, however, *Noah's Garden* is an artistic district that leads to an entirely artificial imagination of the world. Trapped in a labyrinth of mirrors, new species and creatures unfold.

Numerous academics have examined his artistic approach to this current work and have opened up new perspectives of understanding. Many thanks go to them for

Zahlreiche Wissenschaftler haben sich mit seinem künstlerischen Ansatz für diese aktuelle Publikation befasst und neue Perspektiven des Verständnisses erschlossen. Ihnen gilt unser großer Dank für die intensive Zusammenarbeit. Insbesondere aber verdanken wir Deng Guoyuan und seinem Team diese einmalige Kooperation, die zunächst durch die Ausstellung sowie dann durch die wissenschaftliche Recherche im Katalog, der wie eine Quintessenz seiner letzten Jahrzehnte zu interpretieren ist, umfassend dieses künstlerische Werk vorstellen. In seinem unermüdlichen Ringen um Antworten auf die drängenden Fragen und Probleme unserer Zeit, ist es ihm beispiellos gelungen, die Dramatik des weltweiten Transformationsprozesses bis hin zu den aktuellen Genmanipulationen in eine künstlerische Sprache zu überführen, ohne dabei die noch verbleibenden, scheinbar immer unsichtbarer werdenden Bezüge zur chinesischen Tradition gänzlich aufzugeben. Sein Œuvre wird gerade dann am besten verständlich, wenn man es in diesem Bezugsrahmen von chinesischer Tradition und westlicher Moderne verankert.

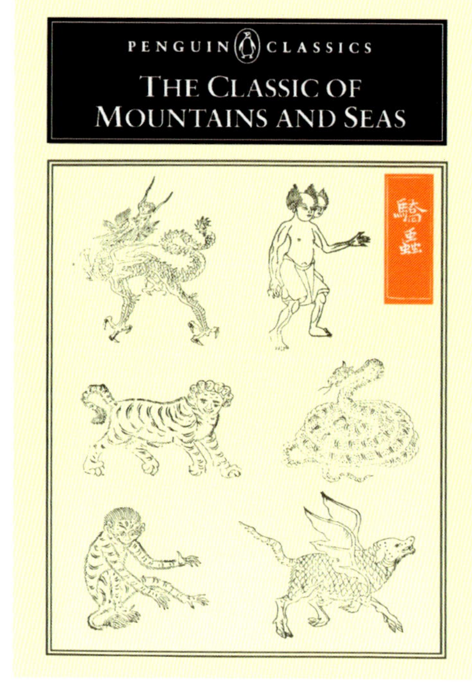

The Classic of Mountains and Seas (Penguin Classics) by Anonymous, 2000

Wir danken zugleich allen weiteren maßgeblichen Unterstützern dieses Projektes, den zahlreichen Sponsoren, die den vitalen Kulturaustausch zwischen China und Deutschland auch finanziell begleiten. Nur so konnte es gelingen, dass die Ausstellung nicht nur im Ludwig Museum in Koblenz zu sehen sein wird, sondern im Herbst dieses Jahres auch in China. Ihnen allen, die ungenannt bleiben wollen, gilt unser aufrichtigster Dank, denn ohne solch maßgebliche finanzielle Mittel wäre eine derart aufwändige Ausstellung nicht denkbar gewesen.

Auch dem Team im Ludwig Museum möchte ich nachdrücklich danken, insbesondere der wissenschaftlichen Mitarbeiterin Suzana Leu, die gewissenhaft den Katalog und die Koordination der Ausstellung betreut hat. Das gesamte Team bei Silvana Editoriale überzeugte – wie immer – durch eine reibungslose und zugleich hoch professionelle, zuverlässige Zusammenarbeit. Ohne sie, insbesondere natürlich ohne seinen Verleger, Michele Pizzi, wäre ein solcher Katalog in dieser umfassenden Form nicht entstanden und nicht im internationalen Buchhandel vertreten. Es bliebe ein wesentliches Fenster zur interessierten Kunst- und Weltgemeinschaft verschlossen. Mit dem Katalog bleibt dem Museum, sowie Deng Guoyuan, die Chance, seine Kunst und seine Mission noch nachhaltiger zu verbreiten. Denn Kunst lebt von Wahrnehmung.

their intensive cooperation. We would also like to thank in particular Deng Guoyuan and his team for this unique cooperation. It was they who first presented this sweeping artistic work through the exhibition and then through academic research in the catalogue, which can be interpreted as the quintessence of Deng in recent decades. In his tireless struggle for answers to the pressing questions and problems of our time, he has succeeded in an unprecedented conveyance of the drama of this worldwide transformation process – including even ongoing genetic manipulation – into an artistic language, without completely abandoning the remaining, apparently increasingly invisible references to Chinese tradition. His oeuvre is best understood when anchored in this frame of reference between Chinese tradition and Western modernity.

We would also like to thank all other key supporters of this project and the many sponsors who provide financial support for the vital cultural exchange between China and Germany. Only with their help was it possible to ensure that the exhibition could be seen both at the Ludwig Museum in Koblenz and in China this autumn. Our sincerest thanks go to all of you who wish to remain unnamed: this elaborate exhibition would have been inconceivable without such substantial financial means.

I would also like to express my sincere thanks to the team at the Ludwig Museum, in particular our Research Assistant Suzana Leu, who conscientiously supervised the catalogue and the coordination of the exhibition. As always, the entire team at Silvana Editoriale impressed with their very professional, reliable cooperation. Without this collaboration, and especially of course without their publisher Michele Pizzi, it would not have been possible to create such a comprehensive catalogue or to have it represented in the international book world. An essential window for the interested art and world community would have otherwise remain closed. With the catalogue, the museum, like Deng Guoyuan, has the opportunity to share its art and mission on a much sustainable scale. As art lives by being perceived.

Deng's Brave New World

Beate Reifenscheid

"Die Menschen werden ihre Unterdrückung lieben, um neue Techologien zu bewundern, die ihnen die Fähigkeit zum Denken abnehmen werden."

(Aldous Huxley, *Schöne neue Welt*, 1932)

Noch in den ersten Jahren des Millenniums entwickelte Deng Guoyuan seine Kunst aus der chinesischen Tuschemalerei. Schon damals arbeitete er aus einem anderen Modus, aus einem anderen Denken heraus. Thematisch kreist das gesamte Werk um die Auseinandersetzung mit der Natur, die er jedoch nicht in ihrer Erhabenheit oder Schönheit interpretiert, sondern immer in ihrer Zerbrechlichkeit, in ihrer Fragmentiertheit und einer fortwährenden Transformation hin zur artifiziellen Existenz.

Diesen Prozess konnte man nun in den mehr als fünfzehn vergangenen Jahren hervorragend miterleben und in ihm seine eigene Reflexion darüber zwischen Begeisterung und Verstörung verorten. Er bleibt immer in dieser spannungsvollen Dualität, die sich auf vielfältige Weise am Werk bricht, vergleichbar dem Licht, das sich im Glasprisma in vielen möglichen Facetten offenbart.

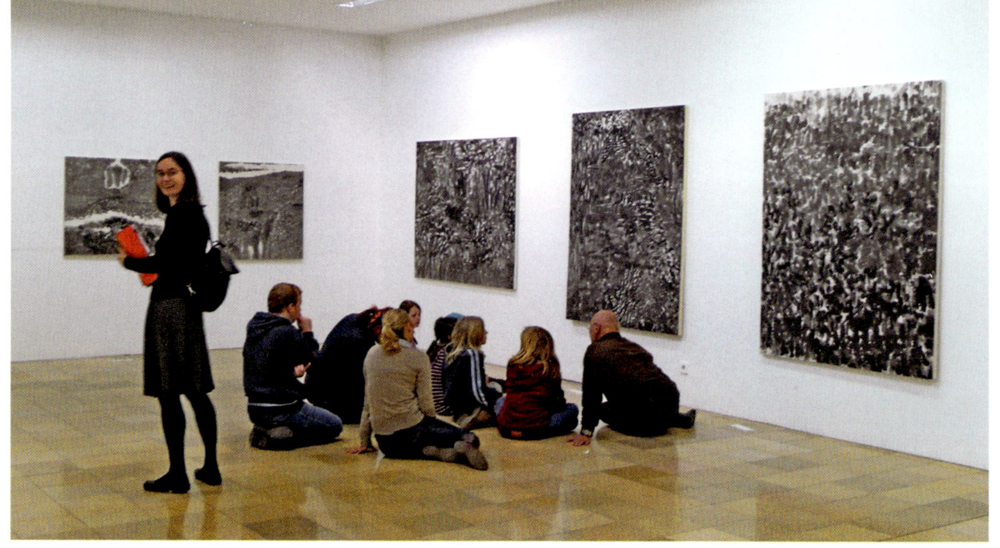

Im Garten, 2008
Ludwig Museum, Koblenz, Deutschland

In the Garden, 2008
Ludwig Museum, Koblenz, Germany

Die zum Teil großformatigen Tuschezeichnungen behielten für einen westlichen Betrachter die Anmutung einer traditionellen chinesischen Malerei, wenngleich Deng auch hier bereits den Prozess seiner radikalen Dekonstruktion begonnen hatte. In seinen stakkatoartigen kurzen Strichzeichnungen entfaltete sich ein rein abstraktes Bild, das aus Rhythmus und nuancierten Farbtonwerten in Schwarz bis Hellgrau abgestuft ist. Jedes für sich war eine abstrakte Entität, letztlich ohne konkrete Bezüge zu Benennbarem oder objektivierbarer Substanz. Vielmehr ergibt sich aus dem

Deng's Brave New World

Beate Reifenscheid

"People will come to love their oppression,
to adore the new technologies – that will undo
their capacity of thinking."

(Aldous Huxley, *Brave New World*, 1932)

Deng Guoyuan was already developing his painting method from Chinese ink painting during the early years of the millennium. Even then he was working from a different mode, with another way of thinking. Thematically, his entire oeuvre revolves around an engagement with nature, which he does not interpret against the context of its sublime aspect or its beauty, but rather against a background of its fragility, its fragmentation and a perpetual transformation towards an artificial existence.

Over the last fifteen years and more it has been possible to witness this process up close and to see in it our own reflection on it, ranging between fascination and perturbation. It is a process that always moves within this tense duality, which refracts in a multitude of ways across the works, not unlike the light that offers up its many facets of possibility as a result of passing through a glass prism.

For a Western observer, the ink drawings, many of them large in format, retain an impression of traditional Chinese painting, even though it is at this level that Deng has already initiated his process of radical deconstruction. In his brief, staccato-like line drawings there develops a purely abstract image, which, in its rhythm and nuanced tones, graduates from black to light grey. Each on its own is an abstract entity, ultimately without any concrete reference to any identifiable or objectifiable substance. Instead, it is the context of his creation and a vision that is intimately acquainted with the natural that give rise to a unique interpretation of the image, an interpretation that positions it within a field of reference, associates it with grasses in the wind, invites floral memories. But instead of a sweeping, overview landscape, familiar to us as a near-trope in the art of the Renaissance through to that of the Romantic period, the artist here draws the viewer's gaze entirely into the close-up perspective: just a little patch of garden, nature bound. This is not another formulation of the concept of a divine power, an omnipotent influence, nor a feeling of grandeur or of all-encompassing isolation. Even in the ink drawing, Deng rejects the current under-

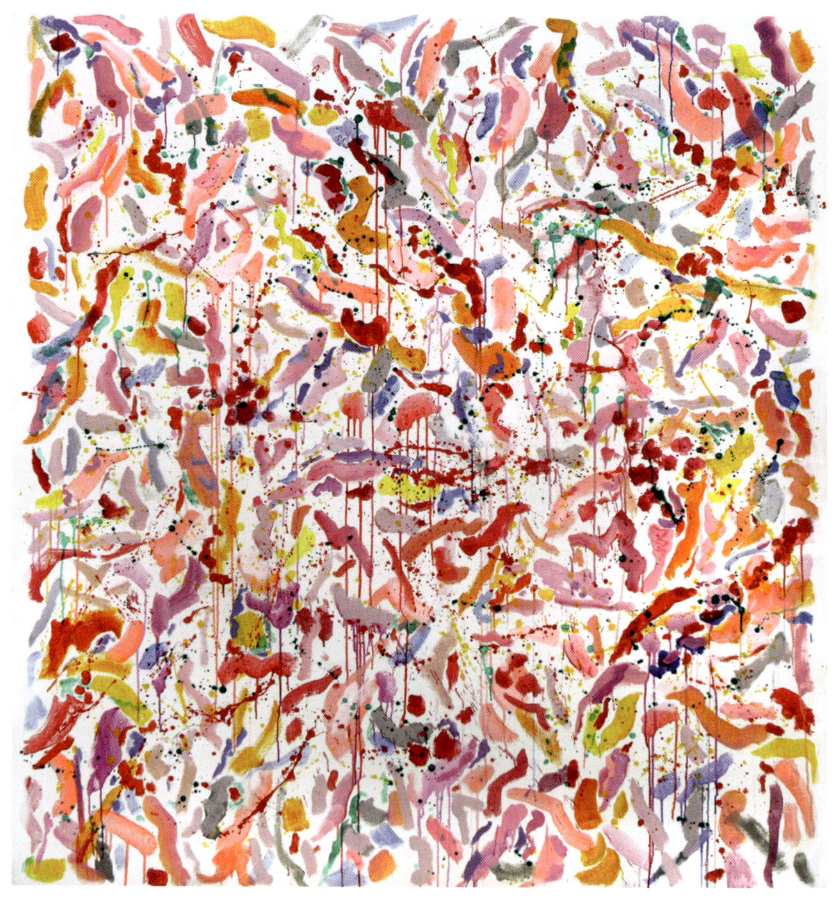

Kontext seiner Schöpfungen und eines naturhaft vertrautem Sehens eine eigene Lesart des Bildes, die dieses in Bezüge versetzt, die es ermöglichen, assoziativ an Gräser im Wind zu denken, an Reminiszenzen von Floralem. Aber statt einer Übersichtslandschaft, wie es in der Renaissance bis zur Romantik geradezu ein Topos war, senkt der Künstler hier das Augenmerk ganz und gar auf die Nahansicht, auf ein nur kleines Fleckchen Garten, auf eine gebändigte Natur. Hier stellt sich nicht das Konzept einer göttlichen Macht, eines allmächtigen Wirkens ein, kein Erhabenheitsgefühl oder Welteinsamkeit. Schon in der Tuschezeichnung verweigert Deng sich der gängigen, über Jahrhunderte tradierten Kunstauffassung innerhalb der Tuschemalerei, die im Shan Shui ihre höchste, zugleich vom spirituellen Ansatz aus betrachtet, sicherlich reinste Form der Einheit zwischen Mensch und Natur formuliert hat. Bei ihm hingegen zeigt sich die Natur gezähmt, vom Menschen bezwungen und deshalb – trotz der Schönheit seiner Zeichnung und Einfühlung in den Naturrhythmus – fragmentiert. Alles, was Menschen von der Natur wahrnehmen, bleibt letztlich ein Ausschnitt, nur Teil eines größeren Ganzen.

Im Feld Nr.5, 2007
Ölgemälde
200 × 180 cm

In the Field No. 5, 2007
Oil painting
200 × 180 cm

In den folgenden Jahren widmet Deng sich unterschiedlichsten Aspekten des Naturhaften, immer aber aus dem Blickwinkel einer zunehmenden Artifizialität. Seien es die Bruchstücke von Natur, die er in Reagenzgläsern scheinbar züchtet, oder die Pflanzen in Vogelvolieren, die getrockneten Palmwedel in Plexiglasboxen oder – sein Hauptthema – Noahs Garten in einem Spiegellabyrinth.

Hier erprobt Deng auf neuartige Weise die Überführung tradierter Landschaftssujets in die auf sich selbst verworfene Natur, die längst nicht mehr ihrer Natürlichkeit frönen darf, sondern in Substitute übersetzt wurde. Der Ausblick auf eine weit in den Raum sich erstreckende Landschaft (als Zeichen des Erhabenen und Grandiosen, der Urgewalten) wird gefangen in Spiegelflächen, an denen der Blick sich immer wieder bricht oder Raumtiefe sich als Illusion erweist. Orientierungslos zuweilen, tastet sich der Nutzer (Betrachter) des neuen Gartens durch diesen. Hier trifft er auf Pflanzen, wundersam bunte Vögel und auf ebenso farbenfroh gestaltete Taihu-Steine, ein eigener Topos im Garten der *Literati*. Noahs Garten liest sich als Reminiszenz an vergangene Traditionen, an ein ungebrochenes Verhältnis zur Natur. Schon in seinem Titel rekurriert er auf die biblische Geschichte aus dem Alten Testament von Noahs Arche. Die Erzählung berichtet von einer riesigen Sintflut, die die ganze Welt erfasste, weil Gott unzufrieden war mit den Menschen und diese auslöschen wollte. Nur mit Noah und seiner Familie hatte er Erbarmen und gab ihnen die Chance, von jeder Spezies zwei auszuwählen und sie mit einem riesigen Schiff vor den Fluten zu retten. Noah sandte nach der Flut eine Taube aus, um zu erfahren, ob es irgendwo wieder Land zum Besiedeln gäbe. Als die Taube mit einem Ölzweig zurückkam, wusste Noah, dass er die Erde wieder neu bewohnen durfte. Dies liest sich

standing of art that pertains within the tradition of ink painting, which has passed down over centuries and which, viewed also from a spiritual perspective, in Shan Shui has assuredly attained the formulation of highest, purest unity between human and nature. In Deng's work, by contrast, nature appears tamed, subjugated by humans and thus – despite the beauty of his drawing and affinity for the rhythm of nature – fragmented. Everything that humans perceive of nature remains, ultimately, a segment, just a part of a larger whole.

In the years that followed, Deng dedicated himself to a hugely diverse range of aspects of the natural, but always from the perspective of an increasing artificiality. Whether it is the fragments of nature that he seemingly grows in test tubes or the plants in aviaries, the dried palm fronds in plexiglass boxes or – his principle theme – Noah's Garden in a mirror maze.

Here, Deng is testing new ways of translating the traditional subject of the landscape to a nature that has itself been rejected, that has long been unable to indulge its naturalness and has instead been translated into substitutes. The view over a landscape that sweeps far into the distance (as a sign of the sublime and the grandiose, of elemental forces) is trapped in reflective surfaces, which refract the gaze and reveal spatial depth to be an illusion. Occasionally disoriented, the users (viewers) of the new garden feel their way through it. Here, they encounter plants, marvellous and brightly coloured birds and equally colourfully painted Taihu stones, a unique topos in the literati garden. *Noah's Garden* appears as a memory of past traditions, of an uninterrupted relationship with nature. Even its title refers to the Old Testament story of Noah's Ark. The story tells of a vast deluge that covered the entire world because God was dissatisfied with humankind and decided to extinguish it. He had mercy on only Noah and his family, giving them the chance to select two of each animal species and save them from the floods in a huge ship. After the flood Noah sent out a dove to discover whether there was any land anywhere that could be settled. When the dove finally returned with an olive twig in its mouth, Noah knew that he could begin resettling the earth. This reads like a new beginning, almost right from

Im Norden Nr.26, 2004
Chinesische Tuschemalerei
122 × 122 cm

In the North No. 26, 2004
Chinese ink painting
122 × 122 cm

Im Garten Nr.47, 2004
Chinesische Tuschemalerei
122 × 122 cm

In the Garden No. 47, 2004
Chinese ink painting
122 × 122 cm

Im Berg Nr.10, 2004
Chinesische Tuschemalerei
122 × 122 cm

In the Mountain No. 10, 2004
Chinese ink painting
122 × 122 cm

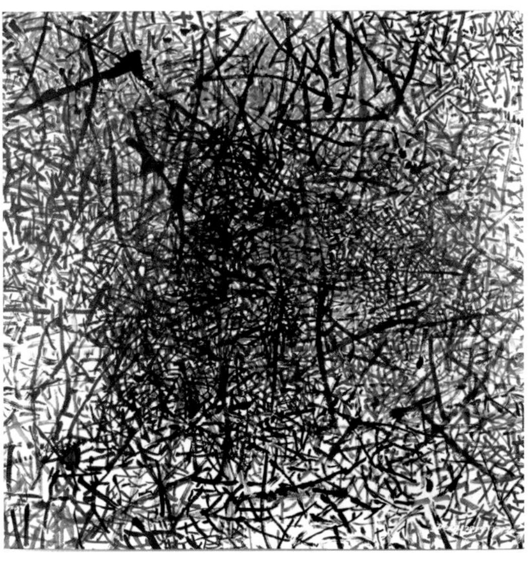

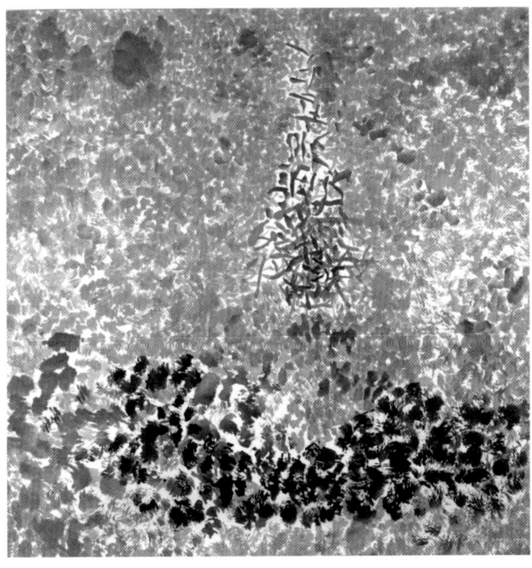

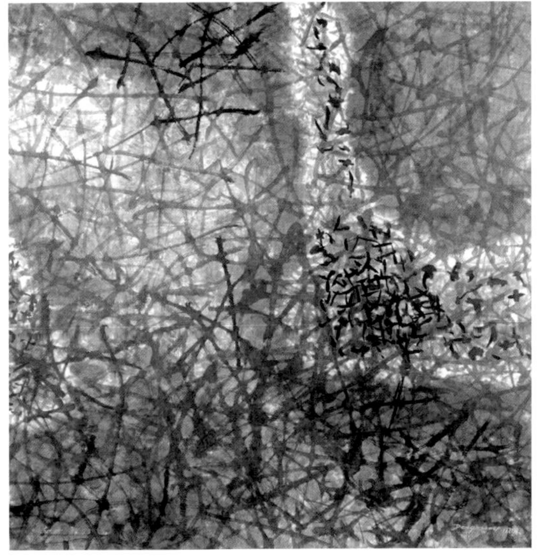

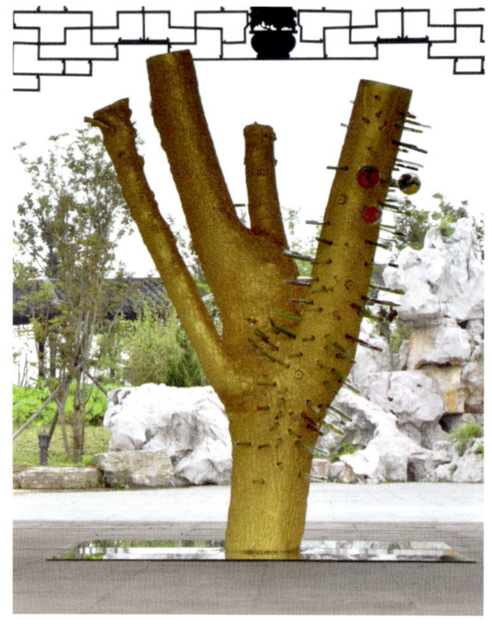

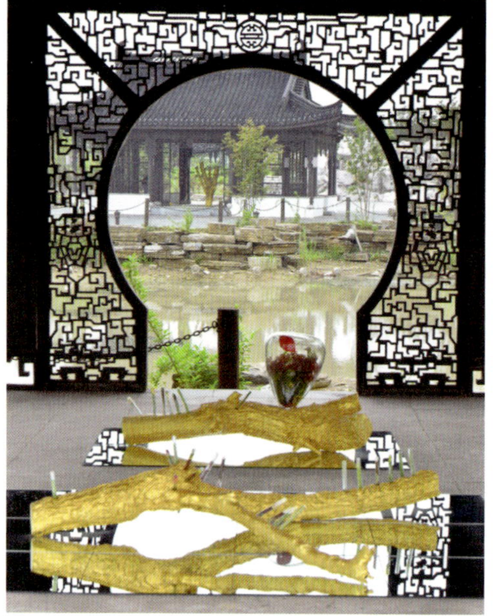

In einer metaphysischen Weise geboren III V Käfig, 2013
Käfig, Pflanze, Versuchsröhre, klassischer Stuhl, Kupfertönung
Variable Maße

Born in a Way of Metaphysics III V Cage, 2013
Cage, plant, experimental tube, classical chair, copper cast tinting
Variable size

In einer metaphysischen Weise geboren III, Detailaufnahme

Born in a Way of Metaphysics III, detail

wie ein Neuanfang, jedenfalls als Chance, diesmal alles besser und richtig zu machen. Daraus spricht auf symbolischer und moralischer Ebene die Erkenntnis, dass der Mensch in seinem Handeln als unvollkommen gesehen wurde, auch jenseits seiner moralisch zu bewertenden Verstrickungen. Deng Guoyuan greift diese Vorlage aus der Bibel auf und verbindet sie zugleich mit der chinesischen Philosophie des Daoismus. Während in der Bibel klare Vorgaben niedergeschrieben sind, denen der Mensch folgen soll, eröffnet der Daoismus eine deutlich liberalere Haltung, die mehr Entscheidungsmöglichkeiten offen lässt. Hier geht es letztlich mehr um die Entwicklung der eigenen Persönlichkeit während eines Lebensprozesses, ohne dabei direkt in den Lebensfluss einzugreifen. In der Bibel heisst es u.a. auch, dass der Mensch sich die Welt untertan machen solle – ein Denkmodell, das für viele Wissenschaftler zum Vorbild wurde.

Dieses jedoch existiert nicht mehr und Deng setzt genau an diesem Bruch, dem Riss, den der Mensch selbst gegenüber der wirkenden Natur erzeugt hat, an. Über die Jahre hat er umfassend die Transformation der Natur begleitet und in immer entschiedeneren Schritten den Verlust eigener Evolutionskraft dargestellt. Von den natürlichen Zweigen in Reagenzgläsern bis hin zu seinen Taihu-Steinen aus Auto-

In einer metaphysischen Weise geboren II Nr. 3, Käfig, Detailaufnahme

Born in a Way of Metaphysics II No. 3 Cage, detail

In einer metaphysischen Weise geboren II Nr. 3, Käfig, Detailaufnahme

Born in a Way of Metaphysics II No. 3 Cage, detail

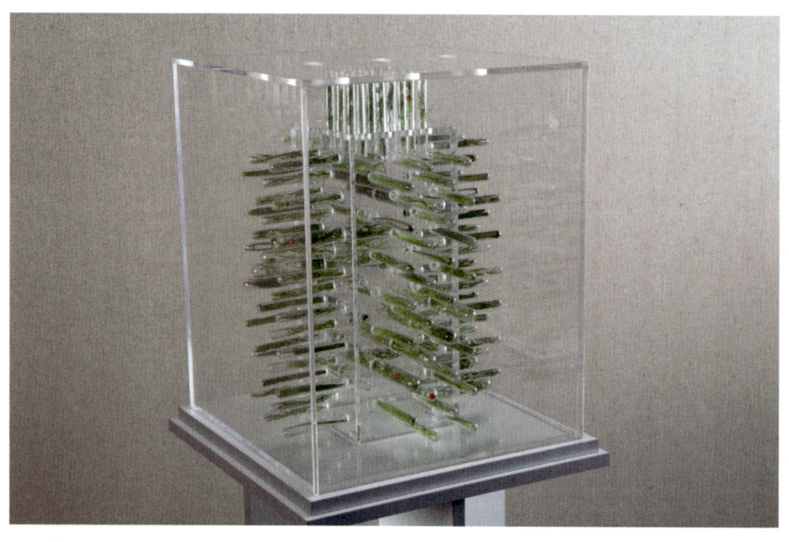

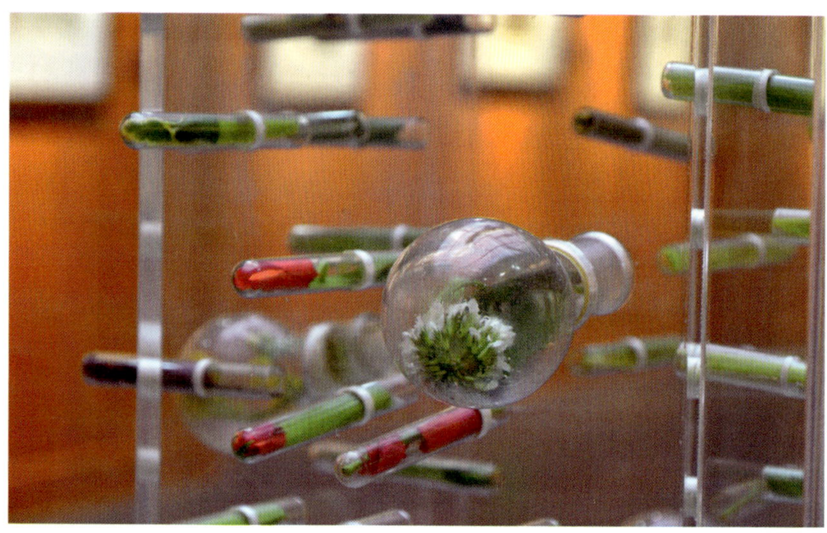

scratch, or at any rate as a chance to do everything better and right this time. From this, on a symbolic and moral level, stems the knowledge that humans and their actions were considered imperfect, quite apart from any deeds that might be subject to moral opprobrium. Deng Guoyuan takes up this model from the Bible and binds it together with the Chinese philosophy of Daoism. While the Bible contains clear rules that humans are to follow, Daoism presents a considerably more liberal position, which allows for more decision making choices. Ultimately, the focus lies here on the development of one's own personality over the course of a life, without interfering directly in the flow of life. The Bible commands, among other things, humans to make the world subject to them – it is a model of thought that became an aspiration for many scholars and scientists.

However, this no longer exists and it is precisely at this fissure, this rupture, which humans themselves have created in active nature, that Deng finds the starting point for his work. Over the years, he has comprehensively traced the transformation of nature and depicted the increasingly decisive stages of the loss of its own power to evolve. From the natural twigs in test tubes through to his Taihu stones made from automobile junk, he has traced a consistent path that has wound ever further from real nature, only to be entirely submerged in the world of artificial creations. Deng Guoyuan does not simply see the continual alterations, but simultaneously also the phenomenon of alienation that humans are engaged in with regard to "Mother Nature." No creature on earth is capable of so radically pursuing this process and yet simultaneously accepting that humankind is sawing through the proverbial branch on which it is sitting.

This is the reason why Deng's works read not just as an ever accelerating history of evolution emerging from the laboratory of artificial insemination, in which an increasingly frequent number of gene mutations are carried out, but also as a history of humankind's alienation from itself. The gesture to tradition is to be seen as a reflex, the consequence of a recollection that nevertheless recedes ever further into the past and will, in its turn, soon be incomprehensible to many because its cultural roots will no longer have any meaning or anything to say. The extent to which Deng

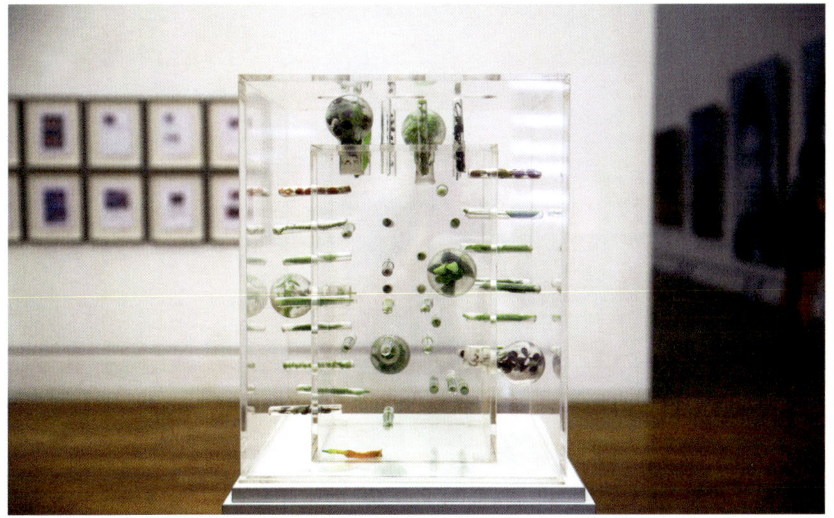

In einer metaphysischen Weise geboren *II Nr. 3, Käfig*, Detailaufnahme

Born in a Way of Metaphysics II No. 3 Cage, detail

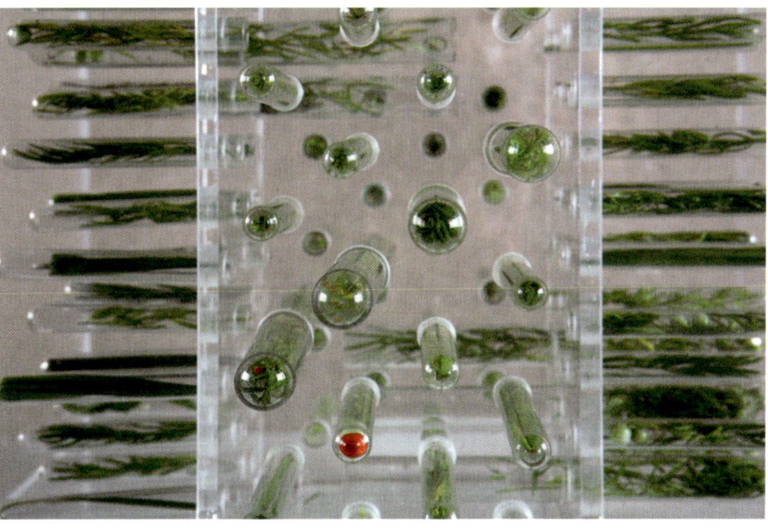

In einer metaphysischen Weise geboren *II Nr. 3, Käfig*, Detailaufnahme

Born in a Way of Metaphysics II No. 3 Cage, detail

schrott war es ein konsequenter Weg, der sich immer weiter von der realen Natur fortentwickelt hat, um gänzlich in die Welt der artifiziellen Kreationen einzutauchen. Es sind nicht nur die fortwährenden Veränderungen, die Deng Guoyuan wahrnimmt, sondern zugleich das Phänomen der Entfremdung, die der Mensch selbst hinsichtlich der „Mutter" Natur betreibt. Kein Lebewesen der Erde ist fähig, diesen Prozess so radikal zu beschreiten und dabei gleichsam wissend in Kauf zu nehmen, dass die Menschheit sich selbst des Lebenszweigs beraubt, auf dem sie sprichwörtlich sitzt.

Deshalb lesen sich seine Werke nicht nur als immer rasantere Evolutionsgeschichte aus dem Labor der künstlichen Befruchtungen, in denen fortschreitend immer öfter unkontrollierte Genmutationen vorgenommen werden, sondern auch als Entfremdung des Menschen von sich selbst. Die Besinnung auf die Tradition versteht sich als Reflexion, als Folge einer Rückbesinnung, die jedoch immer weiter in die Geschichte zurückfällt und ihrerseits bald von vielen nicht mehr verstanden werden wird, weil kulturelle Wurzeln nichts mehr bedeuten werden oder zu sagen haben. Wie weit er dies vorausgesehen hat, zeigt sich bei Deng bereits vor zehn Jahren, als er Baumstämme mit Reagenzgläsern auf Spiegelflächen legt, eine Arbeit, die diese Selbstverwiesenheit bereits betont und somit nur um sich selbst kreist, und schließlich einmündet in „Noah's Garden", als Deng vor circa vier Jahren sein erstes Spiegellabyrinth entwirft.

Mehr als je zuvor, setzt Deng nun alles daran, seine Tuschezeichnungen, sogar seine Ölgemälde in einen dreidimensionalen Kontext zu überführen, wobei er die Disruption von der ursprünglichen Realität hier bereits auf die Spitze treibt. Wie eine Wunderkammer inszeniert, wirkt dieser begehbare Bereich wie eine kleine Enklave, lässt an den Garten Eden denken, an eine neue Form der Kreation, aber erweist sich zugleich auch in seiner trügerischen Dimension, denn diese hier ist nicht fähig, sich selbst zu erschaffen. Nicht so sehr, weil kein Schöpfer diese Welt erschafft, sondern deshalb, weil nichts aus sich selbst erwachsen kann. Vielmehr bleibt in Noahs Garten alles auf Hochglanz poliert und derart übertrieben glatt und bunt, dass kein Einfühlen in eine solche Natur denkbar ist. Spiegel auf Spiegel, alle Wände, alle Böden und der Himmel, multiplizieren immer nur sich selbst, evozieren eine Tiefendimension, die es nicht gibt, und steigern nur alles im Raum selbst in einer scheinbaren Wiederholung und Unendlichkeit. Die Welt, die Natur als Trugschluss – gefangen in sich selbst und ihrer perspektivischen Replikation.

Die Spiegel werfen alles letztlich nur auf sich selbst zurück, sind ausschließlich selbst referenzierend und zeigen wie bei Narziss in der griechischen Mythologie, der selbstverliebt sein Spiegelbild aufsucht und nur mit sich selbst kommuniziert, einzig das eigene Selbst, ohne jedoch zu einer weiterführenden, vertiefenden Erkenntnis zu kommen. Im Spiegellabyrinth steigert sich das Gefühl der sich darin Befindlichen bis hin zur Orientierungslosigkeit und Verwirrung. Bei aller Schönheit, die dort als Reminiszenz an die historischen Gärten dient, indem sie die Taihu-Steine zitiert, die Pflanzen- und Tierwelt imitiert, so ist doch unmissverständlich sichtbar, dass all das Geschaffene hier eine Illusion der natürlichen Landschaft ist, dass diese sogar noch gesteigert ist in der Multiplikation der Spiegelfacetten, die sich überdies zum Teil noch drehen. Die Verwirrung für den Betrachter ist nahezu per-

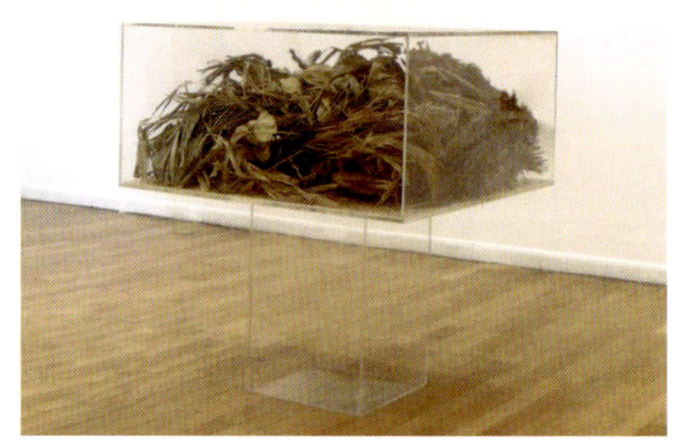

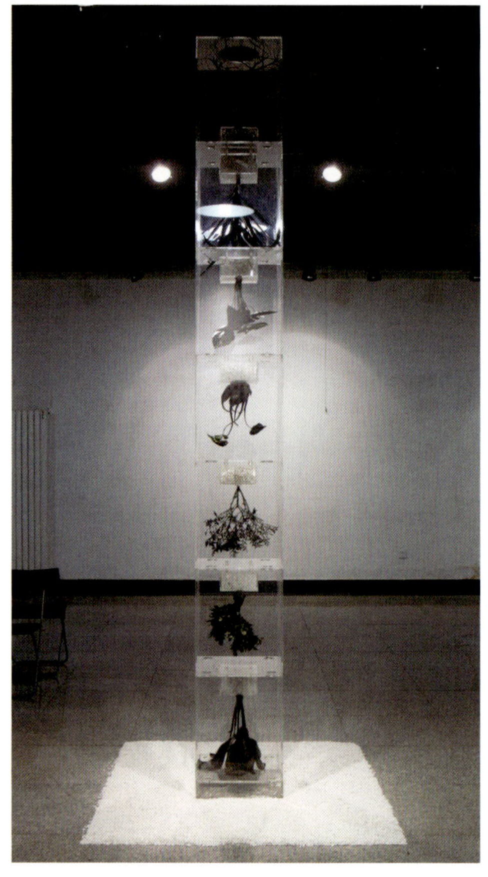

Den chinesischen Meister der Malerei Huo Chunyang, mit Metaphysik begrüßend, 2008
Organisches Glas, Pflanzen, Chinesische Tusche

Saluting Chinese Painting Master, Pan Tianshou, with Metaphysics, 2008
Organic glass, plants, Chinese ink

has been prophetic in this regard can be seen in a work now a decade old, in which he placed tree trunks on mirrored surfaces with test tubes. This work already emphasised that self-referentiality, revolving only around itself and finally flowed into *Noah's Garden*, when, around four years ago, Deng created his first mirror maze.

More than ever before, Deng now began to make every effort to transpose his ink drawings, even his oil paintings, into a three-dimensional context, but now he exaggerated the disruption of the original reality to the highest degree. Staged as a cabinet of curiosities, this physically accessible area is like a small enclave, is reminiscent of the Garden of Eden, of a new form of creation, but it simultaneously reveals its deceptive dimension, because it is incapable of creating itself. Not so much because no creator creates this world, but rather because nothing can arise out of itself. Instead, everything in *Noah's Garden* remains highly polished, indeed, so excessively glossy and colourful that no empathetic feeling for such a nature is conceivable. Mirror on mirror, all walls, all floors and the sky reflect and multiply only themselves, evoking a depth dimension that does not exist and simply enhancing everything in the room in apparent infinite repetition. The world, nature is a fallacy – caught up in itself and its perspectival replication.

Ultimately, the mirrors simply reflect everything back on itself, they are exclusively self-referential and, like Narcissus of Greek mythology, who fell in love with his own reflection and sought communication only with himself, they show only the self, but without ever reaching any further or deeper realisation. The sense of anyone who finds themselves in the mirror maze is there amplified until it reaches disorientation and confusion. For all the beauty that is present there and serves to remind us of the

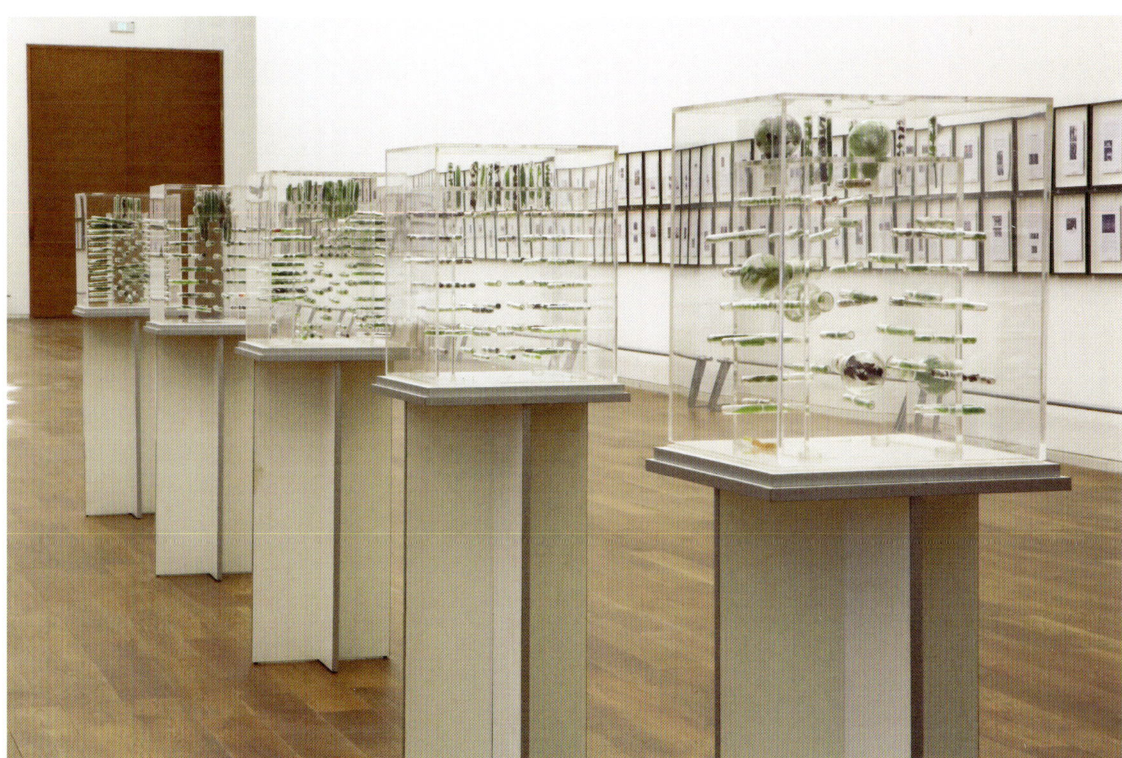

Einzelausstellung, *Lake, Garden*
Deng Guoyuan West Taihu Ink Installation Exhibition
Changzhou West Taihu Art Museum

Solo Exhibition, *Lake, Garden*
Deng Guoyuan West Taihu Ink Installation Exhibition
Changzhou West Taihu Art Museum

fekt, wenngleich dieser letztlich aus dem Labyrinth wieder herausfindet – anders als in der realen Welt, in der die Menschheit sich mehr und mehr selbst in ihrem Handeln verstrickt.

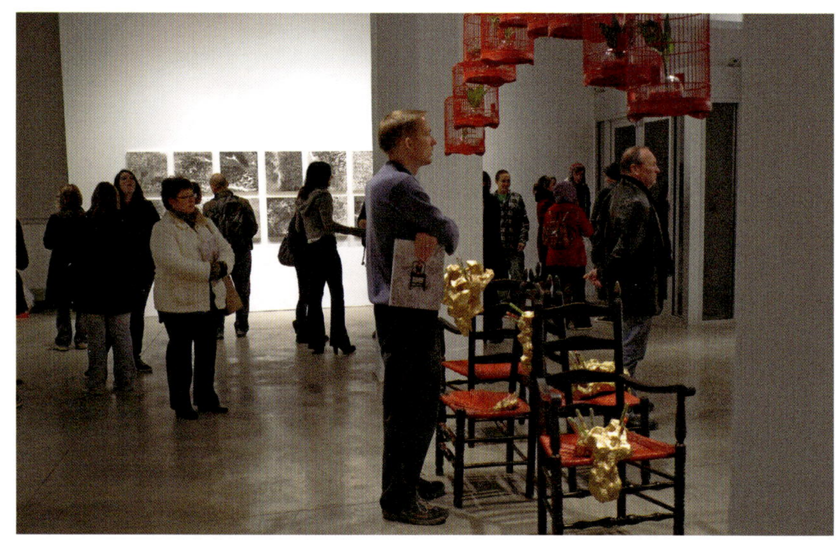

Deng Guoyuan forcierte weitere Perspektiven, indem er Teile seines Spiegelgartens in den urbanen Raum implementierte und diese sich weitgehend mit der Umgebung assimilierten. Realer Raum und dessen Echo im Spiegel verschmelzen dort miteinander. In einem urbanen Umfeld, das kaum noch Natur kennt oder zulässt, vermag der Spiegel wiederum fast eine positive Illusion zu ermöglichen, wenn ein einzelner Strauch oder Baum sich so zu einem multiplizierten Ganzen ausweitet.

Innenansicht der Wanderausstellung *Im Garten*, 2011
Samek Art Museum, Bucknell University, USA
Provenance Center

View of the traveling exhibition *In the Garden*, 2011
Samek Art Museum, Bucknell University, USA
Provenance Center

Zugleich begann er, die Natur in einer neuen Werkserie gleichsam im Spiegel einzufangen: kleine Tiere und menschliche Kreaturen tauchen in facettierten Spiegeln auf und bilden nun einen eigenen Kosmos artifizieller Mutationen. Längst schon von der Natur abgedriftet, sind dies folglich auch durch und durch plastinierte Kreaturen aus der unendlich reichen Welt der Spielzeugindustrie. Überflüssig zu betonen, das China der größte Spielzeugproduzent weltweit ist und vieles tatsächlich hauptsächlich aus Plastikmaterial besteht. Deng belässt die Figurinen nicht wie sie sind, sondern verändert sie fantasievoll, wie in Genlaboren und lässt beständig neue Kreaturen entstehen, die er in seine Welt voller Künstlichkeit ins Spiegeluniversum entlässt. Dabei folgt er anfänglich der Vorlage aus einem historischen Buch, in dem Kreaturen zusammengefasst sind, die schon zur Zeit der Tang-Dynastie die Wandmalerei, Zeichnungen und Gemälde als Fantasiegestalten bevölkerten. (*The Classics of Mountains and Seas*, Penguin Classics, 2000). Hier tauchen Affen mit Menschenköpfen auf, Pferde mit Menschenbeinen und so fort. Sie spielen in der chinesischen Mythologie eine große Rolle, wie überhaupt solche Fabelgestalten zu allen Zeiten die Kulturen der Menschheit begleitet haben. Die Menschen erschufen sich zahlreiche dieser Kreaturen, fantasievoll und wie vorzeitliche Mutationen. Sie fungierten als Schutzgeister oder als abschreckende Wesen, sei es bei den Schamanen, den Urvölkern, oder auch in der eigenen Gegenwart. Schon in der Bronzezeit, in der Antike, in Ägypten, bei den Mayas und Inkas, im Mittelalter in Europa als merkwürdige Drachen und Fratzen an den Außenwänden der gotischen Kathedralen sollten sie das Böse fernhalten oder zeugten als sonderbare Wesen in den historischen Malereien von Grünewald bis Bruegel im Mittelalter von wilden Fantasien. Immer wieder tauchen sie in Zeiten des Schreckens und der Kriege vermehrt auf – bis hinein in die Moderne, insbesondere im Surrealismus von Max Ernst oder Yves Tanguy. Die Gegenwart erschafft sich immer noch ihre

In einer metaphysischen Weise geboren III, Käfig, 2017
Pflanzen, Versuchsröhre, klassischer Stuhl, Kupfertönung
Variable Maße
53 Art Museum, Guangzhou

Born in a Way of Metaphysics III Cage, 2017
Plants, experimental tube, classical chair, copper cast tinting
Dimensions variable
53 Art Museum, Guangzhou

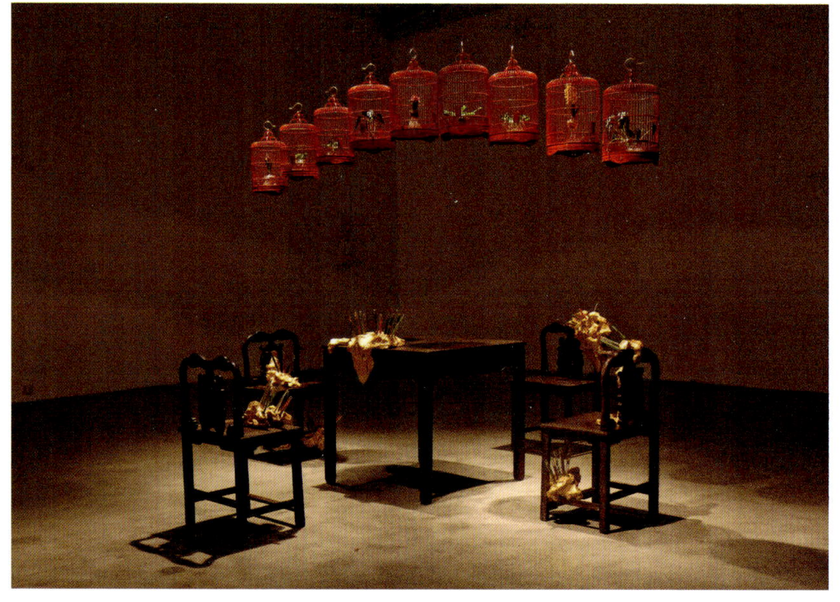

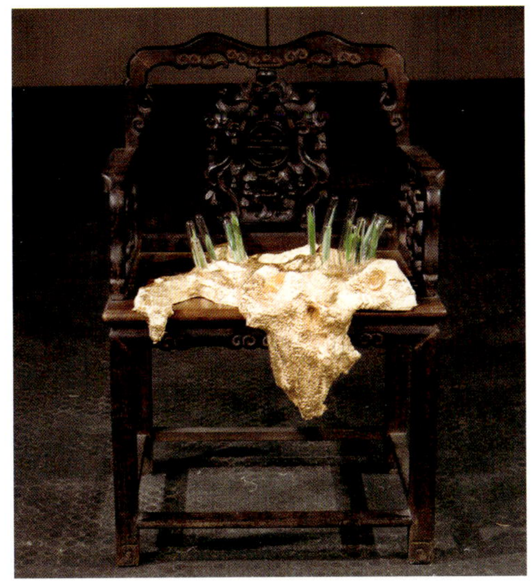

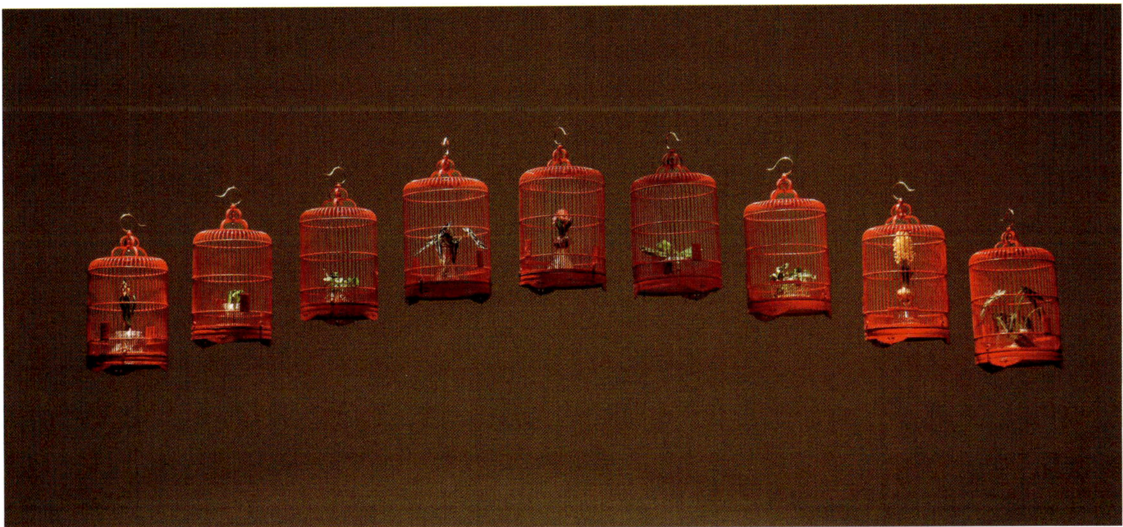

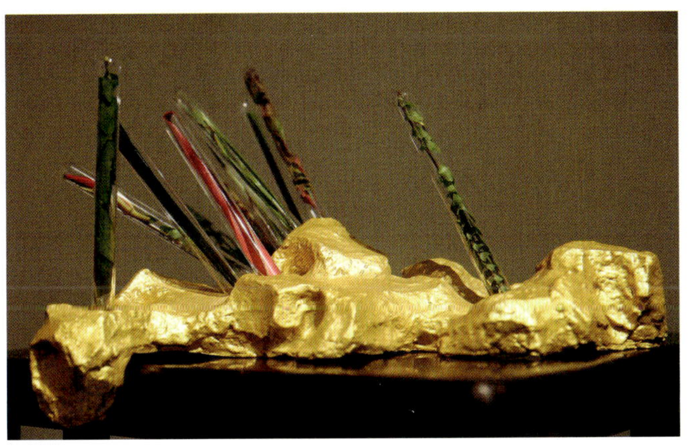

In einer metaphysischen Weise geboren III, Detailaufnahmen

Born in a Way of Metaphysics III, details

gardens of history by referencing the Taihu stones, imitating the flora and fauna, yet it is unmistakably clear that everything here created is an illusion of the natural landscape, that this is even emphasised in its multiplication through the mirrored surfaces (some of which also turn). The confusion of the observer is almost perfect, although ultimately they do find their way out of the labyrinth – contrary to the real world, in which humankind becomes more and more entangled in its own actions.

Deng Guoyuan pushes other perspectives forward by implementing parts of his mirror garden in urban space and assimilating them to a large degree in their surroundings. Real space and its mirrored echo meld together. In an urban environment that barely knows or permits nature, the mirror makes an almost positive illusion possible, as when a single bush or tree extends to a multiplied body through the reflective effect.

At the same time he also began a new work series in which nature would also be captured in the mirror: small animals and human creatures appear in faceted mirrors and form their own cosmos of artificial mutations. Having drifted away from nature long before, these are consequently thoroughly plasticised creatures stemming from the unendingly rich world of the toy industry. It is surely unnecessary to stress that China is internationally the largest producer of toys and that much of what is produced is mainly made of plastic materials. Deng does not leave the figurines as they are, he alters them imaginatively, as in a genetic laboratory, constantly creating new creatures which he releases into his world full of artificiality, into his mirror universe. At the start of this process he followed the precedent given by a history book, in which creatures, fantastical beings, are presented that populated wall paintings, drawings and paintings as early as the Tang Dynasty (*The Classics of Mountains and Seas*, Penguin Classics, 2000). Here, we see monkeys with human heads, horses with human legs and so forth. They play an important role in Chinese mythology, and of course such fantasy figures have always been a part of human cultures. Humans invented multitudes of these creatures, full of imagination and rather like pre-historic mutations. They were intended as guardian spirits or beings that would ward off others, part of the cultures of the shamans, of the aboriginal peoples of the world and even of the present: in the Bronze Age, in antiquity, in ancient Egypt, in the civilisations of of the Maya and the Incas, in the European middle ages as strange

eigenen Fantasiegestalten und deren Herkunft aus dem Reich der Mutationen erscheint nur allzu logisch. Die Fantasyfilme der Hollywood-Industrie geben darüber beredt Zeugnis, sei es Spider-Man, Bat-Man oder Cat-Woman – um noch die Klassiker zu nennen. Sie alle spielen mit der Vorstellung, dass Mutationen, aus welchem Grund auch immer hervorgerufen, zu übermenschlichen oder übersinnlichen Fähigkeiten führen können. Die positiven Eigenschaften der Fairytales täuschen jedoch nicht darüber hinweg, dass in den realen Laboren Versuche unternommen werden, den Menschen zu optimieren, zu klonen und neuerdings auch mit den technischen Möglichkeiten der Artificial Intelligence zu ersetzen. Nach der Überführung der Natur in einen künstlichen Lebensraum, ist es nun der Mensch selbst, der sich damit wohl eher abschaffen wird, als sein eigenes Überleben zu sichern. Seit man in den 1980er Jahren es geschafft hat, erfolgreich zu klonen, ist die Welt in ihrer natürlichen Dimension der Evolution zu Ende gegangen und der Mensch versucht es ihr gleich, respektive besser zu tun.

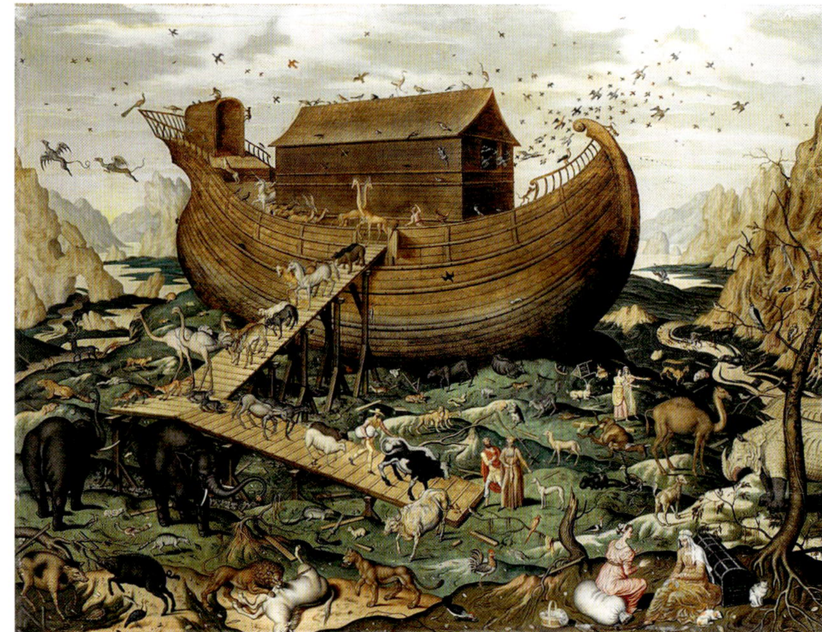

Simon de Myle, *Noahs Arche auf dem Berg Ararat,* 1570, Öl auf Holz, ehemals Musée des Beaux Arts, Lille (Sotheby's 2011)

Simon de Myle, *Noah's Ark on The Mount Ararat*, oil on panel, 1570, formerly Musée des Beaux Arts, Lille (Sotheby's 2011)

Deng Guoyuan bezeichnet deshalb seine museale Inszenierung als Erzählung im Geiste der Apokalypse. Wieder ist es die biblische Vorstellung vom Untergang der Menschheit und der Erde selbst, die im Alten Testament bereits vorhergesagt wird.

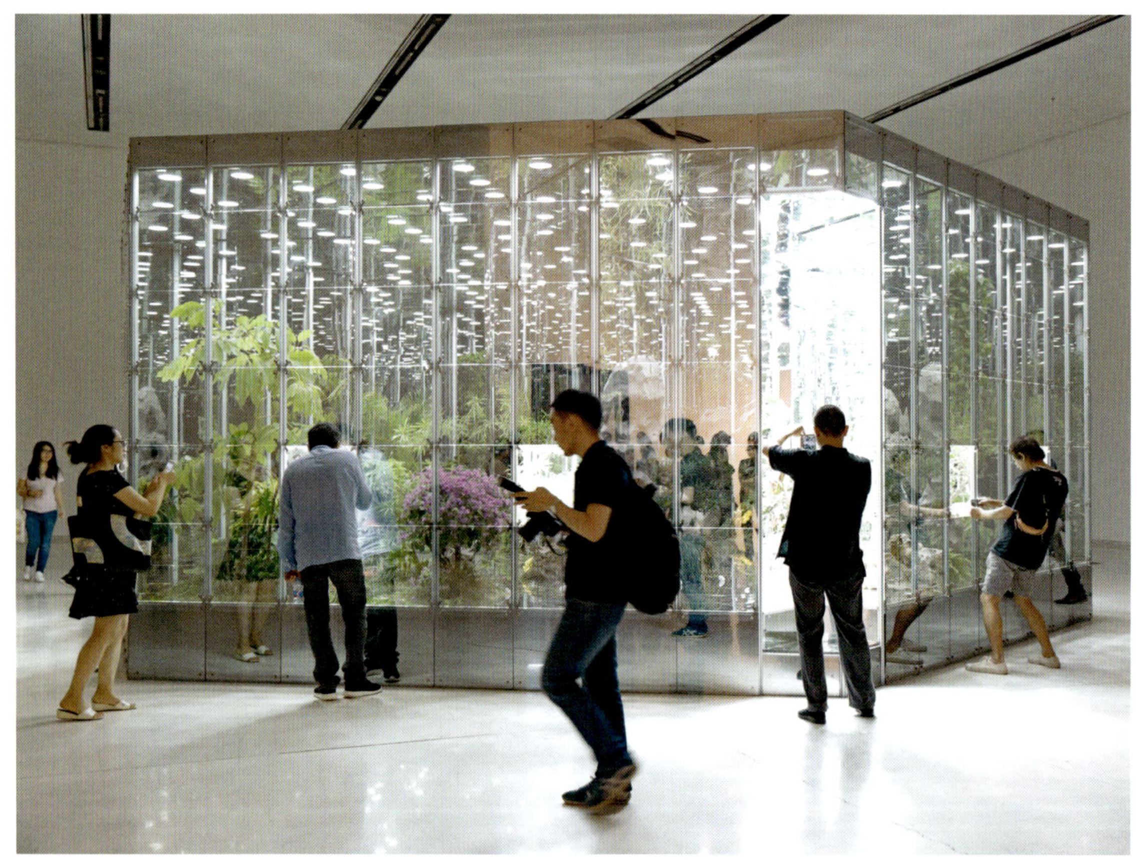

Noahs Garten, Außenansicht

Noah's Garden, outside

dragons and grimacing faces attached to the external walls of Gothic cathedrals to ward off evil, and in the historical paintings of the middle ages executed by artists from Grünewald to Breughel – such strange and marvellous creatures are evidence of wild fantasies. Time and again, they appear in large numbers during times of terror and war – right up to the modern period, in particular in the Surrealist art of Max Ernst and Yves Tanguy. The present continues to create its own fantasy beings and their origins in the realm of mutation seems only logical. The fantasy films produced by the Hollywood industry provide ample evidence of this, whether it is Spider-Man, Bat-Man or Cat-Woman – to name just a few of the classics. They all play with the idea that mutations, brought about by whatever cause, can lead to superhuman or extrasensory abilities. However, the positive fairytale elements cannot hide the fact that real laboratories are undertaking experiments that aim to optimise, clone and, most recently, even to replace humans with the technological possibilities of Artificial Intelligence. Once nature has been transposed into an artificial habitat, now humans, instead of ensuring their own survival, will consequently eliminate themselves. Ever since the first successful cloning experiments in the 1980s, the world's natural dimension of evolution has come to an end and humans have been trying to do it like, or in fact better than, nature.

For this reason Deng Guoyuan describes his museum-like presentation as a narrative in the spirit of the apocalypse. Once again, the biblical idea of the destruction of humankind and of the earth itself is already presaged in the Old Testament. It's an artistic vision that Deng mines for his own work, formulating mirror object after

Noahs Garten II, Innenansicht

Noah's Garden II, inside

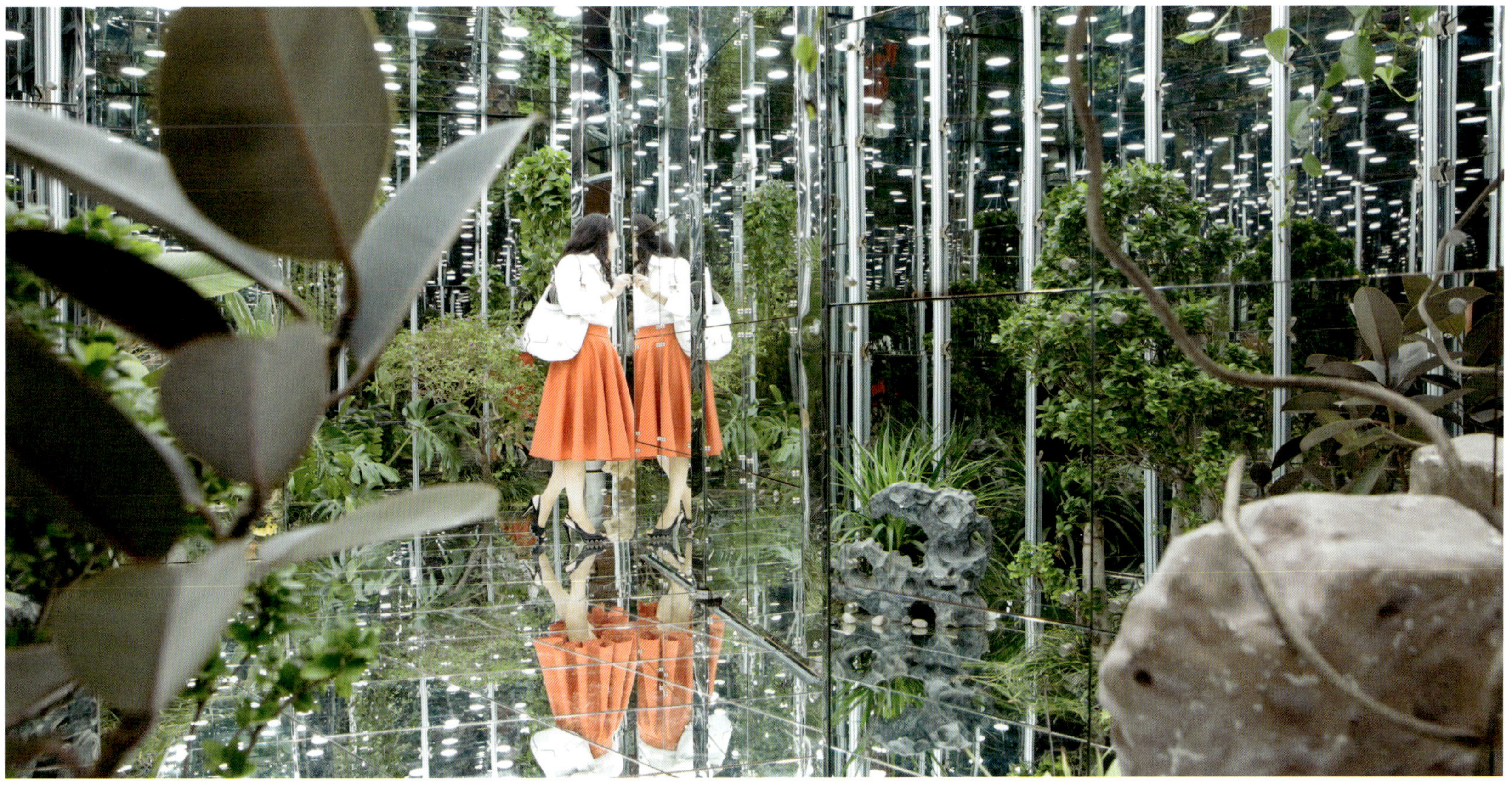

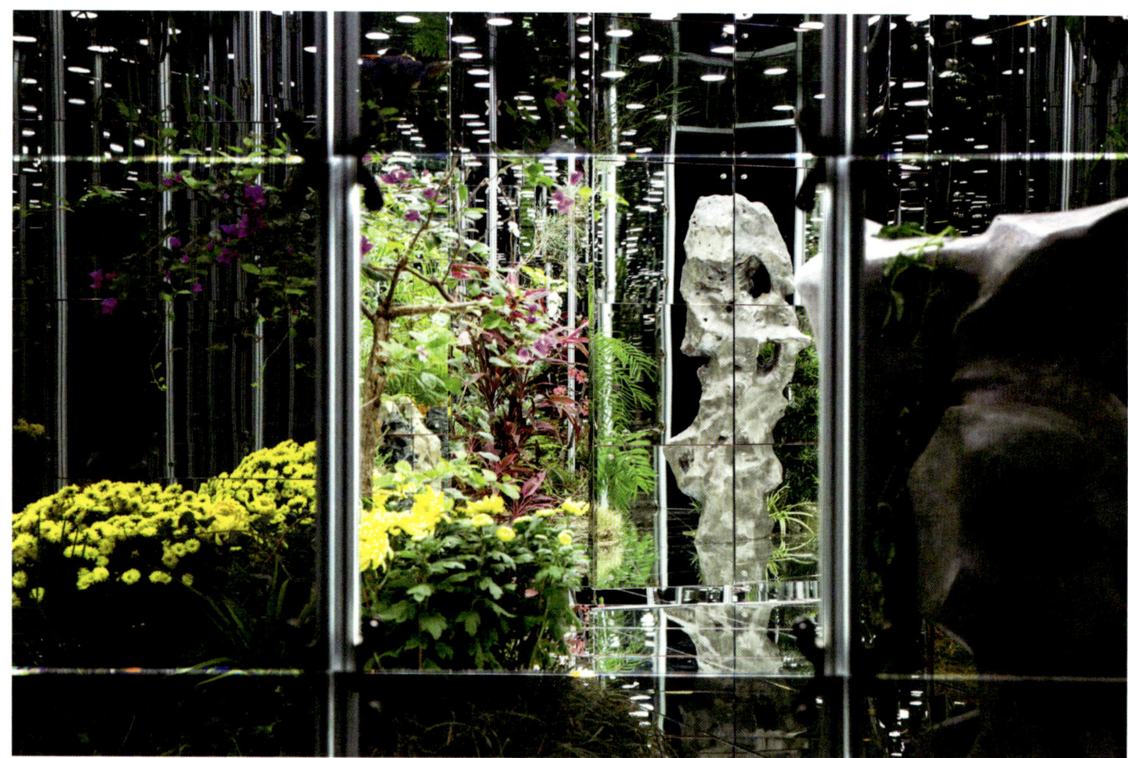

Noahs Garten II, Innenansicht

Noah's Garden II, inside

Eine bildnerische Vorstellung, die sich Deng zunutze macht, und in einzelnen Kapiteln Spiegelobjekt um Spiegelobjekt formuliert. In einzelnen Sequenzen zeichnet Deng diese Vorstellung anhand seiner Spielzeugkreaturen nach, die sich die alte Weltordnung zu eigen machen und überfremden. Es sind hier die kleinen, manchmal als lästig empfundenen Insekten, die, durch Masse übermächtig geworden, sich die Welt untertan machen. Die Schmetterlinge, die den Garten der Dinosaurier erobern, die Marienkäfer, die den Panda-Garten bevölkern oder Libellen, die den Garten der Tiger erobern. In einer realen Welt, in der aufgrund von Umwelteinflüssen die Ozeane vermüllt, die Erde durch Industrieabfälle verseucht, die Luft zutiefst verschmutzt und die schützende Ozonschicht schwindet, die Polkappen schmelzen... bleibt kein Lebensraum mehr für die wilden Tiere, schon gar nicht für die großen und seltenen. Das Aussterben ist im vollen Gange und nur wenige rücken ersatzweise an ihre Stelle.

Deng Guoyuan hat mehr als viertausend kleine Spielzeugtiere und -figuren gesammelt und aufwändig neu komponiert. Die Anmutung des Spielerischen, Wundersamen, mithin Hässlichen bleibt bewahrt und gerade die kleine Dimension seiner Kreaturen löst zunächst die Faszination aus, jedem einzelnen Gedanken folgen zu wollen. In der Überfülle wird dies jedoch rasch unmöglich. Auch dies entspricht der glaubhaften These der Naturwissenschaftler, dass die großen, scheinbar überlegenen Spezies nicht überleben werden, sondern in ihrer natürlichen Welt, die es bald nicht mehr geben wird, die niederen Ordnungen, vom Einzeller bis zum Insekt, sich durchsetzen werden und nur diese eine Überlebenschance haben. Bereits in der Zeit vor dem zweiten Weltkrieg erschufen die Surrealisten Werke, in denen die Natur sich selbst überlassen gezeigt wurde, die sich verlorenes Terrain zurück eroberte und in der es nur noch Insekten als verbliebene Lebewesen gab. Der Mensch war hier bereits nicht mehr existent, sondern ausradiert. Auch damals schon war dies die Apokalypse, die das Desaster des Zweiten Weltkriegs zumindest in seinen Grundzügen zur Vorstellung für die Menschheit, brachte und ganz neu interpretierte.

mirror object, as it were individual chapters. In separate sequences, Deng outlines this vision using his toy creatures, which have overtaken the old world order and thoroughly infiltrated it. These are the small, sometimes pesky insects, which, having found power through sheer numbers, are subjugating the world. The butterflies, which conquer the garden of dinosaurs, the ladybirds, which populate the pandas' garden, or the dragonflies who conquer the tigers' garden. In a real world, in which environmental influences have caused the oceans to be filled with rubbish, the earth to be poisoned by industrial waste, the air to be polluted and in which the protective ozone layer is disappearing, the polar ice caps are melting... there is no living environment left for wild animals, and certainly not for the large or rare species. The rate of extinction is in full swing and only a few new species are emerging to take their place.

Deng Guoyuan has collected over 4000 small toy animals and figurines and carefully reconfigured them. They retain an air of playfulness, of the marvellous, together with the ugly and it is the small dimensions of his creatures in particular that provokes fascination and the desire to follow each individual idea. Their superabundance quickly makes this impossible, however. This, too, is in line with the credible argument presented by scientists that the large, apparently superior species will not survive. Instead, in their natural world, which will soon cease to exist, it will be the lower order animals, from the single-celled organisms to the insect, which will prevail and only these species will have a chance of survival. The Surrealists were already creating works in the period before the Second World War in which nature is shown left to its own devices, reclaiming lost terrain, and in which, of all the animal species, only insects continued to exist. Humans had, in this imagining, already been wiped out, were no longer extant. Even back then, this, at least in its outlines, was the apocalypse which conjured up a vision of the disaster of the Second World War.

In Deng's vision, these little mutants take on a life of their own and leave the narrow world of the mirrored box. They fly away, up and leave, emancipate themselves. Viewed from afar, his mirror works, with their scuttling creatures and mutants, ap-

Noahs Garten II, Innenansicht

Noah's Garden II, inside

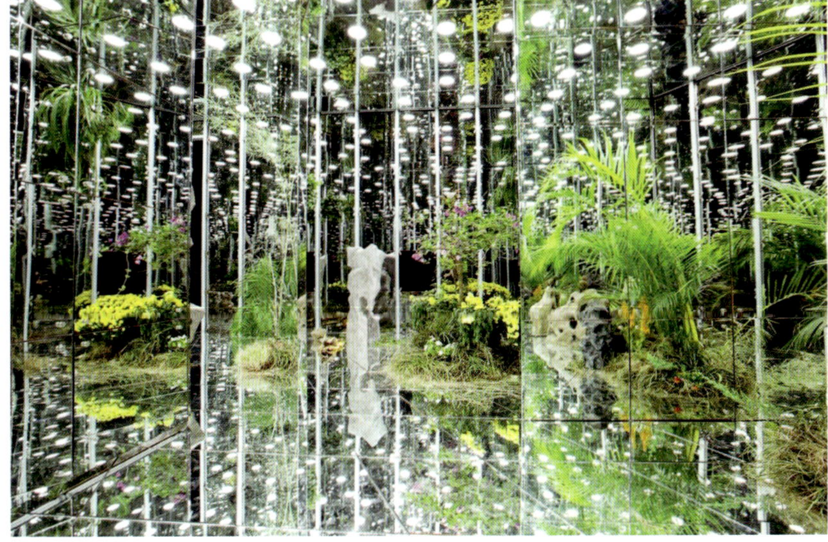

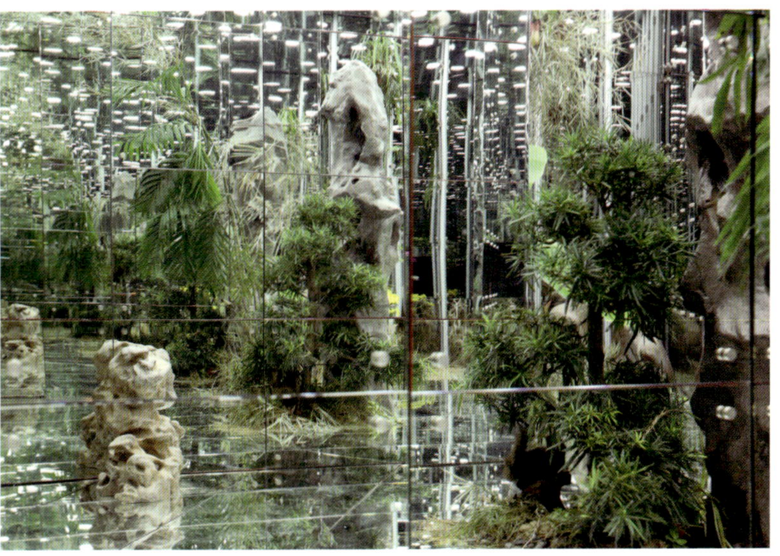

In Dengs Vorstellung verselbstständigen sich diese kleinen Mutanten und verlassen die enge Welt seiner Spiegelkästen. Sie fliegen, machen sich auf und davon, emanzipieren sich. Von Weitem betrachtet erscheinen gerade seine Spiegelarbeiten mit den vor sich hinwuselnden Kreaturen und Mutanten wie seine vor vielen Jahren geschaffenen Ölgemälde, in denen er im abstrakten Farbgestus eine eigene Welt des Natürlichen und des Gartens schuf. Sie wirken beinahe wie die Rückkehr zum Bild – zum Kompositorischen schlechthin.

Dengs künstlerische Haltung, zutiefst geprägt vom Pessimismus der eigenen Zeit gegenüber, orientiert sich an den Entwicklungen im eigenen Land, an Chinas Transformation vom Agrarstaat zu einer der führenden Weltmächte, der jedoch allzu oft die Rücksichtnahme auf das kreatürliche Entstehen und Werden abhanden gekommen ist. Darin steht China anderen Industriestaaten in nichts nach. Den Pessimismus teilt Deng mit vielen Zeitgenossen und Künstler auf der ganzen Welt thematisieren zunehmend die dramatischen Veränderungen unserer Erde, aber in seiner sich über die letzten mehr als zehn Jahre erstreckenden künstlerischen Entwicklung in seinem Werk und den immer neuen Formen, die er mit Materialien aus der Umwelt, der Industrie, der Wegwerfgesellschaft, bis hinzu den Plastikspielzeugen erprobt hat, ist er nicht nur in China ein einzigartiger Künstler, der wie der Rufer in der Wüste zum Umdenken mahnt. Das Spielerische mag auf den ersten Blick darüber hinwegtäuschen, aber Deng meint es bitterernst, wenn er die Versuchsanordnungen, Genmanipulationen und damit den unabwendbar scheinenden Willen des Menschen zur künstlichen Erschaffung hier vorführt und in seinem apokalyptischen Ausmaß andeutet.

Noch erscheinen sie ganz possierlich, diese kleinen Mutanten, aber schon Goethes „Zauberlehrling“ musste bitterlich erkennen, dass er die Geister, die er rief, nicht beherrschen konnte.

pear rather like the oil paintings he created many years before. In these, he created a unique world of the natural and of the garden in an mode of abstract colour. They give the impression of, almost, a return to the image – to the notion of the composition in its pure form.

Deng's artistic philosophy, deeply influenced by a pessimism towards the modern era, takes its cues from developments in his own country, from China's transformation from an agrarian culture to one of the leading world powers, which nevertheless all too often lost sight of a necessary consideration for the development and existence of the natural world. China is second to none in this regard among the industrial nations. Deng shares this pessimism with many of his contemporaries, and artists across the world are increasingly making the dramatic changes to our earth a subject of their work. However, Deng's artistic development as evidenced in his works over the past decade and more, as well as the ever new forms, in which he has experimented with materials from the environment, industry, throw-away society and even plastic toys, shows that he is not simply a unique artist in China, calling like a lone voice in the desert for a fundamental reconsideration of our relationship to nature. The playfulness of his work may deceive us at first glance, but Deng's message is deeply serious as he presents to us experiment designs, gene manipulation and the apparently ineluctable will of humankind to artificial creation.

They may seem quite cute at first, these little mutants, but remember that even Goethe's "sorcerer's apprentice" was forced to the bitter realisation that he could not control the spirits that he himself had conjured up.

Ein wegweisendes Experiment unserer Zeit

Lao Zhu

Heutzutage sind Künstler nicht nur Erschaffer, sondern auch Beobachter und Kritiker der Gesellschaft. Die Entwicklung der neuen Medien und Technologien ist heute an einen Punkt gelangt, an dem Menschen zu „posthumanen" Wesen werden. Einerseits greifen die Menschen durch außerordentliche Errungenschaften in Gottes Schöpfung ein, unter anderem durch die Erschaffung einer virtuellen Welt und posthumane Erfindungen wie Cyborg und Künstliche Intelligenz. Andererseits müssen sich die Menschen mit den folgenreichen Auswirkungen dieser durch die Technologie ermöglichten Interventionen auseinandersetzen. All dies wird durch Technologie ermöglicht. Sie treibt die menschliche Entwicklung an, so wie die Menschen einst erst dank ihrer Fähigkeit, Instrumente zu benutzen, menschlich wurden und sich von anderen Arten abgrenzten. Die technologische Entwicklung kann jedoch auch allzu große Begehrlichkeiten wecken, was wiederum das Überleben der Menschheit gefährdet. Durch die Technologie können die Menschen heutzutage „unmenschlich" oder „übermenschlich" werden, wie im Fall des Cyborgs und der Künstlichen Intelligenz. Der Countdown für die Auslöschung der Menschheit ist demzufolge schon in vollem Gange.

Ein Künstler wie Deng Guoyuan ist nicht nur ein Beobachter, sondern auch eine Leitfigur. Lange Zeit hatte er das Amt des Präsidenten einer Kunstakademie mit tausenden Studenten und hunderten Fakultätsmitgliedern inne. Guoyuans Arbeiten widmen sich den Veränderungen unserer Zeit und regen uns dazu an, das Schicksal der Menschheit und die heutigen Herausforderungen zu reflektieren. Als Präsident einer Kunstakademie realisiert Guoyuan Arbeiten, die der Frage nachgehen, inwieweit Kunst einen Wandel in der Gesellschaft herbeiführen und die drängenden Probleme unserer Zeit angehen kann. Guoyuan spielte eine Schlüsselrolle, als es darum ging, eine renommierte, in der Nähe der Hauptstadt gelegene Kunsthochschule in ein Mekka für experimentelle Kunst umzuwandeln. In diesem Gebiet wachsen Peking, Tianjiin und die Hebei-Provinz zunehmend zusammen und eröffnen viele neue

The Pioneering Experiment of Our Time

Lao Zhu

Artists in our time are not merely creators, but also observers and critics of society. The development of new media and new technology has pushed us to the crossroad where humans are transforming to become "post-human." On one hand, humans intervene with God's Creation through miraculous works, namely, the making of a virtual world and post-human Inventions such as cyborg and artificial intelligence. On the other hand, humans are facing the dreadful consequences of such intervention. These are all made possible by technology. Technology is meant to boost human development, just as the skill of using tools had once separated humans from other species and made humans fully human. Yet, the development of technology can also lead to over-inflation of human desire, which in turn will jeopardize the very survival of mankind. Today, technology can render humans "inhuman" or "superhuman" as in the cases of cyborg and artificial intelligence, the countdown of human extinction has already started.

An artist like Deng Guoyuan is not only an observer, but also a guiding figure. For long time, he has been the president of an art academy that has thousands of students and hundreds of faculty members. To certain extent, his works signal the changes of our time, inspiring us to reflect on the destiny of mankind and the challenges we are facing today. As the president of an art academy, he creates artworks to explore how Art can affect changes in society and address urgent issues of our time. He has played a key part at a crucial moment, transforming a prestigious art academy, close to the Capital, into the mecca for experimental art. In this area, Beijing, Tianjin and the Hebei province are growing tied together, opening up many possibilities. At the middle between Beijing and Tianjin, between the centre and the periphery, and between the classics and experiments, namely, at the margin by the "Centre," Deng has devoted himself to probe into the relationship between humanity and technology. In his hands, experimental art is not merely an art category, but signals various ways of engaging with human creation in the future, both in China and in the world.

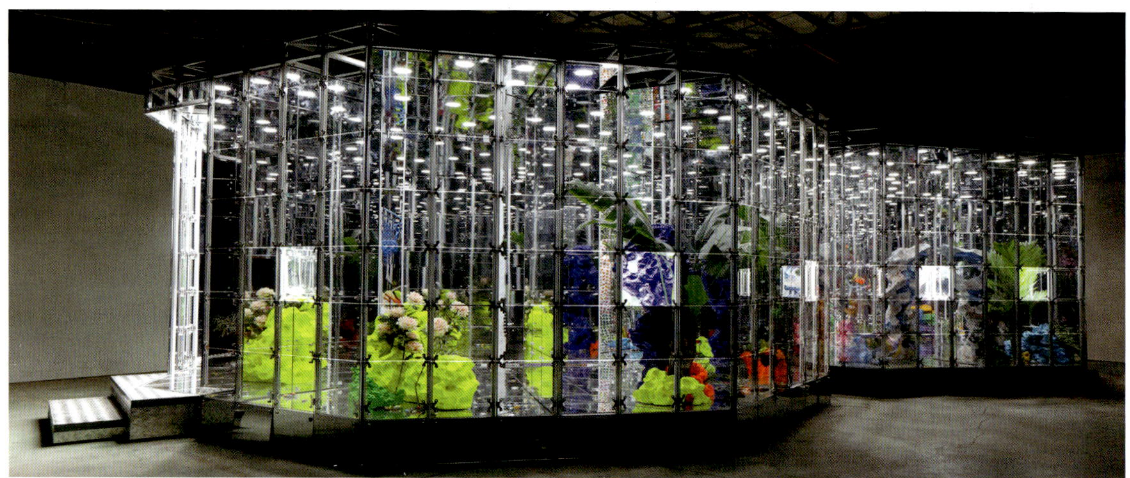

Noahs Garten II, Außenansicht

Noah's Garden II, outside

Möglichkeiten. Zwischen Peking und Tianjin, zwischen dem Zentrum und der Peripherie und zwischen klassischer und experimenteller Ausrichtung erkundet Deng am Rand des „Zentrums" das Verhältnis von Humanität und Technologie. In seinen Arbeiten stellt die experimentelle Kunst nicht nur eine Kunstkategorie dar, sondern zeigt verschiedene Wege, die einen möglichen künftigen Umgang mit der menschlichen Schöpfung in China und auf der ganzen Welt anbieten.

Guoyuans Arbeiten eröffnen den Blick in die Zukunft, auf die er all seine Hoffnungen setzt, und dienen damit als eine Art Leitfaden, welcher uns auffordert, Fragen zu stellen. In China sind die Präsidenten von Kunsthochschulen selbst Künstler (bevor Fan Di'an Präsident der Zentralen Akademie der Bildenden Künste wurde, hatte kein Manager oder Kunsthistoriker je diese Position inne), was eine Ausnahme von der Regel ist. Die Vorteile liegen darin, dass all diese Präsidenten Fachleute auf ihrem Gebiet sind. Ein möglicher Nachteil entsteht jedoch, wenn sie anderen Fakultätsmitgliedern oder Studenten ihre eigenen Anliegen aufzwingen und auf diese Weise die künstlerische Schaffensfreiheit unterwandern. Guoyuan hingegen sucht selbst nach zukunftsweisenden Konzepten für die künstlerische Entwicklung, was auch eine Aufgabe der zeitgenössischen Kunst ist. Dieser Ehrgeiz ist charakteristisch für die Präsidenten der chinesischen Kunstakademien, darunter Pan Gongkai, der frühere Präsident der Zentralen Akademie der Bildenden Künste, Xu Jiang, der Präsident der Chinesischen Hochschule der Künste, Li Xiangqun, der Präsident der Kunstakademie Lu Xun und Pang Maokun, der Präsident der Kunstakademie Sichuan. Vielleicht handelt es sich um ein typisch chinesisches Phänomen.

Obwohl Guoyuan sein Amt als Präsident der Kunsthochschule vor Kurzem niedergelegt hat, tat dies seinem sozialen Engagement keinerlei Abbruch. Aus diesem Grund ist es opportun, seine Arbeitenå nicht nur aus einem künstlerischen Blickwinkel zu betrachten. Wenn etwas Wahres daran ist, dass jede künstlerische Arbeit, „Herz und Seele" des/der Künstlers/erin zum Ausdruck bringt, dann legen Guoyuans Arbeiten nahe, dass sich dieser kontinuierlich mit der Zukunft der Menschheit auseinandersetzt, gesellschaftliche Fragestellungen entschlossen in Angriff nimmt und den gesellschaftlichen Wandel in China dokumentiert. Folglich sollten wir uns seinen Arbeiten aus einer neuen Perspektive annähern und diese nicht als Werke einer spezifischen

His works provide a glimpse of the future he is hoping for. His works serve as a kind of guidance, inspiring us to raise questions. Rather peculiarly, presidents of art academies in China are all artists themselves. (Before Fan Di'an became the president of the Central Academy of Fine Arts, no manager or art historian had ever taken such positions). The advantage lies in that these presidents are all experts in the field. But there is also a disadvantage, namely, they might impose their own agendas on other faculties or students, thus compromise the freedom of artistic creation. In contrast, Deng Guoyuan has devoted himself to explore forward-looking plans for artistic development, which is also a task for contemporary art. Such ambition is common among presidents of art academies in China, including Pan Gongkai, the former president of the Central Academy of Fine Arts, Xu Jiang, the president of the Chinese Academy of Art, Li Xiangqun, the president of the Lu Xun Academy of Fine Arts, and Pang Maokun, the president of the Sichuan Academy of Fine Arts. Perhaps this is a phenomenon unique to China.

Although Deng had just resigned his official post as the president of an art academy, his sense of social responsibility has not abated even a bit. Therefore, we shall not approach his works only from artistic perspectives. If it is right to say that any work by an artist always reveals the artist' "heart and mind," Deng's works prove that he is always concerned about the future of mankind, addressing social issues unflinchingly and highlighting social transformation of China. Hence we shall approach his works from a unique perspective, regarding them not as works by a specific person, but as the representation of a kind of role, just like in Greek tragedy, where every character wears a mask. The mask serves not only to camouflage the actor, but also to assign a kind of responsibility, a kind of role to the actor. In the voice of such role, the actor ruminates on various issues and expresses his views. In the case of Deng Guoyuan, the voice of such role conveys the formidable charge of destiny and his motivation to address urgent issues of our time.

In light of this, Deng's works show another kind of consistency. The three series of works he recently created all echo with the social development of China, the modernization of a developing country and the revolution of science and technology ongoing in our time.

The first series, titled *Noah's Garden*, tackles the possibility of human creation in the future. It shows a cutting edge on virtual reality and the hope of mankind, inspiring us to seek for ways to return to nature, recover the sense of reality, and maintain intimate human relationships when suffering alienation inflicted by modern technology and knowledge. The series is like a passage, set at the crossroad of mankind, prior to the boom of new technology. He is calling for a different kind of human beings. Not ordinary producers or daydreamers baffled by society and indulging in bitterness or futile resistance, this kind of human beings can take firm actions, make elaborate plans, and constantly venture to fulfil their ideals. Through the passage laid out in *Noah's Garden*, they arrive at the "other shore" of human spirit, attaining self-salvation and also saving others. The series shows no clear-cut conceptual makeup, but carries on experiment and creation freely. The passage it lays out is wide open, inviting us to walk through and tread our own path. As for

Person betrachten, sondern als die Wiedergabe einer Art Rolle, vergleichbar mit der griechischen Tragödie, in der jeder Darsteller eine Maske trägt. Die Maske dient nicht nur dazu, den Darsteller zu verbergen, sondern weist diesem mittels der Rolle auch eine gewisse Verantwortung zu. In dieser Rolle erörtert der Darsteller dann verschiedene Themen und legt seine Ansichten dar. In Guoyuans Fall erhalten wir Einblick in die gewaltige, mit dem menschlichen Schicksal verbundene Verantwortung und Guoyuans Motivation, die drängenden Probleme unserer Zeit anzugehen.

Noch eine weitere Konstante durchzieht Guoyuans Arbeiten. Seine drei aktuellen Werkserien setzen sich allesamt mit der gesellschaftlichen Entwicklung in China, dem Modernisierungsprozess eines Entwicklungslandes und den heutigen bahnbrechenden Umbrüchen in Wissenschaft und Technologie auseinander.

Die erste Werkserie, die den Titel *Noah's Garden (Noahs Garten)* trägt, erkundet die Möglichkeiten künftiger menschlicher Schöpfungen. Sie wirft neues Licht auf die virtuelle Realität und die Hoffnungen der Menschheit, und fordert uns dazu auf, nach einem Weg zurück zur Natur zu suchen, unseren Realitätssinn neu zu entdecken und enge menschliche Beziehungen zu knüpfen, wenn wir unter der durch die moderne Technologie und das moderne Wissen herbeigeführten Entfremdung leiden. Die Werkserie gleicht einem Schlupfloch, das sich für die Menschheit am Scheideweg vor dem Boom der neuen Technologie auftut. Guoyuan sehnt eine andere Art menschlicher Wesen herbei. Keine gewöhnlichen Produzenten oder Tagträumer, die von der Gesellschaft ausgebremst werden und sich der Verbitterung oder dem nutzlosem Widerstand hingeben. Die menschlichen Wesen, die sich Guoyuan ausmalt, handeln entschlossen, feilen Pläne aus und treten für ihre Ideale ein. Durch das Schlupfloch, das *Noah's Garden* eröffnet, gelangen sie ans „andere Ufer" des menschlichen Geistes und können sich und die anderen retten. Die Werkserie folgt keinem eindeutigen konzeptuellen Aufbau, sondern zeichnet sich durch einen experimentellen Charakter und freien Realisierungsprozess aus. Das Schlupfloch, das sie erschafft, ist weit geöffnet und lädt uns dazu ein, dieses zu passieren und dann unseren eigenen Weg einzuschlagen. Unabhängig davon, ob die Arbeiten eine transzendentale oder erfüllende Wirkung auslösen, kann der/die Betrachter/in den Garten betreten und sich den eigenen Gedanken hingeben.

Die zweite Werkserie namens *Rockeries* besteht aus „Steingärten", die zu verschiedenen Zeiten unter Verwendung unterschiedlicher Materialien errichtet wurden. Der Steingarten ist eines der charakteristischen Elemente der traditionellen chinesischen Kultur. Guoyuans *Steingärten* sind jedoch keine Steingärten *per se*, sondern genau das Gegenteil, und zwar „künstliche Steingärten", die auf Technologie, Materialien, Farben und Überreste aus dem Industriezeitalter zurückgreifen. Als Symbol des untergehenden Industriezeitalters werden Autos zerquetscht und verschrottet. Mit diesen Überbleibseln – den „Relikten" des Industriezeitalters – erschafft Guoyuan dann seine „Steingärten". Das Ergebnis ist emotional aufwühlend. Der Metallschrott, der in dem Ausstellungsraum zu Haufen aufgetürmt ist, ähnelt Wucherungen, Abfall und Schreckgestalten, und vermittelt auf diese Weise ein beklemmendes Gefühl von Unterdrückung. Den Steingärten haftet ein elegischer Tonfall an, während sie den Niedergang des Industriezeitalters verkünden. Gebrauchtwagen stehen für das Ende des Industriezeitalters und das Aufkommen des Informationszeitalters.

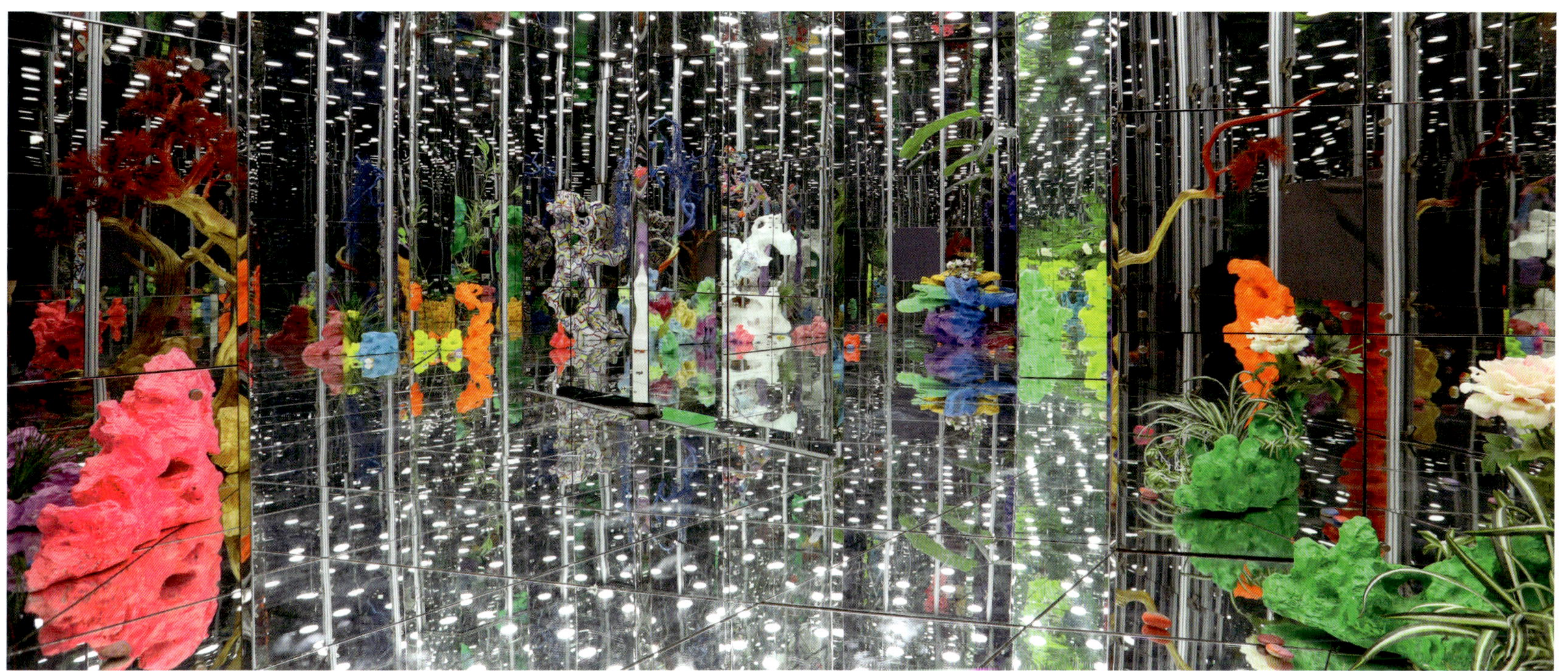

Noahs Garten II, Innenansicht

Noah's Garden II, inside

whether it will lead to transcendence and fulfilment, you may enter the Garden and think for yourselves.

The second series, titled *Rockeries*, are "rockeries" built at different times, using different materials. Rockery is one of the trademarks of traditional Chinese culture, but Deng's "rockeries" are not rockeries per se, but the very opposite, namely, "faked rockeries" that draw upon technology, materials, colours and residues from the industrial age. As the twilight symbol of the industrial age, used automobiles are crushed and compressed into scraps. Using such residues – the "carcasses" of the industrial age, Deng built his "rockeries." The result is emotionally shocking. Scrap metals are piled up in the exhibition hall, looking like tumours, wastes and bogeys, conveying a suffocating sense of oppression. They ring an elegiac tone while addressing the decline of the industrial age. Used automobiles symbolize the eclipse of the industrial age at the dawn of the information age. When scrap metals from used automobiles are turned into "rockeries," they look grotesque, like giant abscesses. What is florid in *Noah's Garden* changes tonality in *Rockeries*, capturing the twilight gloom of an era's coming to end. Deng has always been keen to address social changes, tackle urgent issues of our time and keep pace with artistic development at large. Not surprisingly, he has set out to create the third series, *Gene Mutations*.

On November 26, 2018, the day before the 2nd International Summit on Human Genome Editing was inaugurated in Hong Kong, He Jiankui, a Chinese biologist, announced a bioengineering project that shocked the world. Using the genome-editing technology, he mutated two human foetuses and "created" two girls, named "Lulu" and "Nana." As human genome can be mutated against rules to create "new kinds of human beings," the "post-human" issue becomes all the more urgent. He

Wenn sich verschrottete Gebrauchtwagen in „Steingärten“ verwandeln, dann nehmen diese groteske Züge an und gleichen riesigen Abszessen. *Noah's Garden* wirkt überladen. Die *Rockeries* zeichnen sich hingegen durch eine andere Gesinnung aus und fangen die letzten Zuckungen einer sich nun zu Ende neigenden Ära ein. Guoyuan setzt sich seit jeher mit gesellschaftlichen Umbrüchen auseinander, stellt sich den Problemen der heutigen Zeit und verfolgt aufmerksam die aktuellen künstlerischen Entwicklungen. Daher verwundert es nicht, dass er seine dritte Serie, die *Gene Mutations*, in Angriff genommen hat.

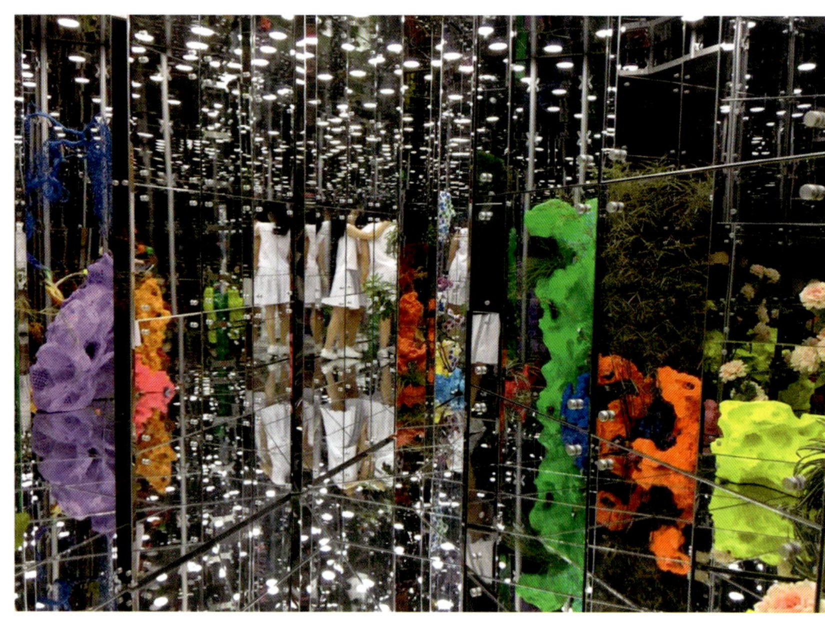

Noahs Garten II, Innenansicht

Noah's Garden II, inside

Am 26. November 2018, einen Tag vor der Eröffnung des zweiten Internationalen Gipfels zur Bearbeitung von Humangenomen in Hong Kong verkündete der chinesische Biophysiker He Jiankui ein Bioengineering-Projekt, das weltweit für Entsetzen sorgte. Mithilfe der Genom-Editierung manipulierte er zwei menschliche Föten und „erschuf“ zwei Mädchen namens „Lulu“ und „Nana“. Da das menschliche Genom auf missbräuchliche Weise manipuliert werden kann, um neue „Arten von menschlichen Wesen“ hervorzubringen, stellt sich das „posthumane“ Problem umso dringlicher. He Jiankuis Projekt wurde in China in der breiten Öffentlichkeit zur Sprache gebracht und diskutiert. Wie aber verhält es sich mit ähnlichen Fällen in anderen Teilen der Welt? Werden diese geheim gehalten? Bei der Manipulation des menschlichen Genoms zur Erschaffung neuer Organismen handelt es sich nicht um einen Science-Fiction-Plot oder eine Fantasie, sondern um die heutige Realität, besser gesagt, um einen Alptraum, der bedrohliche Züge annimmt. Heutzutage bedroht die Technologie die menschliche Existenz, was direkt mit dem Schicksal der Menschheit verbunden ist. Guoyuan setzt sich mit diesem Thema in seinen Arbeiten umfassend auseinander. Die Form der zeitgenössischen Kunst, die seine Arbeit repräsentiert, verbindet politische Aktualität mit ästhetischer Zeitmäßigkeit. Beim Versuch, die beiden Aspekte miteinander zu verbinden, verknüpfen viele Zeitgenossen die Kunst mit Industrie und Mode. Guoyuan geht es hingegen um die durch die Technologie im Informationszeitalter verursachte menschliche Entfremdung. Auf diese Weise entfalten seine Arbeiten ihre ganze Wirkkraft und fördern das Groteske, den Prunk, die Eigenartigkeiten und wilden Fantasien zutage, die die Welt von morgen ausmachen.

Gene Mutations umfasst vier Unterserien – *Loreley's Garden* (*Loreleys Garten*), *Revelations* (*Offenbarungen*), *The Gods' Garden* (*Der Göttergarten*) und *Images of the Gods* (*Götterbilder*), die sich alle durch ihr seltsam anmutendes Erscheinungsbild kennzeichnen. Die dritte Unterserie legt den Fokus auf die Genkombination und gibt dabei Schmetterlinge wieder, die in den Dinosauriergarten eindringen, Libellen, die in den Tigergarten eindringen, Meerestiere, die in den Nilpferdgarten, Käfer, die in den Elefantengarten, Spinnen, die in den Pandabärengarten, Kakerlaken, die in den Löwengarten, Honigbienen, die in den Orang-Utan-Garten und Götter, die in den Robotergarten eindringen. Die Genome von Tigern und Honigbienen werden beispielsweise miteinander kombiniert, um ihren Nachwuchs hervorzubringen. Wie

Jiankui's project got reported and discussed openly in China, but how about similar cases in other parts of the world? Are they being kept secret? To mutate human genome to create new organisms is not a sci-fi plot or a fantasy, but a reality we are facing today – more exactly, a nightmare that looms large. Today, technology is jeopardizing the very existence of mankind. This urgent issue directly relates to the destiny of mankind. Deng Guoyuan addresses the issue intensely in his works. The kind of contemporary art that his works represent features both political contemporaneity and aesthetic contemporaneity. When trying to combine the two, many have focused on how to associate the arts with industry and fashion. In contrast, Deng is concerned about human alienation inflicted by technology in the information age. His works thus becomes so powerful, featuring grotesqueness, gaudiness, oddities and wild fantasies the world will encounter in the future.

Gene Mutations comprises four subseries – *Loreley's Garden*, *Revelations*, *The Gods' Garden*, and *Images of the Gods*, which all have a strange outlook. The third subseries focuses on gene combination, portraying butterflies invading dinosaurs' garden, dragonflies invading tigers' garden, marine organisms invading hippos' garden, beetles invading elephants' garden, spiders invading pandas' garden, cockroaches invading lions' garden, honeybees invading orangutans' garden, and the gods invading robots' garden. For instance, the genomes of tigers and honeybees are combined to yield their offspring. How do their offspring look like? We see not only flying tigers, but also carnivorous honeybees. On a honeybee's belly grows a human foot, and on a tiger's buttock grows a flower in full bloom, bathed in sunlight.

Drawn upon imagination, *Noah's Garden* shows a glimpse of hope for mankind. *Rockeries*, a tragic rendition of the eclipse of the industrial age at the dawn of the information age, more or less has a realistic touch. In contrast to both, *Gene Mutations* alerts us of a crisis on the horizon, namely, technology poses a threat to the very validity and legitimacy of human existence. When anthropocentrism can no longer be taken for granted, humans will suffer an excruciating sense of self-doubt

Noahs Garten II, Innenansicht

Noah's Garden II, inside

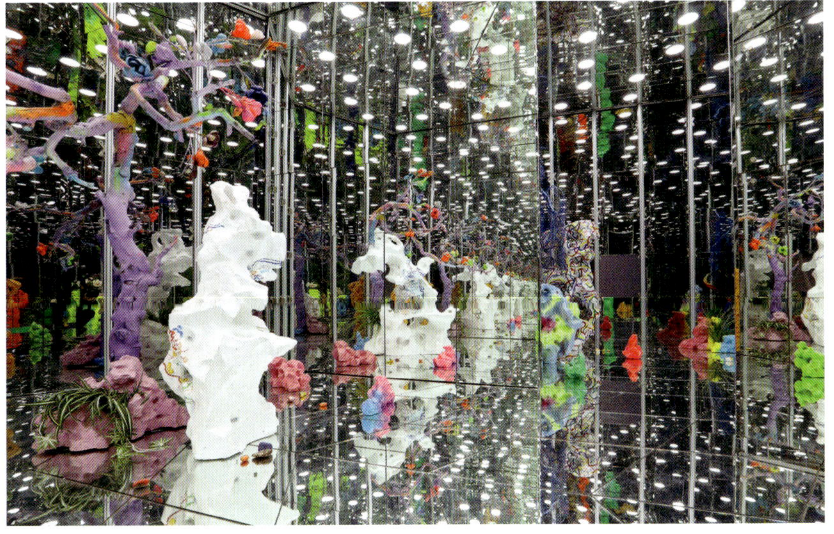

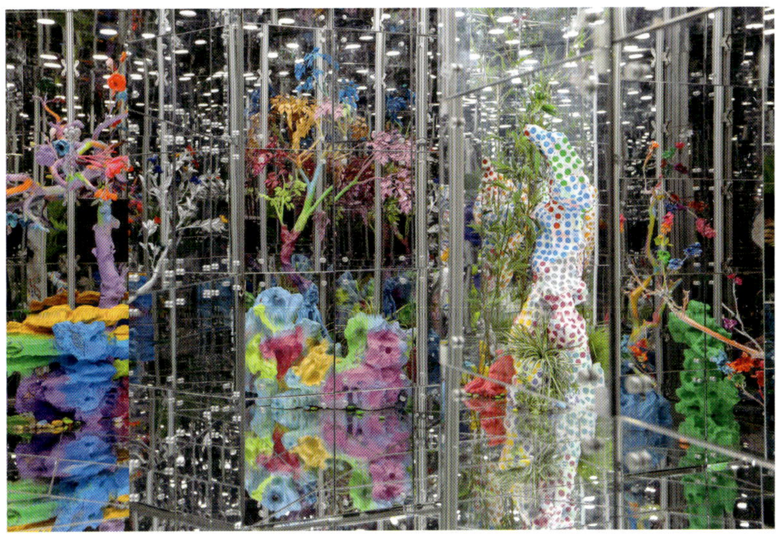

aber sieht dieser Nachwuchs aus? Wir entdecken nicht nur fliegende Tiger, sondern auch fleischfressende Honigbienen. Auf dem Bauch einer Honigbiene wächst ein menschlicher Fuß und am Hinterteil eines Tigers sprießt eine Blüte, auf die das Sonnenlicht fällt.

Die Werkserie *Noah's Garden*, die an unsere Vorstellungskraft appelliert, versprüht einen Funken Hoffnung für die Menschheit. Die Werkserie *Rockeries*, die auf tragische Weise den Untergang des Industriezeitalters und den Beginn des Informationszeitalters verkündet, zeichnet sich hingegen durch ihren realistischen Charakter aus. Im Vergleich zu diesen beiden Werkserien warnt uns *Gene Mutations* vor einer aufziehenden Krise, und zwar vor der Technologie, die die Gültigkeit und Legitimität der menschlichen Existenz infrage stellt. Wenn der Anthropozentrismus nicht länger als selbstverständlich gilt, werden die Menschen unter einem quälenden Gefühl von Selbstzweifel und Hoffnungslosigkeit leiden. Von Guoyuans Arbeiten nehmen wir keine Geräusche wahr. Wir sehen nur die Schmetterlinge, die in das Gebiet der Dinosaurier eindringen, was die folgende Perspektive impliziert: Jeder Genotyp kann auf die Menschheit übertragen werden. Menschen können somit zu allen Arten von „unmenschlichen" Organismen werden – kraftvoll, intelligent, rücksichtslos und schön. Letztendlich werden die Menschen zu rein körperlichen Kreaturen degradiert, die von Maschinen überflügelt werden und abhängig sind von künstlichen Arten, die durch Genkombination entstehen. Aus diesem Blickwinkel gesehen rüttelt die Serie *Gene Mutations* den Betrachter auf.

Wenn man Guoyuans Werkserien in Form von virtuellen Bilder präsentieren würde, würden sie eine Art virtuelle Realität darstellen. Genauso wie wir uns dem Orakel eines Propheten annähern, neigen wir dazu, der virtuellen Realität auf eine respektvolle und zugleich desinteressierte Weise zu begegnen. Guoyuan realisiert zusammen mit seinen Mitarbeiter eine Vielzahl von Skulpturen, die Tausende Fälle von Genmutation wiedergeben – ein endloser Prozess, der außer Kontrolle geraten kann. Die Ausstellung zeigt nur einen Teil dieses Prozesses. Analog zum Genombearbeitungsunfall im November 2018 ist die Genmutation anfangs vielleicht nur ein Gesprächsthema. Sie kann aber zu Veränderungen führen, die den modifizierten Spiegelfunktionen in Guoyuans Arbeiten vergleichbar sind, die eine vollständige Umkehr bedeuten. In *Noah's Garden* zaubert der Spiegel ohne Unterlass bizarre Illusionen hervor, sodass der Betrachter kurzweilig dem Alltag entfliehen kann. Die Anspielung auf die Arche Noah verweist hierbei auf den menschlichen Überlebensinstinkt. Die düstere Situation, die die Werkserie *Gene Mutations* erzeugt und der die Menschheit heute ausgesetzt ist, kann jedoch nicht länger als Illusion oder Vermutung abgetan werden. Die Spiegel werden folglich zum Realitätshintergrund. Wenn der Betrachter die Miniskulpturen betrachtet, die Fälle von Genmutation wiedergeben, entdeckt er fragmentierte Bilder seiner selbst in den Spiegeln. Guoyuans Werkserien gelingt es somit, uns die Rolle anschaulich vor Augen zu führen, die das Genetic-Engineering für die Mutation und den Eingriff am Menschen spielt.

and despair. In front of Deng's works, we hear no sound, only see butterflies invading dinosaurs' territory, which implies the following prospect. Any genotype, and literally anything can encroach on humanity, humans can be changed into all kinds of "inhuman" organisms – powerful, intelligent, ruthless and beautiful. In the end, humans will degrade to become merely corporeal creatures, outwitted by machines and at the mercy of man-made species born of gene combination. In this regard, *Gene Mutations* is really shocking.

If the series is presented as virtual images, it would remain as a kind of virtual reality. Just as how we deal with a prophet's oracles, we tend to treat virtual reality in a respectful but dismissive manner. But the fact is, Deng is leading a team to create a multitude of sculptures, portraying thousands of cases of gene mutation – an endless process that may grow out of control. The exhibition only shows part of such creation. Just like the genome-editing incident in November 2018, gene mutation might only be a topic for discussion at the start. But it may lead to changes comparable to how the mirror's function changes in Deng's works, namely, a total reversal. In *Noah's Garden*, the mirror constantly conjures up fancy illusions, so the audience can momentarily escape hardships in real life. The allusion to the Noah's Ark endorses the human instinct for survival. Whereas in *Gene Mutations*, the dire situation that mankind is facing today can no longer be dismissed as illusion or speculation. Mirrors become the backdrop of reality. Whenever the audience look at the mini-sculptures portraying cases of gene mutation, they see fractured images of themselves in the mirrors. Thanks to the series, the role that genetic engineering plays in mutating and intervening with humanity has become a reality so tangible to us.

Deng Guoyuan
Kunst und Parallelrealität

Robert C. Morgan

Die Rolle, die die Quantifizierung in unserem Alltag spielt, stellt einen der umstrittensten Glaubenssätze in unserer sich rasant beschleunigenden globalisierten Welt dar. Man hat quasi den Eindruck, als ob alle Bereiche des menschlichen Lebens zunehmend von verschiedenen Codes, Passwörtern und Zahlen bestimmt werden, die die unausweichliche Hyperstruktur in unserem Alltag zu bilden scheinen. Am anderen Ende des Spektrums mag sich mancher fragen: Kann es sein, dass die Bedeutung, die heutzutage der Menge beigemessen wird, in die Irre führt? Bewegen wir uns in die falsche Richtung? Es gilt als erwiesen, dass viele Menschen keinen Sinn mehr in ihrem Leben sehen – nicht nur aus materialistischen Gründen –, sondern in einem weitaus einschneiderenden Maße. Eine der wichtigsten, unausgesprochenen Fragen in der heutigen, von den kommerziellen Medien durchdrungenen Welt lautet, wie wir in Anbetracht eines sich anbahnenden Lebens mit der Künstlichen Intelligenz die richtige Balance finden, um unser grundlegendes menschliches Bedürfnis nach Stabilität zu erfüllen. Einige glauben, dass die Antwort nicht nur mit großen Investitionen, Blockchain-Technologie und anderen finanziellen Belangen zu tun hat, sondern auch mit einer natürlichen Suche nach Qualität und Bedeutung im Kontext einer Kunst, die auch unseren emotionalen und spirituellen Anliegen entgegenkommt.

In diesem Zusammenhang möchte ich einen Einblick in das Werk des Künstlers Deng Guoyuan geben, der viele komplexe und faszinierende Gebiete künstlerisch erkundet. Der vielschichtige Charakter seiner Arbeiten zeichnet sich durch eine metaphysische und biomorphe Seite aus, da er sich mit Inhalt und Form auf eine Weise auseinandersetzt, die über die normierte Welt mit ihren gewöhnlichen Ereignissen und Wahrnehmungen routinierten Verhaltens hinausgeht und weit in imaginäre Gefilde vordringt. Was mich an Guoyuans Arbeiten besonders beeindruckt, ist seine Fähigkeit, eine alternative Welt zu erschaffen, die auf einer Parallelrealität gründet. Diese Realität umfasst die chinesische Tradition des Künstlers, der sich aber gleichzeitig durch andere gedankliche Galaxien bewegt, die Einfluss auf den Lauf des menschli-

Deng Guoyuan
Art and Parallel Reality

Robert C. Morgan

The role of quantification in everyday life constitutes one of the most conflicted tenets in our rapidly accelerating global society. It would appear that all aspects of human life are in the process of becoming subjected to various codes, passwords, and numbers that presumably represent the inevitability of a hyper-structure in our everyday lives. At the other end of the spectrum, one might ask: is it possible that this overriding emphasis on quantity in today's world is misleading? Are we going in the wrong direction? There is evidence that a significant number of human beings have lost the notion of meaning in their lives – not solely from a materialist perspective – but in more significant ways. One of the major, unspoken questions in today's environment – deliberately evaded by commercial media – is how to find a balance in a way that satisfies our fundamental human need for stability as we embark on a course of living with artificial intelligence. There are some who believe the answer is not solely related to high-level investments, block chain technology, and other financial proprieties, but may also be discovered through an innately discernable search for quality and meaning in the presence of art that would also include our desire to find emotional and spiritual fulfilment.

In the context of this statement, I would like to introduce the work of the artist, Deng Guoyuan, whose involvement in art has taken him to many areas of investigation, both complex and intriguing. The complexity has a metaphysical aspect as well as a biomorphic one in that he appears to be dealing with matter and form in ways that go beyond the normative world into a vast imaginative territory that surpasses ordinary events and perceptions of routine behaviour. What strikes me as significant in Deng's work is his ability to construct an alternative world based on the parallel reality of the imagination. This reality encompasses the artist's Chinese tradition as he concurrently moves through other galaxies of thought that propose to impact the course of human life. As Deng has made clear, the world of his imagination is one removed from how he lives in the reality of the present. It is a vastly different

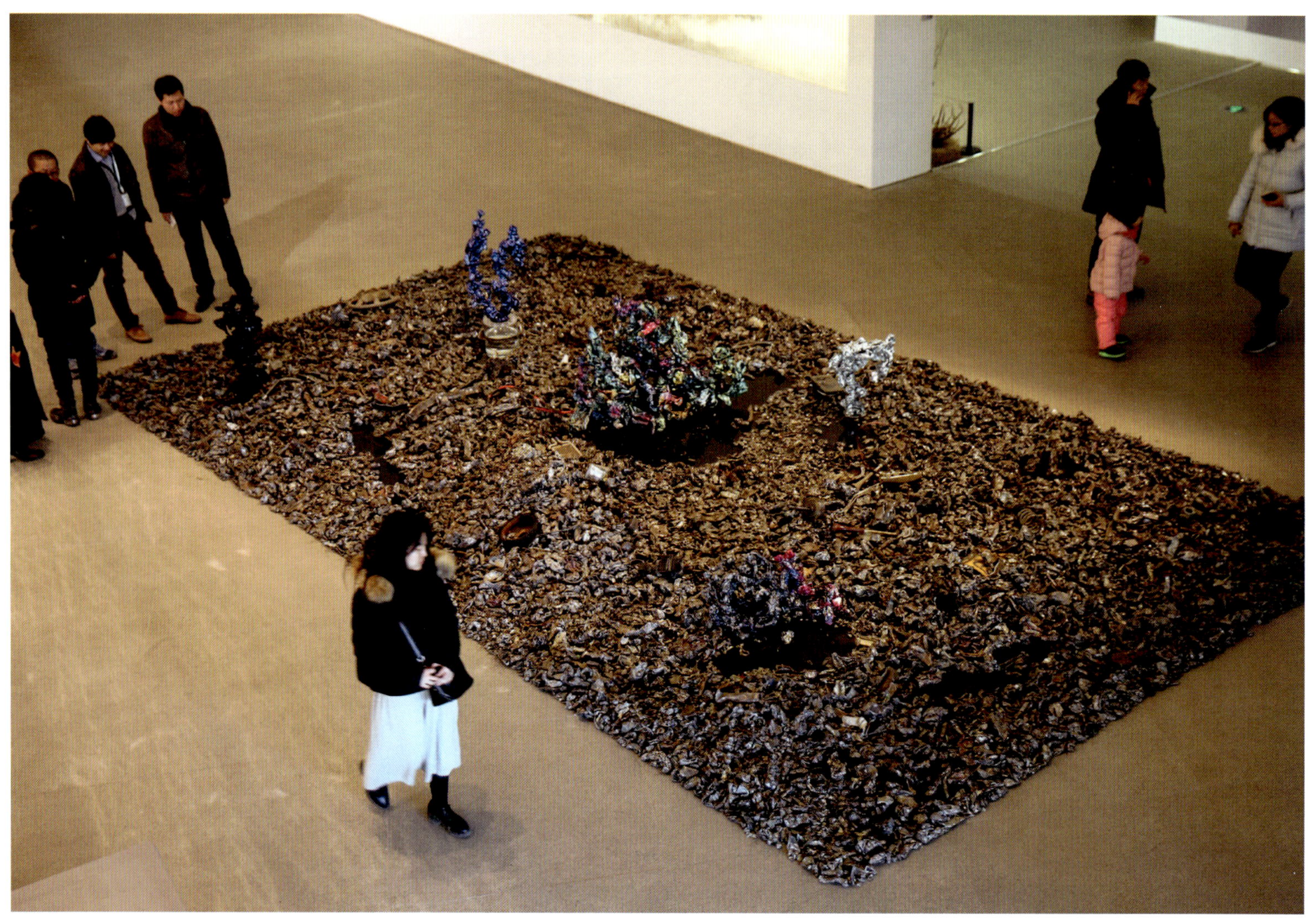

Ein zerstörter Garten, 2017
Autoschrott, Autolack, Aquarium
Variable Maße
Beijing Minsheng Modern Art Museum, Peking, China

A Ruined Garden, 2017
Scraped automobile waste, car paint, aquarium
Dimensions variable
Beijing Minsheng Modern Art Museum, Beijing

chen Lebens nehmen. Dabei macht Guoyuan aber deutlich, dass seine Vorstellungswelt nichts gemein hat mit seinem Leben in der gegenwärtigen Realität. Es handelt sich um eine vollkommen andere Welt, um eine Welt, die wir mit Künstler/innen in Verbindung bringen, die fortwährend damit beschäftigt sind, neue Denksysteme zu erspinnen, die größtenteils außerhalb oder jenseits der Alltagssphäre liegen.

Wie viele Künstler hat Guoyuan eine mythologische Welt erschaffen, die eine andere Realität umfasst, eine Realität, die er in seinem Atelier von einem Tag auf den anderen immer wieder neu erfindet. Sein mythischer Kontext ist komplex und offen für verschiedene Deutungsideen und -formen. Kriker setzen häufig das, was sie sehen oder denken, in Beziehung zu dem künstlerischen Werk: Guoyuans Arbeiten sollten aber aus einem unabhängigen Blickwinkel betrachtet und gedeutet werden: Guoyuan ist durch die alten chinesischen Legenden und die Geschichten der klassischen Literatur geprägt, die sich um das drehen, was sich in den Bergen und Flüssen des Landes ereignete. Diese Mythen und Volksmärchen sind in verschiedenen Gegenden eingebettet, größtenteils spielen sie sich im Landesinneren Chinas ab. Einige Geschichten bieten sich für das transformative Kunstkonzept des Künstlers an, wieder andere enthalten Wahrheiten, die er aus der Vergangenheit gezogen hat.

Zugleich ist Guoyuan von den mit der Natur verbundenen Traditionen geprägt, wobei er sich auch der Unmenge an massenproduzierten Objekten bewusst ist, die unser schnelllebiges, kommerziell geprägtes Umfeld überschwemmen – Plastikspielzeug,

world, one that we might expect from artists who are perpetually in the process of inventing new systems of thought, which is, for the most part, outside or beyond the reaches of everyday life.

Like many artists, Deng has constructed a mythological world that encompasses another reality, a reality that he invents and re-invents in his studio from one day to the next. His mythical context is complex and open to many different ideas and forms of interpretation. Critics will often read what they see or how they think in relation to the artist's work; but Deng's work should be seen and understood from an independent, autonomous point of view. He has been influenced by the ancient Chinese legends and the stories born from Classical literature that revolve around the history of what has occurred in the mountains and rivers throughout his country. These are myths and folklore embedded in different geographies. Their various locations are largely in the interior of China. They are stories that lend themselves to the artist's transformative idea of art, and stories that embed the truths he has learned from the past.

At the same time that Deng is influenced by these traditions in the context of nature, he is also cognizant of the deluge of mass-produced objects that have come into our fast-paced commercial environment – plastic toys and dolls and machine parts that are designed for children to play. But in the case of Deng, they are not merely for play, they also suggest a future world in which the problems of everyday life are surmounted through fakery and the encroachment generated by artificial intelligence. As a kind of prediction of the future, the artist takes these manufactured toys, animals, machines parts, and life-like dolls into his reality. As he mutates these animal toys with one another, he is also reflecting on the process that genetic mutations will inevitably come through scientific laboratories and ultimately will integrate themselves into the human population. What happens when the genetic structure of a marine creature – a shark or a whale or a crab or a lobster – is mutated with a mammal whose history has always been on the land? Will this hybrid creature have a better life in the throes of trying to exist in a foreign, unknown environment? And what happens if machine parts replace intestines or armatures of the human body as they are already doing? What will be the impact of further experimentation on human life and on the world as we know it today?

For the artist, Deng Guoyuan, the schemata he has outlined moves from the ancient past into the present and ultimately to an unknown future. He begins with his *Loreley's Garden* in which he constructs cubistic Taihu stones. Instead of the natural form of rocks, the structures are geometrically constructed using steel pipes and LED lamps. The variety of these structures, when seen together in a darkened space, is mesmerizing. Whether of not, one thinks of the ancient past is almost irrelevant. The fact of the matter is that these forms give a new look to "scholars' rocks" and are perhaps more in keeping with the postmodern present. Another work referred to as *The Gods of New Species* is also a provocation, but in a vastly different way. Here the artist is morphing the appearance of dolls and various toys through his own set of mutations. His suppressed anxieties relate to the future and begin to reveal themselves both in terms of "scientific" mutations and the out-of-control usage of artificial intelligence.

Puppen und Maschinenteile für Kinder. In Guoyuans Fall sind diese jedoch nicht nur zum Spielen gedacht: Sie verweisen auf eine künftige Welt, in der die Probleme des Alltagslebens durch Vortäuschungen und die durch die Künstliche Intelligenz (KI) verursachten Beeinträchtigungen überschattet werden. Als eine Art Vorankündigung der Zukunft überführt der Künstler diese Spielzeuge, Tiere, Maschinenteile und lebensecht wirkenden Puppen in seine Realität. Indem er diese Spielzeugtiere untereinander verändert, setzt er sich auch mit dem Prozess auseinander, demzufolge die genetischen Mutationen durch wissenschaftliche Labors zur unvermeidbaren Realität werden und sich letztendlich selbst in die menschliche Bevölkerung integrieren. Was passiert, wenn die genetische Struktur eines Meerestieres – eines Haies, eines Wals, einer Krabbe oder eines Hummers – mit einem Säugetier verändert wird, das immer auf dem Land gelebt hat? Wird dieses hybride Wesen ein besseres Leben führen, wenn es in einem fremden, unbekannten Umfeld um sein Überleben kämpft? Und was passiert, wenn Maschinenteile Eingeweide oder Glieder des menschlichen Körpers ersetzen, wie es bereits geschieht? Was sind die Auswirkungen weiterer Experimente mit dem menschlichen Leben und der Welt, wie wir sie heute kennen?

Die von Guoyuan entwickelten Konzepte reichen von der Vergangenheit bis zur Gegenwart und hin zu einer unbekannten Zukunft. Er beginnt mit *Loreley's Garden*, in dem er einen kubistischen Taiku-Felsen errichtet. Anstelle ihrer natürlichen Form sind diese Gebilde mit Stahlröhren und LED-Lampen geometrisch gestaltet. Die Vielfalt dieser Gebilde übt in einem verdunkelten Raum eine beinahe hypnotische Wirkung aus. Es spielt dabei keine Rolle, ob einer an die Vergangenheit denkt. Das was zählt, ist die Tatsache, dass diese Formen dem „Gelehrten-Felsen" eine neue Gestalt verleihen, die eher im Einklang mit der postmodernen Gegenwart zu stehen scheint. Auch eine als *The Gardens of the Gods and Gods of a New Classicism of Mountains and Rivers* bekannte Werkkategorie stellt eine Herausforderung dar, auch wenn auf ganz andere Weise. Der Künstler verwandelt hier die Erscheinungsform von Puppen und Spielzeugen durch seine Mutationen. Seine unterdrückten Ängste beziehen sich auf die Zukunft und beginnen sowohl im Hinblick auf wissenschaftliche Mutationen als auch auf die unkontrollierte Verwendung der Künstlichen Intelligenz zum Vorschein zu kommen.

In der Werkserie *Revelation* geht Guoyuan noch einen Schritt weiter und arbeitet mit Neonzeichen und -wörtern. Er betritt eine virtuelle Welt, in der eine Künstliche Intelligenz herrscht, die die Kontrolle über ihre eigenen Möglichkeiten verloren hat. In *The Passing of the Gods and Apocalypse* basieren seine imposanten Lichtinstallationen direkt auf genetischen Mutationen, KI-Kodierungen und Quantenphysik. Guoyuan setzt sich anhand dieser Projekte mit der Zukunft auseinander, er realisiert diese Gebilde jedoch auch als biomorphe, über die Natur wirksame Systeme, die er zu einem hypersurrealen Environment erhebt. Es handelt sich um eine metaphorische Welt, parallel zur Realität einer anderen Welt. Wir haben es mit einer echten Traumwelt zu tun, deren Ausbeutung und Entwicklung unser Verständnis von all dem verschleiert, an das sich die Menschen im Laufe von Tausenden von Jahren gewöhnt haben. Guoyuans künstlerische Position scheint die Realität der Vergangenheit herauszufordern, indem wir in Spiegelinstallationen blicken, in denen es von winzigen, bizarren Lebensformen nur so wimmelt. Auch wenn wir nicht genau

In a series of works referred to as Revelation, Deng goes further in working with neon signs and words. He enters into the virtual world of a heightened artificial intelligence that has lost control of its own facility. In the four works – *Butterfly, Dinosaur*, *Dragonhorse*, and *Dragonfly* – of *The Gods of New Species*, his exorbitant light installations are directly based on genetic mutations, AI codifications, and quantum physics. Deng claims to worry about the future as he proceeds to work on these projects – all part of a grand myth – yet he also appears committed to realizing these structures as biomorphic systems emanating through nature as he elevates these systems into a hyper-surreal environment. Essentially this is a metaphorical world that one might consider parallel to the reality of another world. It is a dream world exploited and developed in a manner that obscures our understanding of what human beings have grown accustomed to over thousands of years. It would appear that Deng Guoyuan's position as an artist is to challenge the reality of the past in such a way that we stare into his mirrored installations where tiny specimens of fantastical life abound. While we may not know exactly what we

Ein zerstörter Garten

A Ruined Garden

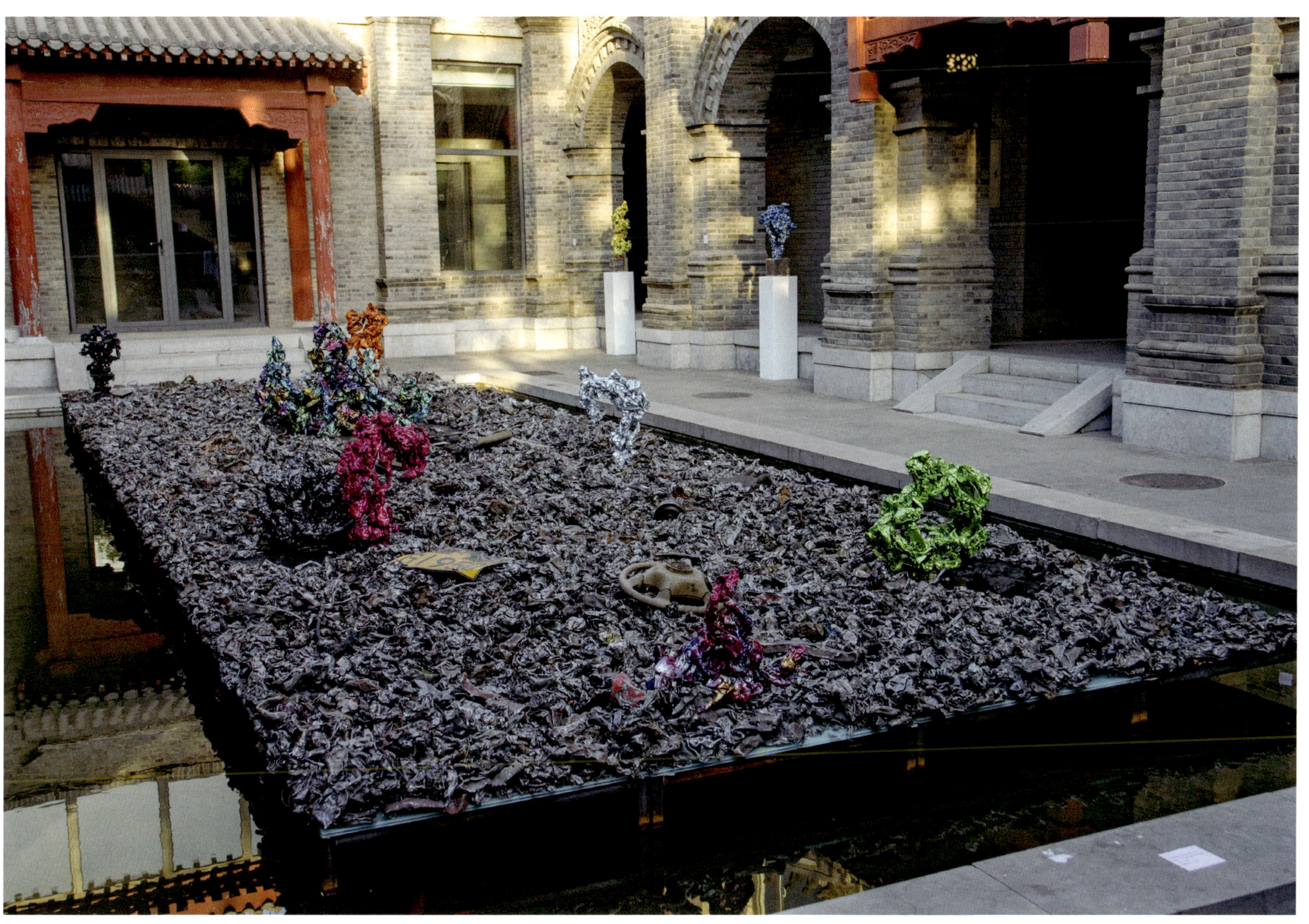

wissen, was wir wahrnehmen, verstehen wir, dass es sich um etwas Unbewusstes handelt, das plötzlich in der bewussten Welt auftaucht.

Haben wir es mit einer neuen Art des Denkens und Sehens zu tun? Wäre dies möglich, oder ist dies nur ein Klischee? Dasselbe wurde auch über die Arbeiten der Surrealisten, Hyperrealisten und Neo-Dadaisten behauptet, um nur einige zu nennen. Hierbei aber handelt es sich um westliche Kunstformen, die sich grundlegend von den chinesischen unterscheiden. Daher ist es vielleicht Zeit, den Spieß umzudrehen und Guoyuans strenge Installationen als das Ergebnis einer Kultur zu betrachten, die den Modernismus außer Acht ließ und von einer oppressiven Vergangenheit direkt in eine postmoderne Phase überging, die jetzt zu etwas hinführt, das weit über das hinausgeht, was sich die westliche Welt ein halbes Jahrhundert zuvor vorgestellt hätte. Jetzt ist für einen Künstler wie Guoyuan der Moment gekommen, abzuwarten, wie die bevorstehende Zukunft mit ihrem wissenschaftlichen und pseudowissenschaflichen Gepäck die Richtung der chinesischen Kunst beeinflussen wird. Seine bizarren Kreaturen legen nahe, dass das Leben auf der Erde auch weiterhin die impulsgebende Inspirationsquelle für die menschliche Imagination sein wird. Zudem ermöglichen sie es, über den kulturellen Austausch ein besseres gegenseitiges Verständnis zu gewinnen.

are perceiving, we understand they are something from the unconscious than has suddenly come into our conscious world.

Might we call it a new way of thinking and seeing? This is possible, but also commonplace. It has been said before in the work of the Surrealists, the Hyperrealists and the Neo-Dadaists, among countless others. But these are Western forms of art, not necessarily Chinese. Therefore, it may be the right time to turn the tables and to look at Deng's array of intensely severe installations as being the result of a culture that skipped over modernism and moved directly from an oppressive past into a post-modern phase that has now begun to blossom into something far beyond what the Western world would have imagined a half-century ago. Indeed, this is the time for an artist like Deng Guoyuan to emerge in coming to terms with how the impending future with all its scientific and pseudo-scientific baggage impacts the direction of Chinese art. His fabulous creatures exert a resonance that life on Earth may still be the source for the human imagination to spring forth. They offer fantastic qualitative possibilities for how to think and understand one another through the medium of cultural exchange.

Der Schöpfer neuer Welten

Liang Kegang

Die Chinesen sind seit jeher ein gefühlsbetontes Volk. Meiner Meinung nach ist dieser Wesenszug auf die piktographischen Wurzeln der chinesischen Zeichen zurückzuführen. Die chinesischen Zeichen waren einst Bilder, die später in der Schrift vereinfacht wurden, um die ideographischen geschriebenen Wörter und das entsprechende linguistische System zu bilden, das sich grundlegend von der Schrift und der Sprache der romanischen Sprachen des Mittelmeerraums unterscheidet, die selbst aus einer Vielzahl von abstrakten Symbolen hervorgekommen sind. Seit der Antike verwenden die Han-Chinesen Konzepte und Bedeutungen, die gleich Bildern mit einer ideographisch geprägten, visuellen Wahrnehmung verbunden sind, um die Welt zu verstehen und zu beschreiben und mit dieser zu interagieren. Daher zeichnen sich die Han-Chinesen auch durch ihr sentimentales Gemüt aus. In alten Zeiten liebten die Mitglieder der gebildeten Schicht sich zu versammeln, um über die Gegenwart nachzudenken und die Erinnerungen der Vergangenheit wach zu halten. Darüber hinaus hatten sie großes Interesse an einer illusorischen Form der Realität, die sich in der Seele einprägt, ähnlich dem Mond, der in einem Spiegel reflektiert wird. Im Laufe der Zeit entsprangen genau aus diesem Rahmen viele große Werke der Dichtkunst, der Literatur, des Drama, der Malerei, der Bildhauerei.

Zeitgenössische Künstler bilden heutzutage eine Gruppe, die sich durch besondere Vorstellungskraft und Kreativität auszeichnet. Sie sind ausgesprochen geschickt, gewöhnliche Materialien zu verwenden um virtuelle Welten und unerklärliche Wahrnehmungen hervorzubringen.

Mit Jörg Immendorff in seinem Atelier, 1996

With Jörg Immendorff in his studio, 1996, photo Deng Guoyuan Studio

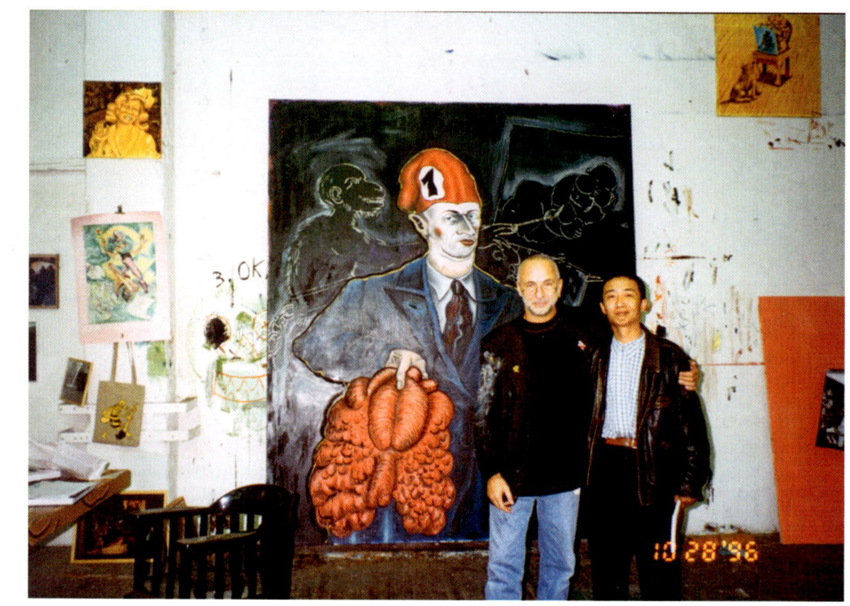

Creator of Folding Universes

Liang Kegang

The Chinese have always been an emotionally perceptive people. I think this is perhaps connected to the pictographic roots of Chinese characters. Chinese characters in remote antiquity were basically pictures, which were later simplified in the writing to form the unique ideographic written words and corresponding linguistic system that seems to differ in very essential ways from the writing and language of the Latin languages of the Mediterranean, which themselves emerged from clusters of abstract symbols. Thus, since ancient times, the Han Chinese people have used the concepts and meanings reflected through an ideographic visual perception akin to pictures to understand, describe and interact with the world. This has also made the Han Chinese quite a sentimental people. In ancient times, the more educated literati class enjoyed gathering to reflect on the present and reminisce about the past, and were particularly interested in illusions of reality projected in the heart like the moon reflected in a mirror. Throughout history, many great works of poetry, literature, drama, painting and sculpture emerged from precisely this background.

Zeichnung aus *The Classic of Mountains and Seas*, Penguin, 2000

The sketch of *The Classic of Mountains and Seas*, Penguin, 2000

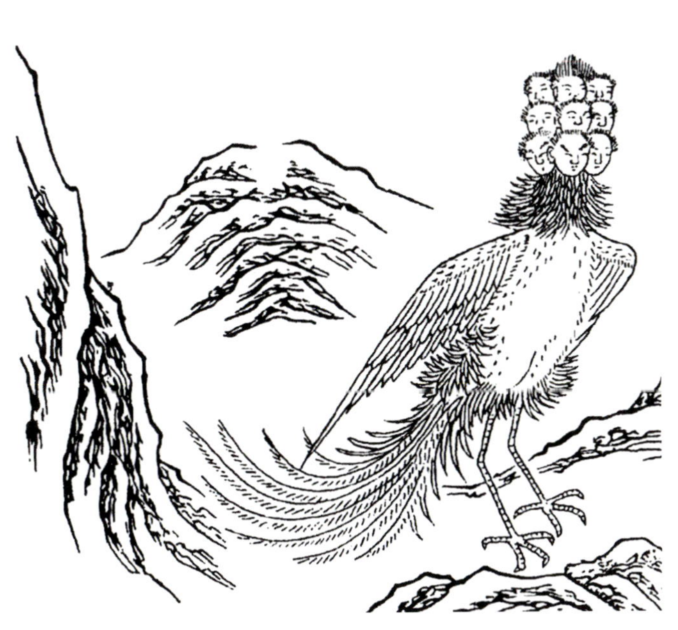

Contemporary artists today are a group with even more extraordinary imagination and creativity. They are particularly adept at the use of ordinary materials to produce virtual worlds and inexplicable perceptions.

Now a mature contemporary artist, Deng Guoyuan in his early days was subject to a very rigid and traditional Western art education system, and furthered his studies over many years in Germany, where he came to a deep understanding of the concepts and developmental threads of international modern and contemporary art. In recent years, however, he has not been satisfied by merely following the developmental logic of Western art history or the creative method-

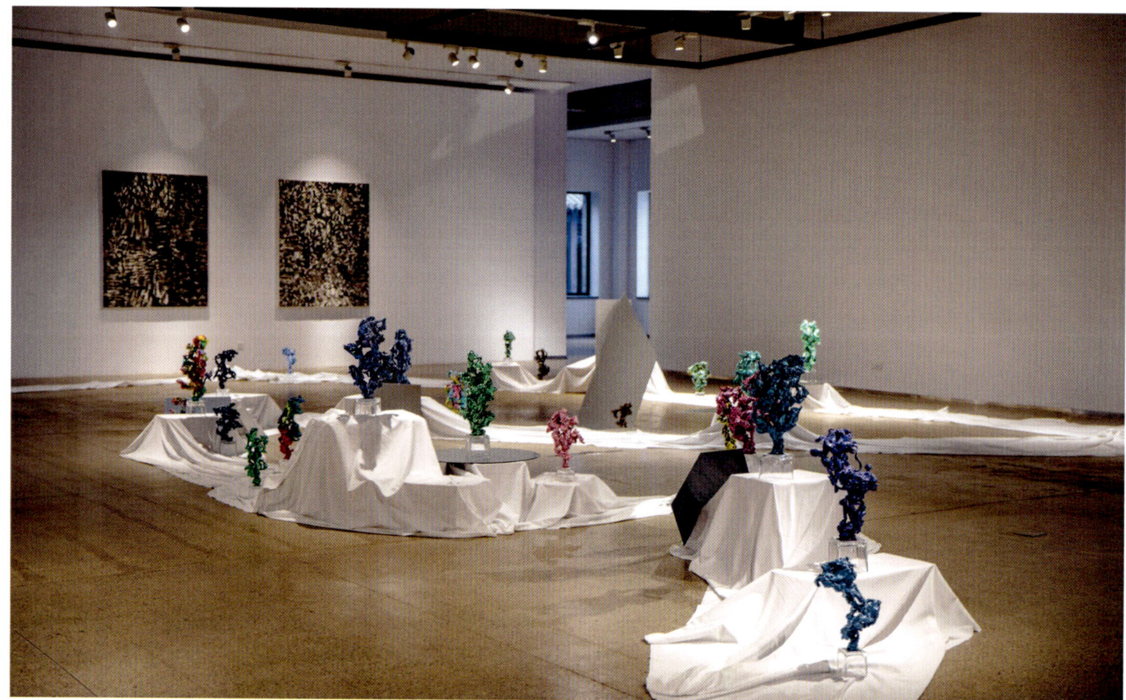

Bild eines ruinierten Gartens, 2018
Autoschrott, Autolack, Aquarium, Kleidung, Spiegel
Variable Maße
Tianjin International Design Week

Image of Ruined a Garden, 2018
Scraped automobile waste, car paint, aquarium, cloth, mirror
Dimensions variable
Tianjin International Design Week

Deng Guoyuan, der heute ein etablierter zeitgenössischer Künstler ist, durchlief zu Beginn seines künstlerischen Schaffens eine westliche Kunstausbildung, die sich durch ihren starren Akademismus kennzeichnete. Er vertiefte seine Studien mehrere Jahre lang in Deutschland, wo er sich umfassende Kenntnisse der Konzepte und Entwicklungsgrundlinien der internationalen modernen und zeitgenössischen Kunst aneignete. In letzten Jahren gab er sich jedoch nicht mehr damit zufrieden, der Entwicklungslogik der westlichen Kunstgeschichte oder den kreativen Methoden der internationalen zeitgenössischen Kunst zu folgen. Guoyuan begann hingegen, die traditionellen chinesischen Kulturressourcen mit der aktuellen Realität zu verbinden und in neue künstlerische, zeitgenössisch geprägte Ausdrucksformen umzuwandeln. Hierbei handelt es sich um ein kulturelles Bewusstsein, das sowohl der Familie und dem Land eines traditionellen konfuzianischen Intellektuellen als auch den Werten und der Gewissheit der Mission des zeitgenössischen Künstlers Tribut zollt. Der entscheidende Einschnitt in Guoyuans künstlerischer Praxis kündigte sich bereits vor langer Zeit in Werkserien wie *In the Garden* und in *Noahs Garten* an.

Als Inspirationsquelle diente Guoyuan das alte chinesische Kuriositätenbuch *Klassiker der Berge und Meere*, das Mythologie, Geographie, Volksbräuche und Phantasie verknüpft. Darüber hinaus prägten ihn die Erzählstruktur der griechischen Mythen sowie die radikalen Umbrüche und absurden Realitäten der rastlosen zeitgenössischen chinesischen Gesellschaft. Er verwendet Spielzeuge, Puppen und komplexe Spiegelräume um einen bizarren, fantastisch anmutenden Raum zu entwickeln, der tausende von seltsamen Lebensformen enthält.

Guoyuan hat zuerst eine virtuelle, parallele Welt erschaffen, die unabhängig von der realen existiert. Dann hat er diese Welt genommen und in drei miteinander verbundene und sich überschneidende Hauptbestandteile unterteilt. Das Ergebnis ist

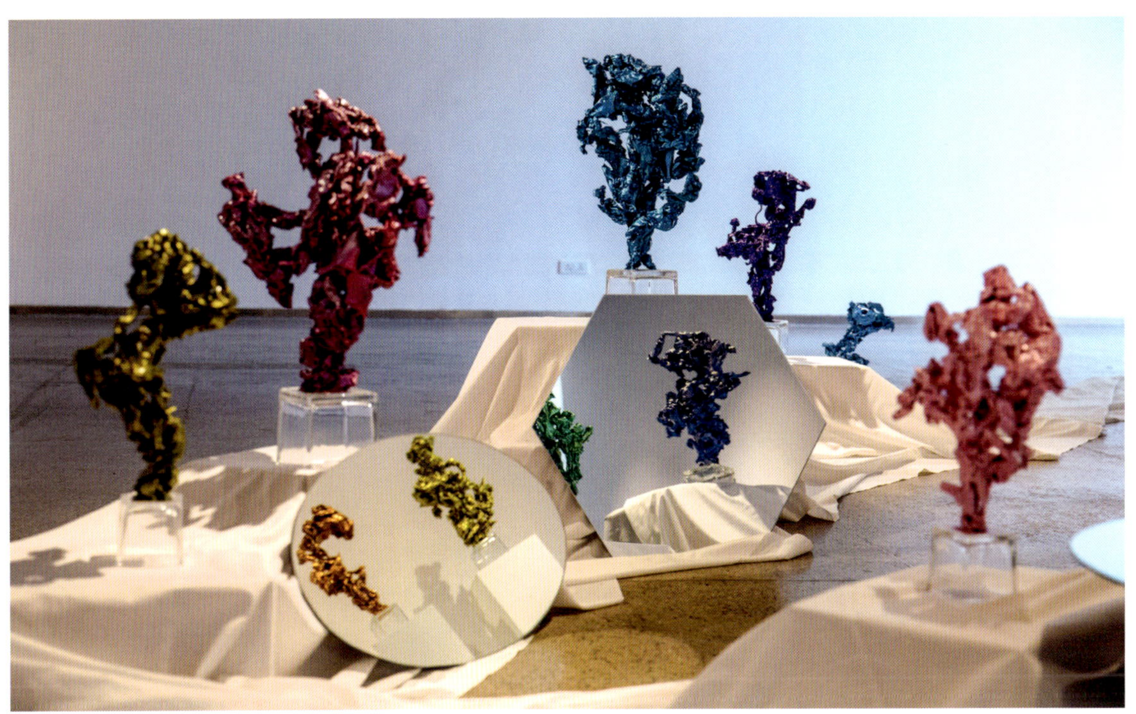

Bild eines ruinierten Gartens, Detailaufnahme

Image of a ruined Garden, details

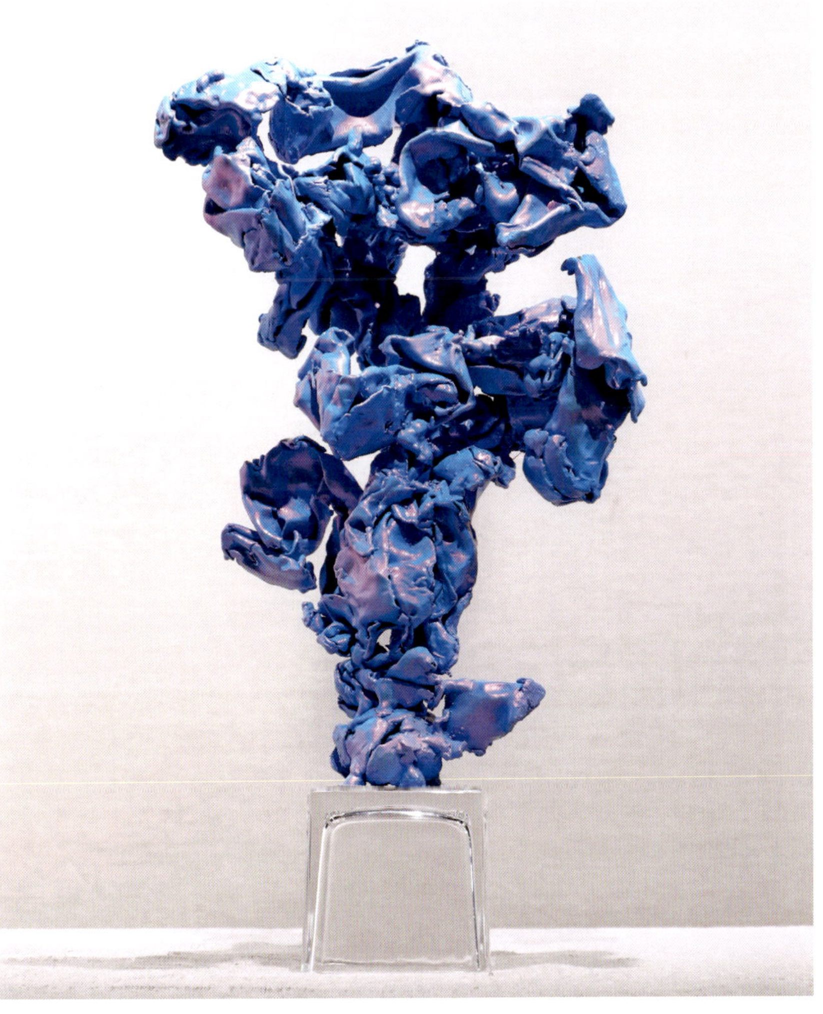

ologies of international contemporary art, but has instead begun to ponder how to combine China's own traditional cultural resources with its current state of reality, and transform them into new artistic forms with contemporary significance and traits. This is a cultural consciousness that possesses both the devotion to family and country of the traditional Chinese Confucian intellectual, and the values and sense of mission of the contemporary artist. This crucial shift in Deng Guoyuan's individual creative trajectory had already begun to manifest long ago in such series as *In the Garden* and *Noah's Garden*.

He found inspiration in that ancient Chinese book of oddities combining mythology, geography, folkways and imagination, *The Classic of Mountains and Seas*. He drew from the narrative structure of Greek mythology, and was also moved by the drastic changes and absurd realities of China's frenzied contemporary society, using toys, dolls and complex mirror spaces to construct a bizarre, fantastical space that contains thousands of strange life forms.

The artist has created a virtual, parallel world independent of reality. Deng Guoyuan has then taken this complete world and structured it into three key interrelated and overlapping components, an environmental

ein räumliches System, das dem Naturraum der realen Welt entspricht. Analog zur Funktion der Taihu-Steine der alten chinesischen Gelehrten, geben Guoyuans Installationen die Berge und Flüsse einer imaginierten Welt wieder. Der weitläufige Spiegelraum seiner Arbeiten steigert das allumfassende Gefühl von Unwirklichkeit und enthüllt die illusorische Beschaffenheit jeder und aller Welten.

Guoyuan hat ein den ökologischen Nischen und Ökosystemen der Natur entsprechendes System von Lebewesen hervorgebracht, indem er verschiedene Spielzeuge und Puppen zu Tausenden von fiktionalen Kreaturen und Arten zusammensetzte und darüber hinaus Hunderte von göttlichen Wesen kreierte. Aus seiner kindlichen Phantasie entsprangen auch Kämpfe und Eroberungen zwischen diesen Tieren und Gottheiten.

In jeder Welt, egal ob real oder imaginiert, existieren unsichtbare Grundsätze, die den Ablauf des Systems garantieren. Aus diesem Grund verwendet Guoyuan eine imposante Lichtinstallation über dem Spiegelraum, in der verschiedene Symbole aufblitzen, die mit der Genetik, der Künstlichen Intelligenz und der Quantenmechanik verbunden sind und auf die Entwicklung eines Systems verweisen, das auf Ordnung und Wahrheit basiert. Die Installation bringt darüber hinaus das Gespür und das Engagement des Künstlers für mögliche künftige Krisen in der realen Welt zum Ausdruck, darunter Klima- und Umweltkatastrophen, Genmutationen oder dem Kontrollverlust über die Künstliche Intelligenz. Schließlich setzt der Künstler auch verstärkt archäologische und wissenschaftliche Methoden ein, um seine Pseudo-Dokumentation der von ihm erzeugten Arten fortzuführen.

Guoyuan ist es gelungen, ein magisches Paralleluniversum voller Fiktionen und Metaphern erstehen zu lassen, dessen innere Logik und Ausdrucksfülle seine Reflexionen zur traditionellen Kultur, seine entschiedene Haltung gegenüber der heutigen Realität und sein großes Interesse für die Zukunftsperspektiven einprägsam widerspiegelt.

system to correspond to the spatial field of nature in the real world. In a method akin to the Taihu stones of China's ancient literati, his environmental installations reflect the mountains and rivers of his imagined world. The large mirror space of the artworks heightens the overall sense of unrealness, revealing the illusory essence of any and all worlds.

A system of living beings corresponds to the ecological niches and ecosystems of nature, which the artist has created by piecing together various toys and dolls into thousands of fictional creatures and species. He is even creating hundreds of deities. With his eternally childlike mind, he has also imagined battles and conquests between these beasts and gods.

Another thing that exists in every world, whether real or imagined, is an invisible set of principles that maintains the operations of the system. For this, Deng Guoyuan employs a massive light installation above the mirror space flashing with various symbols from genetics, artificial intelligence and quantum mechanics, alluding to the construction of a system underpinned by order and truth. It also profoundly reflects the artist's sensitivity and concern for the potential for future crises in the real world, such as climate and environmental catastrophes, genetic mutations, or loss of control over artificial intelligence. He also employs over-the-top fake archaeological and scientific methods to continue the counterfeit documentation of these fabricated species.

In this way, a magical world of the artist's imagination and fabrication has come into being in Deng Guoyuan's hands. He has fully constructed a complete, parallel world of speculation and metaphor, the inner logic and rich manifestations of which reveal a sensitive artist's profound thinking on traditional culture, incisive attitude toward the present reality, and deep concern for the prospects of the future.

Frühe Arbeiten

Early Works

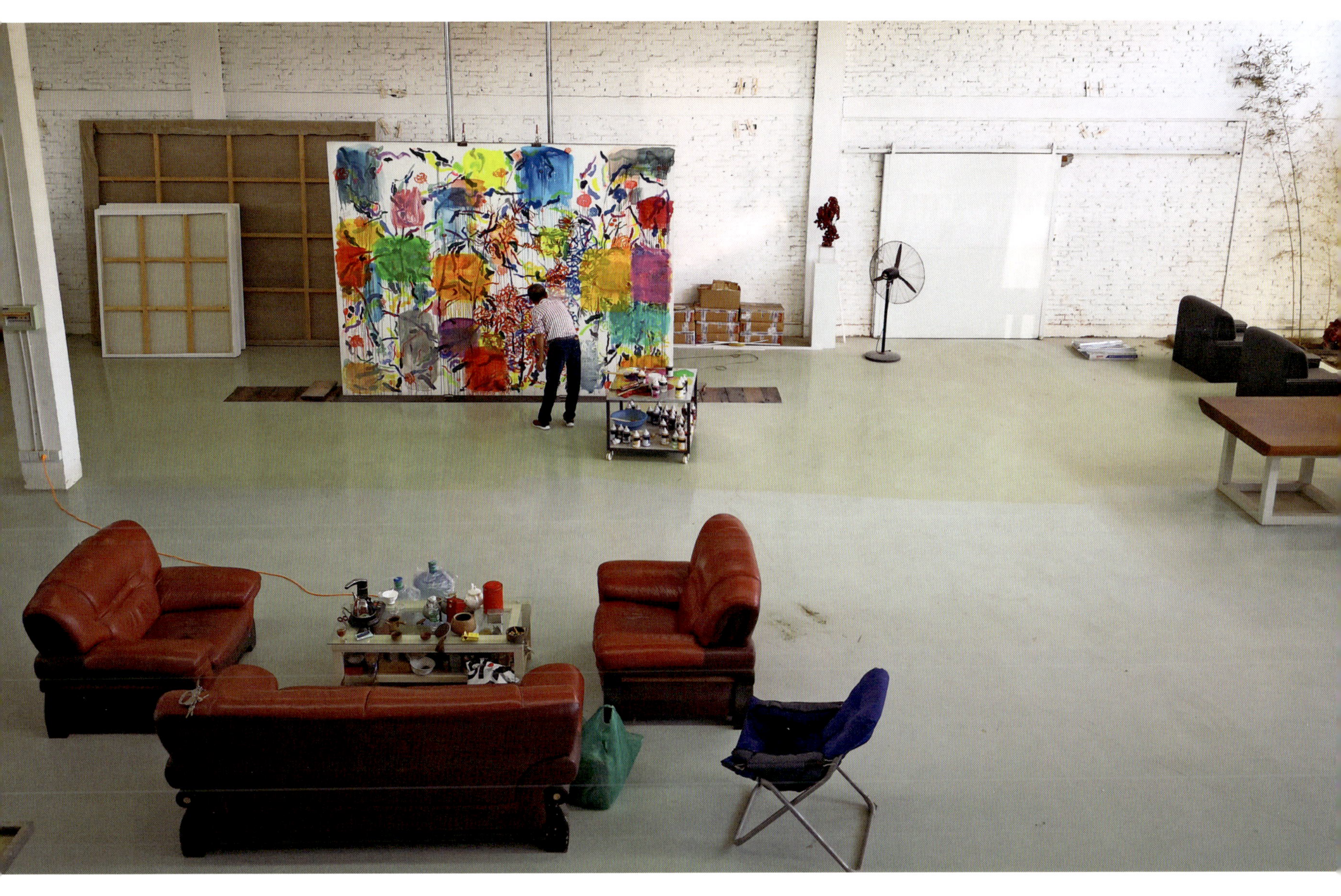

Deng Guoyuan bei seiner Arbeit im Atelier, 2018

Deng Guoyuan painting in his studio, 2018

Deng Guoyuan
Das Naturschöne und die durch die Kunst domestizierte Natur: Über das Naturideal

Unter den Arbeiten seiner bedeutenden Serie *In the Garden*, liegt – neben der virtuosen Maltechnik – ein Naturkonzept zugrunde, welches unter formellen Gesichtspunkten weit über die traditionelle chinesische Malerei hinausgeht, die sich niemals wirklich zur Abstraktion bekannte und stattdessen einen narrativen Kontext mittels einer figürlichen Darstellungsweise anstrebte. Guoyuan hingegen unternimmt das Wagnis, die Natur in rein abstrakte malerische Begriffe zu fassen, die nur durch die Sichtweise des Betrachters, die man als erkennende Wahrnehmung beschreiben könnte, in einen lesbaren, narrativen Kontext übertragen und auf ihre Ursprünge als Garten und Natur zurückgeführt werden. Dies ist insbesondere in Anbetracht der Tatsache von Interesse, dass sich Guoyuans neuere Arbeiten von Malerei abwenden und sich hin zu dreidimensionalen Objekten und vollständigen Environments entwickeln.

Beate Reifenscheid

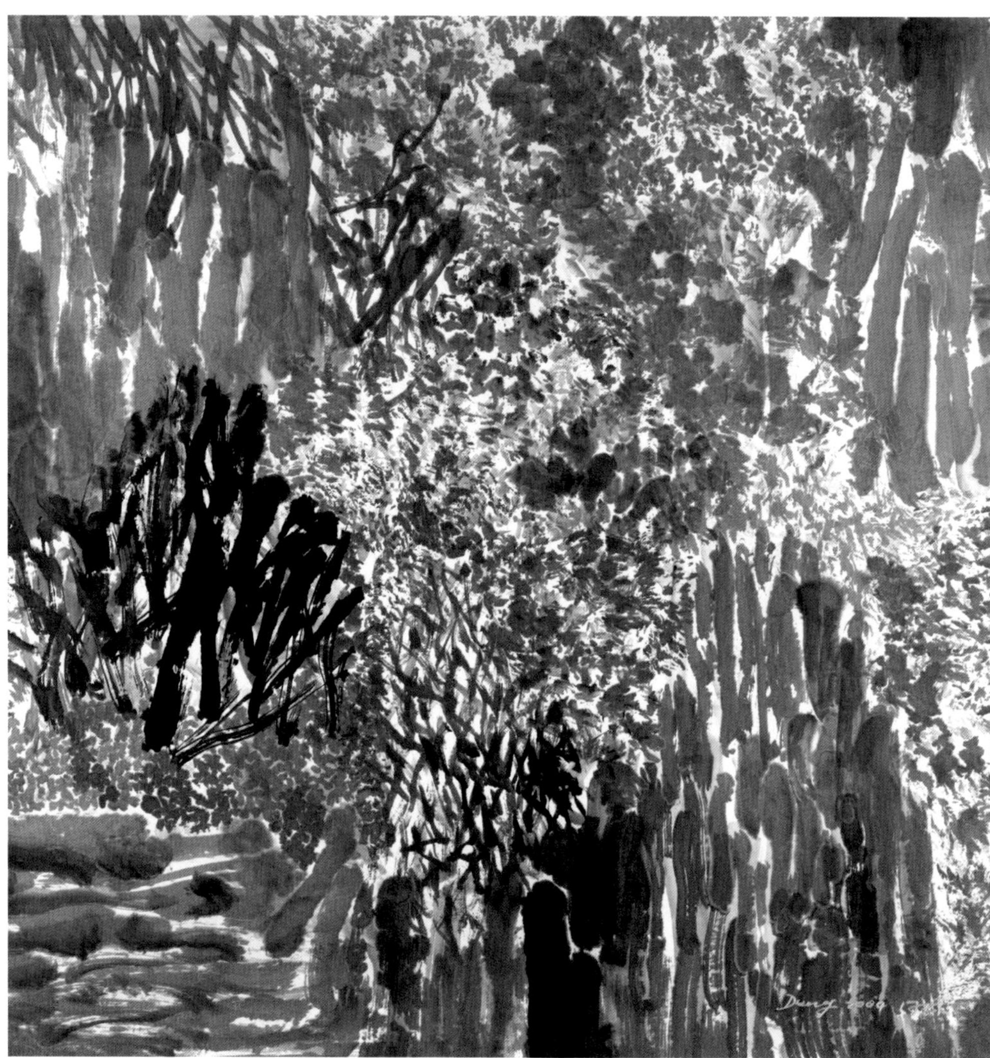

Im Garten Nr. 48, 2004
Chinesische Tusche, Reispapier
122 x 122 cm

In the Garden No. 48, 2004
Chinese ink, rice paper
122 × 122 cm

Deng Guoyuan
Naturally Beautiful and Domesticated by Art: On the Ideal of Nature

Underlying the works of his important *In the Garden* series is – besides the virtuoso application of painterly technique – a concept of nature that, in formal terms, radically transcends traditional Chinese painting. The latter advances not nearly as resolutely into abstraction, instead always seeking the narrative context and expressing it in, by and large, figuratively based painting. Deng Guoyuan, on the other hand, ventures on a translation of nature into purely abstract pictorial terms, which are transferred into a readable, narratively intended context – and traced to their origin in garden and nature – only through a mode of seeing on the part of the viewer that can be described as recognitive perception. This is particularly interesting considering that Deng Guoyuan's most recent works leave the realm of painting behind and, instead, "grow" into three-dimensional objects and entire environments.

Beate Reifenscheid

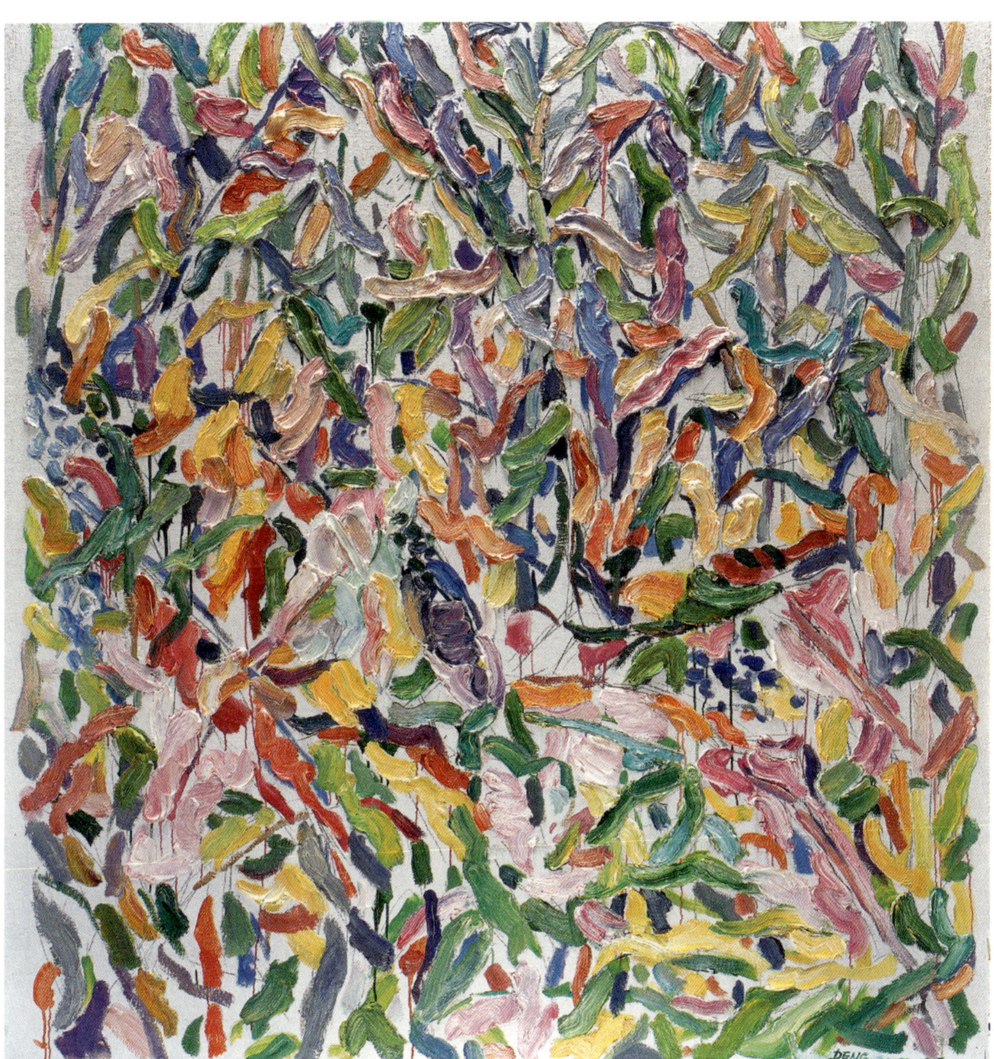

Das Feld Nr. 4, 2007
Öl auf Leinwand
200 x 180 cm

The Field No. 4, 2007
Oil painting
200 × 180 cm

Deng Guoyuan

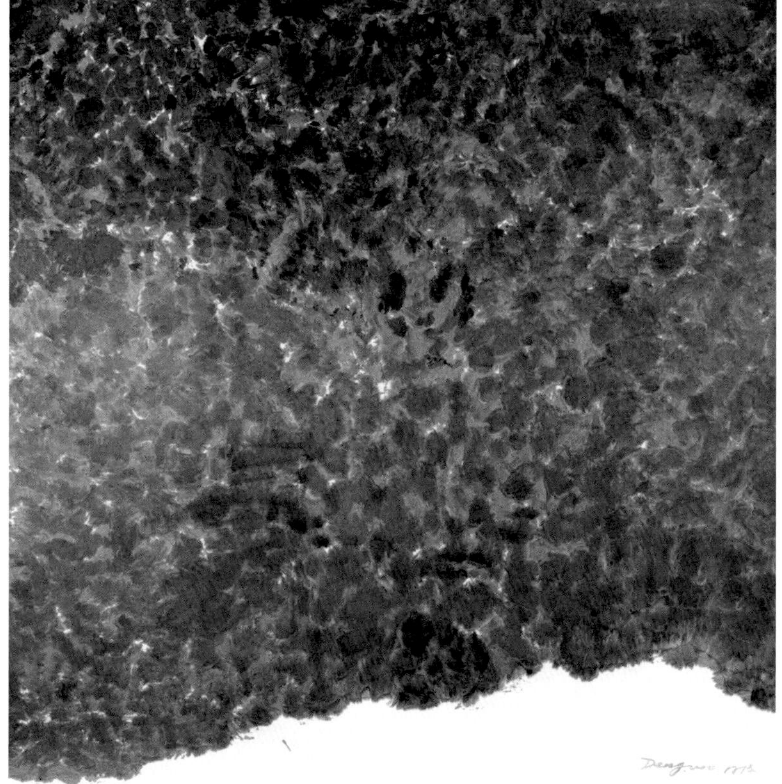

Auf dem Berg Nr. 5, 2004
Chinesische Tusche, Reispapier
122 x122 cm

In The Mountain No. 5, 2004
Chinese ink, rice paper
122 × 122 cm

Die fortschreitende Internationalisierung der Kunst stellt für den Verfasser ein oftmals beunruhigendes Thema dar. Werden wir wirklich die charakteristischen Merkmale jeder Kultur, insbesondere die unserer eigenen, über Bord werfen? Die Herausforderung, der sich heutige Künstler stellen, kann als ein Identitätsproblem betrachtet werden, nicht so sehr in Form von persönlichen Charakteristika als vielmehr unter dem Aspekt der Zugehörigkeit, der im Laufe jeder künstlerischen Laufbahn von Relevanz ist. Die Frage, die den chinesischen Maler Deng Guoyuan betrifft, dem sich die Ausstellung im Ludwig Museum widmet, dreht sich ganz um die Vorstellung einer kulturellen Bindung, die einem westlichen Menschen ein wenig befremdlich anmuten mag. Seit dem Beginn der Moderne trugen westliche Künstler gleich Elstern eine Vielzahl von visuellen Stimuli zusammen, die von weit entfernten Kulturen zu stammen scheinen. Und sie tun dies weiterhin – wir müssen uns nur den US-amerikanischen Maler Brice Marden in Erinnerung rufen, dessen Werkserie *Cold Mountain* der chinesischen Kalligrafie sehr viel zu verdanken hat. Im Laufe der Zeit wurde eine wahre Flut von kulturübergreifendem Material in die asiatische und westliche Kunstwelt geschwemmt. Sie haben versucht, die Wirkung des fremden Einflusses abzukanten. Die chinesischen Künstler/innen, deren mit dem Tuschpinsel realisierten Landschaftsgemälde der westlichen Ölmalerei von ihrer Auffassung und Form her diametral entgegenstehen, haben in den letzten hundert Jahren bevorzugt mit Öl gemalt. Ihr technisches Können in diesem Medium ist beachtlich, ihre Themenwahl erscheint jedoch manchmal unzeitgemäß. Guoyuan begann interessanterweise als Ölmaler, bevor er sich im Jahr 2000 seinen Tuscharbeiten auf Papier zuwandte. In kleinem Umfang nahm er so an der Öffnung der chinesischen Kunst für westliche Einflüsse teil, zumindest in Bezug auf seine Materialien. Seine Rückkehr zur traditionellen chinesischen Malerei wurde durch seine Erfahrung mit der westlichen Kunst, die er teilweise auf seinen Reisen nach Europa und in die USA kennenlernte, beeinflusst. Die Frage, die ihn sowie die aktuelle Praxis der Tuschmalerei betrifft, handelt davon, inwieweit seine Arbeiten *aktiv* an einem Stil teilhaben, der in irgendeiner Form die Tradition der westlichen Kunst widerspiegelt. Wie wir beobachten können, suggeriert Guoyuan auf geniale Weise einen Einfluss, ohne diesem zu unterliegen. Er oszilliert zwischen Abstraktion und Figuration – ein Ort, der mit keiner besonderen kulturellen Bindung in einem Zusammenhang gebracht werden kann. Folglich erweist es sich als nützlich, Guoyuan nicht aufgrund eines visuellen Einflusses zu bewerten, der von woanders herrührt. Es stellt sich vielmehr die Frage nach einer Verschmelzung – wie ausgeprägt ist die kulturelle Kombination, die sich in Guoyuans kompositorischen Ideen auf Papier niederschlägt? Wenn wir wie viele davon ausgehen, dass Guoyuans Leistung darin liegt, eine Welt erschaffen zu haben, in der zwei vollständig unterschiedliche Traditionen koexistieren, dann akzeptieren wir stillschweigend die Vorstellung, nach der die Einflüsse aus anderen Kulturen in einer globalen Kultur nicht verneint werden können, in der die Bilder aus den Zeitschriften, dem Fernsehen und dem Internet frei zur Verfügung stehen.

Jonathan Goodman

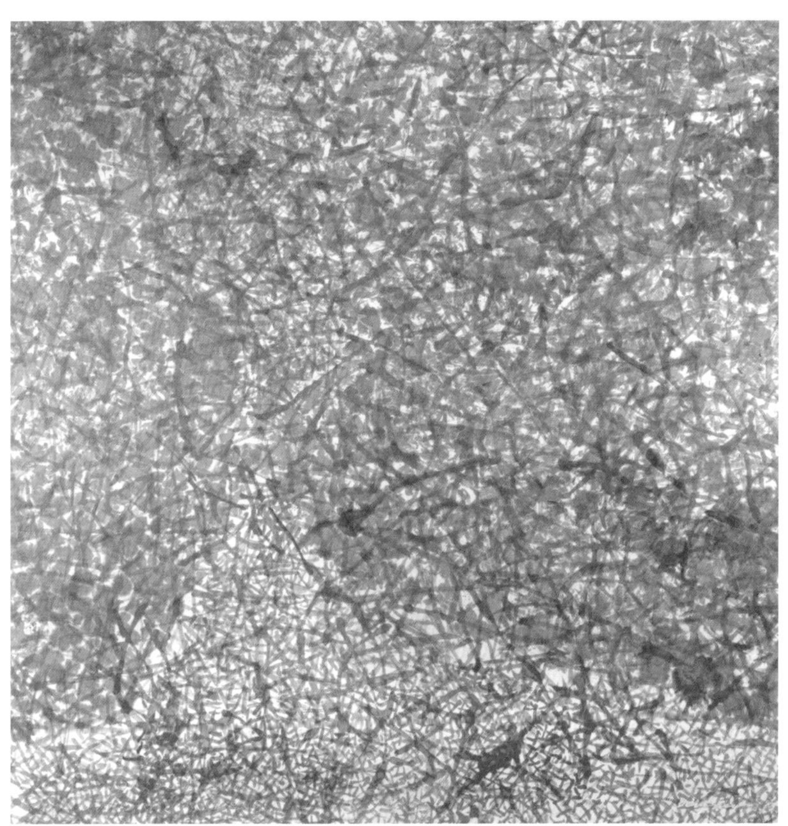

Im Norden Nr. 28, 2004
Chinesische Tusche, Reispapier
122 x 122 cm

In The North No. 28, 2004
Chinese ink, rice paper
122 × 122 cm

Deng Guoyuan

The progress of art's internationalization often proves a daunting topic for the writer to consider. Will we really throw away the particulars of any given culture, most especially those of our own? The challenge facing artists today can be seen as a problem of identity, not in the terms of personal characteristics so much as in the kinds of affiliation a serious painter makes during the course of his career. The question regarding the Chinese painter Deng Guoyuan, the subject of the Ludwig Museum exhibition, revolves around the notion of a cultural loyalty that may seem a bit idiosyncratic to a Westerner. Ever since the start of modernism, Western artists have been magpies, accumulating for themselves a broad range of visual stimuli that may come from cultures far away; and they continue to do so – think, for example, of the American painter Brice Marden, whose *Cold Mountain* series owes a considerable debt to Chinese calligraphy. As time has gone on, there has been a flood of cross-cultural materials in the art world of both Asia and the West; they have tended to blunt the impact of foreign influence. The Chinese, whose ink-and-brush landscape paintings couldn't be further in spirit and form from the Western oil tradition, have in the last one hundred years been actively painting with oils; their technical prowess in this medium is remarkable, but their choice of subject matter seems old-fashioned at times.

Deng, interestingly enough, began as an oil painter before turning to ink-on-paper works in the year 2000. So in a small way, he too has participated in the opening of Western influence in Chinese art – at least on the level of materials. His return to Chinese traditional painting has indeed been modified by his experience with Western art, partially gotten through travels in Europe and America. The question facing him – and indeed the question facing the current practice of ink painting generally – is whether his work *actively* participates in a style that reflects in any way the tradition of Western art. As we shall see, Deng brilliantly intimates influence without succumbing to it. He resides in the gap between abstraction and figuration – a place that carries with it no particular cultural allegiance. As a result, it proves useful not to judge him in light of any visible impact coming from somewhere else; instead, the question to emphasize becomes that of a merger – just how much of a cultural combination has the artist made in his use of compositional ideas on paper? If we say, as many would, that Deng's accomplishment is to have created a world in which two highly differing traditions are comfortable, then we are tacitly accepting the notion that influences from other cultures cannot be denied in a world culture where images are freely gotten from magazines, television and the Internet.

Jonathan Goodman

Deng Guoyuan

Das Naturschöne und die durch die Kunst domestizierte Natur: Über das Naturideal

Von den Sitzflächen, den Rücklehnen und den Querträgern der Stühle „fließen" schwere Goldmassen hinab zusammen mit kleinen, schmalen Reagenzgläsern, die mit Pflanzen gefüllt sind und an den Stuhlgestellen angebracht sind. Über den Stühlen hängt eine Reihe von rot bemalten Vogelkäfigen, in denen Pflanzen wachsen. Der harmonische Kontrast zwischen Schwarz (die Stühle) und Gold, zwischen Rot (die Vogelkäfige), schimmerndem Glas und grünen Blättern könnte kaum schöner und harmonischer anmuten. Diesem Arrangement wohnt etwas Kontemplatives, Eigenständiges inne, was jedoch bald in Verwirrung ausartet. Trotz all seiner Schönheit macht uns dieses Arrangement auf zaghafte und zugleich unerfreuliche Weise bewusst, dass die Freiheit der Natur der durch den Menschen offenbarten Vereinnahmung aller kreatürlichen Dinge preisgegeben wurde. Guoyuan eignet sich folglich eine Sichtweise der Natur an, die die Zeichen der Zeit kritisch verinnerlicht und reflektiert, wobei diese an den Betrachter weitergegeben werden. Kritik wendet sich gegen das, was möglicherweise glaubhaft ist, gegen die Überschreitung der natürlichen Grenzen zum Schutz der Natur und zur Bindung in all ihrer Fülle an den Kreislauf von Geburt, Wachstum und Verfall. Guoyuan verfolgt vermutlich das Ideal, welches Adorno unter dem Konzept des Naturschönen fasst, „im ‚Naturschönen' die Spur des Nichtidentischen an den Dingen im Bann universaler Identität erkennen."

Beate Reifenscheid

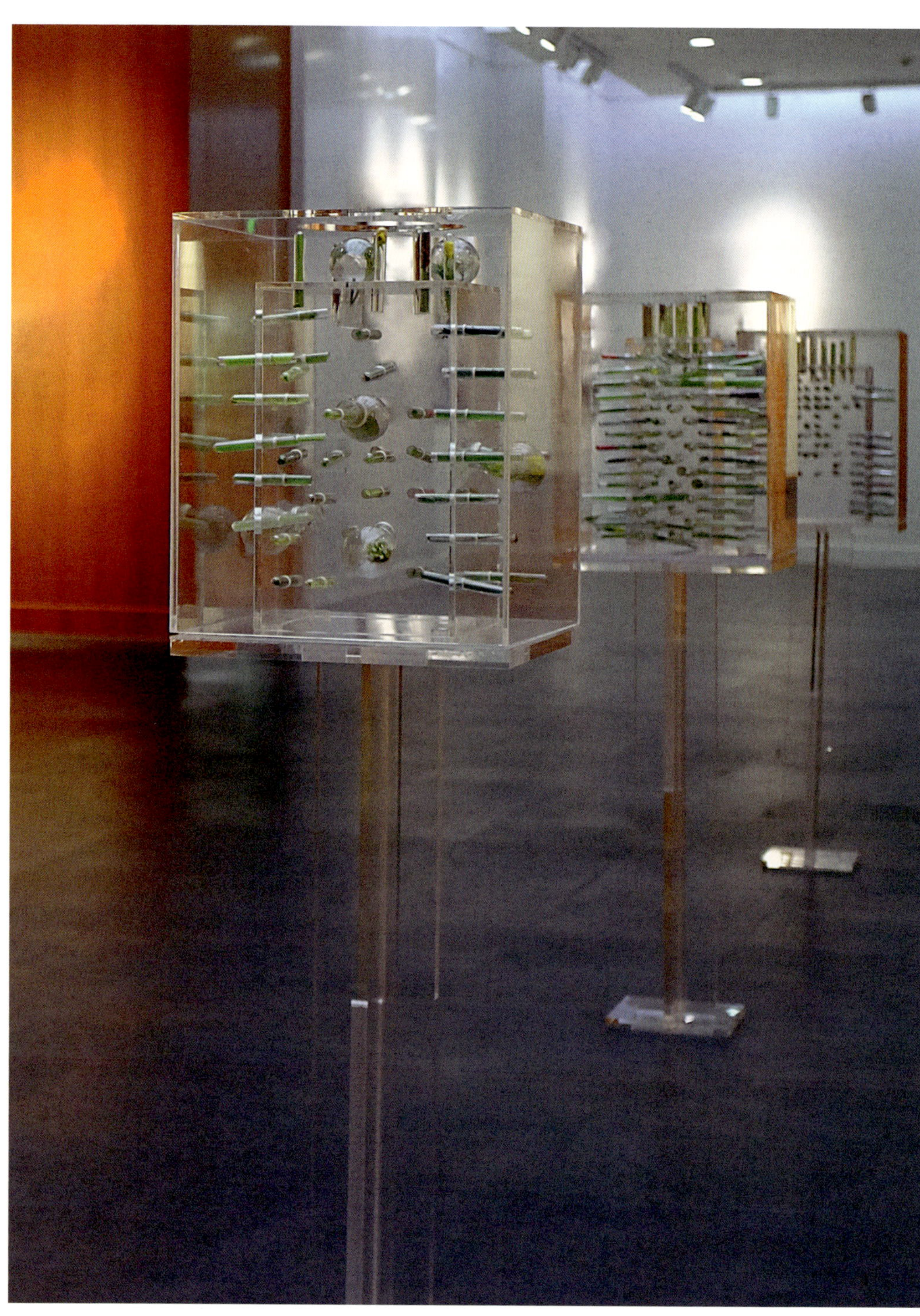

Auf eine Art Metaphysik geboren II, Käfig, 2009
Pflanzen, organisches Glas
Variable Maße
West Taihu Art Gallery, Changzhou

Born in a Way of Metaphysics II No. 3 Cage, 2009
Plants, organic glass
Dimensions variable
West Taihu Art Gallery, Changzhou

Deng Guoyuan
Naturally Beautiful and Domesticated by Art: On the Ideal of Nature

From the seats, backs and crosspieces of the chairs heavy masses of gold "flow" down, with small, narrow test tubes filled with plants plugged into the bodies of each of them. Hanging above the chairs is a series of red painted birdcages with plants growing in them. The consonant contrast between black (the chairs) and gold, between red (the birdcages), shimmering glass and the green of leaves could hardly be more beautiful and harmonious. There is a sense of the contemplative, of the self-contained to this arrangement. However, this quickly changes into irritation. For all its beauty, the arrangement makes us faintly, yet irksomely aware that the freedom of nature has been abandoned in the usurpation – made manifest by man – of all things creaturely. Deng thus adopts a view of nature that critically internalizes the signs of the times and, in reflecting on them, passes them along to the viewer. Criticism turns against what is conceivably feasible, against the transgressing of natural boundaries, in favour of protecting nature and committing it, in all its opulence, entirely to the cycle of becoming, growing and decaying. Deng likely pursues that very ideal that Adorno aptly encapsulated in the concept of *das Naturschöne*, or "natural beauty," "seeing in 'natural beauty'... the trace of the non-identical in things under the spell of universal."

Beate Reifenscheid

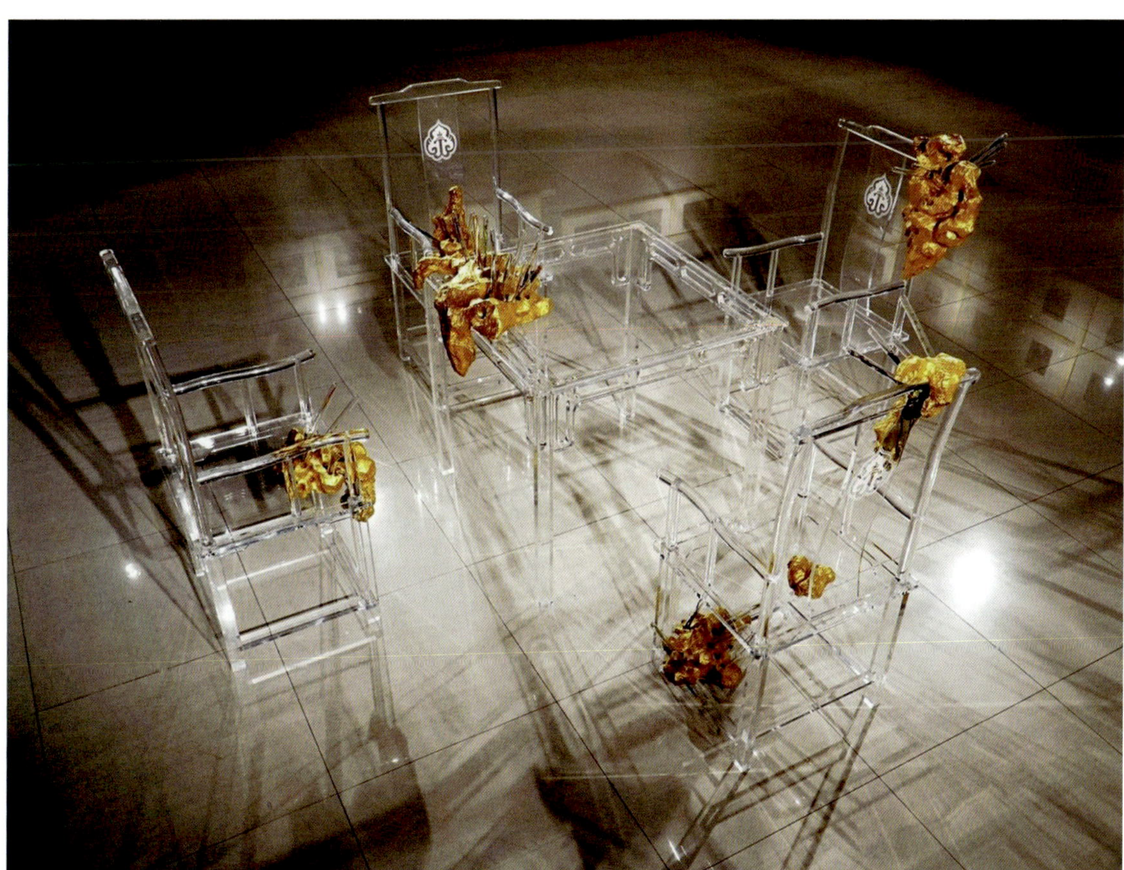

Auf einer metaphysischen Weise geboren III, Käfig, 2017
Pflanzen, Versuchsröhre, klassischer Stuhl, Kupfertönung
Variable Maße
53 Art Museum, Guangzhou

Born in a Way of Metaphysics III Cage, 2017
Plants, experimental tube, classical chair, copper cast tinting
Dimensions variable
53 Art Museum, Guangzhou

Deng Guoyuan führt eine Gruppe von Personen an,um diesen Wandel zu bewirken
Noahs Garten

Obwohl *Noahs Garten* ein Garten ist, stellt dieser eine noch größere Arche dar, die durch die Informationsflut gleitet. In *Noahs Garten* experimentiert Deng Guoyuan mit verschiedenen Möglichkeiten, die den Menschen dabei helfen können, die gewaltige Flut zu durchqueren. Die Möglichkeiten, die sich in Zukunft herausbilden, führen in fiktive Welten und geben Anlass zur menschlichen Hoffnung. Wenn wir uns mit den Dilemmas auseinandersetzen, die mit der Entfremdung durch die modernen Technologien und das moderne Wissen zusammenhängen, entdecken und erschaffen wir neue Wege, die uns zur Natur, zur Wahrheit, zu unserem physischen Körper und zu den intimen und wunderbaren menschlichen Beziehungen zurückführen können. In der Originalgeschichte kehrte die Taube mit dem Olivenzweig in ihrem Schnabel zur Arche zurück. Heute erschafft Noahs Garten einen Weg sowohl für die Verbannung als auch für die Rückkehr. Am Schnittpunkt von industrieller Revolution und individueller Existenz werden wir zu neuen Menschen. Diese neuen Menschen unterscheiden sich von gewöhnlichen Produzenten oder Träumern, die ihre Zeit mit Verlusten, Missgunst oder starkem Widerstand gegen die Gesellschaft verschwenden. Da sie praktische Fähigkeiten und einen präzisen Plan haben, erweitern sich ihre Ideale kontinuierlich. Indem diese Menschen dem Weg folgen, den *Noahs Garten* vorgibt, betreten sie ein spirituelles „Paradies". *Noahs Garten* liegt kein konkretes Konzept zugrunde, während sich Kreativität und Experimentierlust hingegen frei entfalten können. Auf diese Weise weiten und durchkreuzen sich die Wege, auf denen man entlangschreiten und sich seinen Gedanken hingeben kann. Diejenigen, die zu diesen Wegen gelangen, können Künstler/innen sein, die zu den neuen Menschen einer künftigen Gesellschaft werden.

Zhu Qingsheng

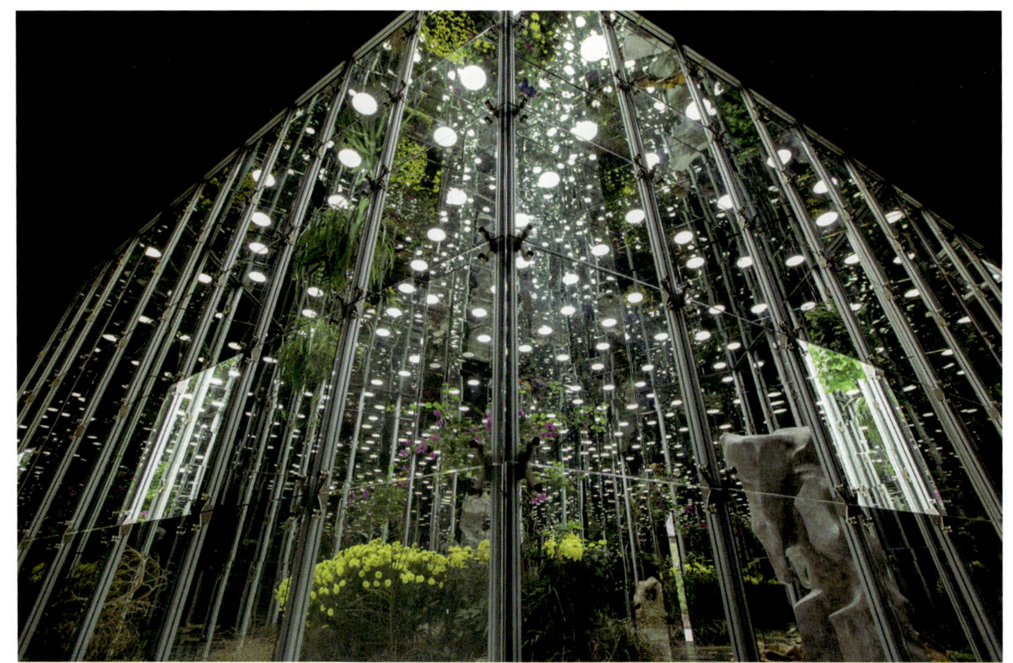

Noahs Garten, 2015
Stahlrahmen mit Aluminiumlegierung,
Einscheiben-Sicherheitsglas, LED-Licht, Licht,
halbautomatische Drehtür, Pflanzen,
künstliche Felsen
900 × 450 × 350 cm
Red Brick Art Museum, Peking

Noah's Garden, 2015
Aluminium alloy steel frame, toughened mirror glass,
LED light, light, semi-automatic revolving door,
plants, fake rocks
900 × 450 × 350 cm
Red Brick Art Museum, Beijing

Deng Guoyuan is Leading a Group of People to Make this Transition
Noah's Garden

Although *Noah's Garden* is a garden, it represents an even larger Ark floating on the flood of knowledge. In *Noah's Garden*, Deng Guoyuan experiments with various possibilities for humans crossing this massive flood, and the possibilities created in the future are entrances to fictitious worlds and human hope. When we confront the predicaments created by the alienation of modern technologies and modern knowledge, we seek out and create paths that could return us to nature, to truth, to the physical body, and to the intimate and marvellous relationships between people. In the original story, the dove holding an olive branch in its mouth returned to Noah and the Ark, and today, Noah's garden creates a path for both banishment and return. At the intersection of the Industrial Revolution and individual existence, we are becoming new people. These new people are different from ordinary producers or dreamers who idle away their time in loss, resentment, or intense resistance to society; since they have practical skills and a precise plan, their ideals are always expanding. In following the path indicated by *Noah's Garden*, these people enter into a spiritual "paradise." In *Noah's Garden*, there is no explicit concept; there is only creativity and experimentation that is no longer controlled or hindered. It makes the paths wide and intersecting, giving everyone a place to walk and think. The people who can find their way to these paths may be artists, who may become the new people of a future society.

Zhu Qingsheng

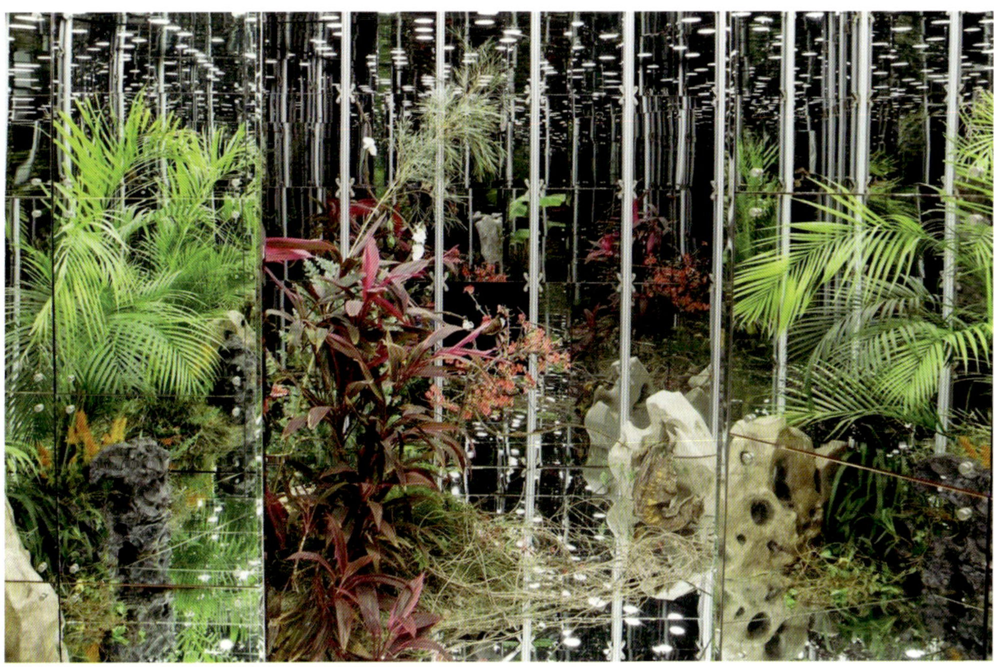

Noahs Garten, Innenansicht

Noah's Garden, inside

Deng Guoyuans *Noahs Garten II*

In *Noahs Garten II* nimmt der Künstler eine entscheidende Änderung vor, indem er die natürliche Vegetation aus Pflaumenbäumen, Orchideen, Bambus, Chrysanthemen und Kiefern, die er in seinen früheren Garteninstallationen einsetzte, gegen Kunstpflanzen in grellen Farben eintauscht. Darüber hinaus führt der Künstler das Konzept der Landkarte in sein Werk ein. Die Farben der Kunstpflanzen und die Punkte, Linien und Farben auf dem Gelehrtenstein basieren folglich auf einer Weltkarte. Die Farben, die die verschiedenen Landschaften, Gebiete und Länder symbolisieren, haben hier jedoch ihre ursprüngliche identifizierende Funktion verloren.

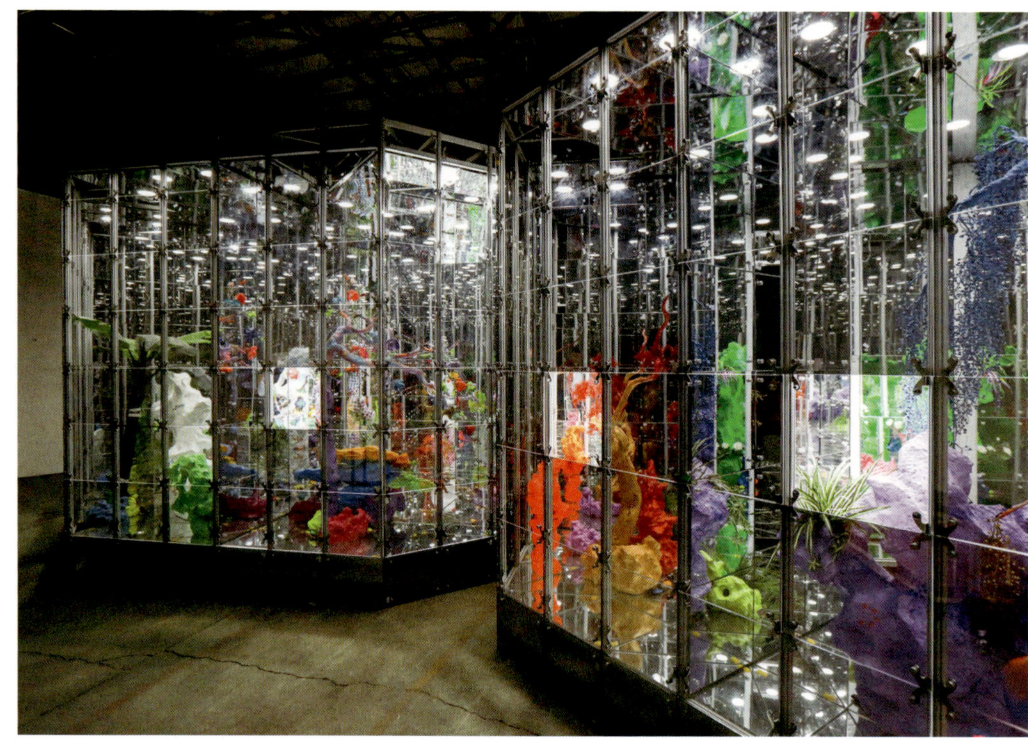

Noahs Garten II, 2016
Stahlrahmen mit Aluminiumlegierung, Einscheiben-Sicherheitsglas, LED-Licht, Licht, halbautomatische Drehtür, Pflanzen, künstliche Felsen
1160 × 650 × 320 cm
Singapore Art Museum, Singapur

Noah's Garden II, 2016
Aluminium alloy steel frame, toughened mirror glass, LED lights, semi-automatic revolving door, plants, fake rocks
1160 × 650 × 320 cm
Singapore Art Museum, Singapore

Während der Künstler anfangs Tusche verwendete, um echte Pflanzen zu färben, das repräsentativste Material der traditionellen chinesischen Kultur, erschuf er dann einen Garten, in dem er diese durch „aufgemachte" Kunstpflanzen ersetzte und versuchte, die Gartengestaltung von einem eleganten, poetischen Akt in einen Zustand der Naturversunkenheit zu überführen, in einen Prozess, der farbenfrohe Industrieprodukte mit Albereien im Stil der Pop-Art kombiniert. Der Garten wird somit zu einem Vergnügungspark. Handelt es sich hierbei um ein Heilmittel gegen die zunehmende Entfremdung zwischen Menschen und Natur oder um eine Beschönigung unserer exzessiven Ausbeutung und Zerstörung der Natur?

Offensichtlich basiert die Herrschaft des Menschen über die Natur nicht länger auf „Kultivierung", oder noch eindringlicher, auf Kultur und Wissen, wie dies vorher der Fall war.

Xiang Liping

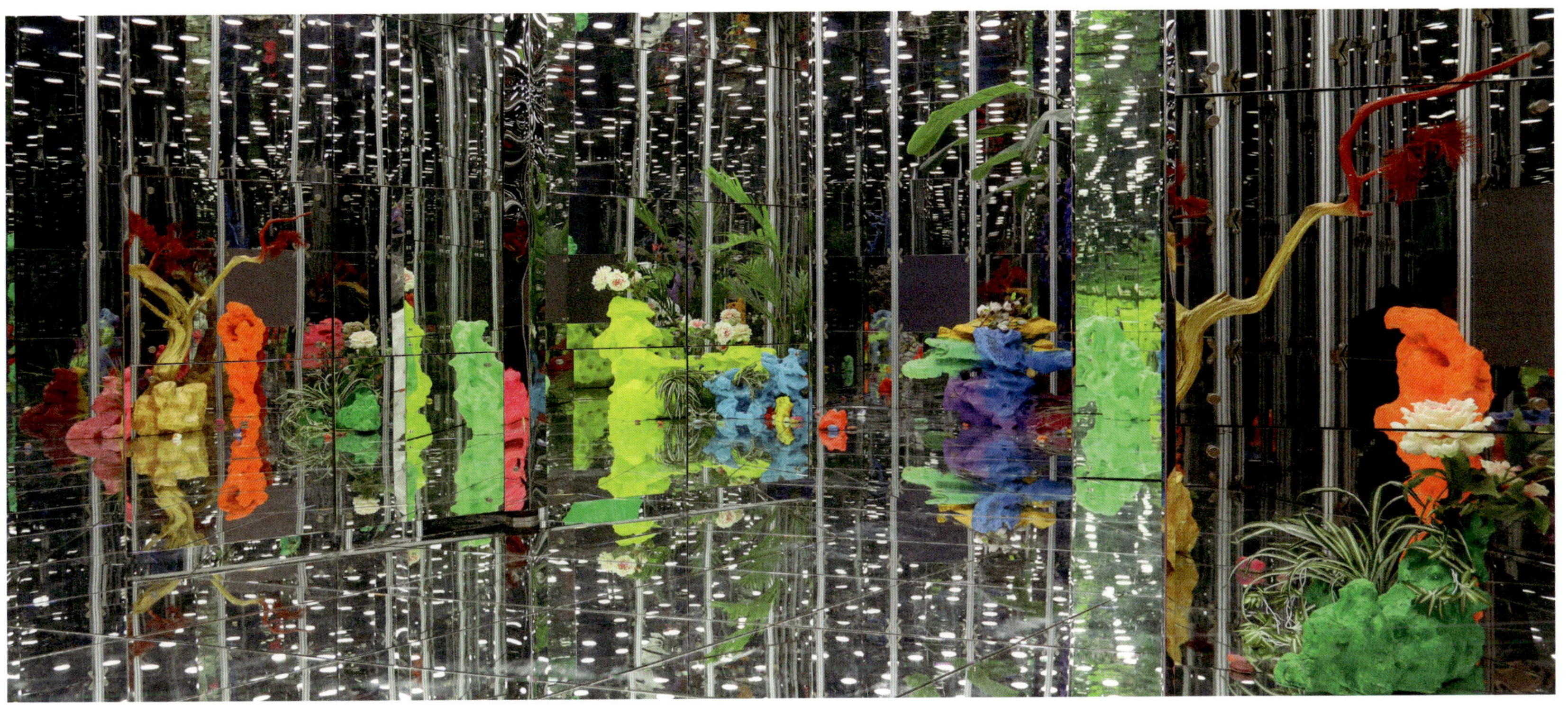

Noahs Garten II, Innenansicht

Noah's Garden II, inside

Deng Guoyuan's *Noah's Garden II*

In *Noah's Garden II*, the artist made a crucial adjustment by replacing natural vegetation, such as plum trees, orchids, bamboo, chrysanthemum, and pine trees, which were used in his garden installations before, with fake plants coated in dazzling colours. Moreover, the artist has specifically introduced the concept of the map into the work. The fake plant colours and the points, lines, and colours on the scholar stone are based on a map of the world. The colours, which symbolize different landscapes, territories, and countries, lose their original identifying function here.

From originally using ink to stain real plants, which is the material most representative of traditional Chinese culture, to create a garden, to replacing them with "make-up heavy" fake plants, the artist has tried in his work to transform landscape gardening from a type of elegant, poetic act in the abandoning of oneself to nature, to a process that combines gaudy industrial products with a Pop-Art-style banter. The garden turns into an amusement park. Is this a remedy for the gradual estrangement between humans and nature, or a whitewashing of our excessive exploitation and destruction of nature?

Apparently, mankind's mastery over nature is no longer based on "cultivation" or, even more pointedly, culture and knowledge as it was before.

Xiang Liping

Loreleys Garten

Loreley’s Garden

Modell für Loreley Nr.1, 2019
Stahlplatte, Stahlröhre, Autolack
Originalmaße
600 × 560 × 580 cm

Model for Loreley No. 1, 2019
Steel plate, steel pipe, automobile paint
Dimensions of full scale work
600 × 560 × 580 cm

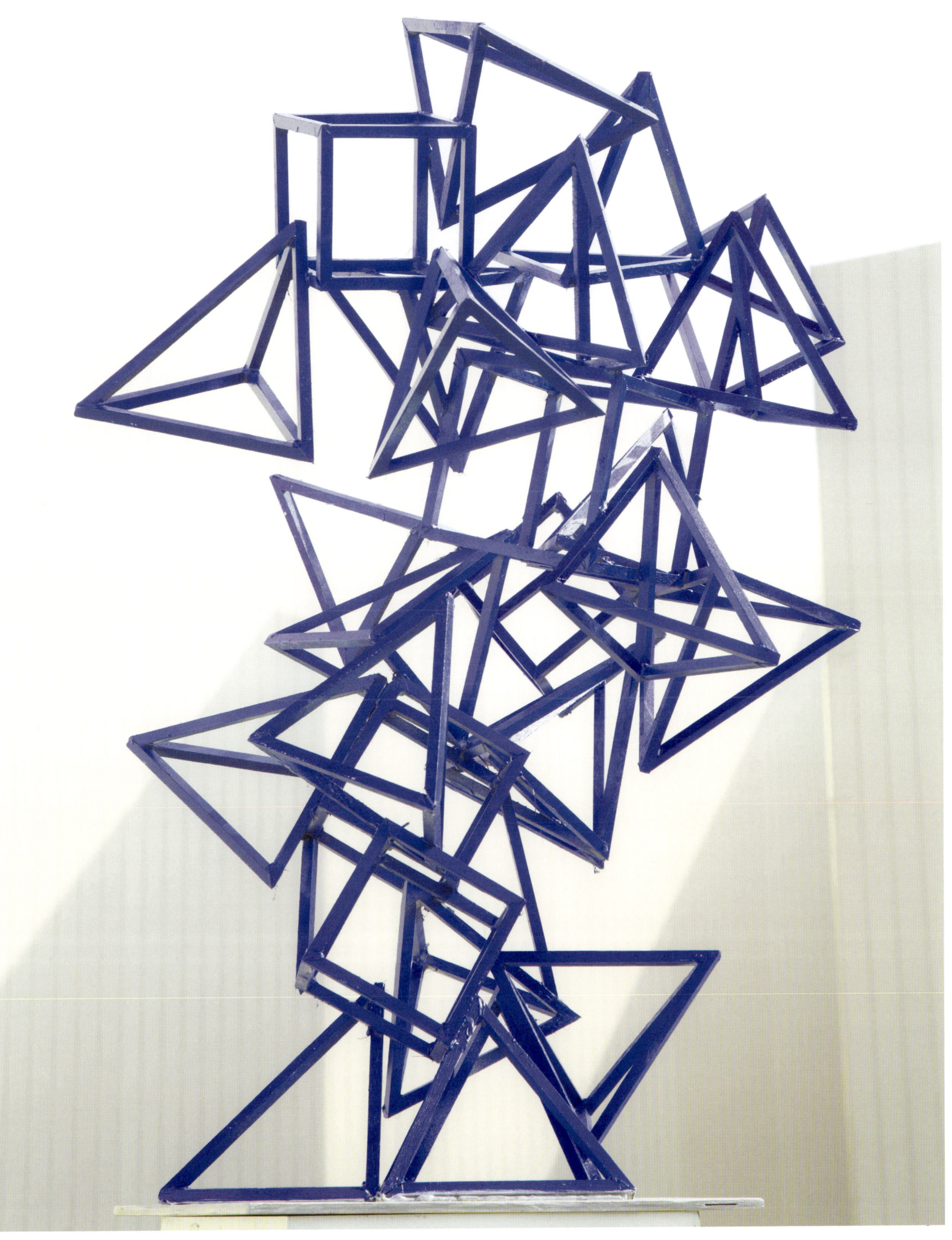

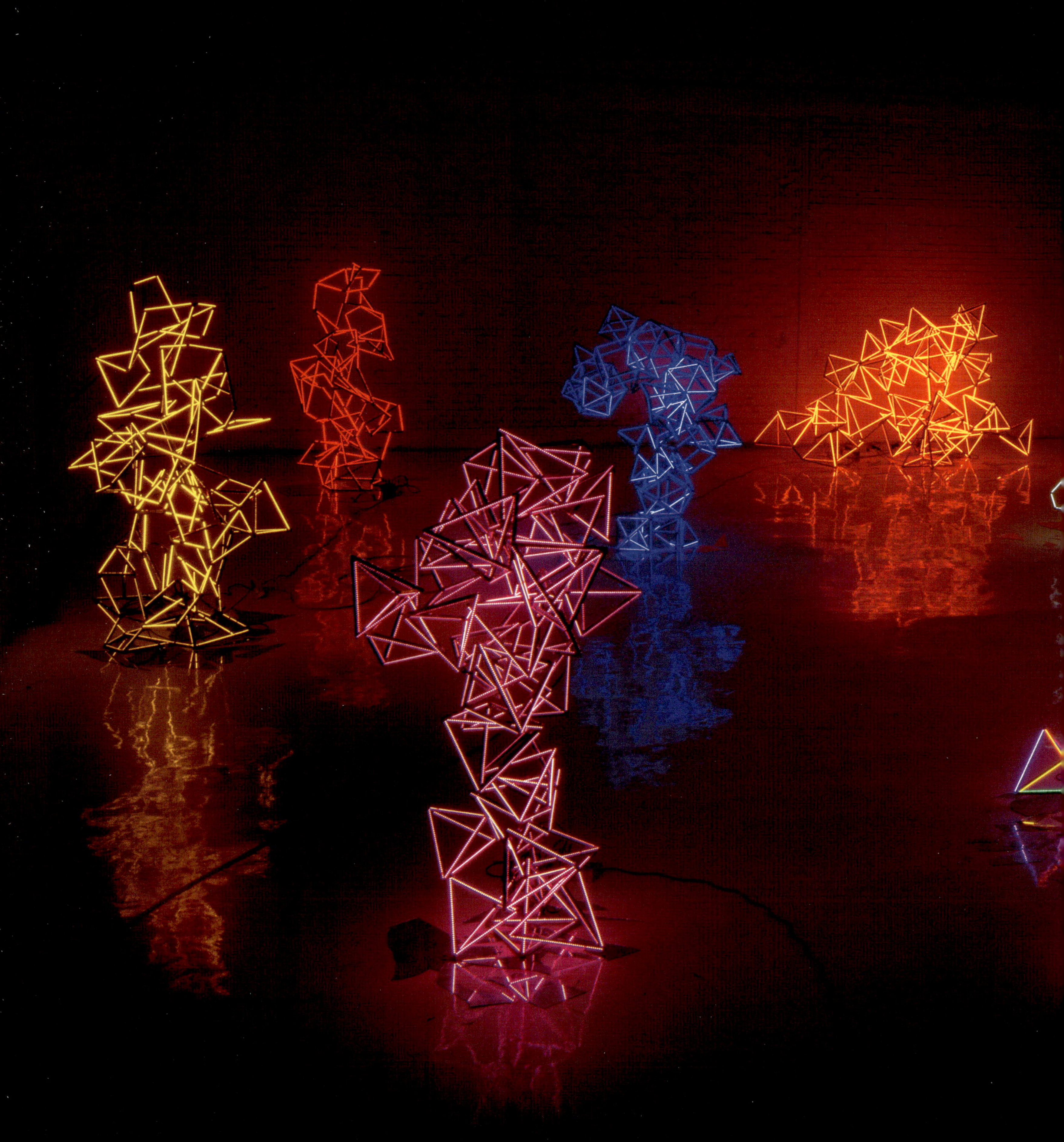

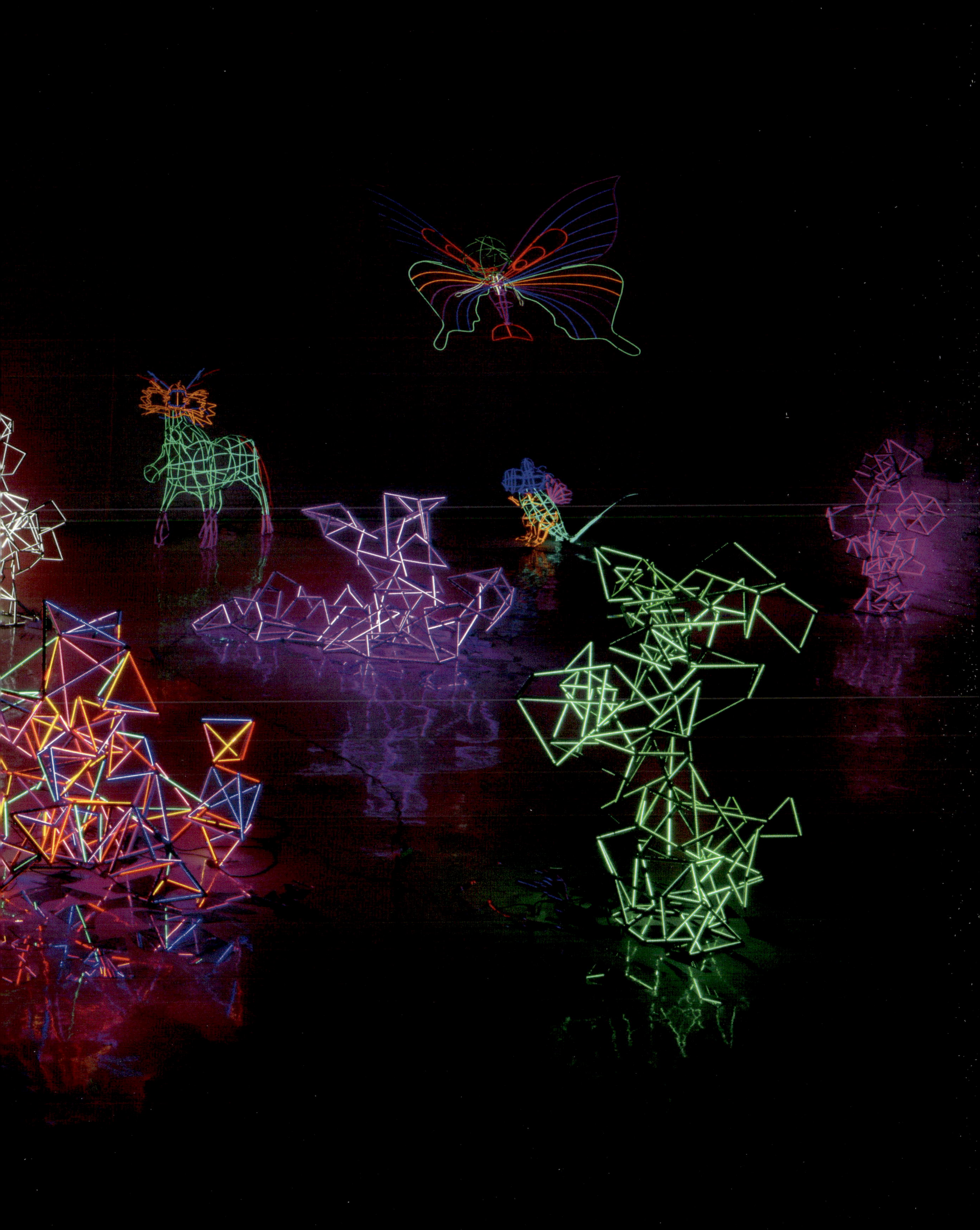

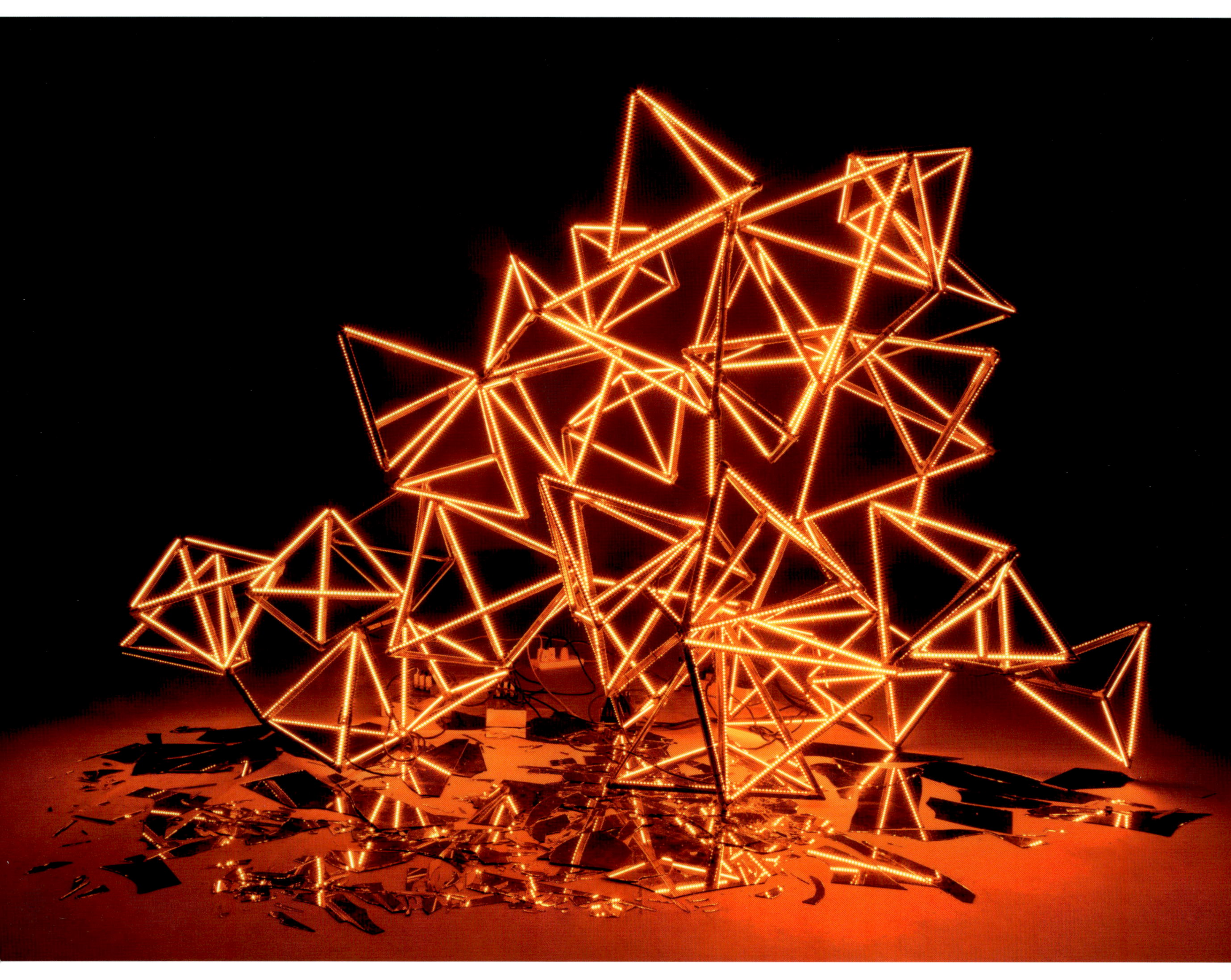

Loreley Nr.2, 2019
Stahlröhre, LED-Lampen
290 × 149 × 175 cm

Loreley No. 2, 2019
Steel pipe, LED lamps
290 × 149 × 175 cm

Vorherige Seiten:
***Loreleys Garten* (Vollständige Werkserie)**

Previous pages:
***Loreley's Garden*, full series**

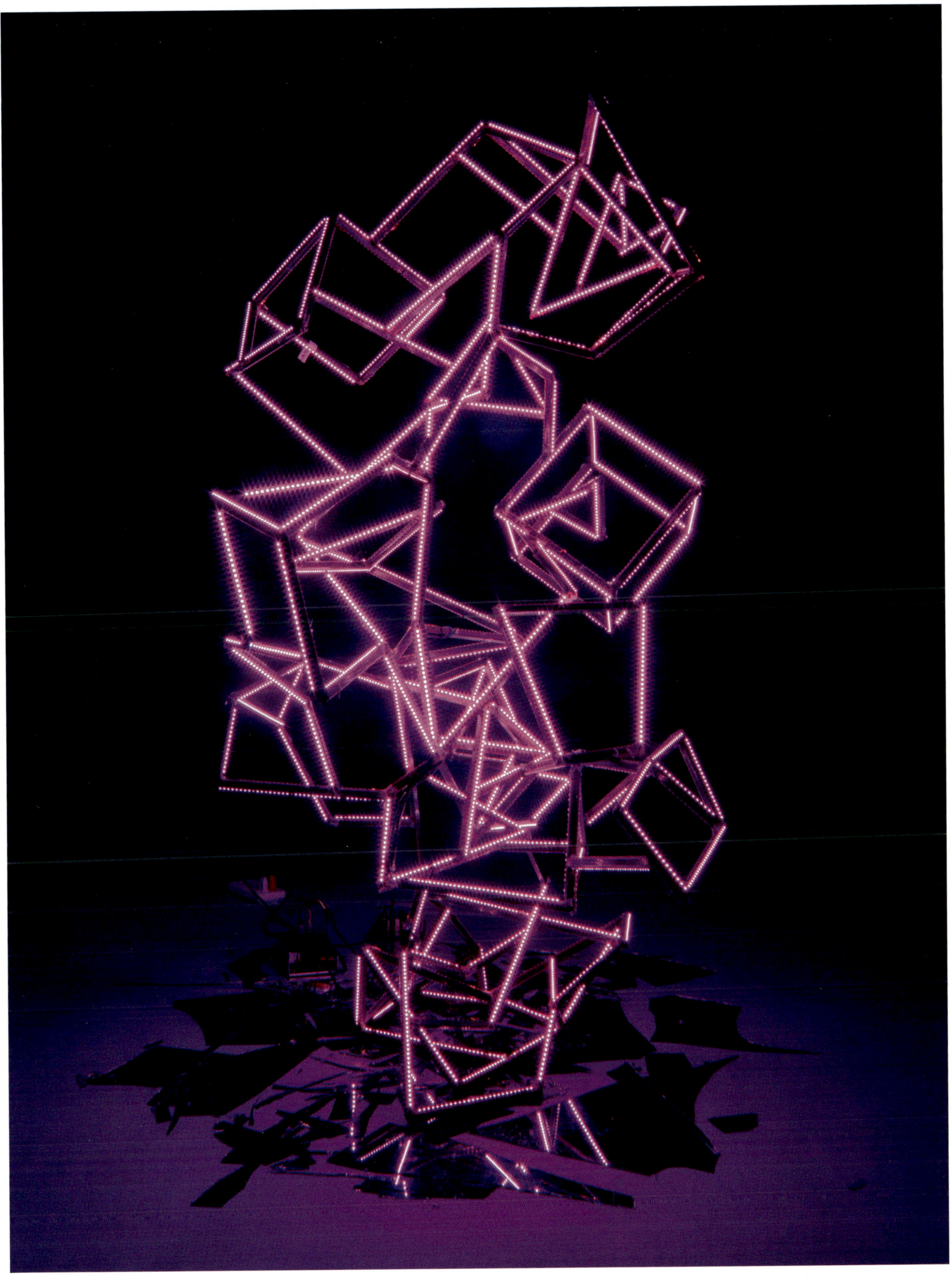

Loreley Nr.3, 2019
Stahlröhre, LED-Lampen
115 × 120 × 220 cm

Loreley No. 3, 2019
Steel pipe, LED lamps
115 × 120 × 220 cm

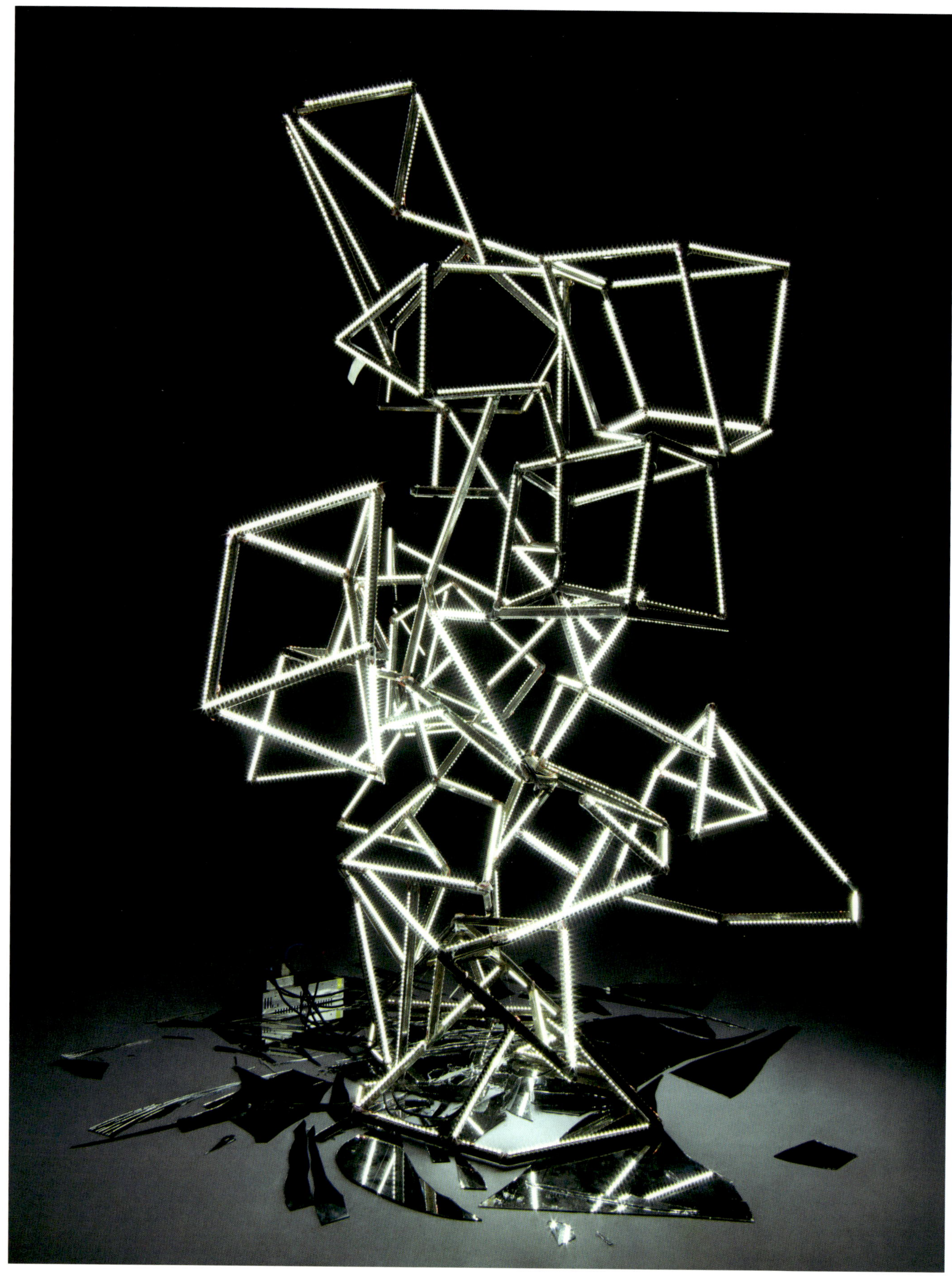

Loreley Nr.4, 2019
Stahlröhre, LED-Lampen
182 × 143 × 240 cm

Loreley No. 4, 2019
Steel pipe, LED lamps
182 × 143 × 240 cm

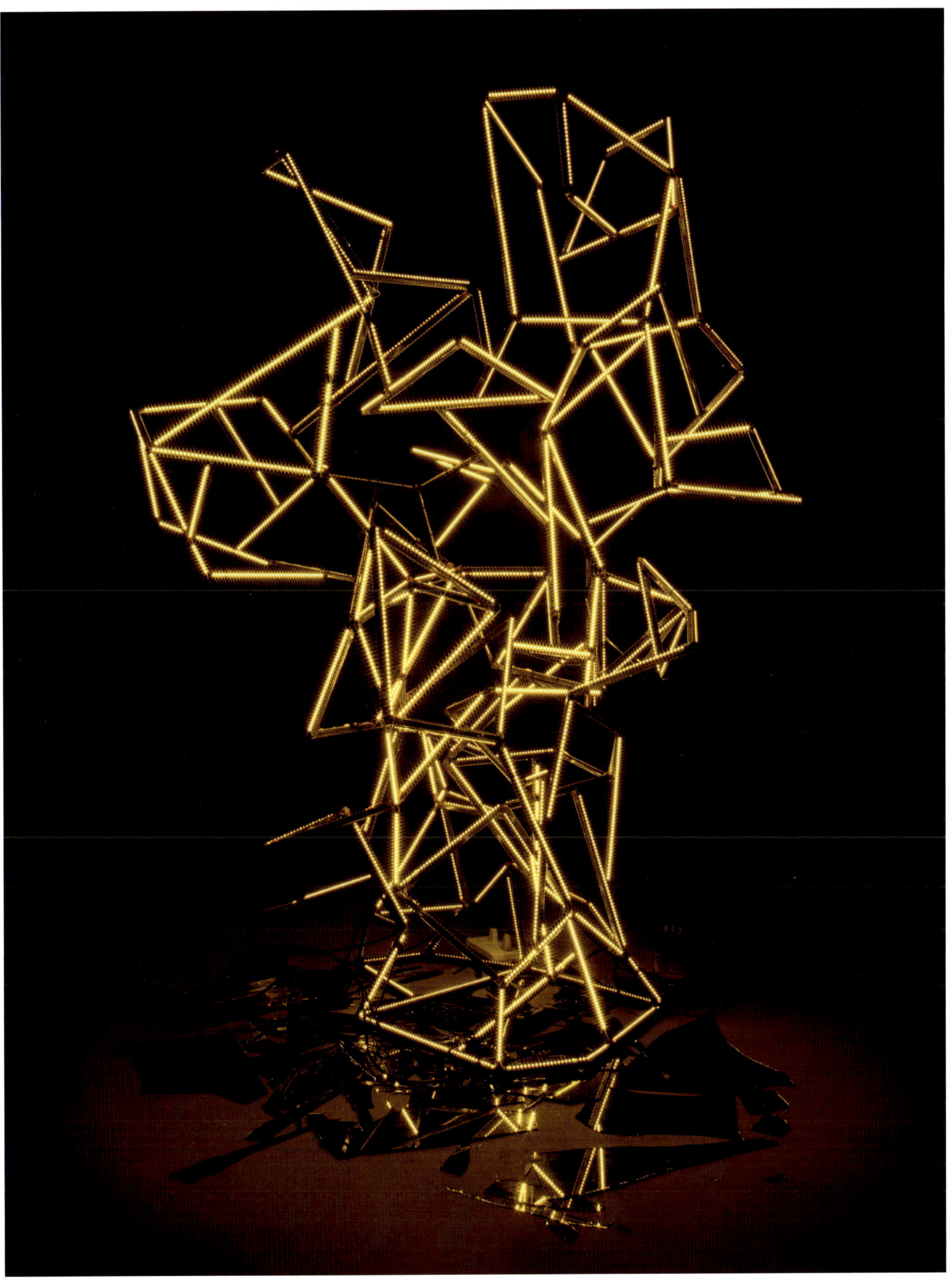

Loreley Nr.5, 2019
Stahlröhre, LED-Lampen
105 × 145 × 220 cm

Loreley No. 5, 2019
Steel pipe, LED lamps
105 × 145 × 220 cm

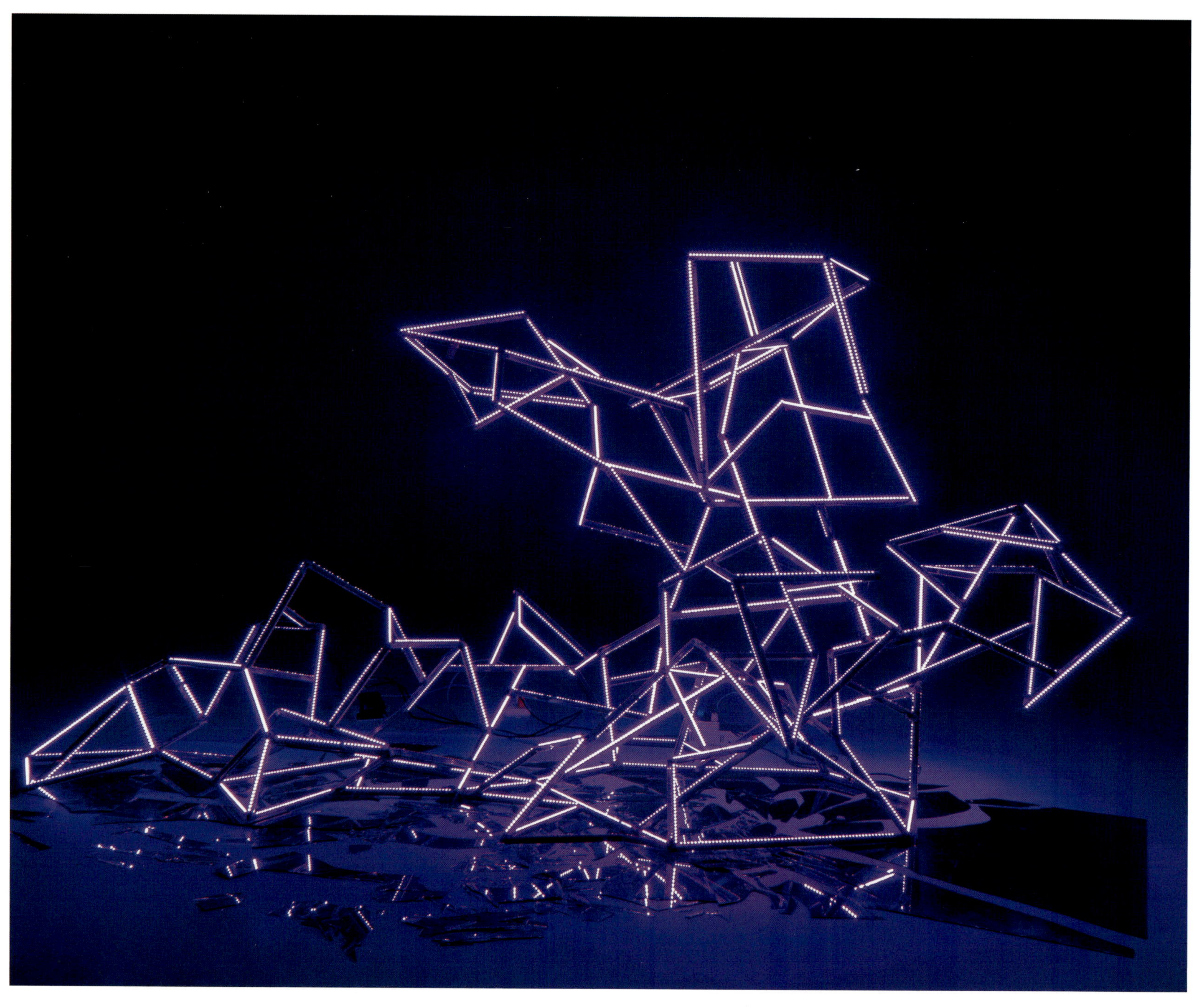

Loreley Nr.6, 2019
Stahlröhre, LED-Lampen
290 × 155 × 157 cm

Loreley No. 6, 2019
Steel pipe, LED lamps
290 × 155 × 157 cm

Rechts:
Loreley Nr.7, 2019
Stahlröhre, LED-Lampen
100 × 125 × 210 cm

Right:
Loreley No. 7, 2019
Steel pipe, LED lamps
100 × 125 × 210 cm

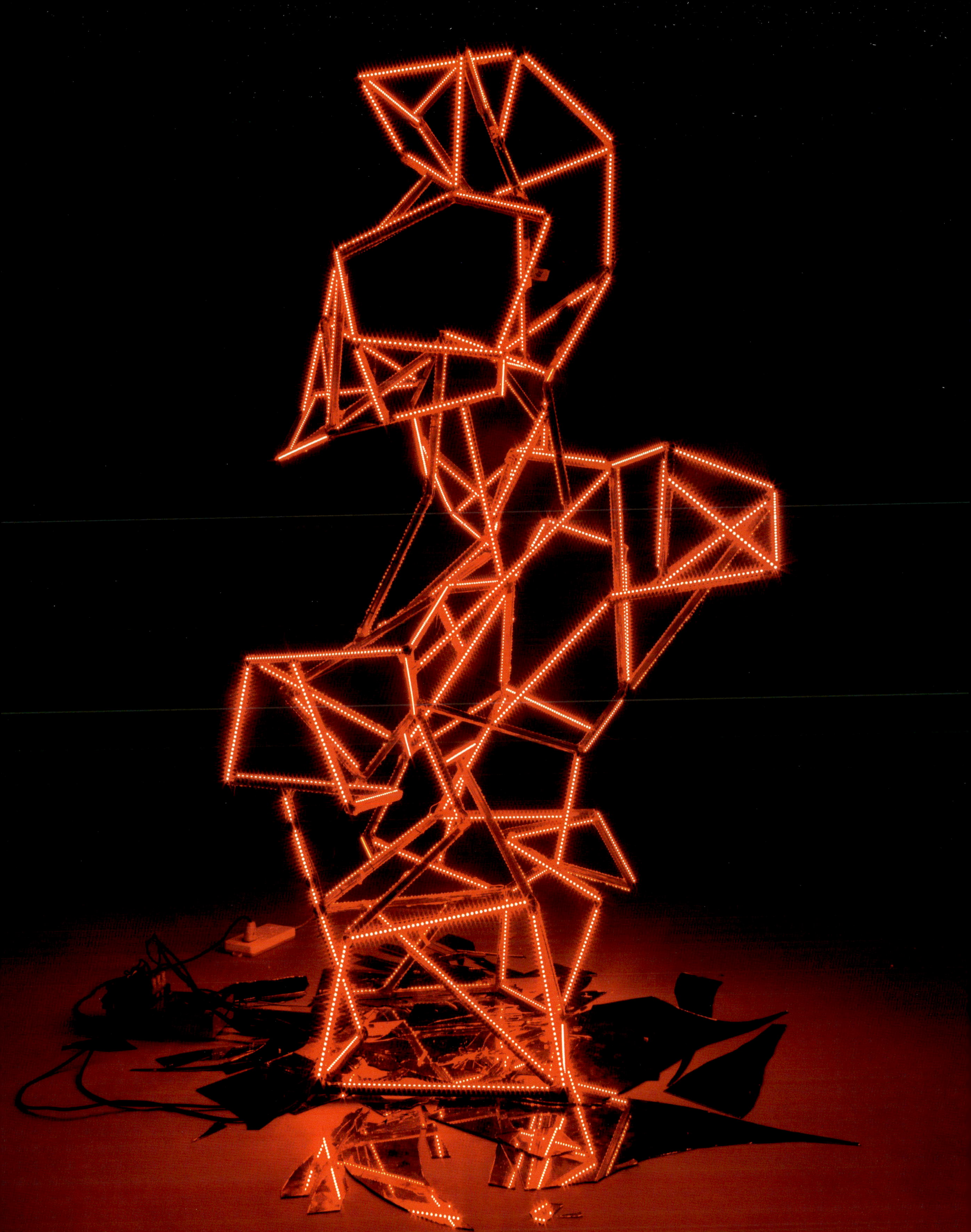

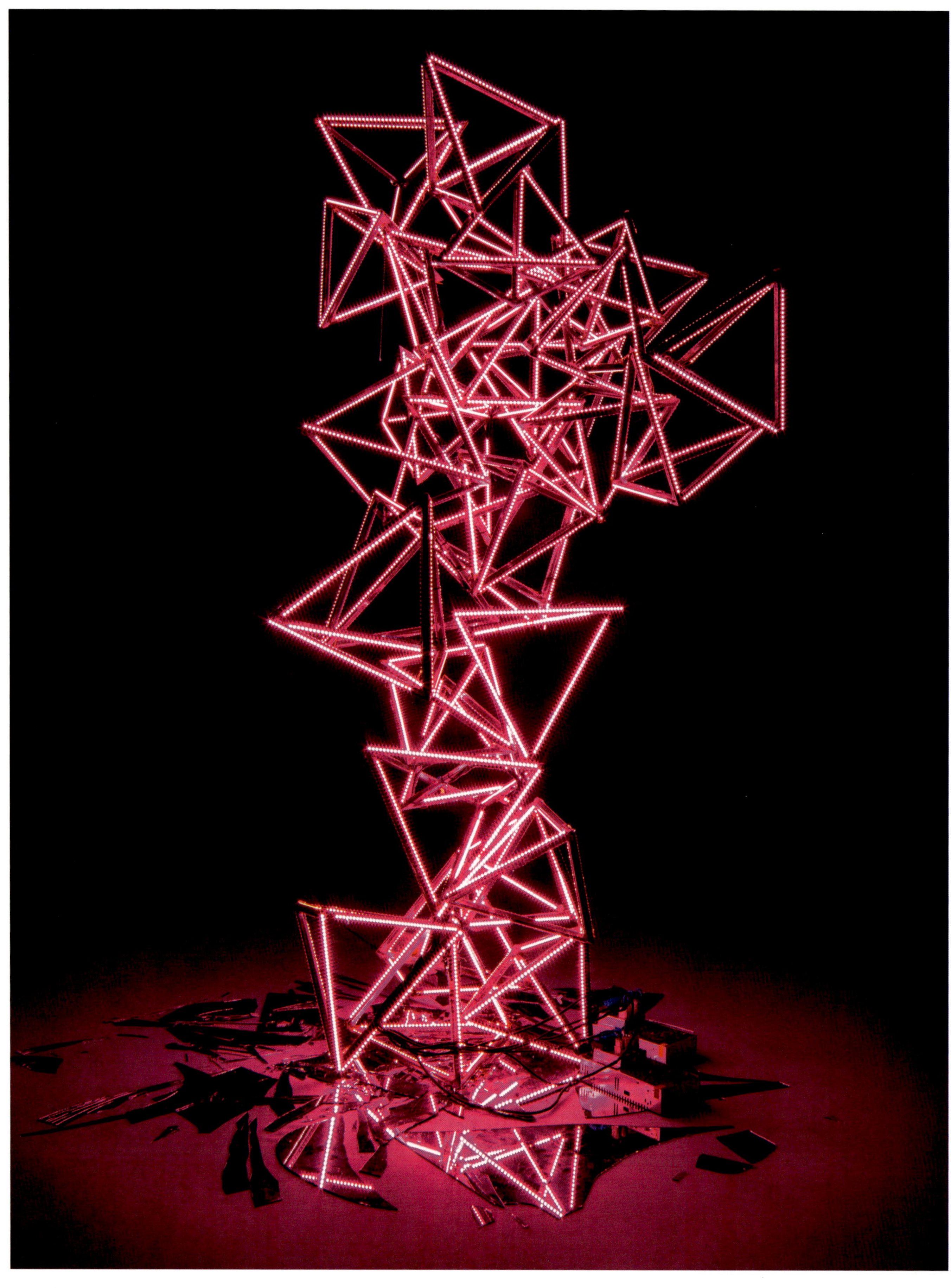

Loreley Nr.8, 2019
Stahlröhre, LED-Lampen
120 × 110 × 220 cm

Loreley No. 8, 2019
Steel pipe, LED lamps
120 × 110 × 220 cm

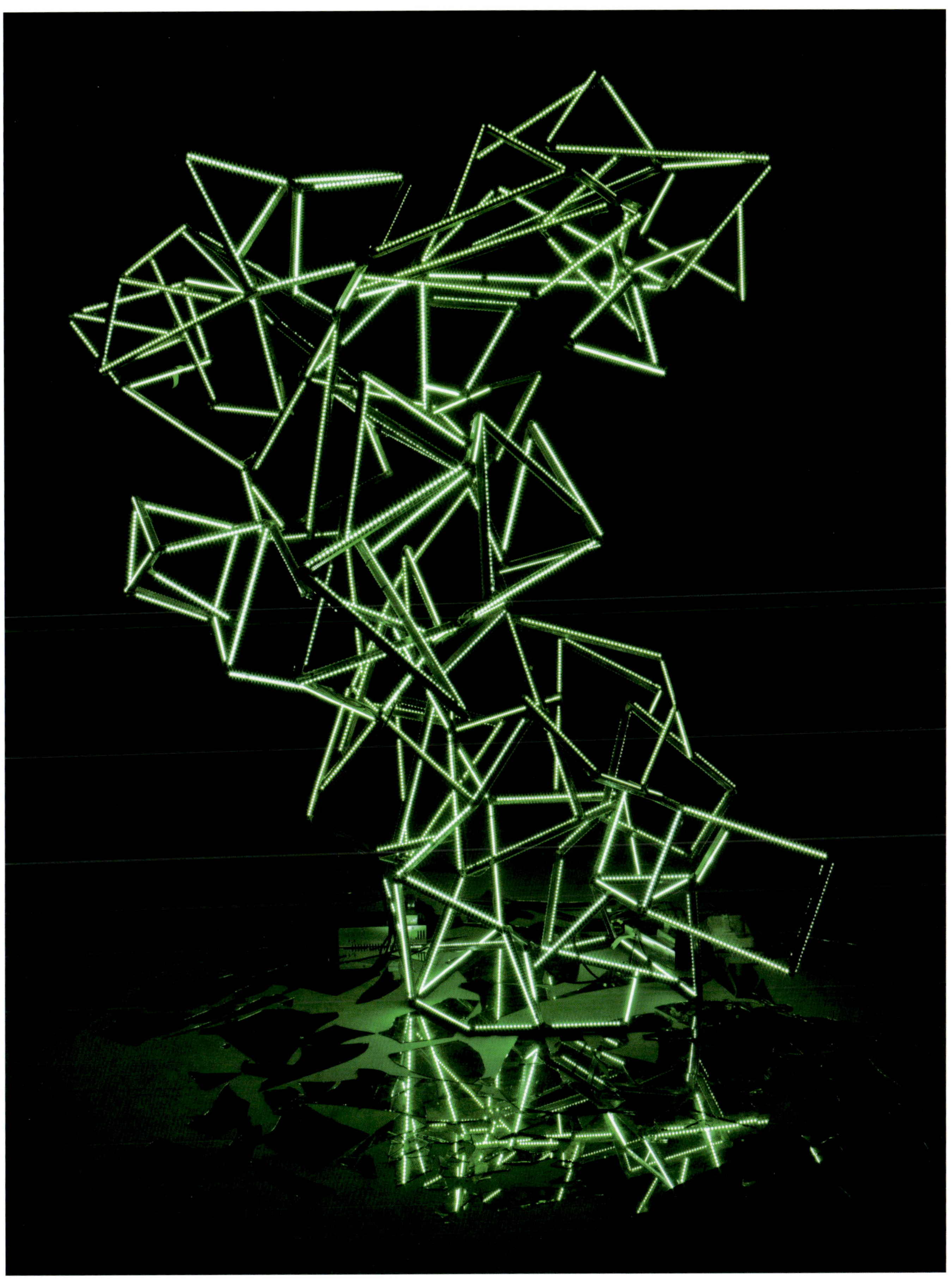

Loreley Nr.9, 2019
Stahlröhre, LED-Lampen
152 × 185 × 215 cm

Loreley No. 9, 2019
Steel pipe, LED lamps
152 × 185 × 215 cm

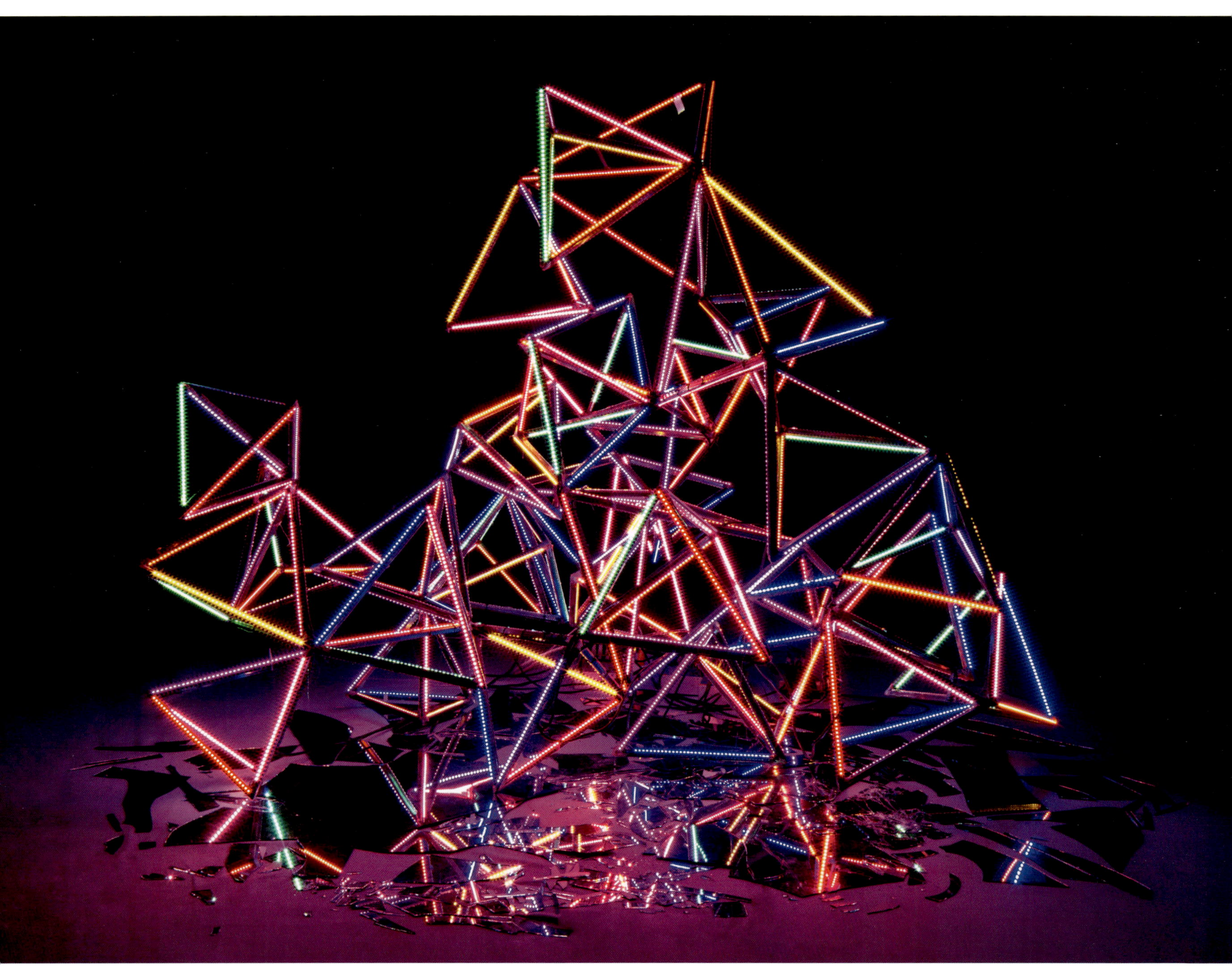

Loreley Nr.10, 2019
Stahlröhre, LED-Lampen
150 × 210 × 167 cm

Loreley No. 10, 2019
Steel pipe, LED lamps
150 × 210 × 167 cm

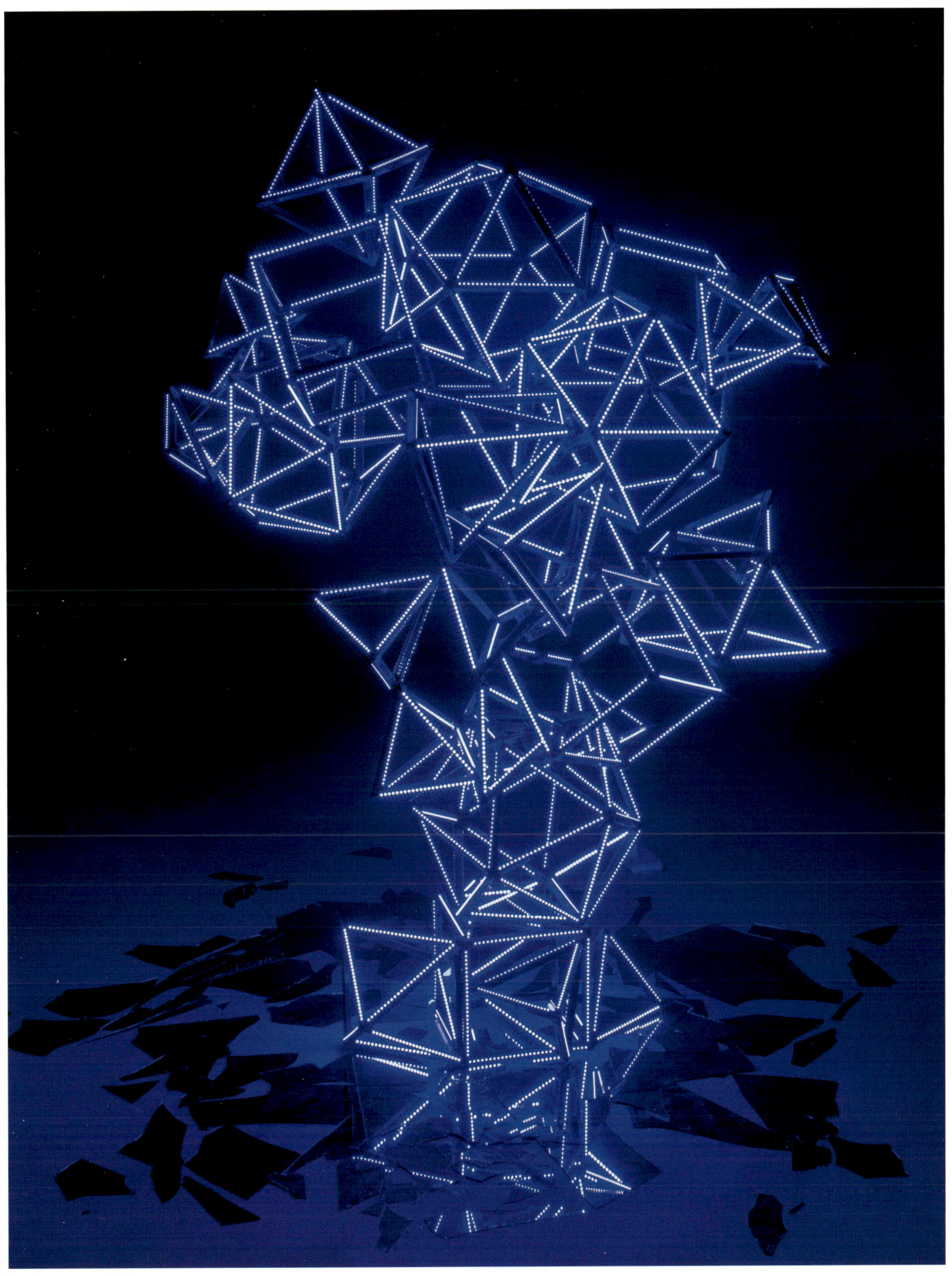

Loreley Nr.11, 2019
Stahlröhre, LED-Lampen
148 × 124 × 200 cm

Loreley No. 11, 2019
Steel pipe, LED lamps
148 × 124 × 200 cm

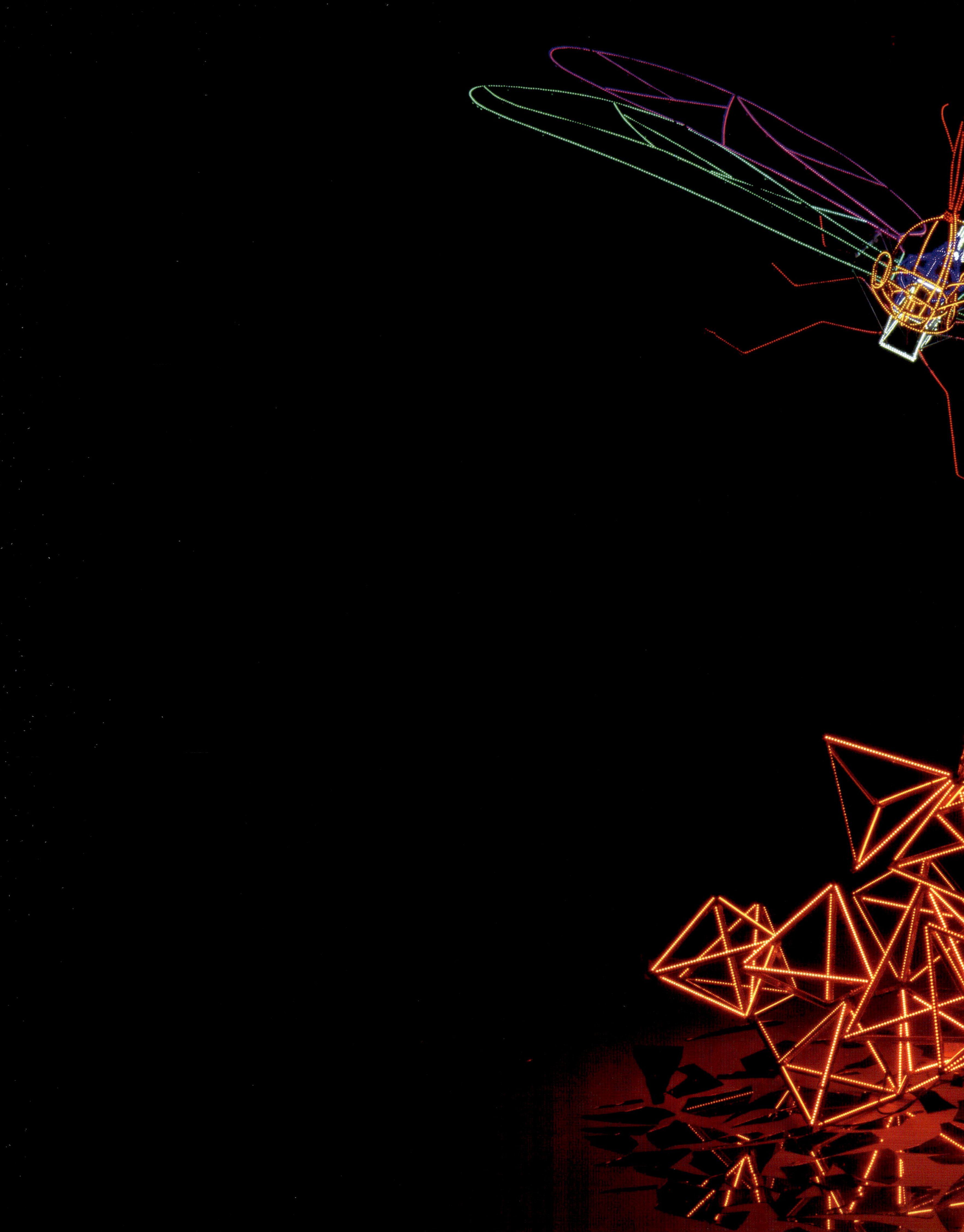

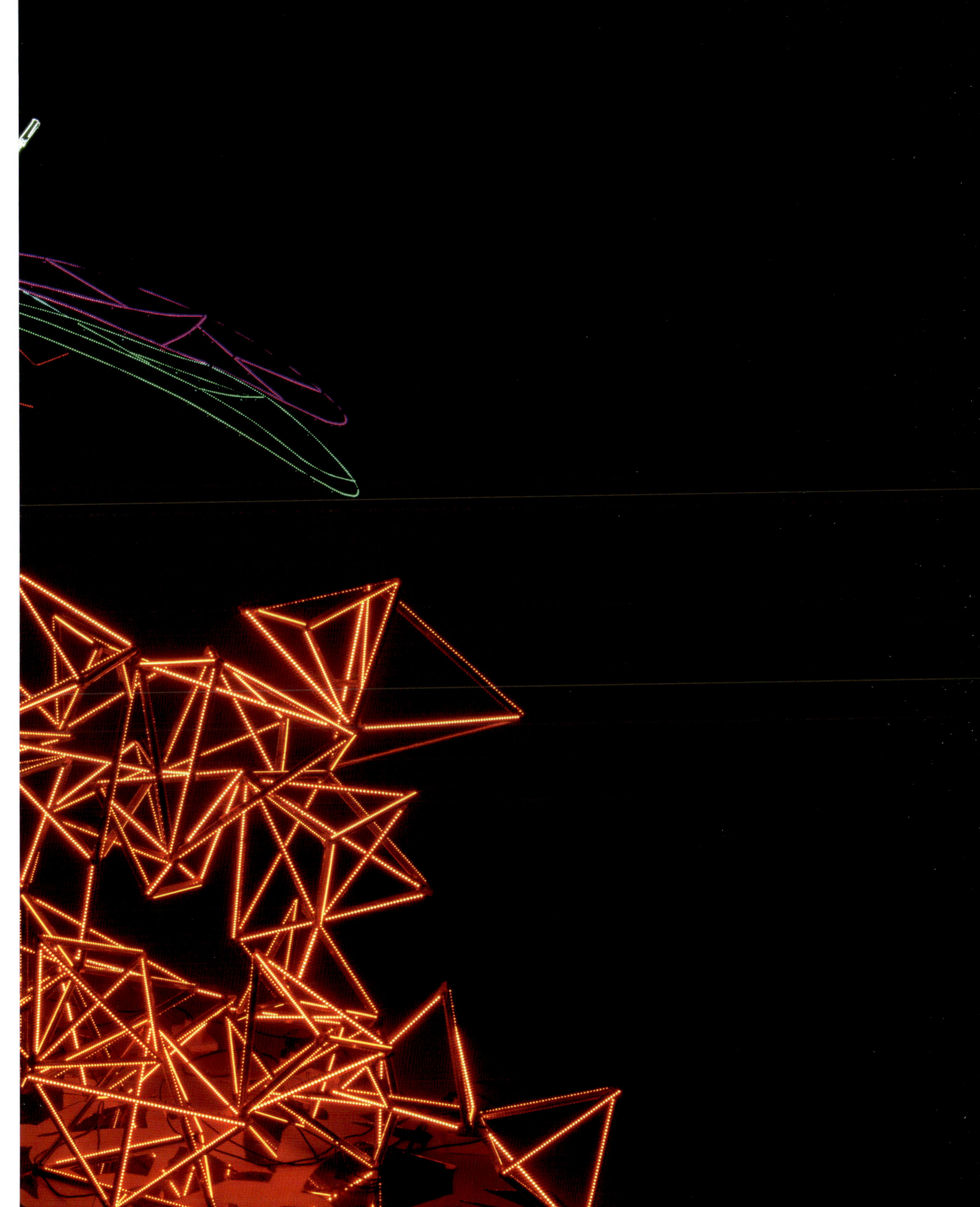

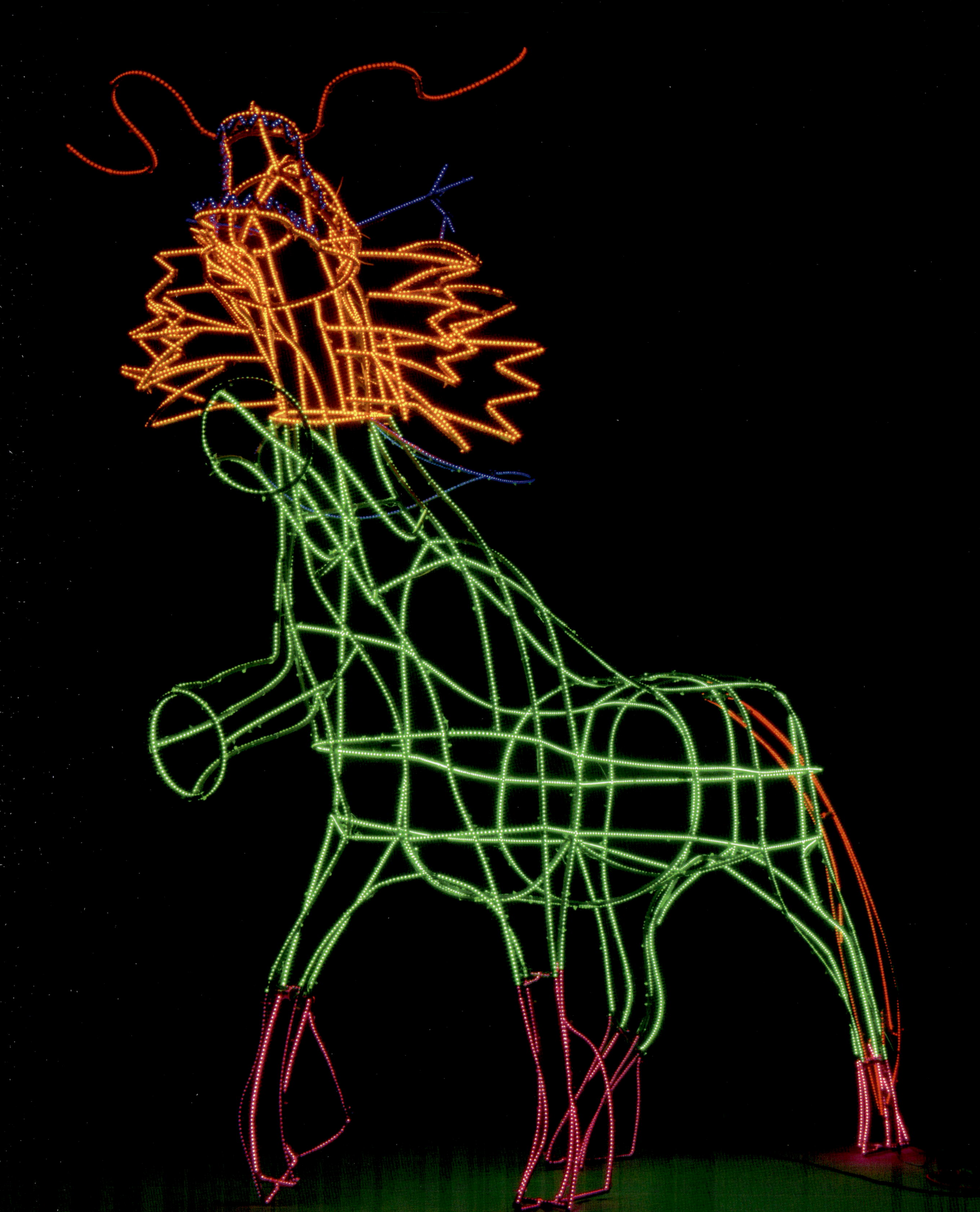

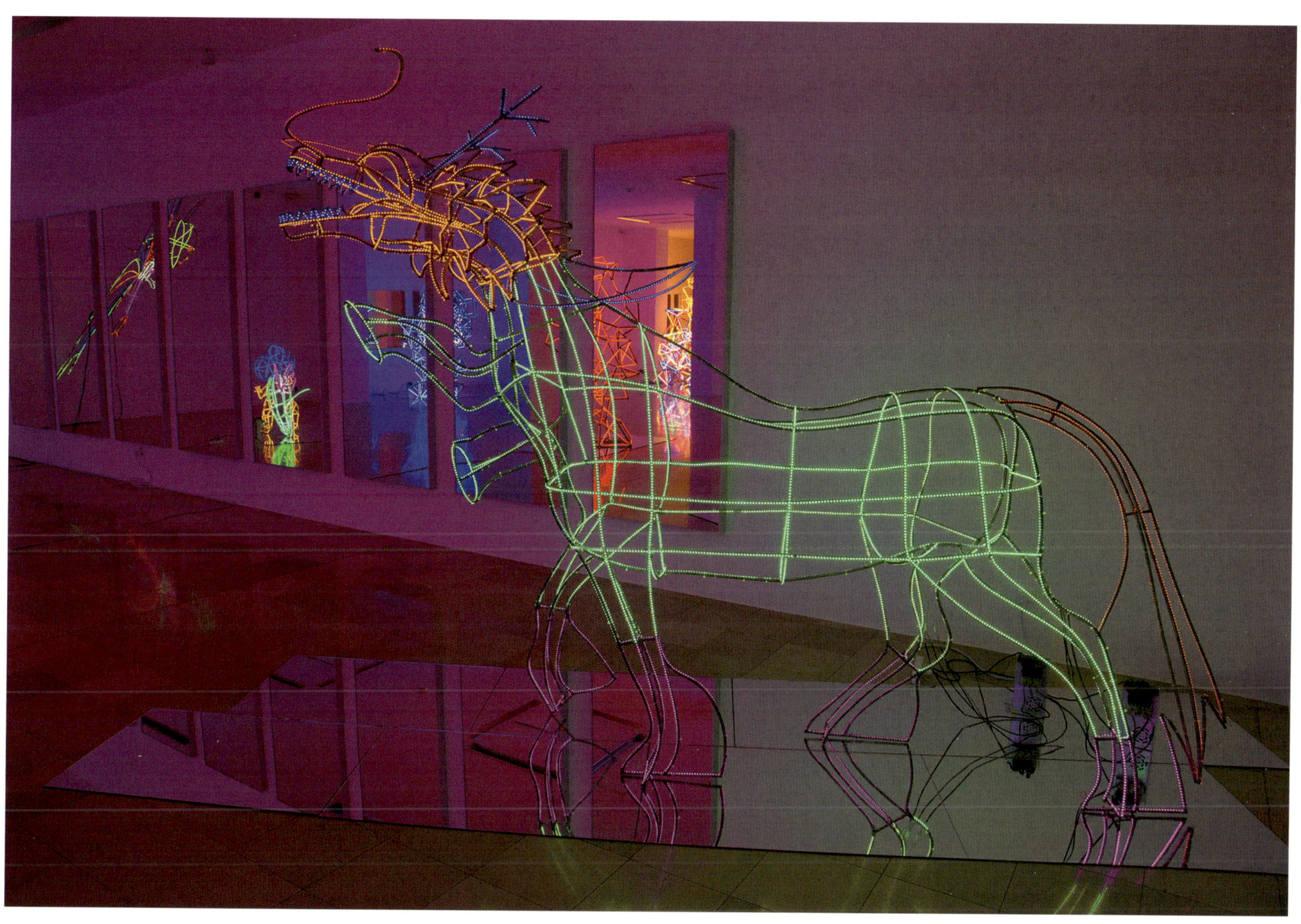

Links:
Drachenpferd, aus der Serie Die Götter der neuen Arten, 2019
Stahlröhre, LED-Lampen
295 × 110 × 210 cm

Left:
Dragonhorse, The Gods of New Species, 2019
Steel pipe, LED lamps
295 × 110 × 210 cm

Oben:
Ansicht der Installation im Ludwig Museum,
Koblenz, 2019

Above:
View of the installation in the Ludwig Museum,
Koblenz, 2019

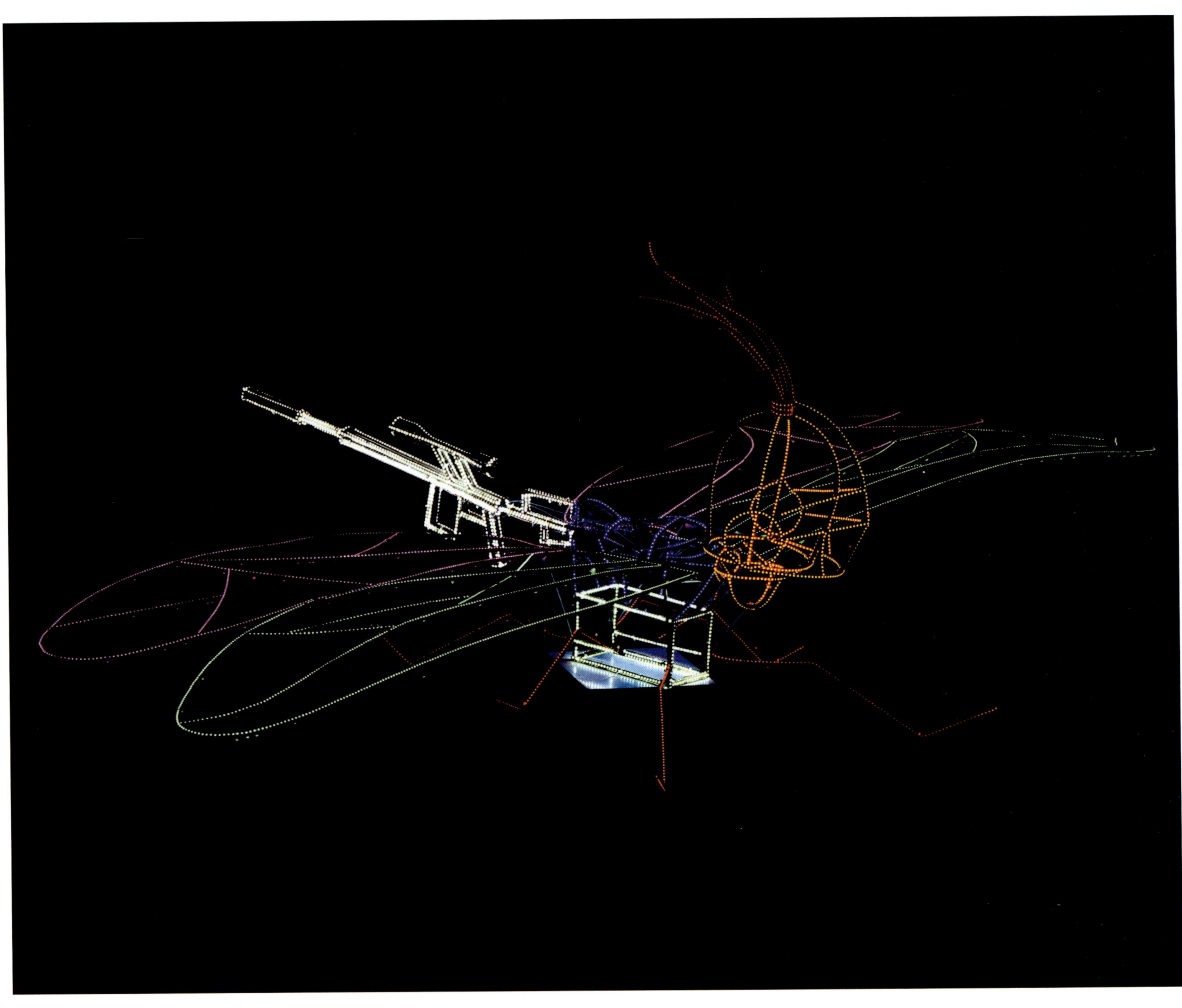

Libelle aus der Serie Die Götter der neuen Arten, 2019
Stahlröhre, LED-Lampen
300 × 160 × 110 cm

Dragonfly, The Gods of New Species, 2019
Steel pipe, LED lamps
300 × 160 × 110 cm

Rechts:
Dinosaurier und Schmetterling,
aus der Serie Die Götter der neuen Arten, 2019
Stahlröhre, LED-Lampen
300 × 160 × 110 cm

Right:
Dinosaur, The Gods of New Species
and *Butterfly, The Gods of New Species*, 2019
Steel pipe, LED lamps
300 × 160 × 110 cm

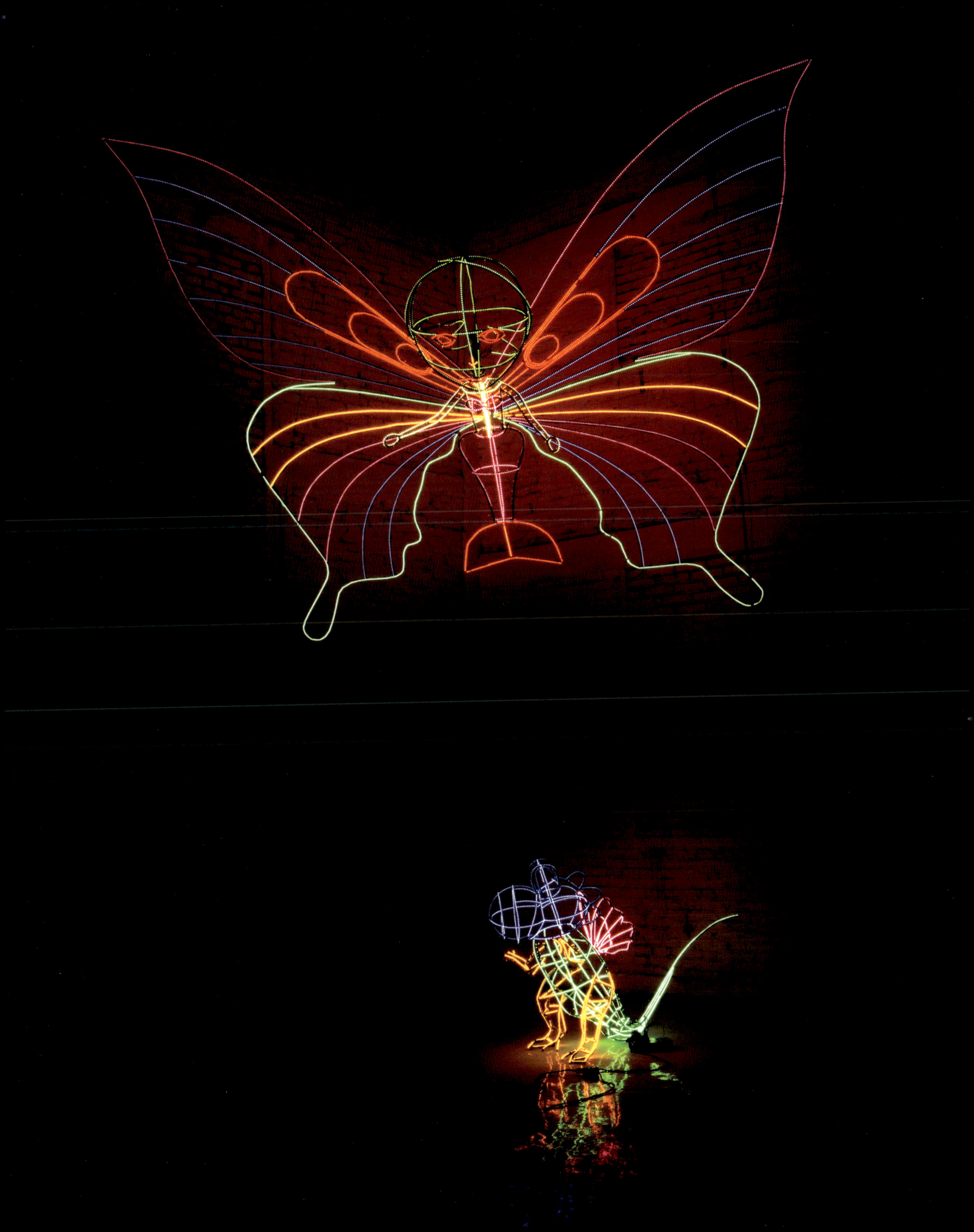

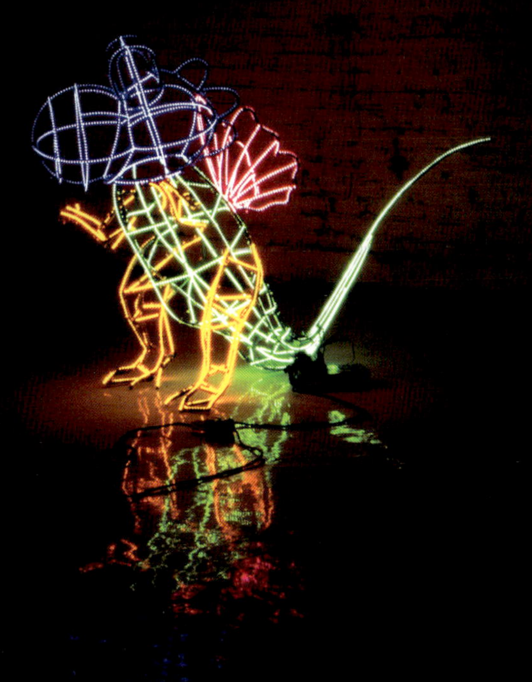

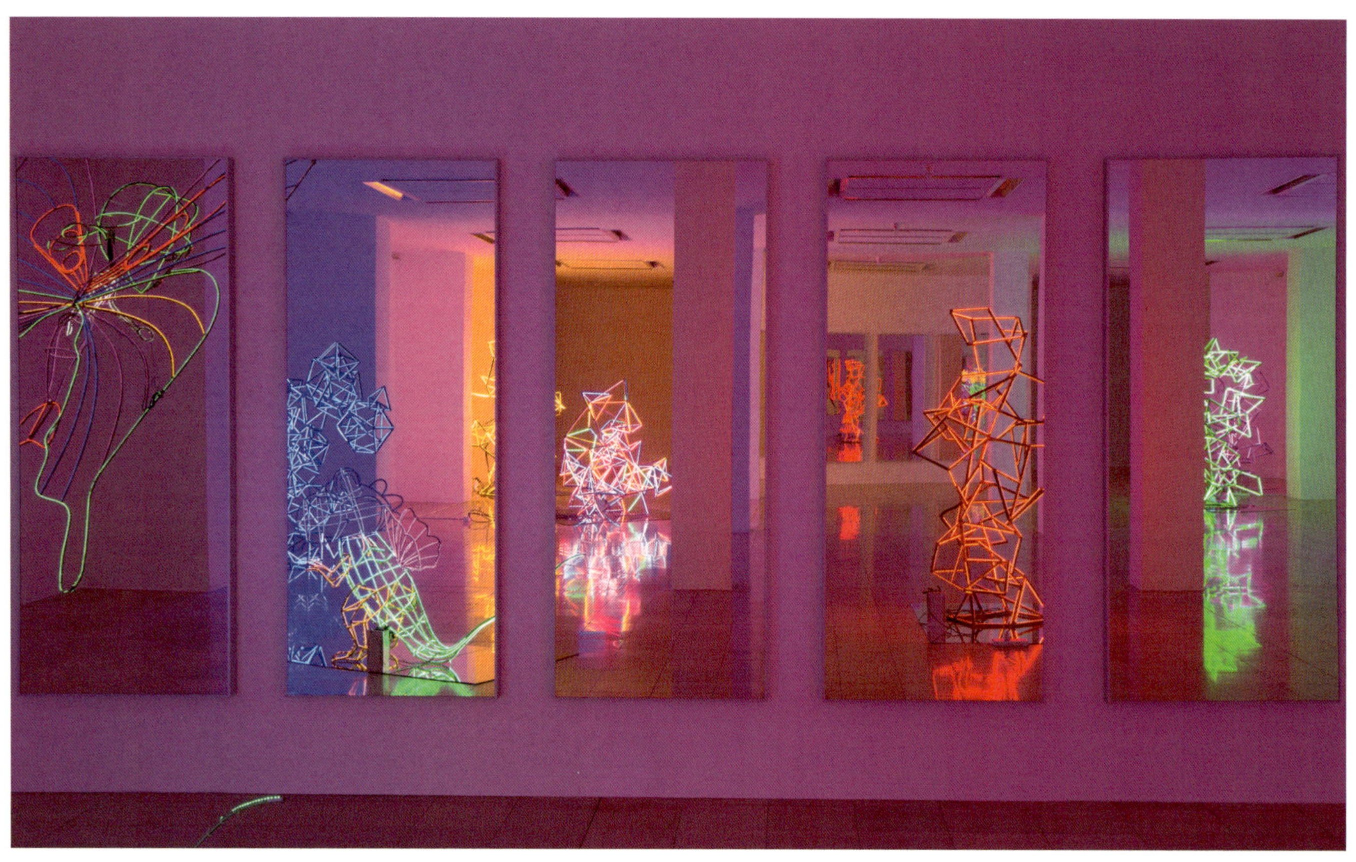

Oben und unten:
Ansicht der Installation im Ludwig Museum, Koblenz, 2019

Above and below:
View of the installation in the Ludwig Museum, Koblenz, 2019

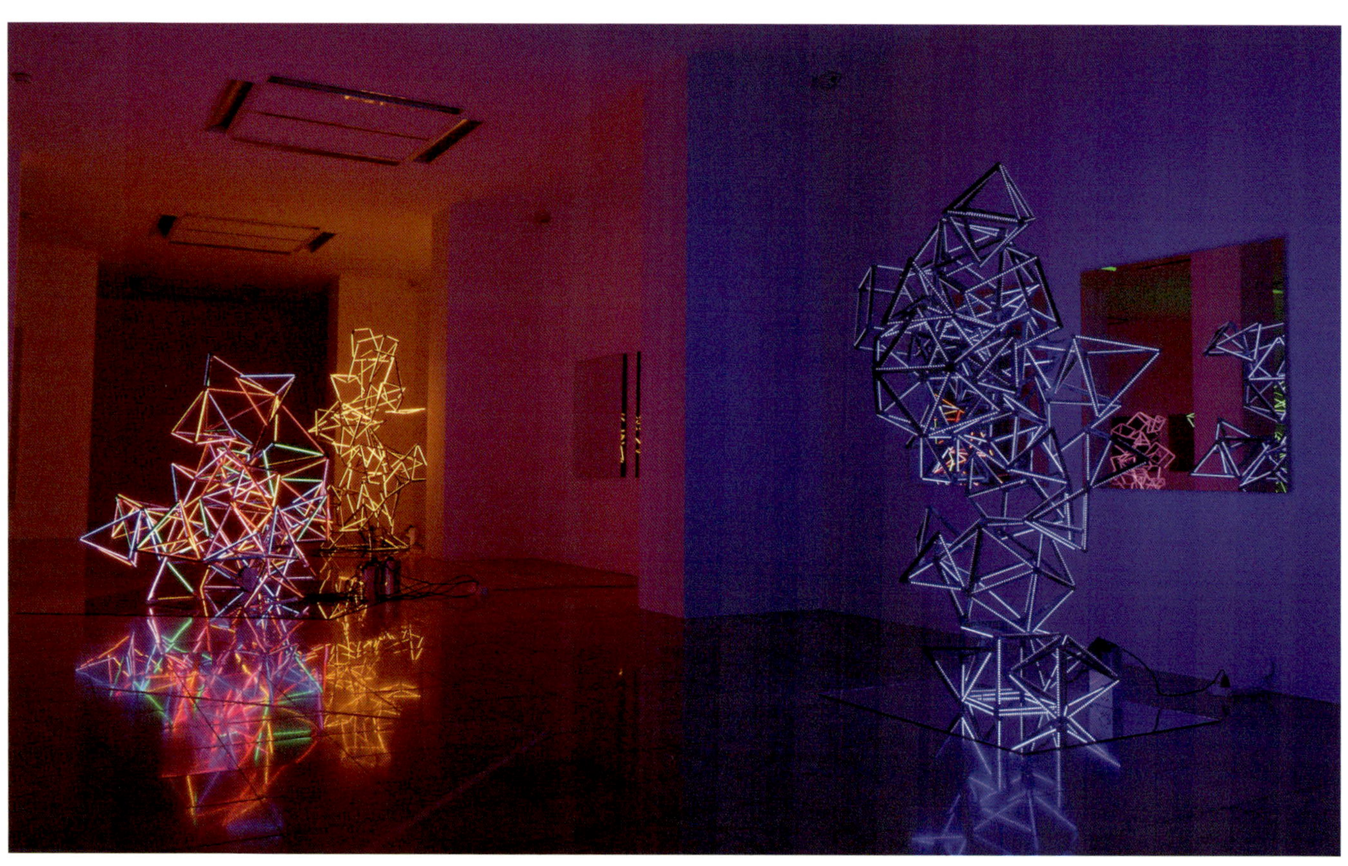

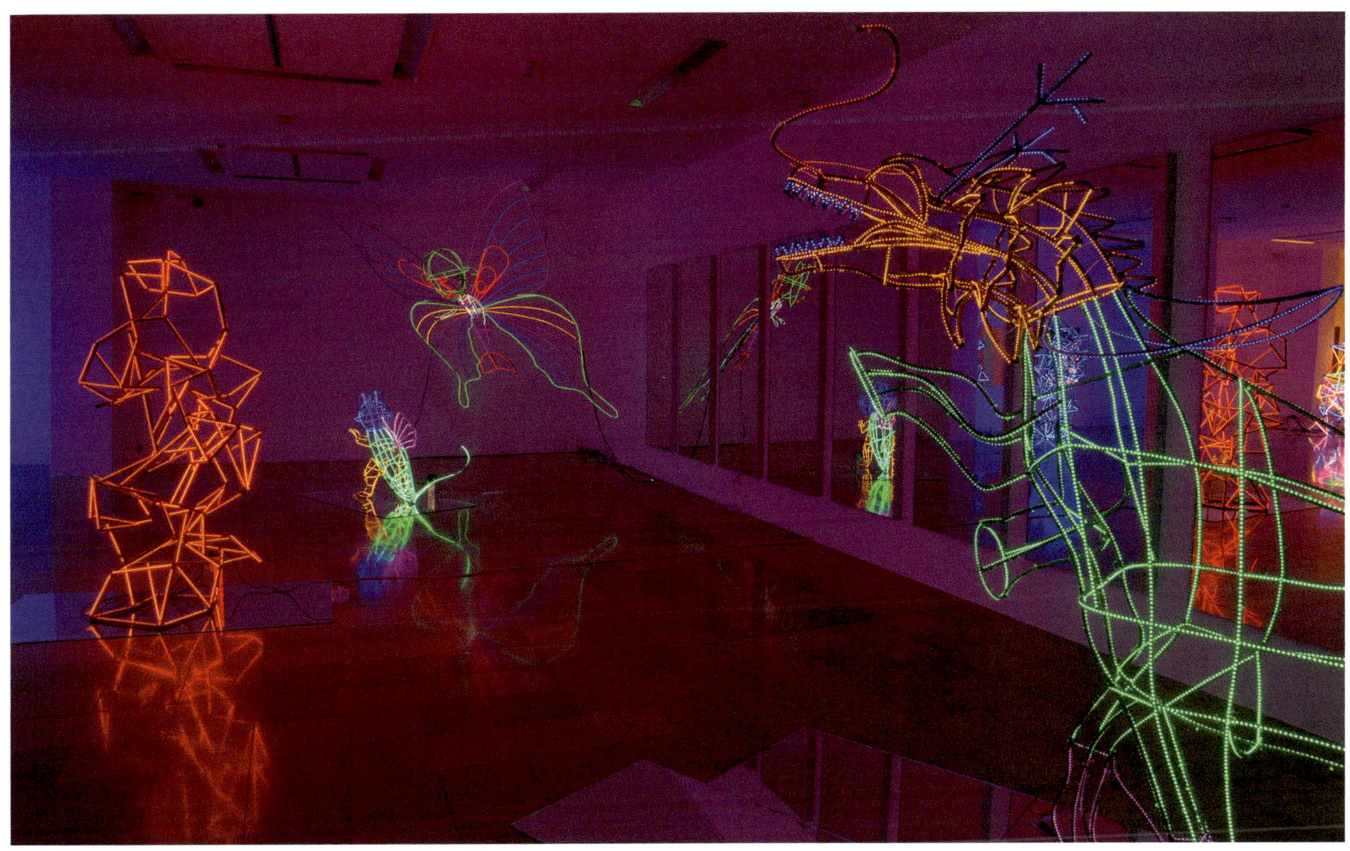

Oben und unten:
Ansicht der Installation im Ludwig Museum, Koblenz, 2019

Above and below:
View of the installation in the Ludwig Museum, Koblenz, 2019

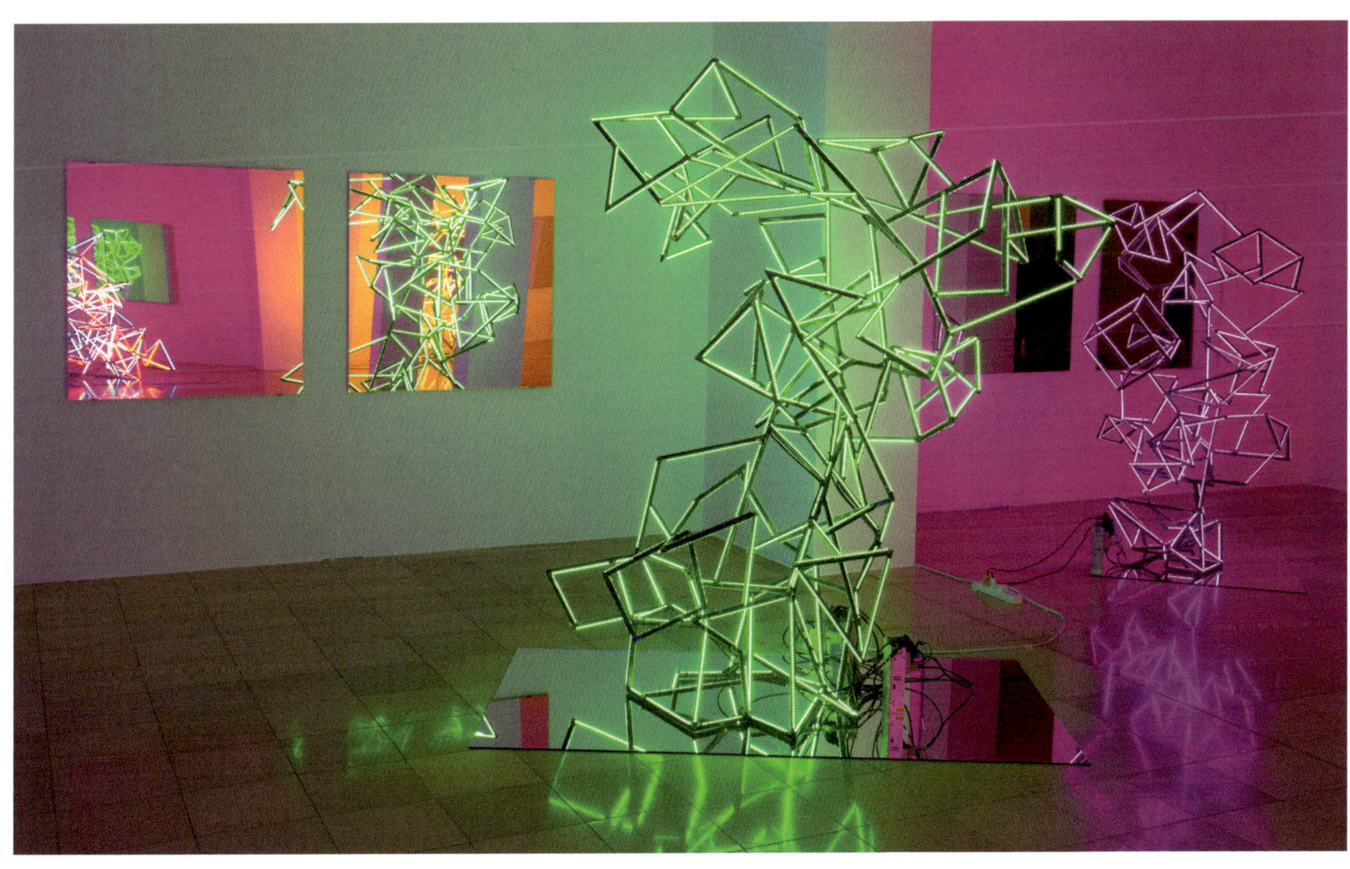

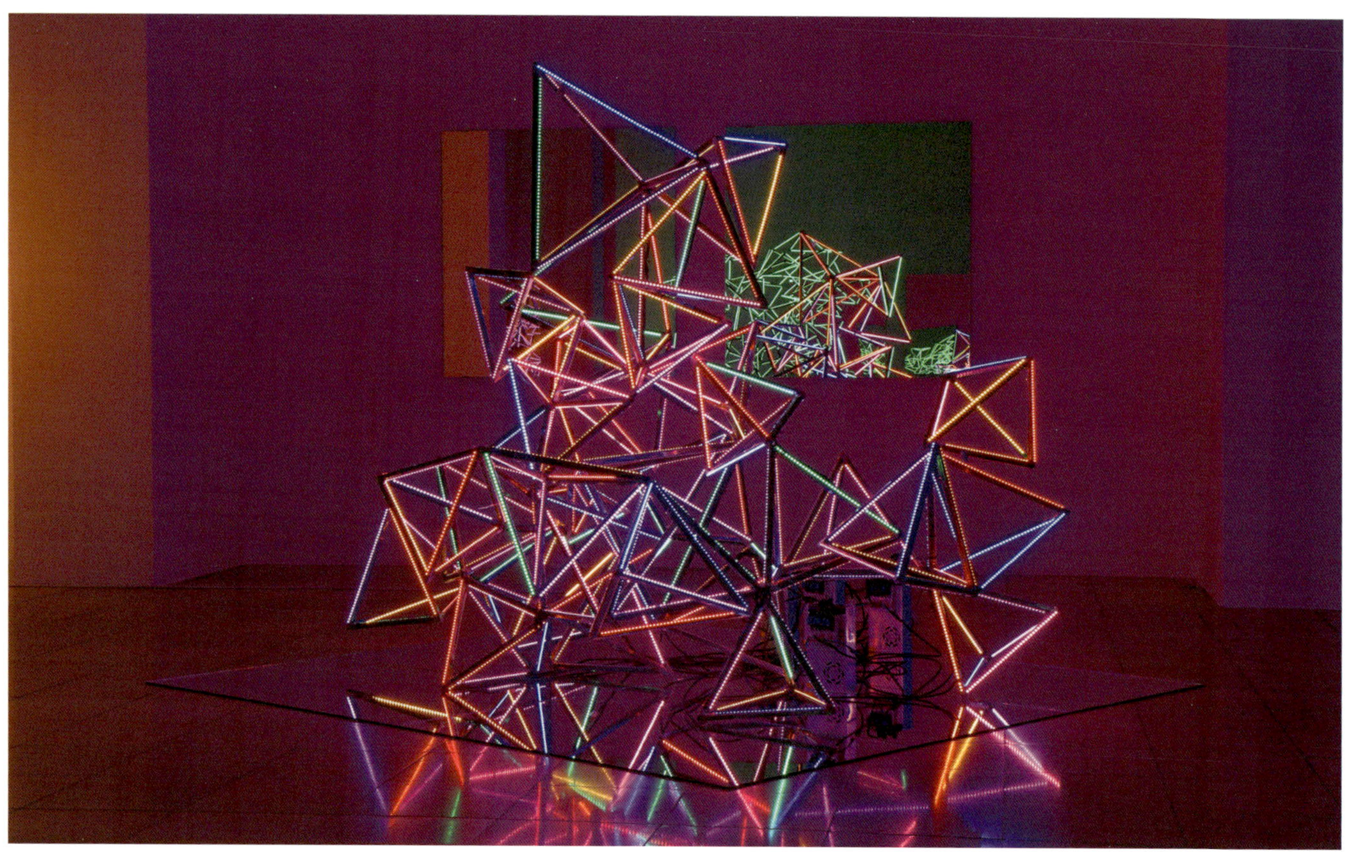

Oben und unten:
Ansicht der Installation im Ludwig Museum, Koblenz, 2019

Above and below:
View of the installation in the Ludwig Museum, Koblenz, 2019

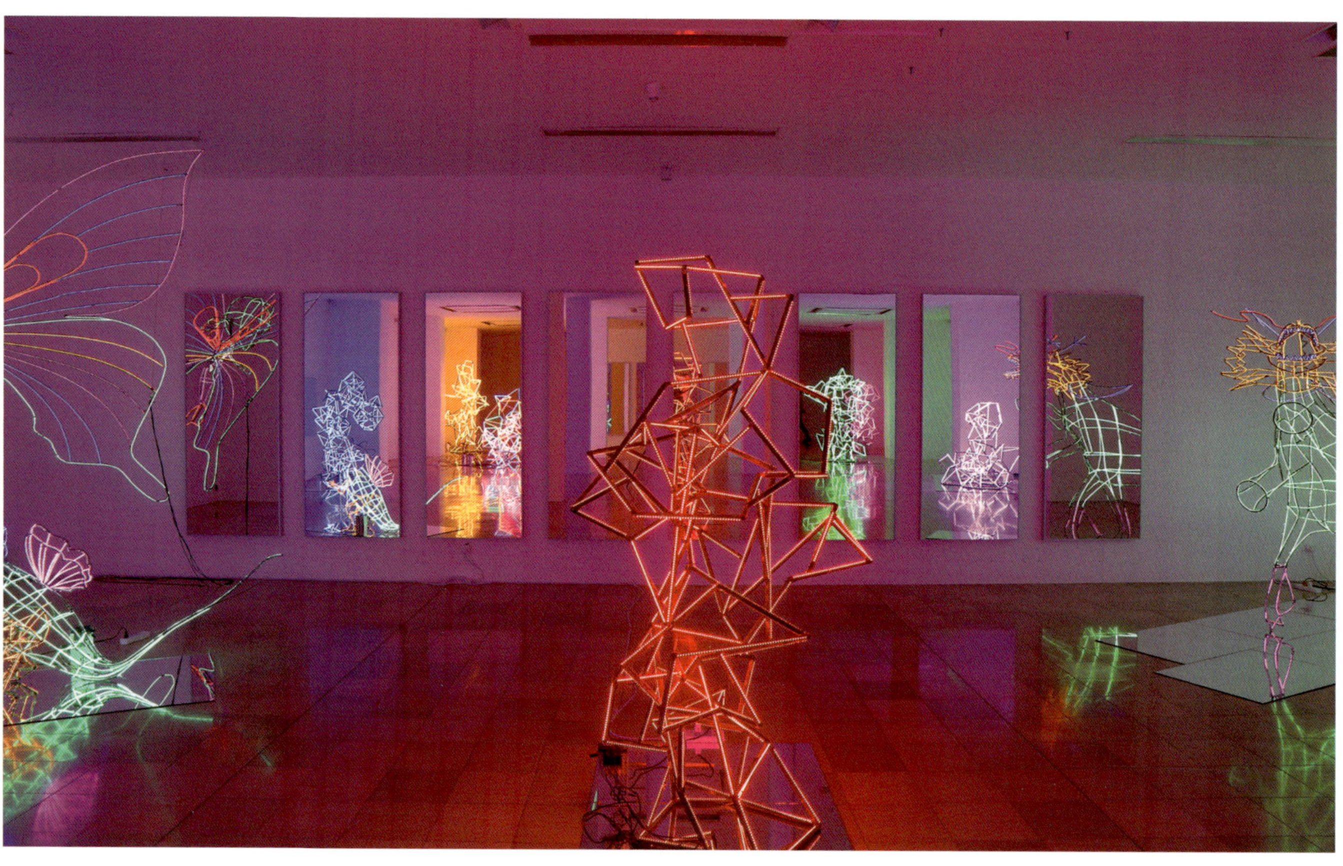

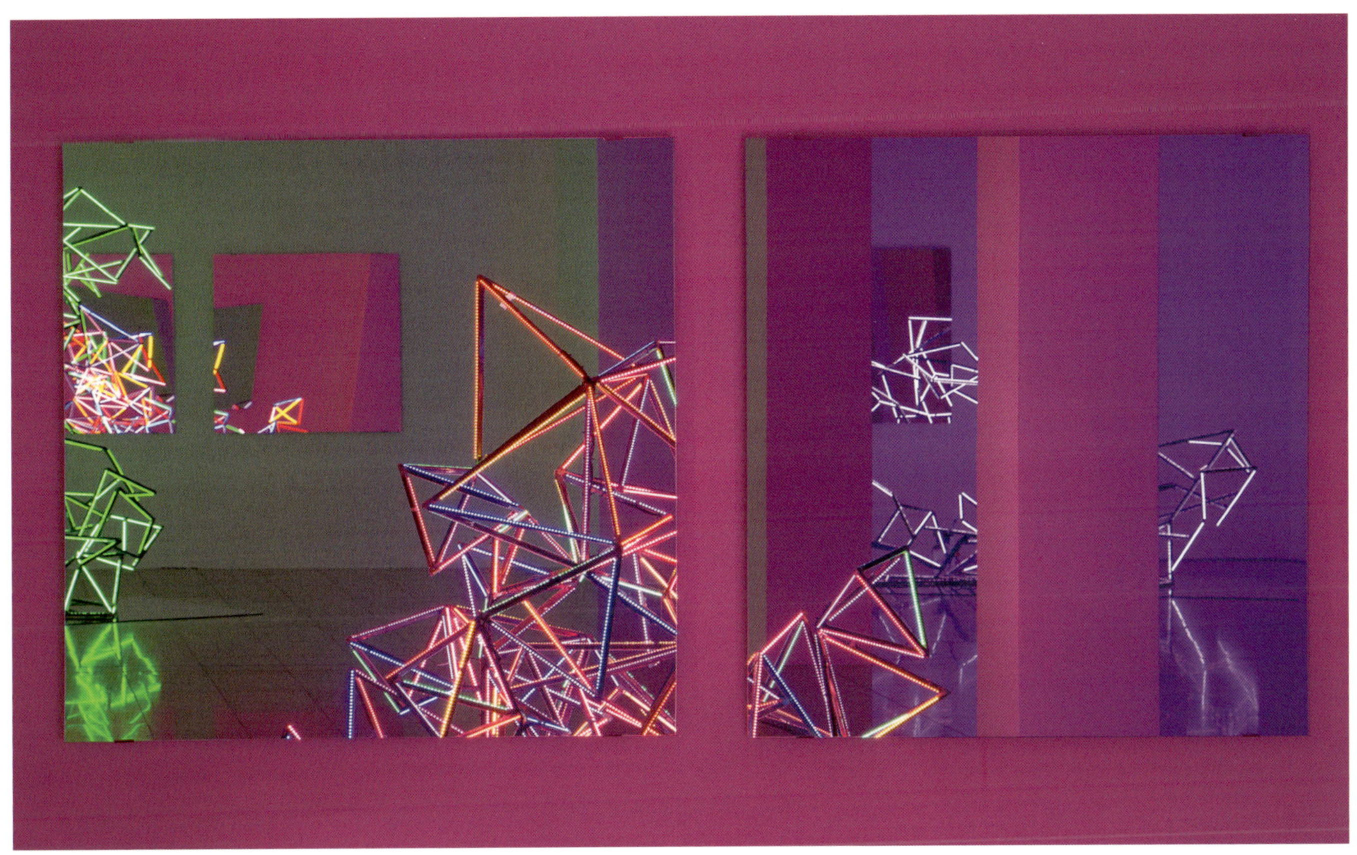

Oben und unten:
Ansicht der Installation im Ludwig Museum, Koblenz, 2019

Above and below:
View of the installation in the Ludwig Museum, Koblenz, 2019

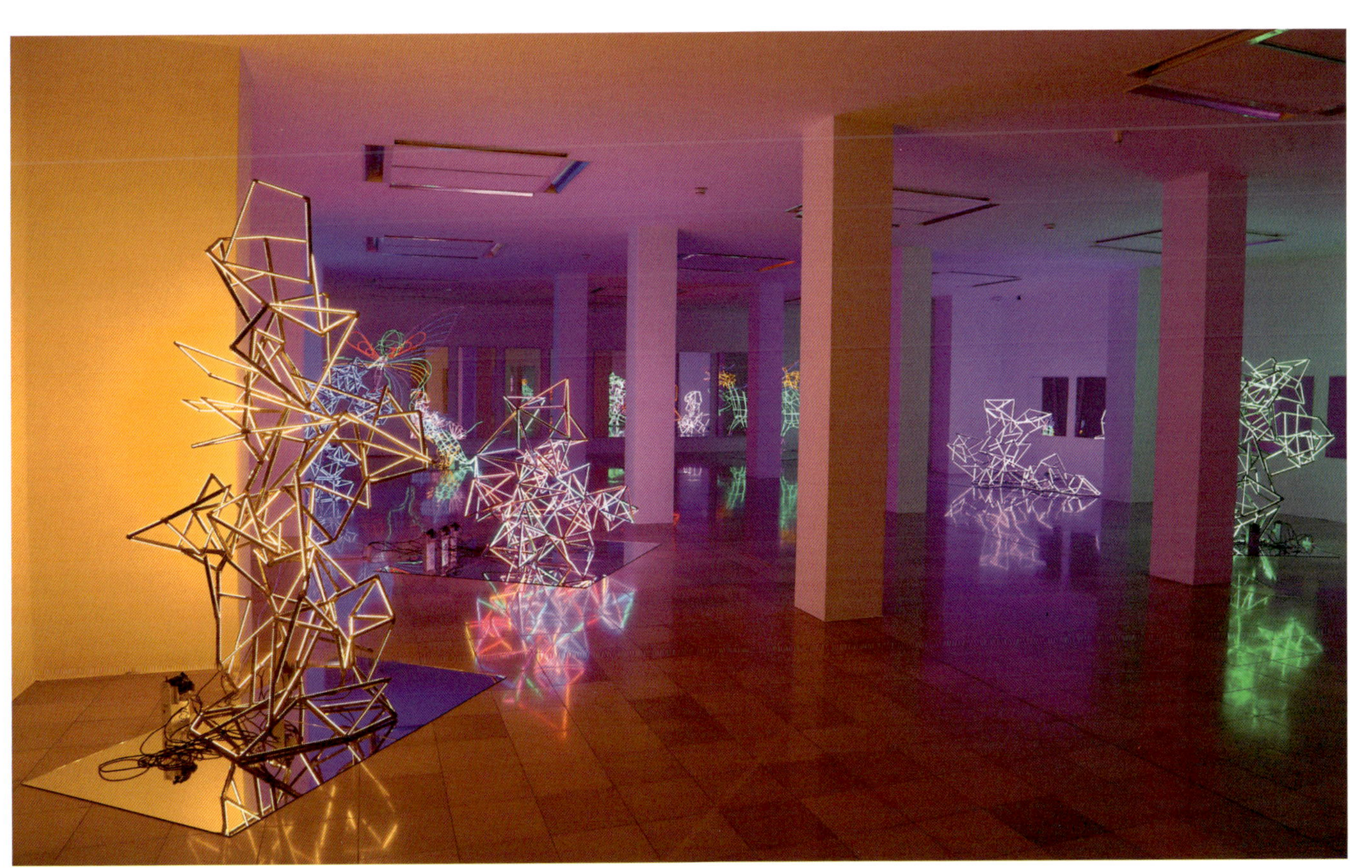

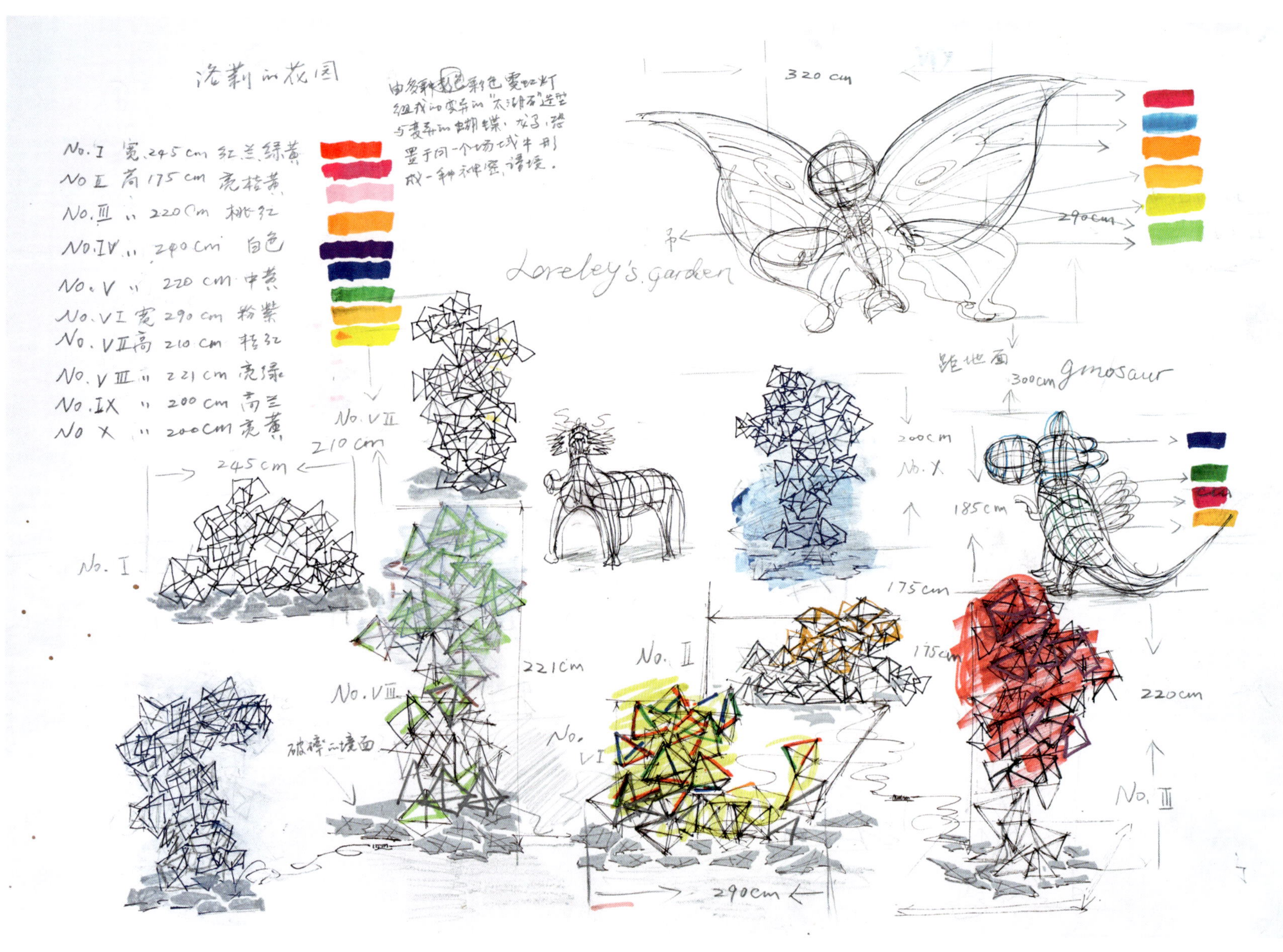

Loreleys Garten, 2019
Mixed Media auf Papier
39 x 53,8 cm

Loreley's Garden, 2019
Mixed media on paper
39 x 53.8 cm

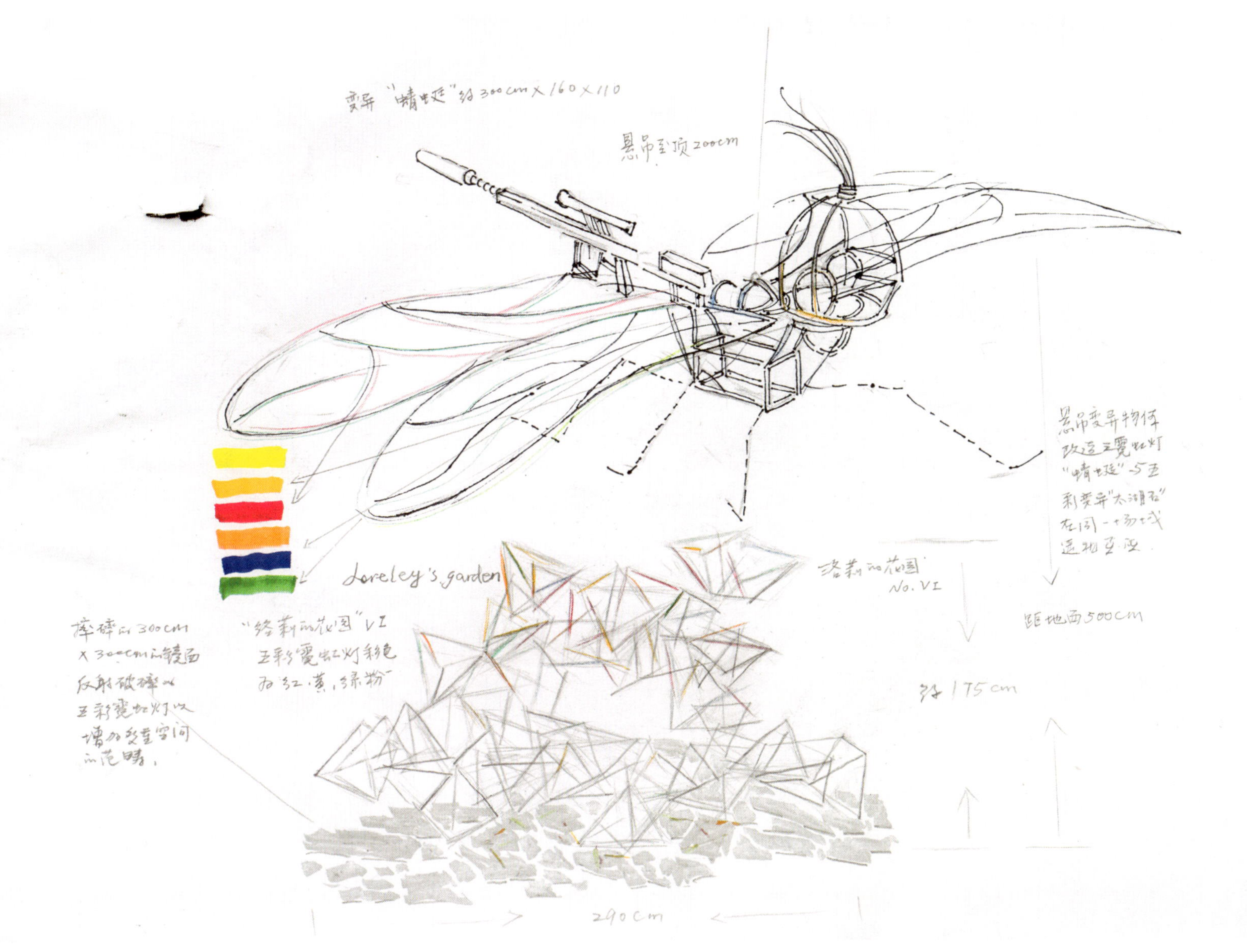

Libelle, 2019
Mixed Media auf Papier
37,5 x 52,5 cm

Dragonfly, 2019
Mixed media on paper
37.5 x 52.5 cm

Offenbarung

Revelation

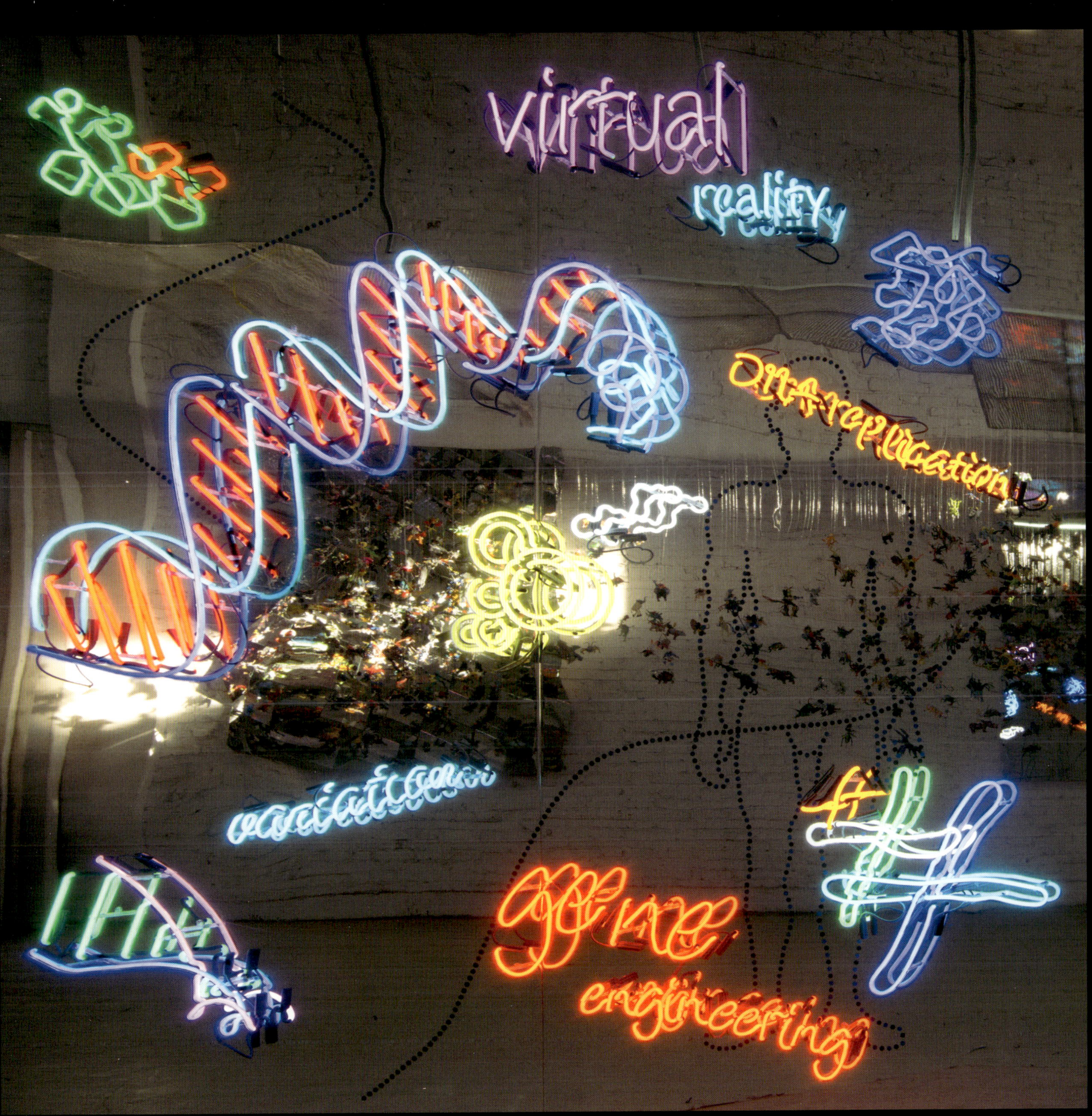

Offenbarung Nr.1, 2019
Spiegel, Edelstahl, Neonröhren, Acrylfarbe
244 × 244 × 7 cm

Revelation No. 1, 2019
Mirror, stainless steel, neon tube lights, acrylic paint
244 × 244 × 7 cm

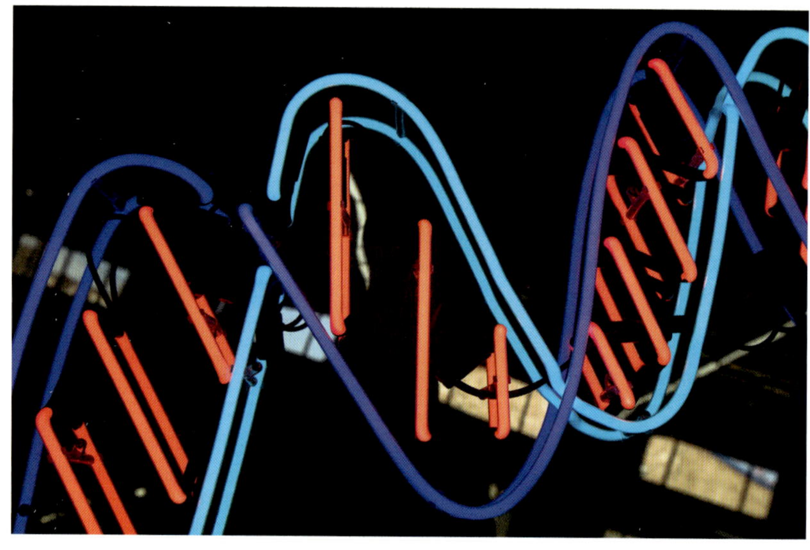

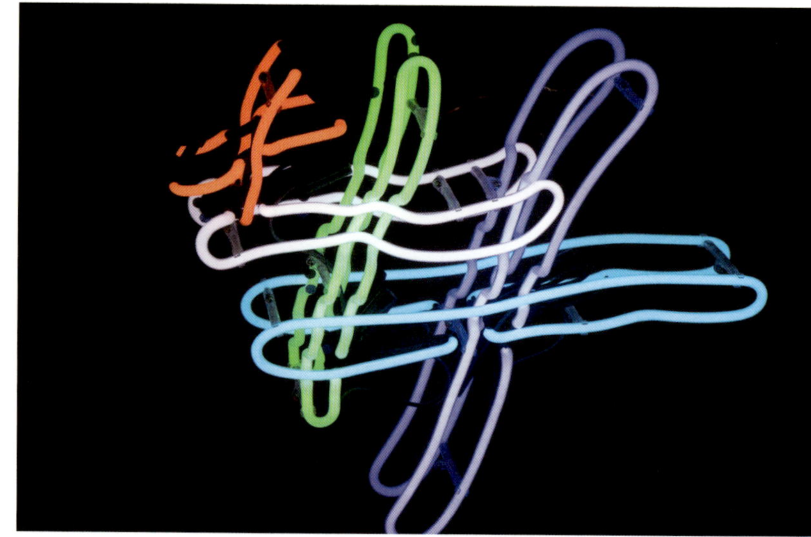

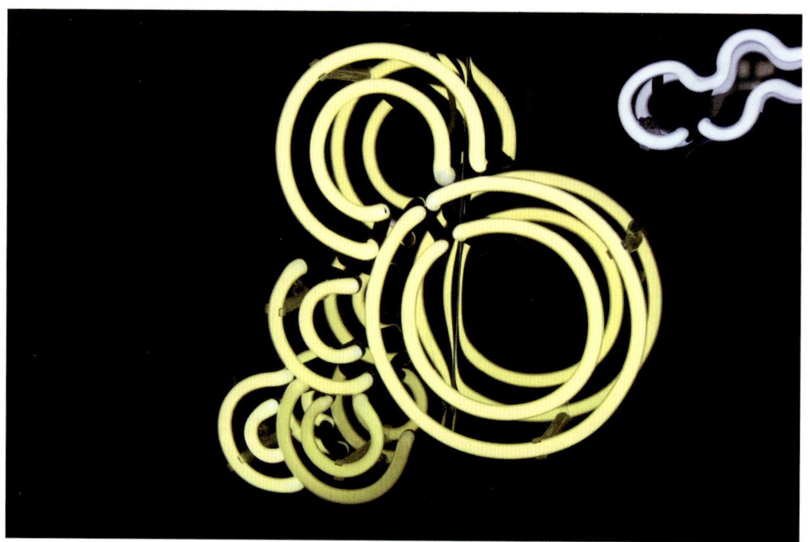

Offenbarung Nr.1, Details

Revelation No. 1, details

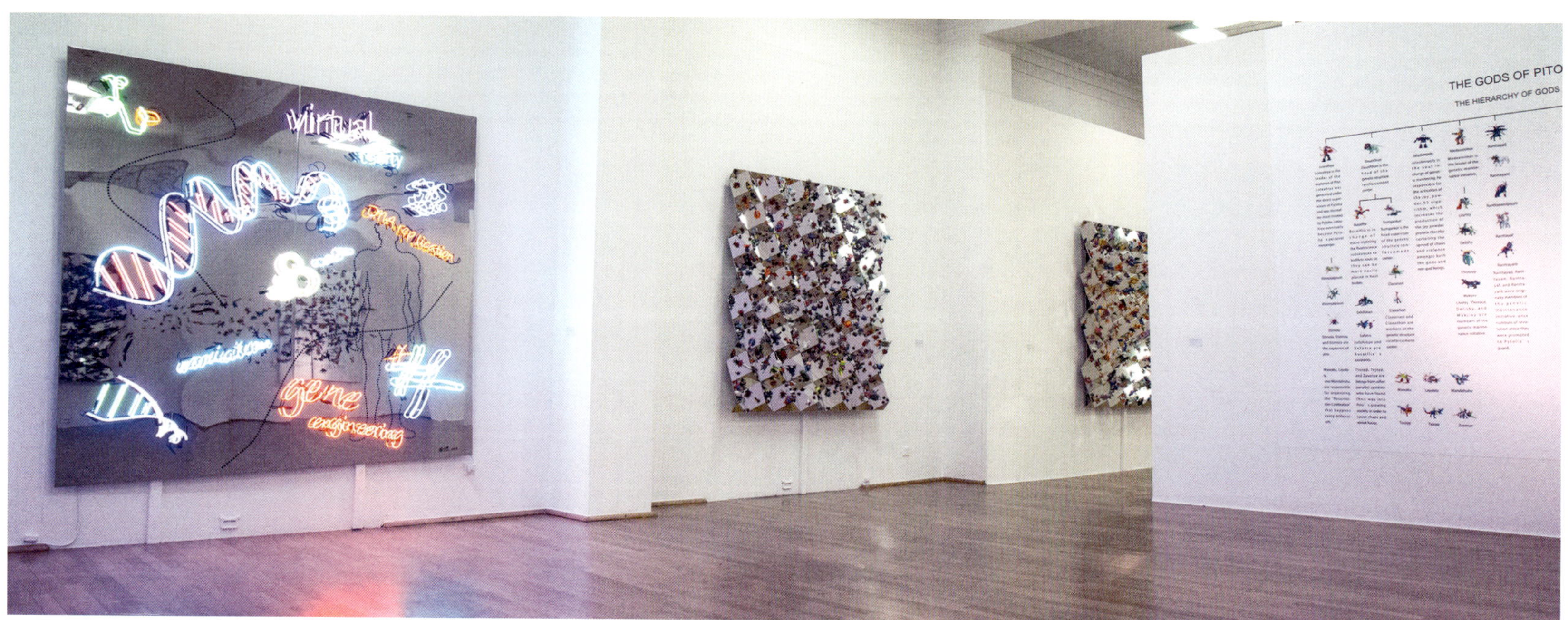

Offenbarung Nr.1, Ansicht der Installation im Ludwig Museum, Koblenz, 2019

Revelation No. 1, view of the installation in the Ludwig Museum, Koblenz, 2019

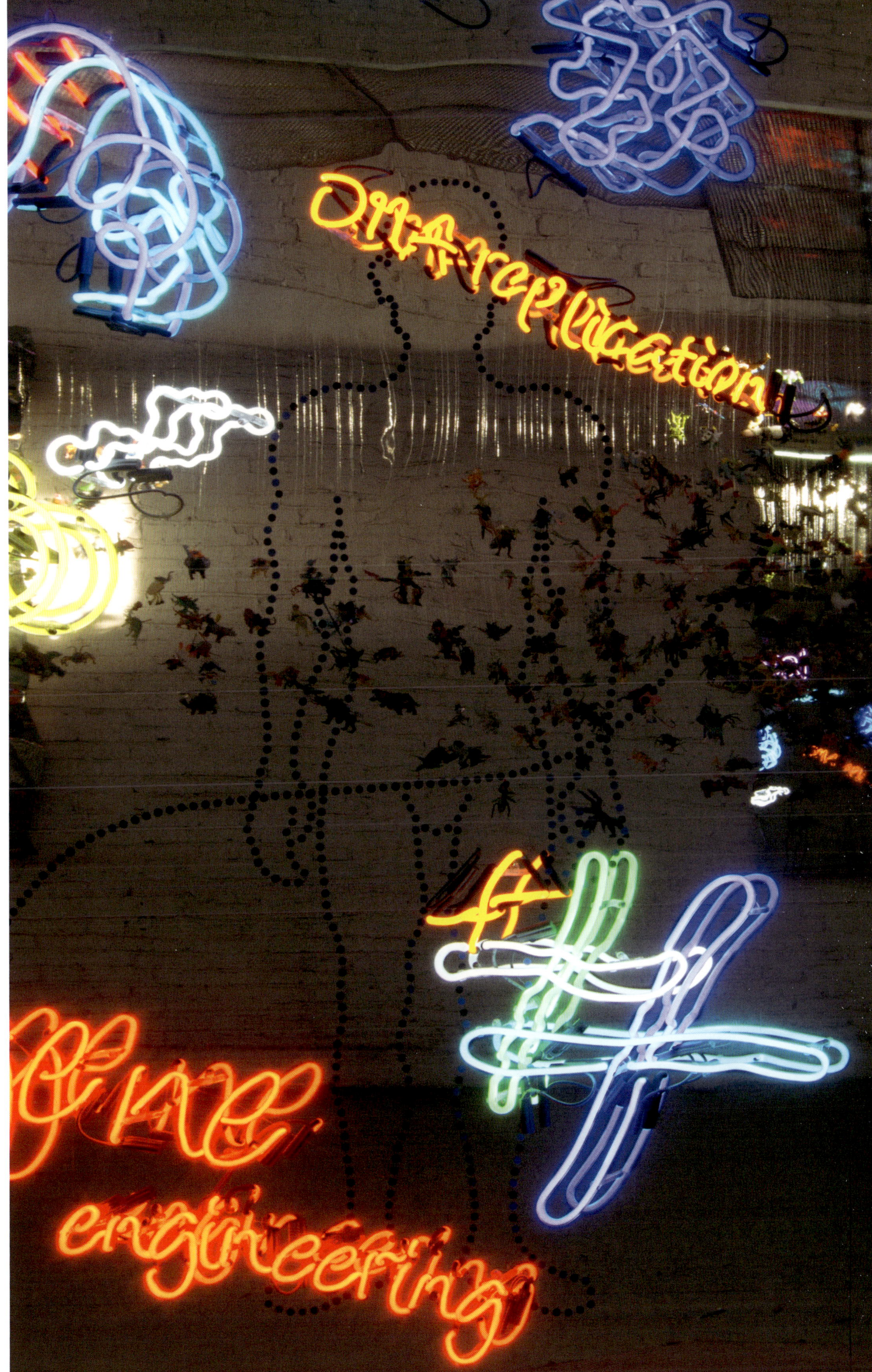

Offenbarung Nr.1, Detail

Revelation No. 1, detail

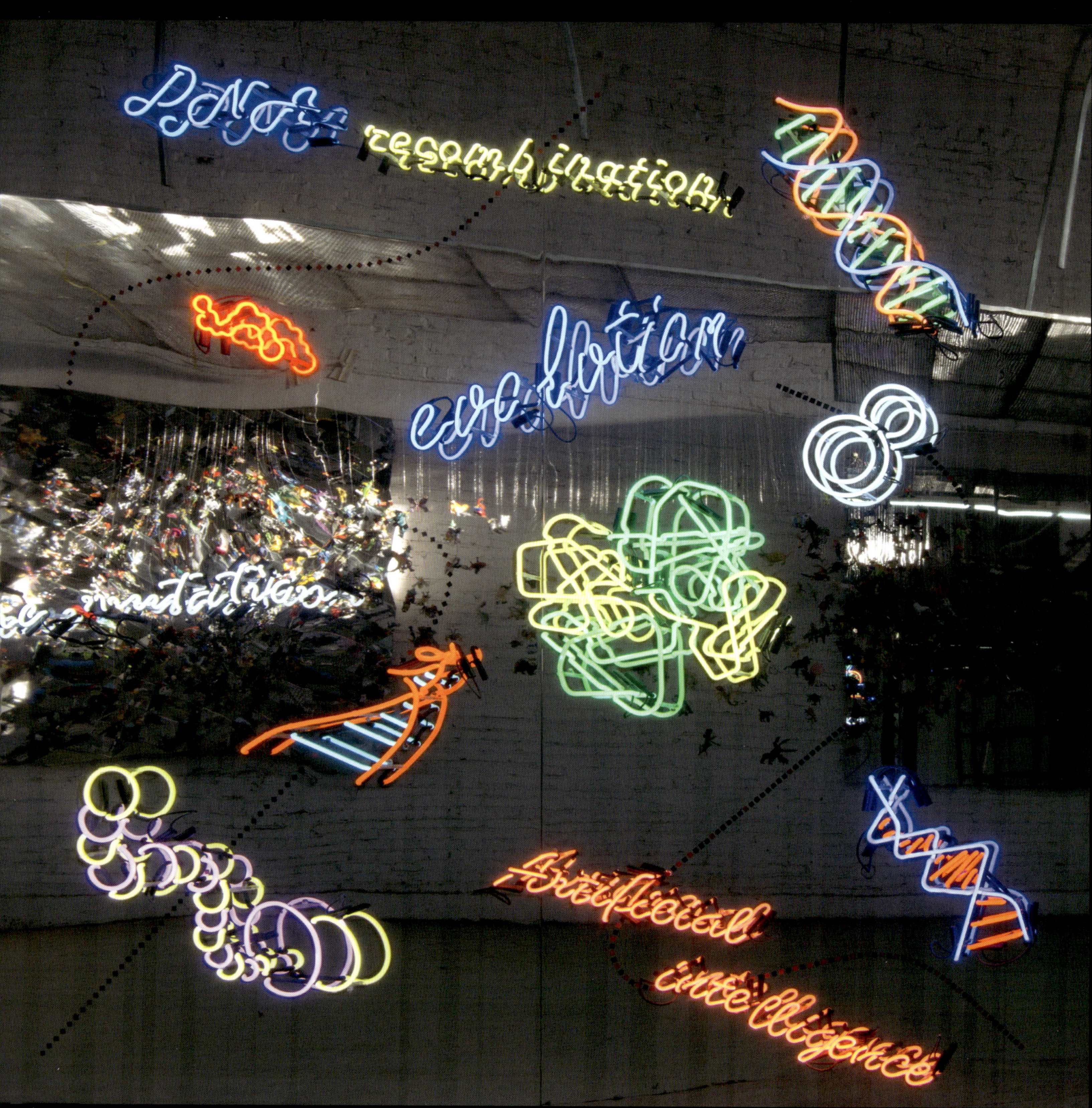

Offenbarung Nr.2, 2019
Spiegel, Edelstahl, Neonröhren, Acrylfarbe
244 × 244 × 7 cm

Revelation No. 2, 2019
Mirror, stainless steel, neon tube lights, acrylic paint
244 × 244 × 7 cm

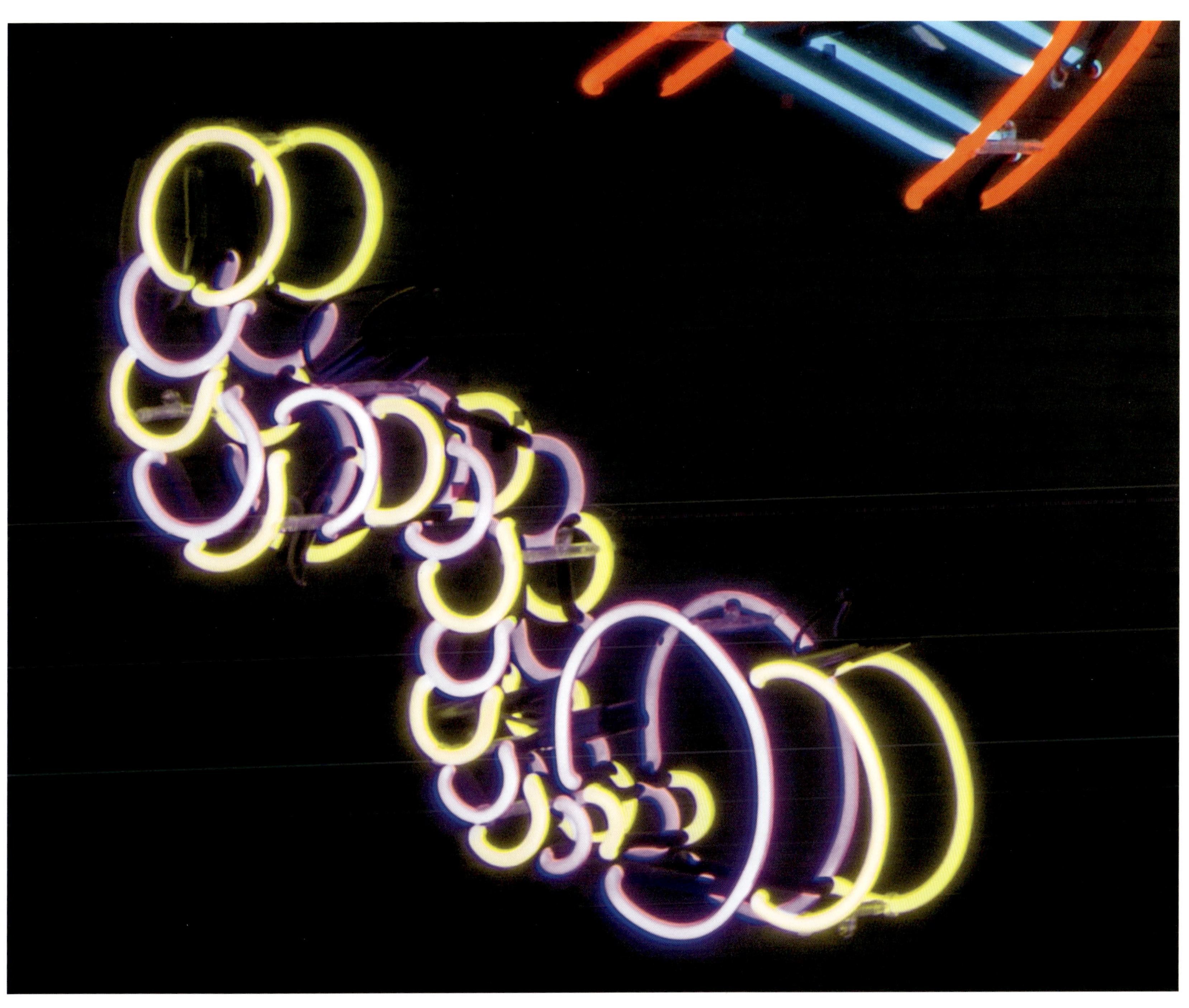

Offenbarung Nr.2, Detail

Revelation No. 2, detail

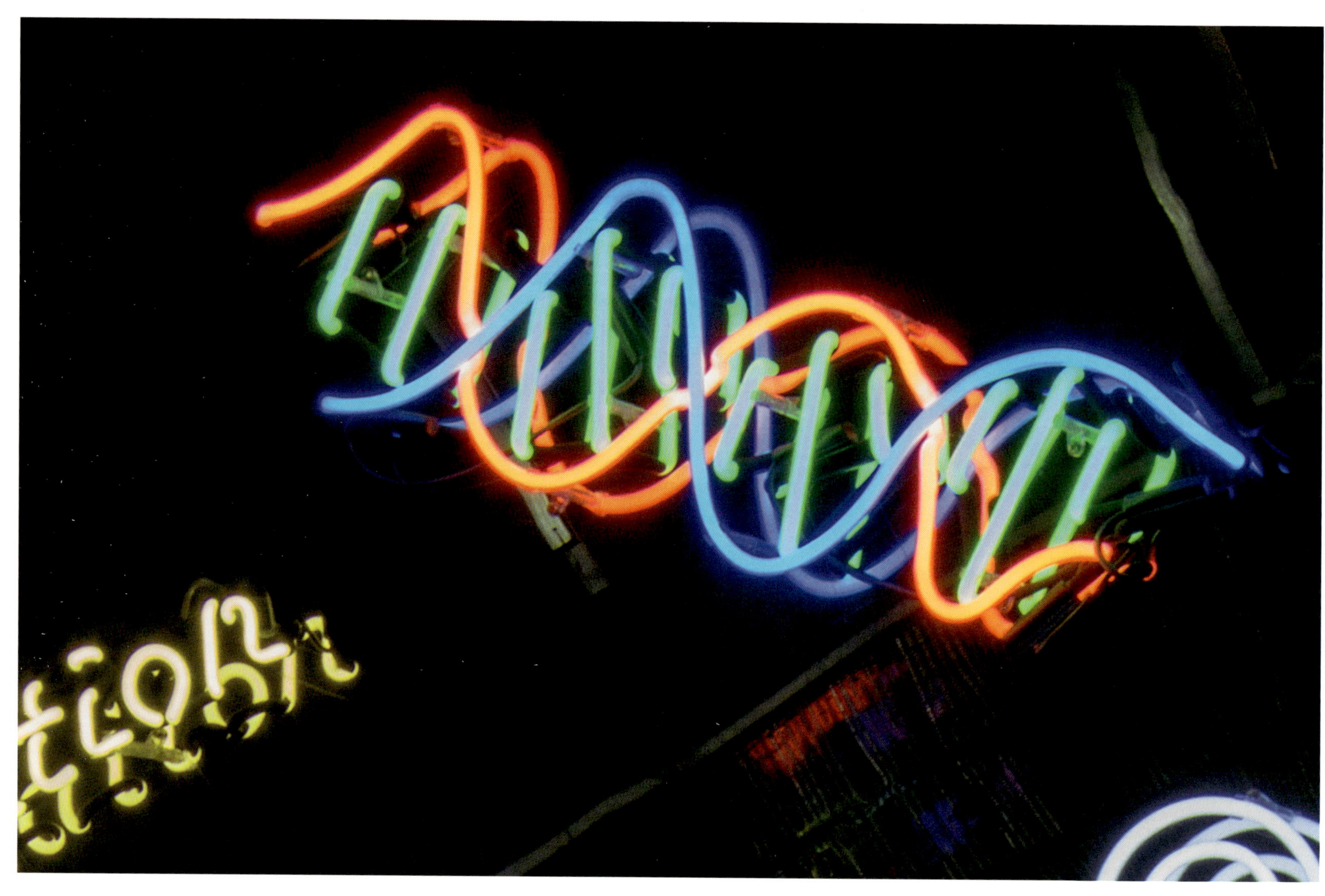

Offenbarung Nr.2, Detail

Revelation No. 2, detail

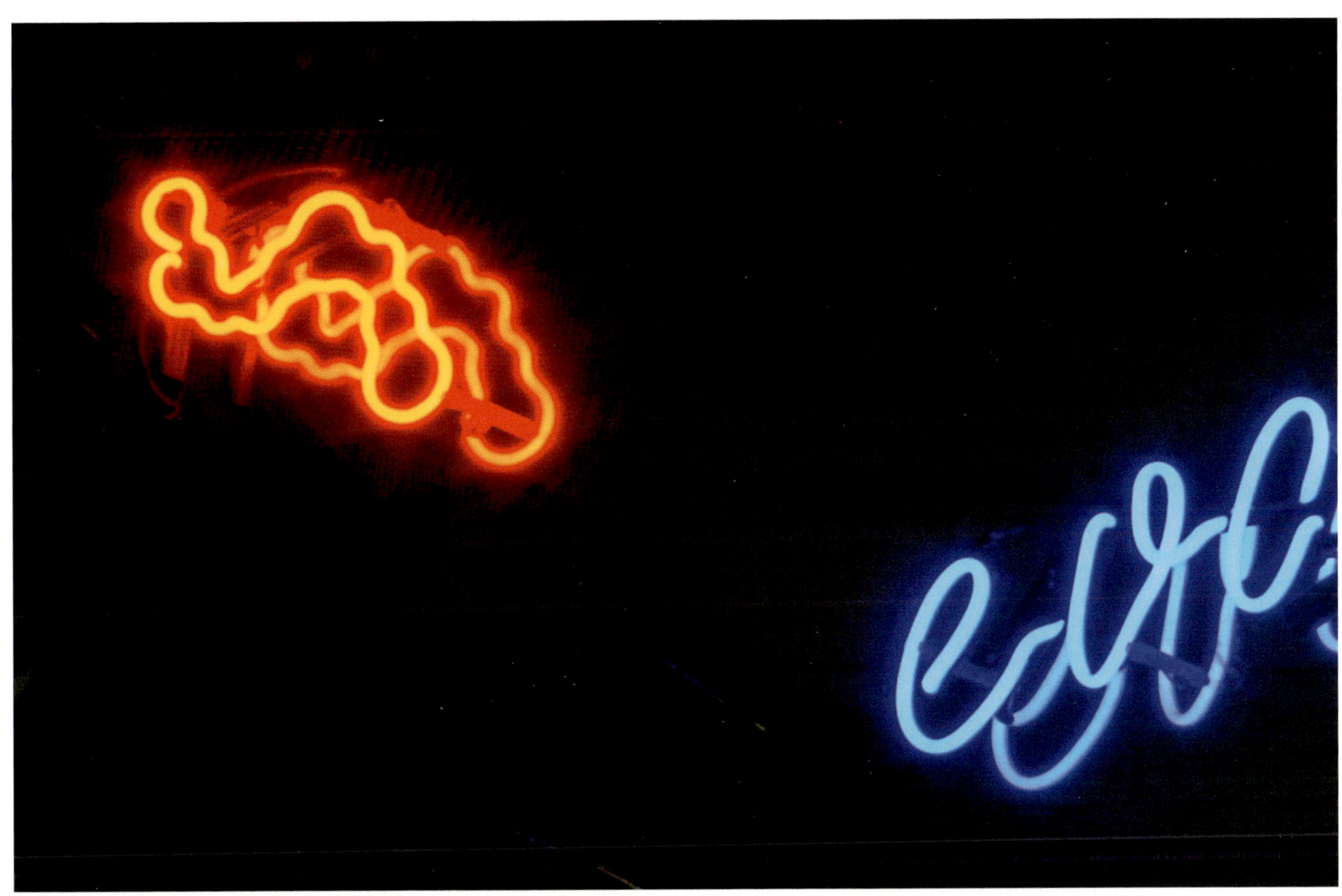

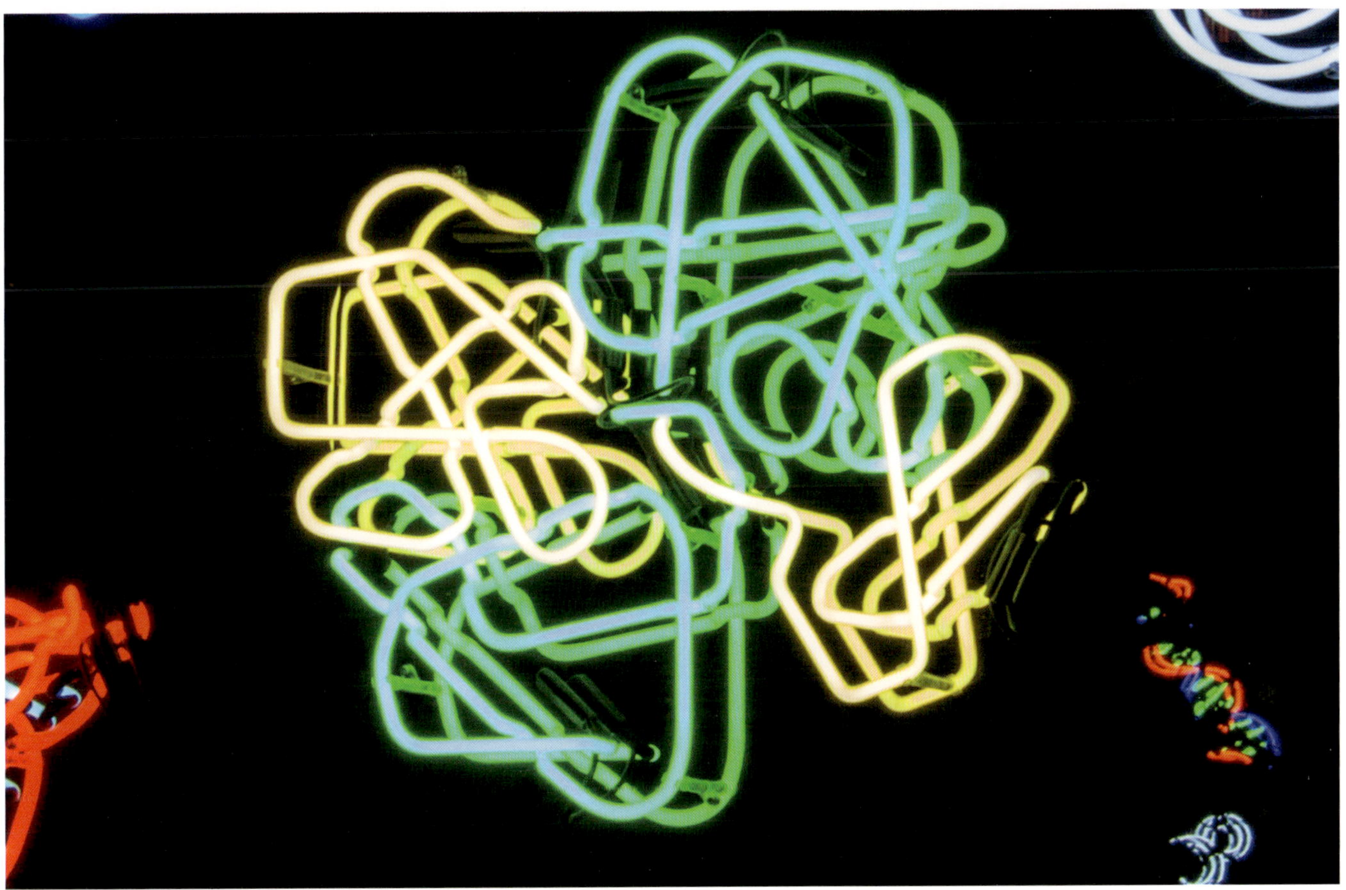

Offenbarung Nr.2, Details

Revelation No. 2, details

Sterben der Götter

Passing of the Gods

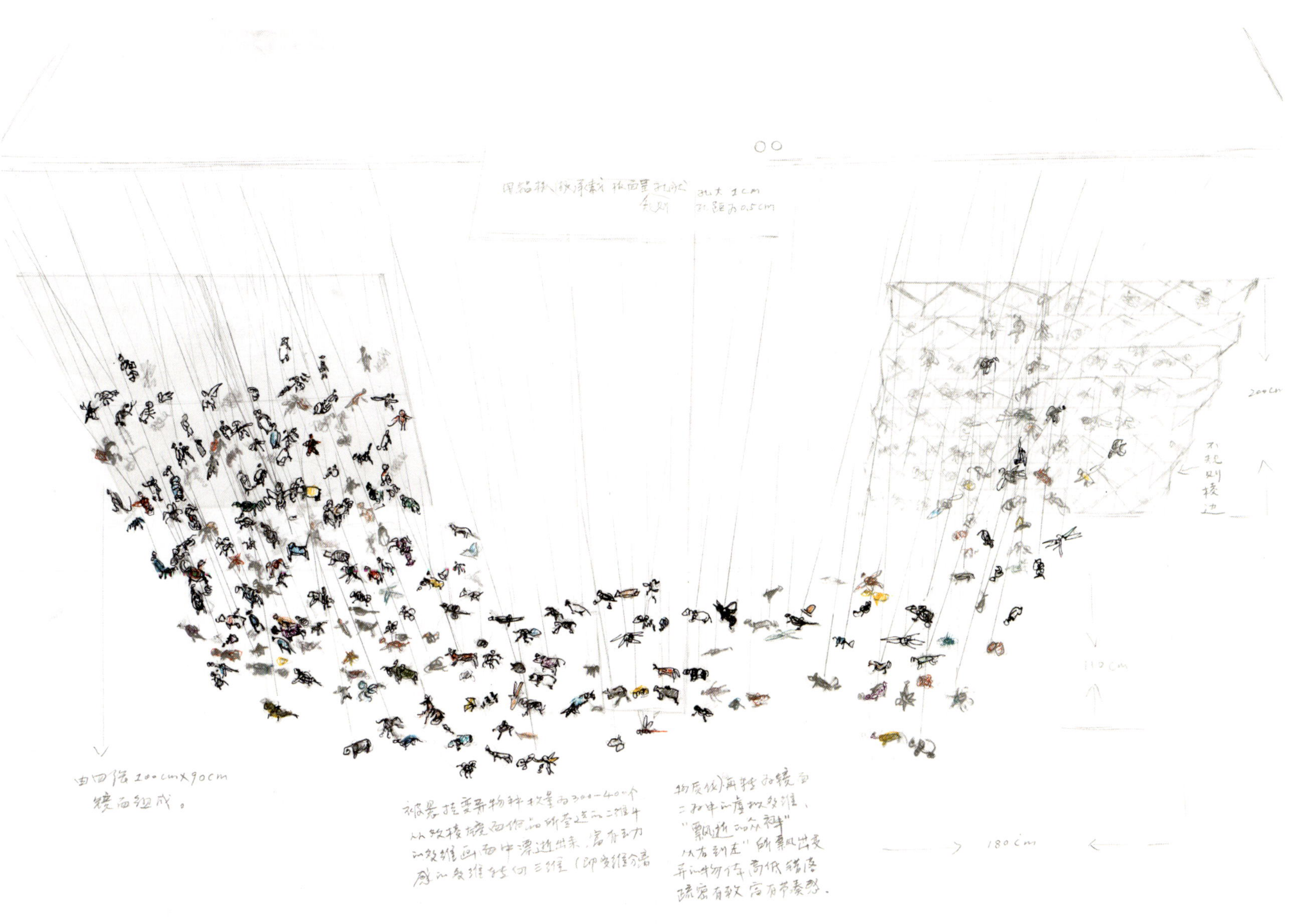

Sterben der Götter, 2019
Mixed Media auf Papier
42 x 58,8 cm

Passing of the Gods, 2019
Mixed media on paper
42 x 58.8 cm

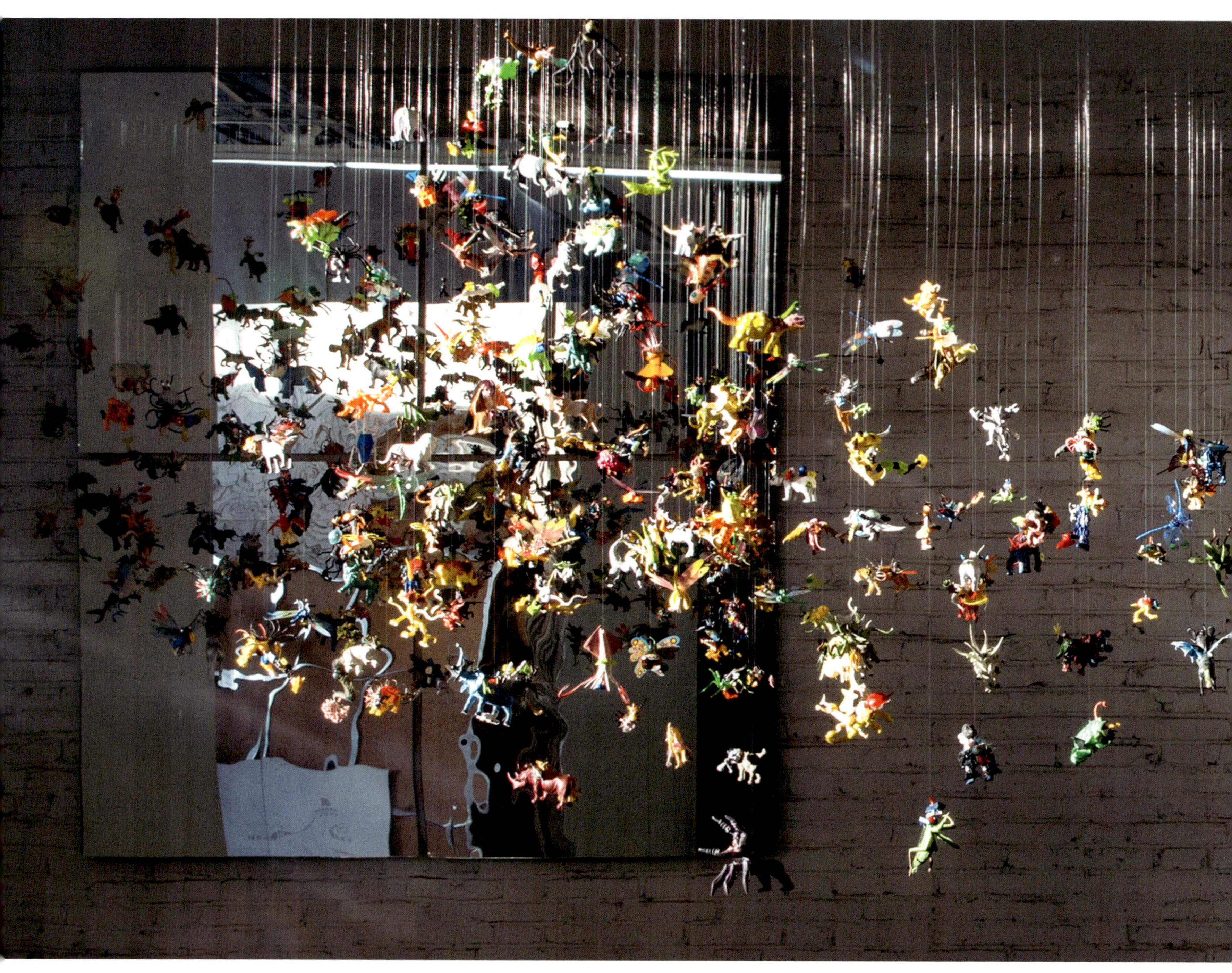

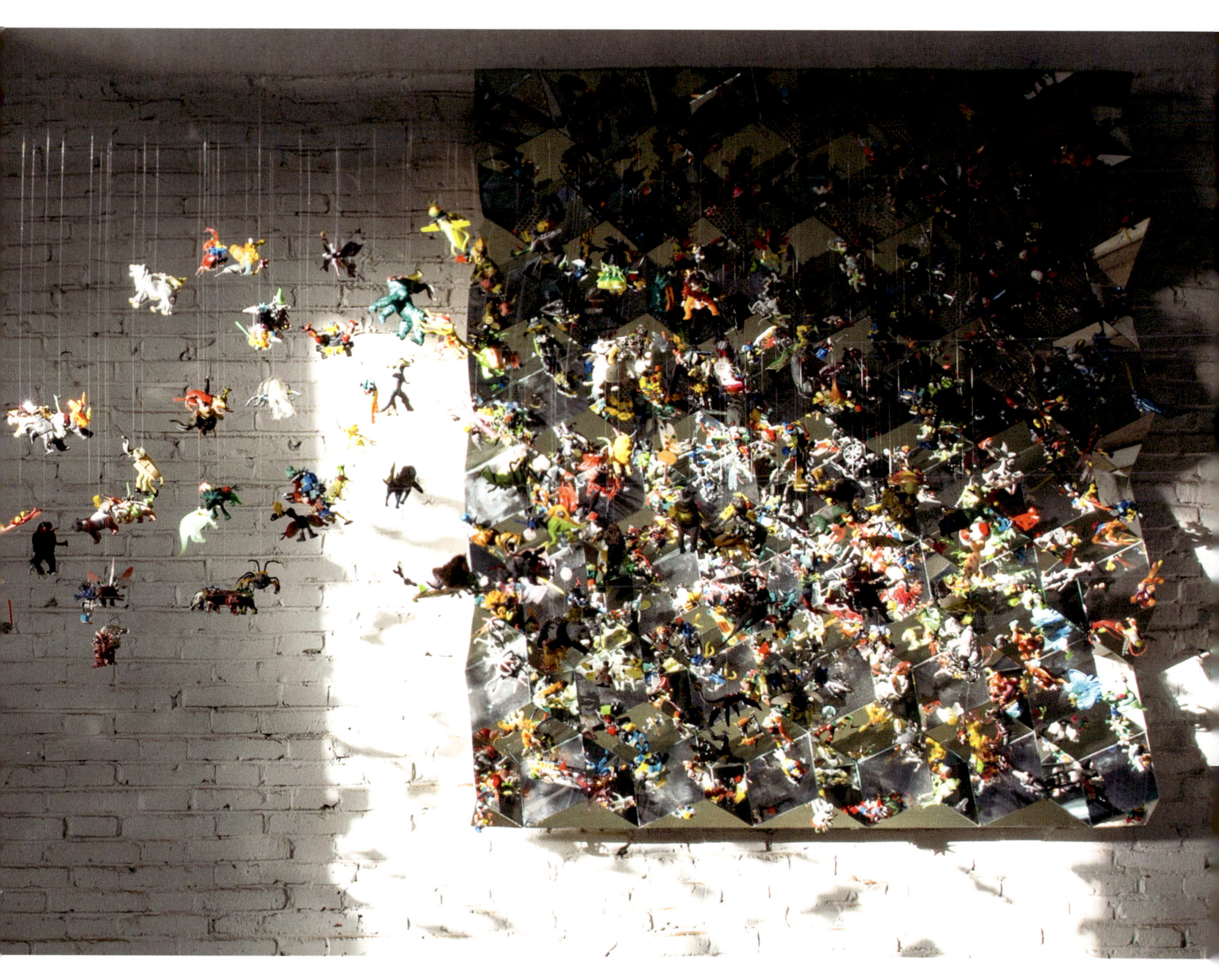

Sterben der Götter, 2019
Verändertes Spielzeug, Acrylfarbe, Emailfarbe
630 × 200 × 380 cm

Passing of the Gods, 2019
Modified toys, acrylic paint, enamel paint
630 × 200 × 380 cm

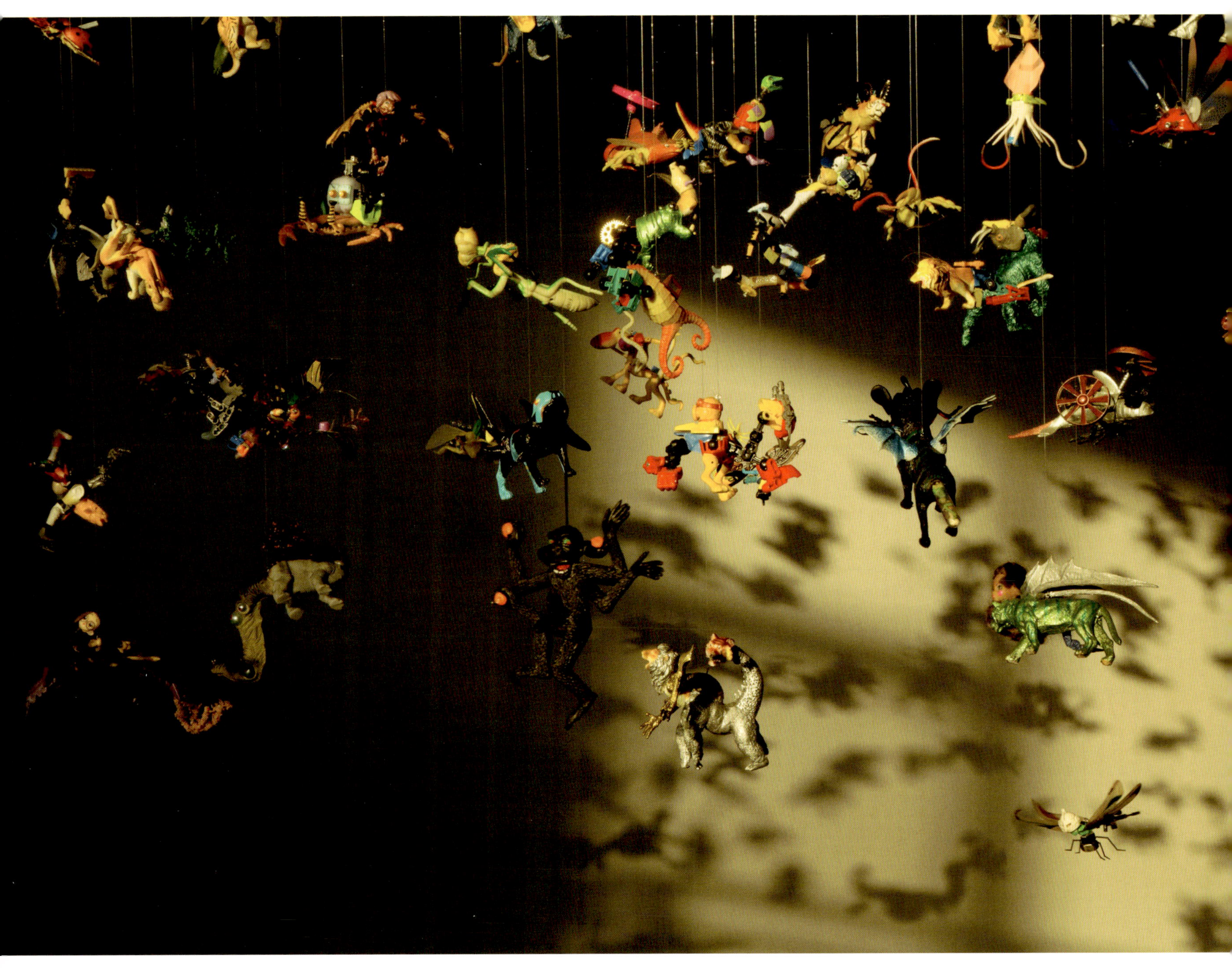

Sterben der Götter, Detail

Passing of the Gods, detail

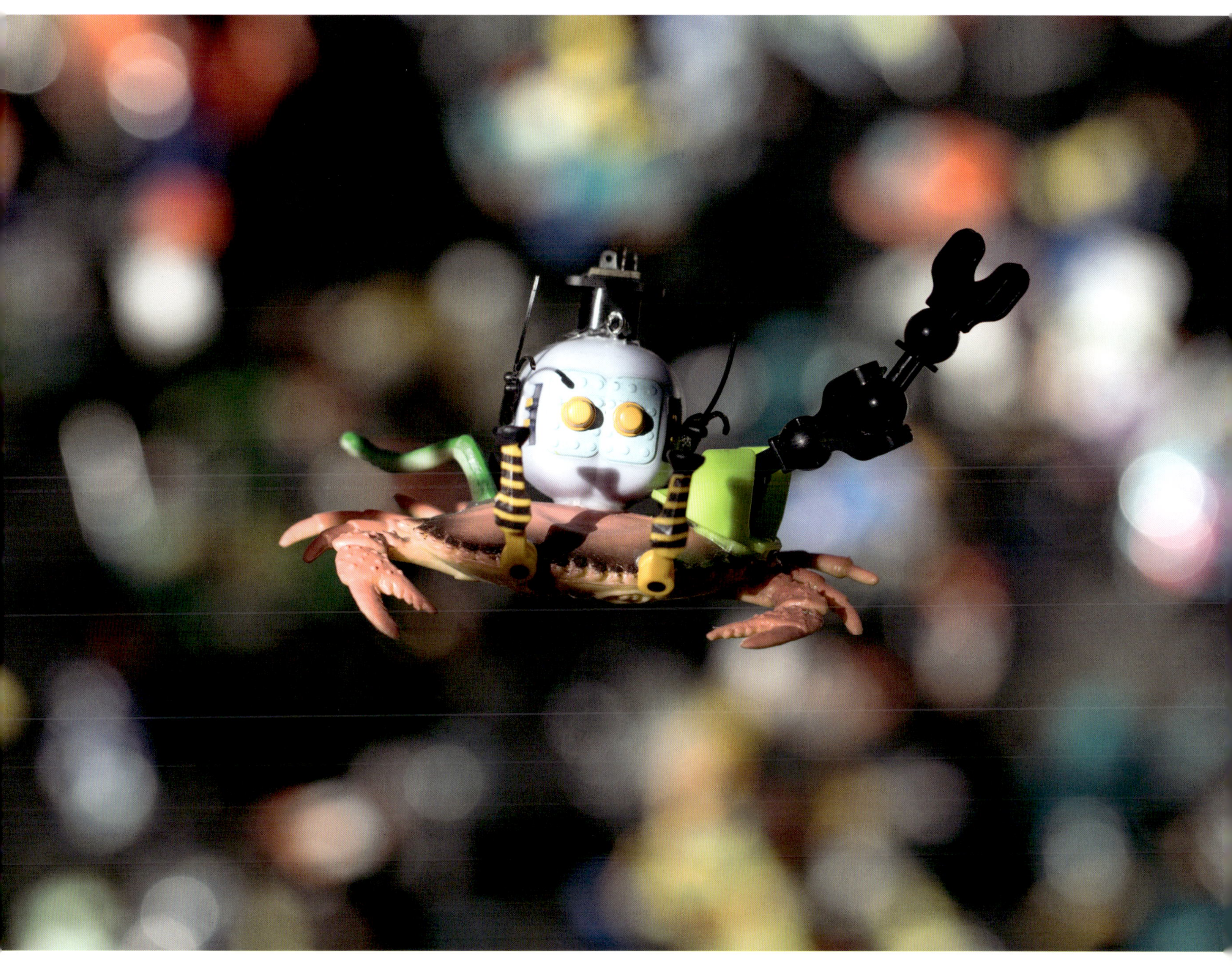

Sterben der Götter, Detail

Passing of the Gods, detail

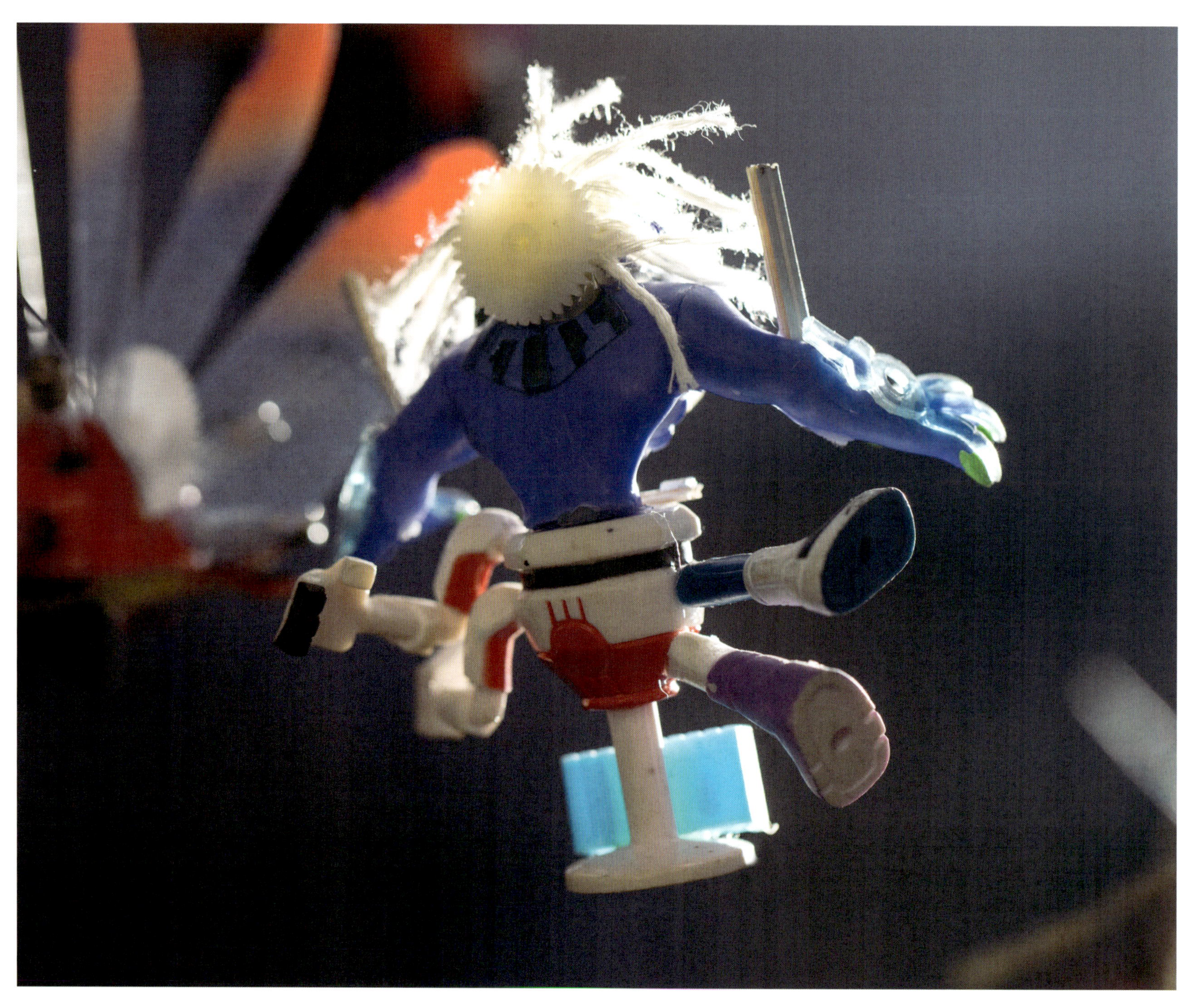

Sterben der Götter, Details

Passing of the Gods, details

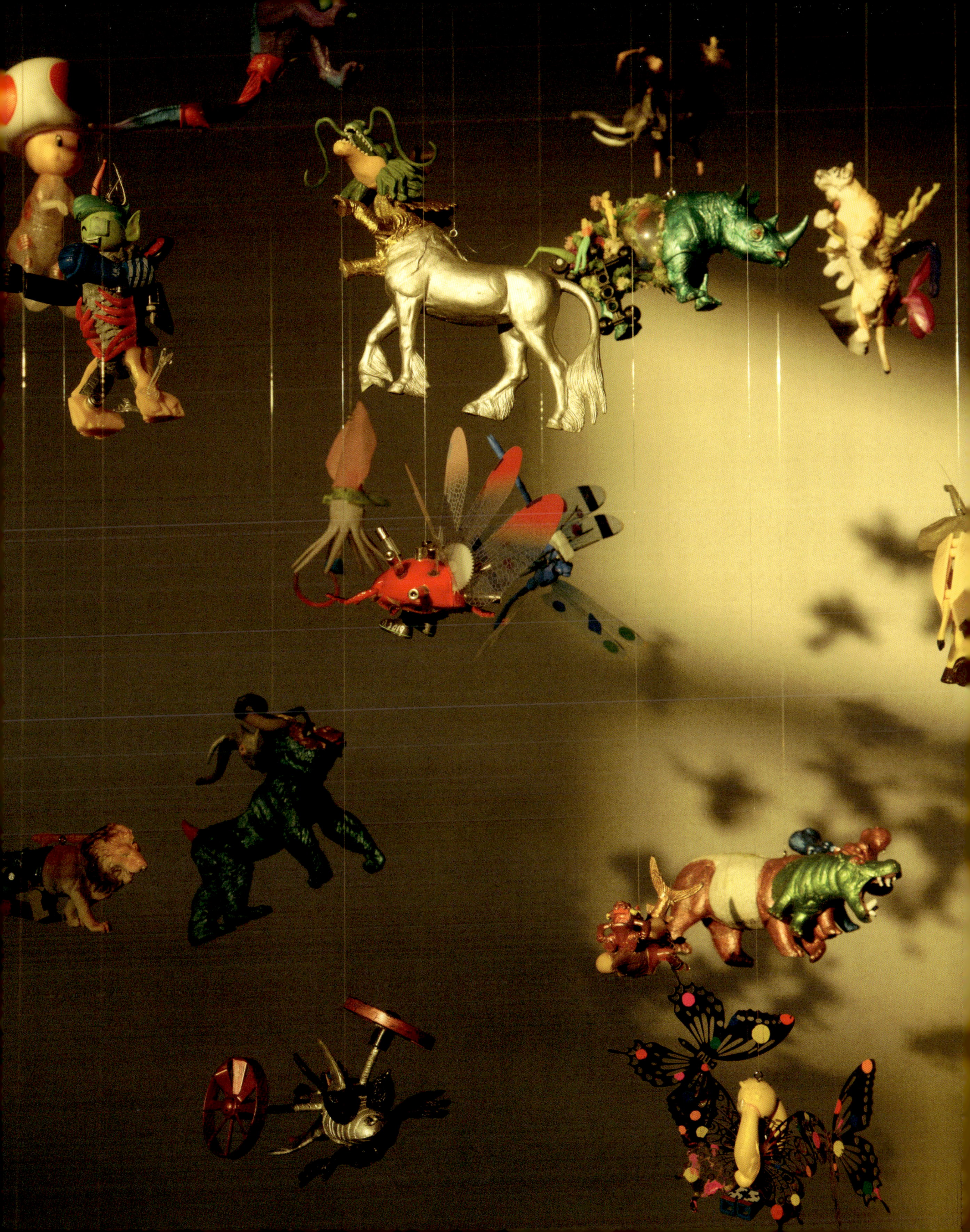

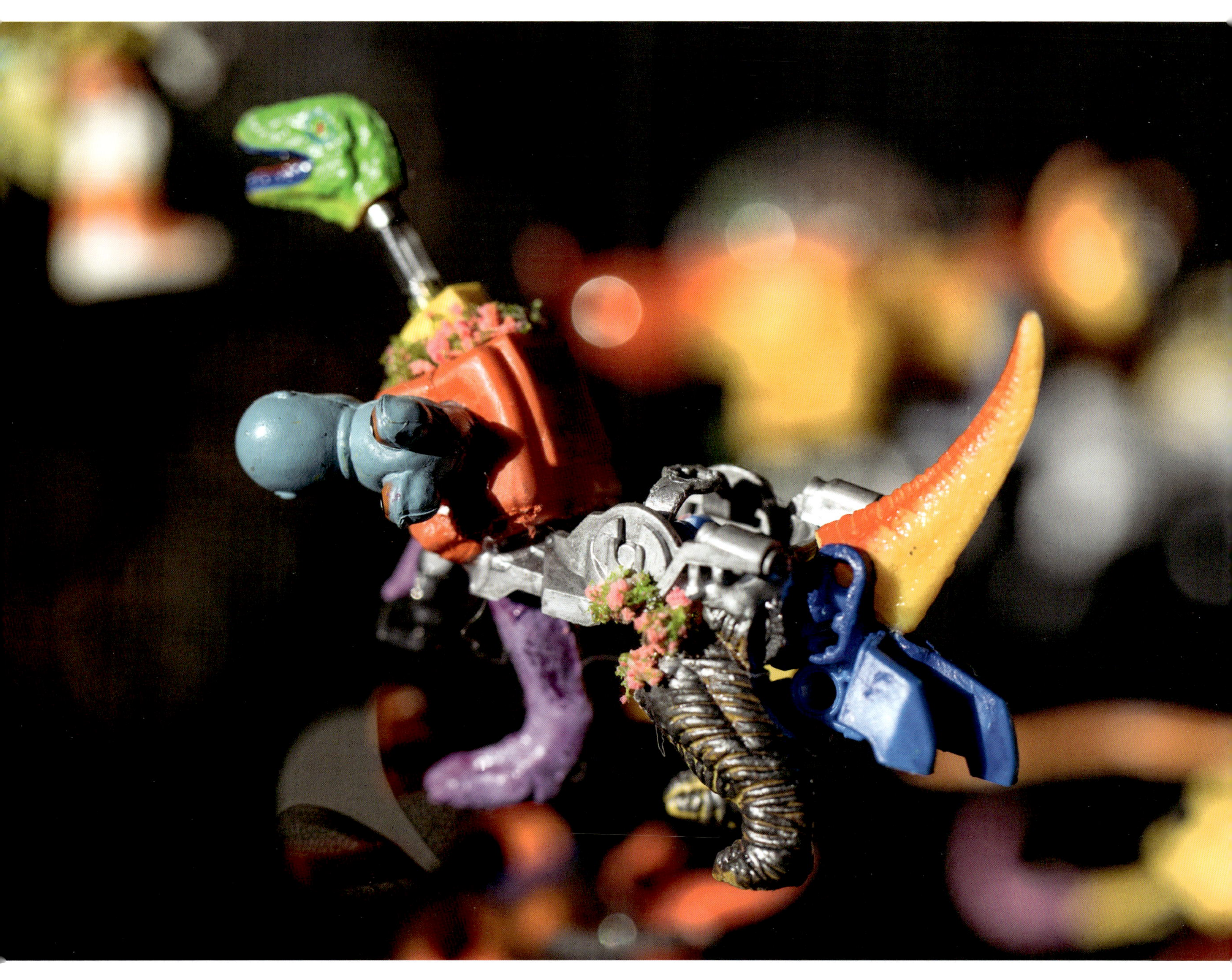

Sterben der Götter, Detail

Passing of the Gods, detail

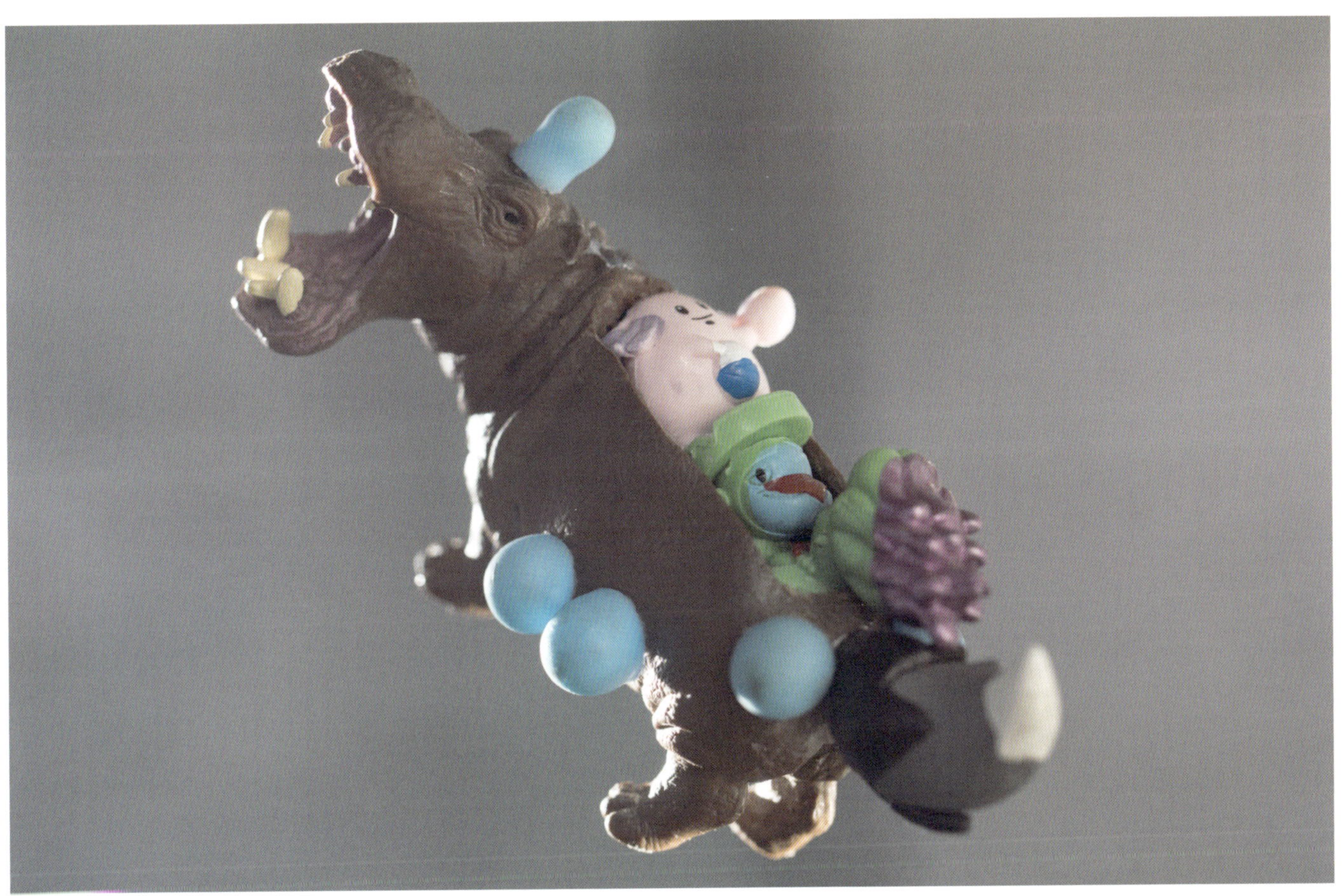

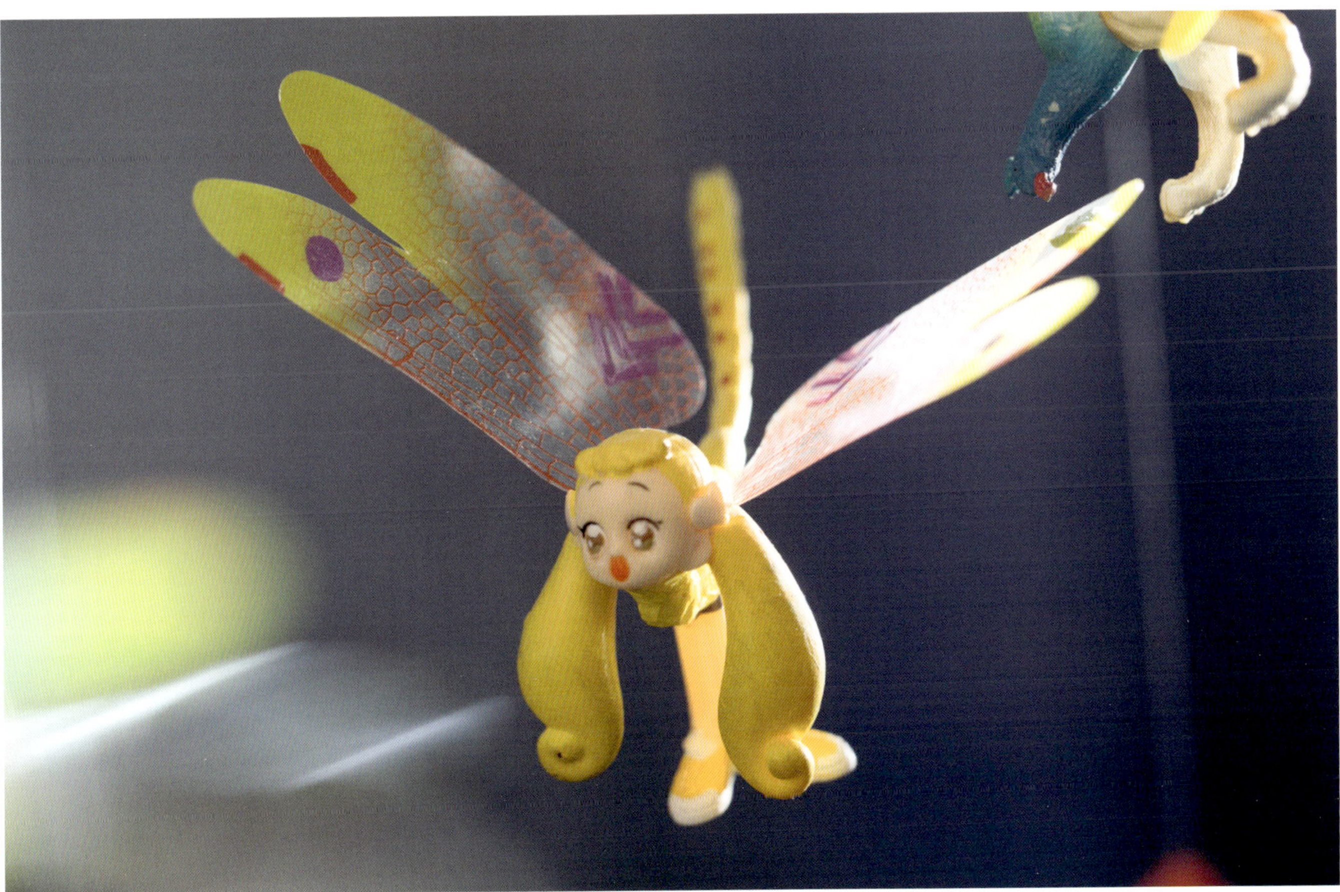

Sterben der Götter, Details

Passing of the Gods, details

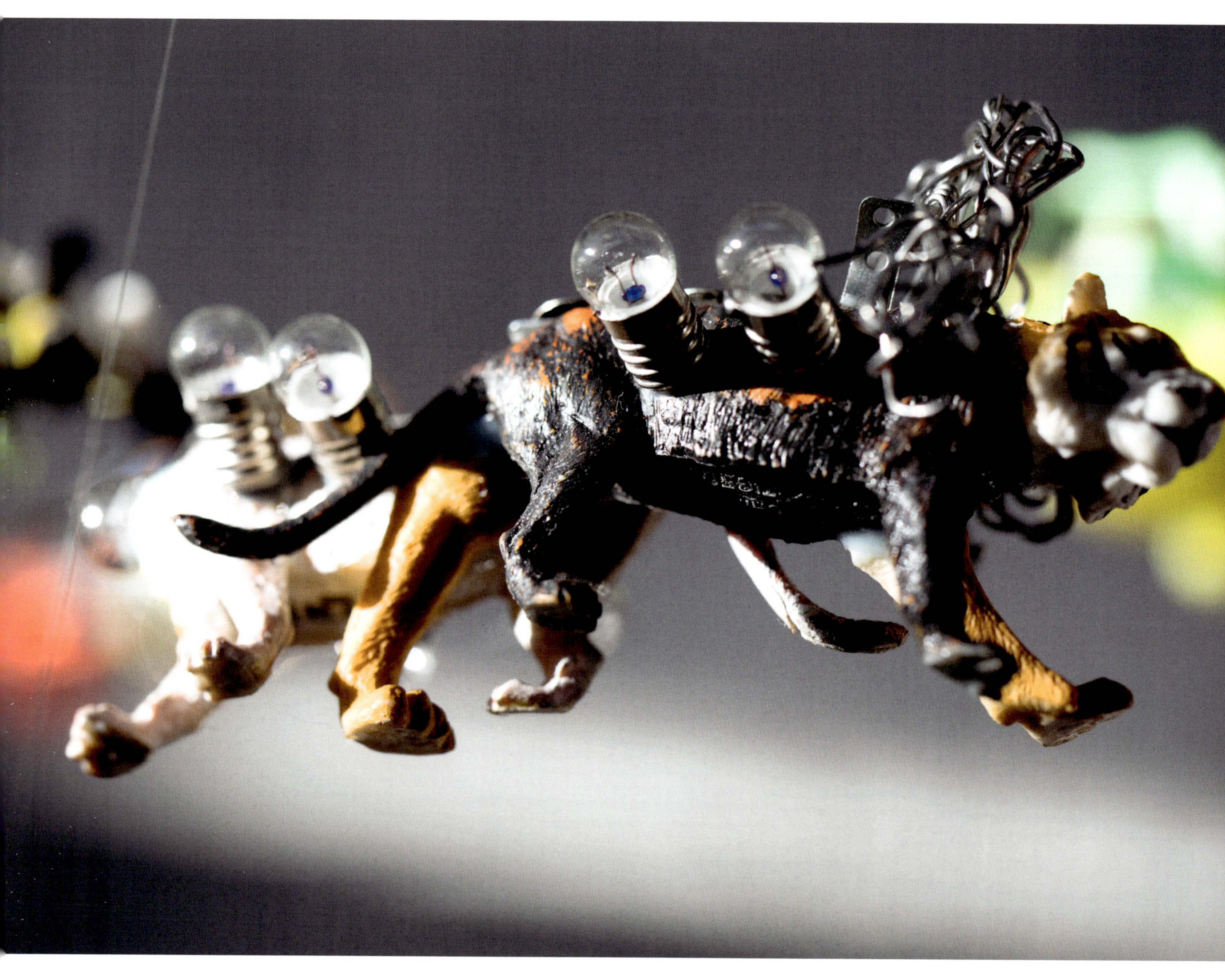

Sterben der Götter, Detail

Passing of the Gods, detail

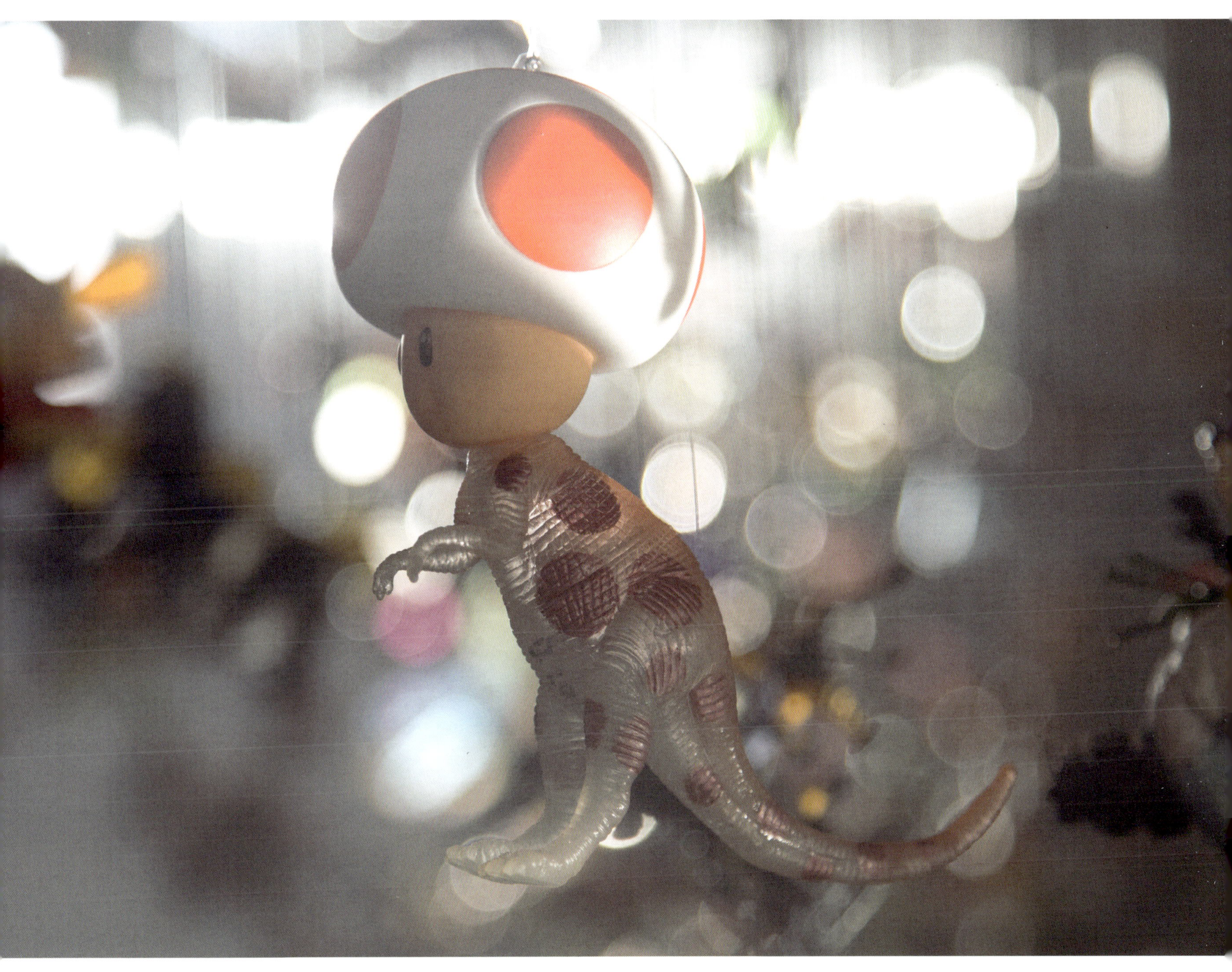

Sterben der Götter, Detail

Passing of the Gods, detail

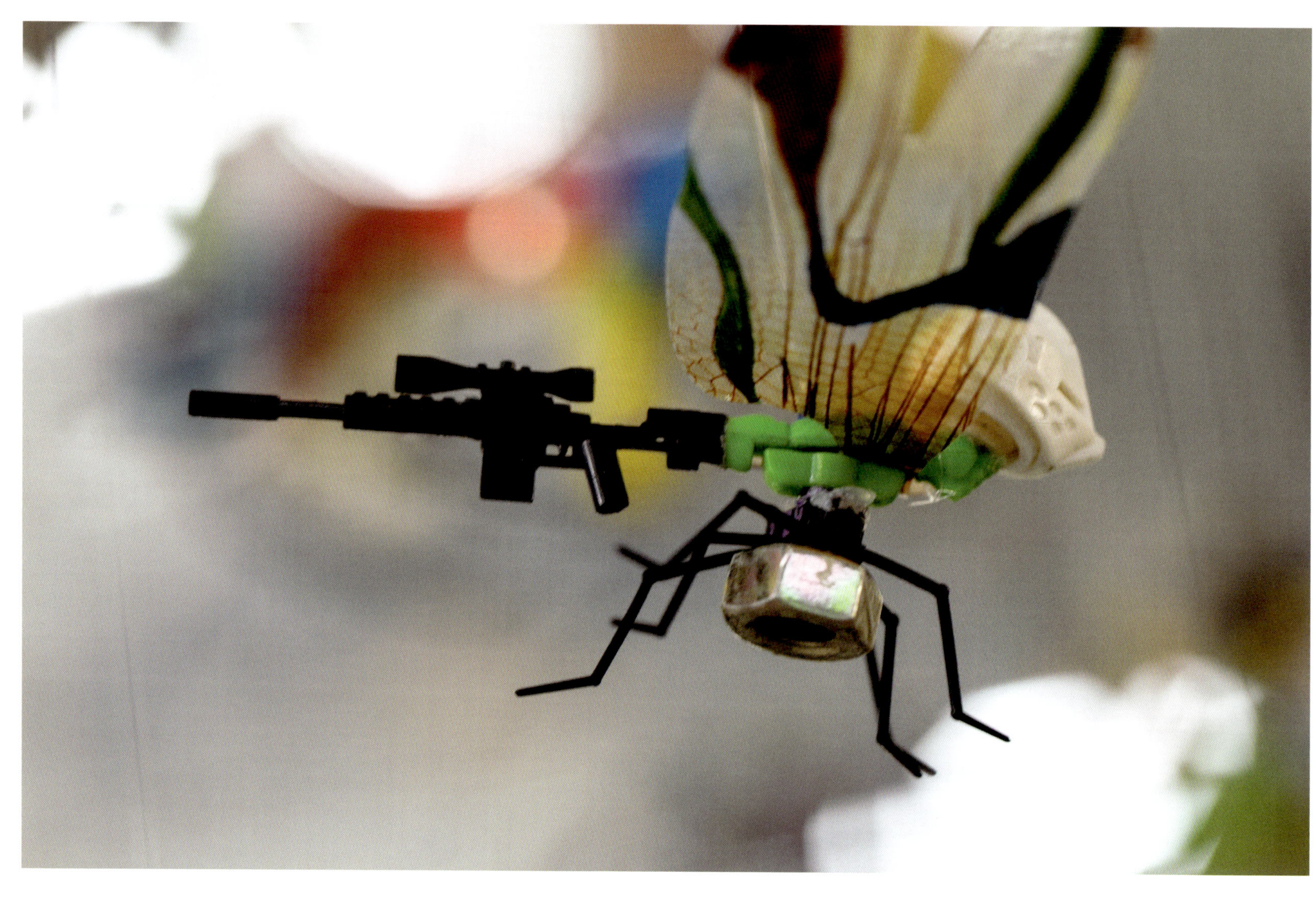

Sterben der Götter, Detail

Passing of the Gods, detail

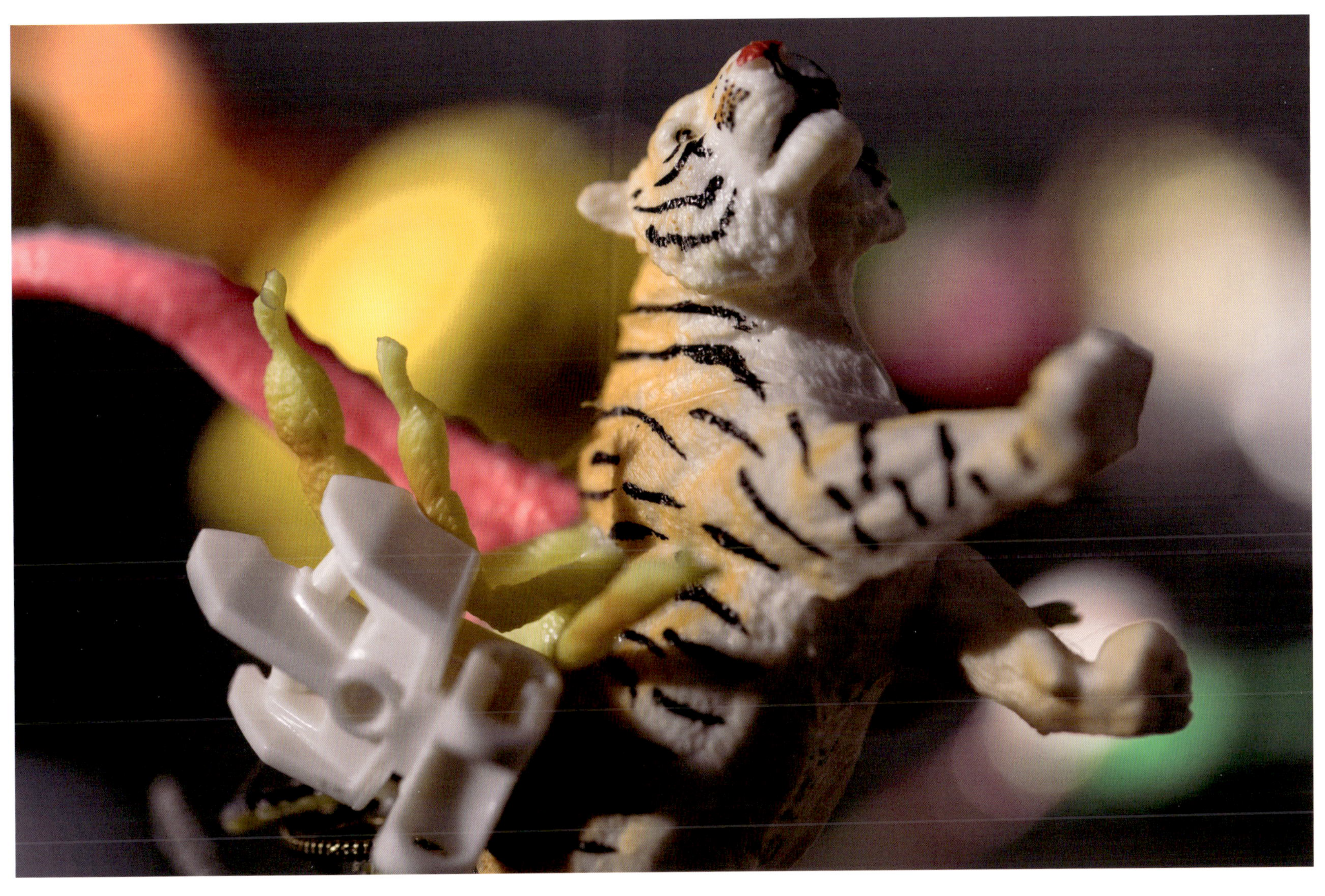

Sterben der Götter, Detail

Passing of the Gods, detail

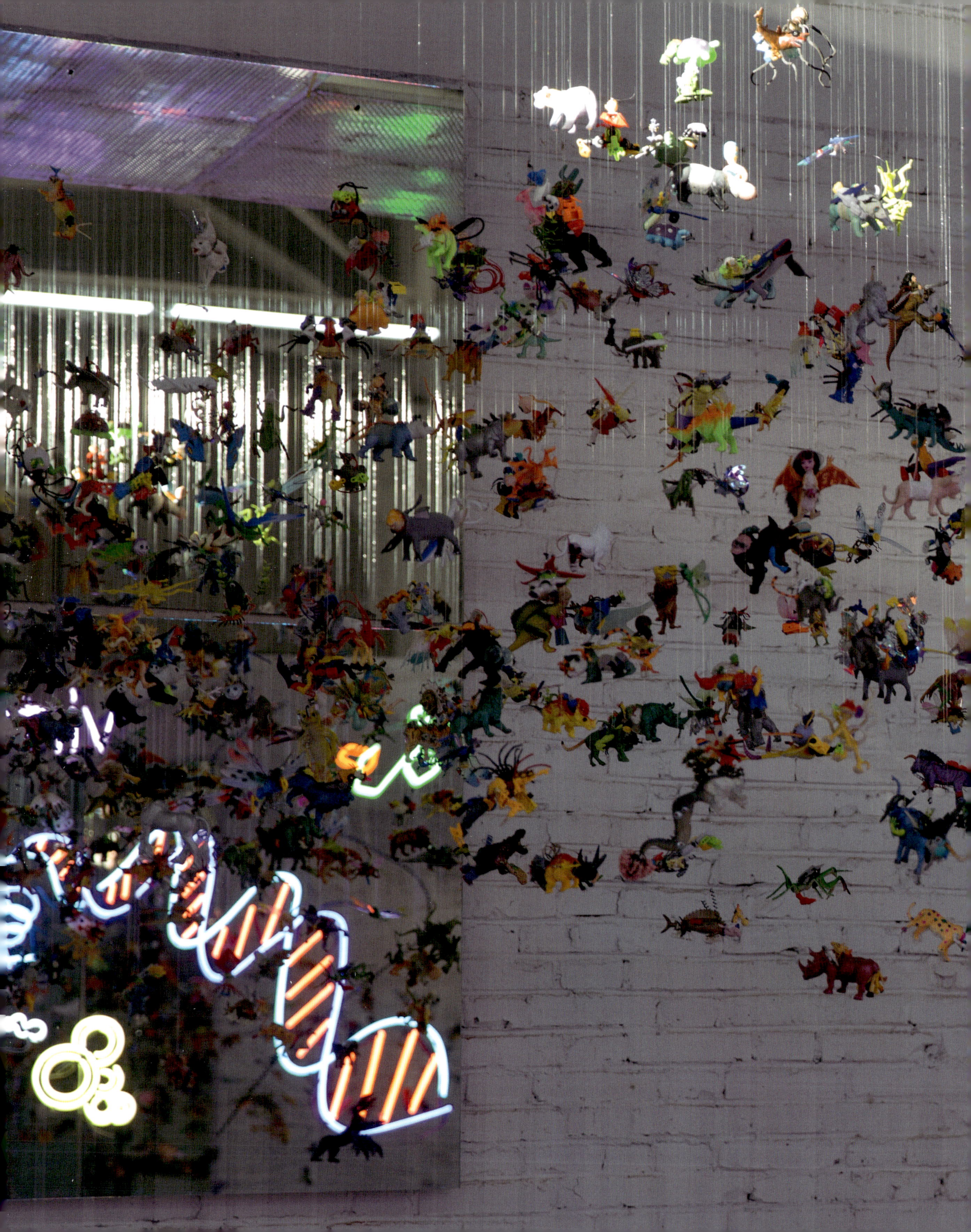

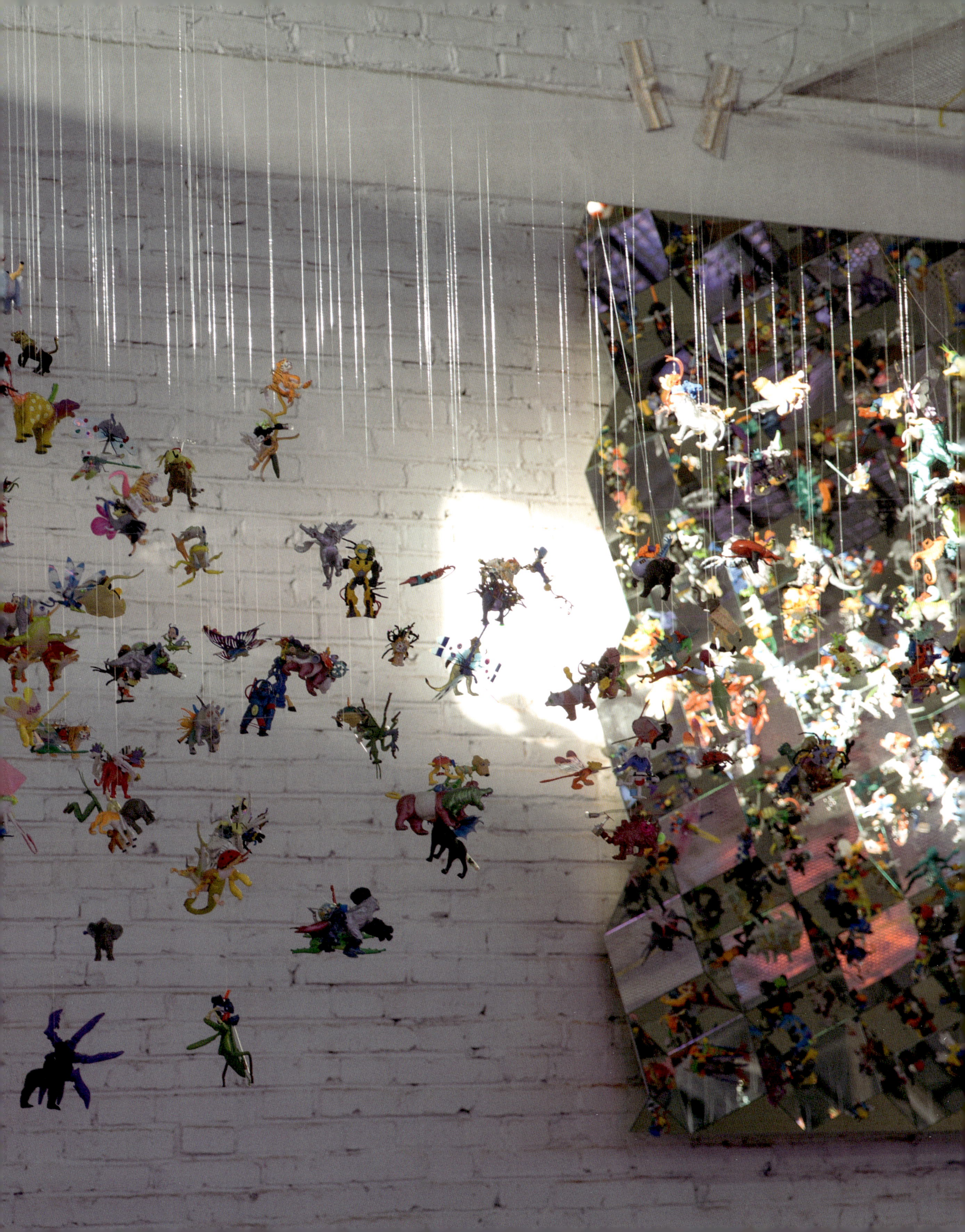

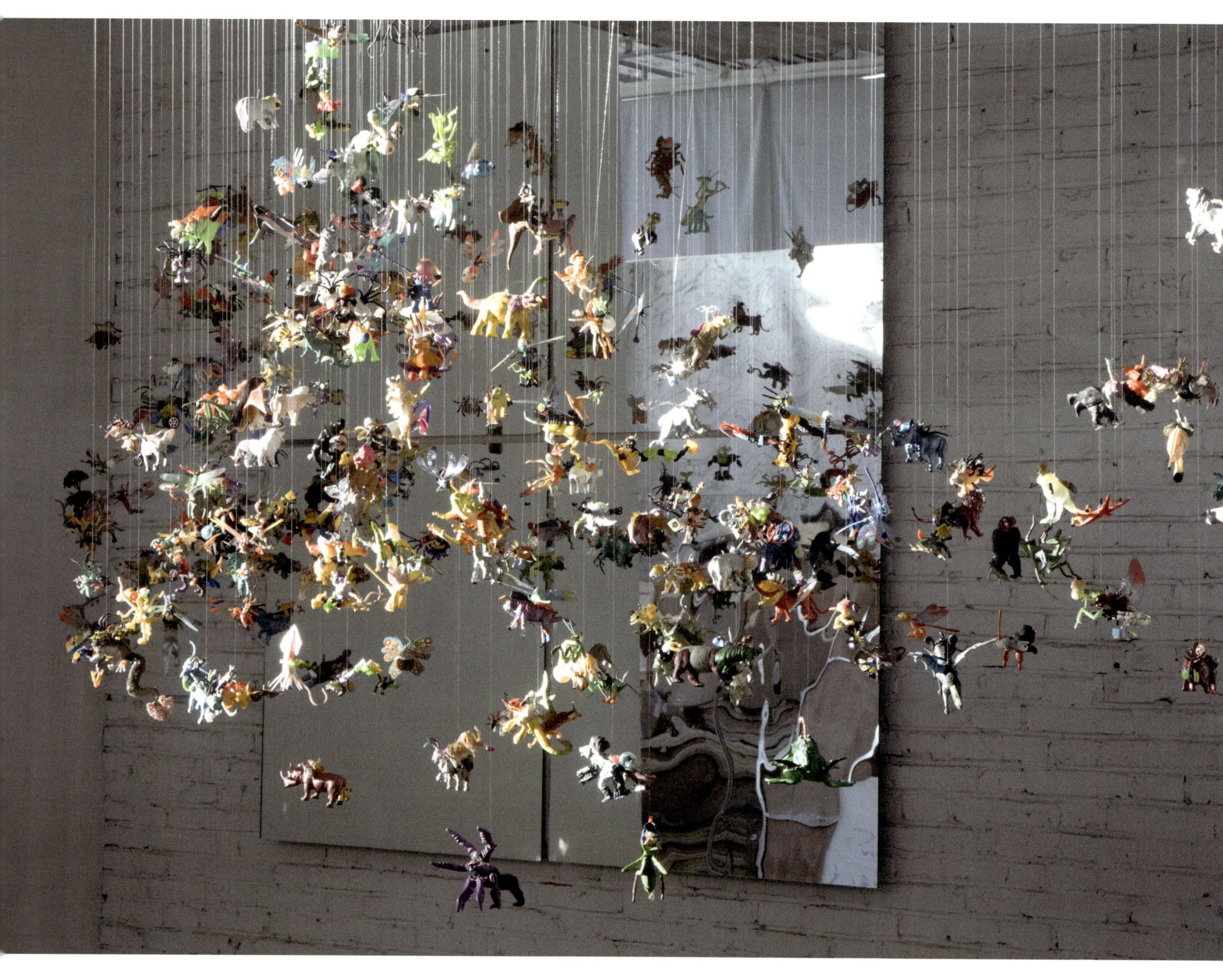

Sterben der Götter, Detail

Passing of the Gods, detail

Vorherige Seiten:
Sterben der Götter, Gesamtansicht

Previous pages:
Passing of the Gods, overall view

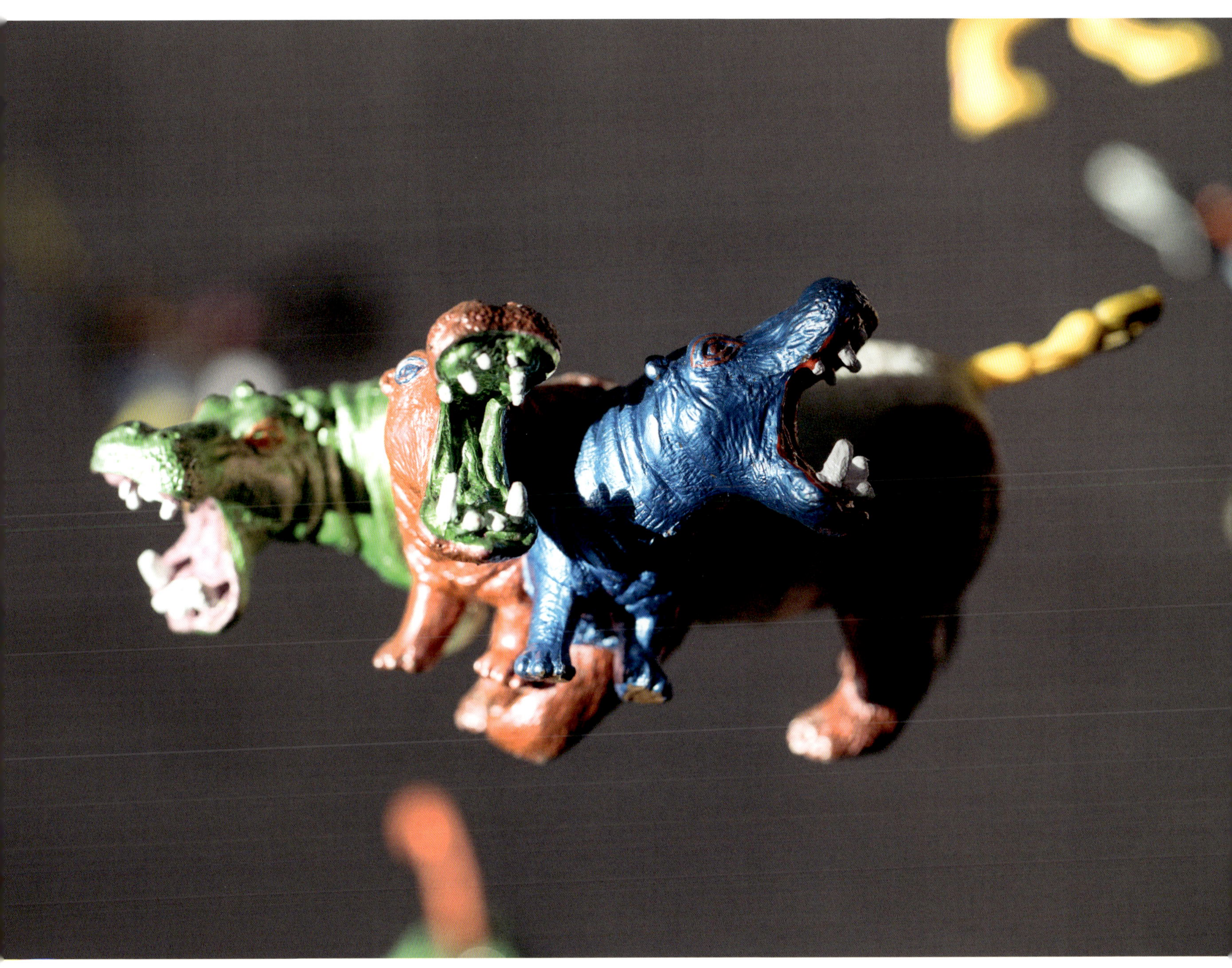

Sterben der Götter, Detail

Passing of the Gods, detail

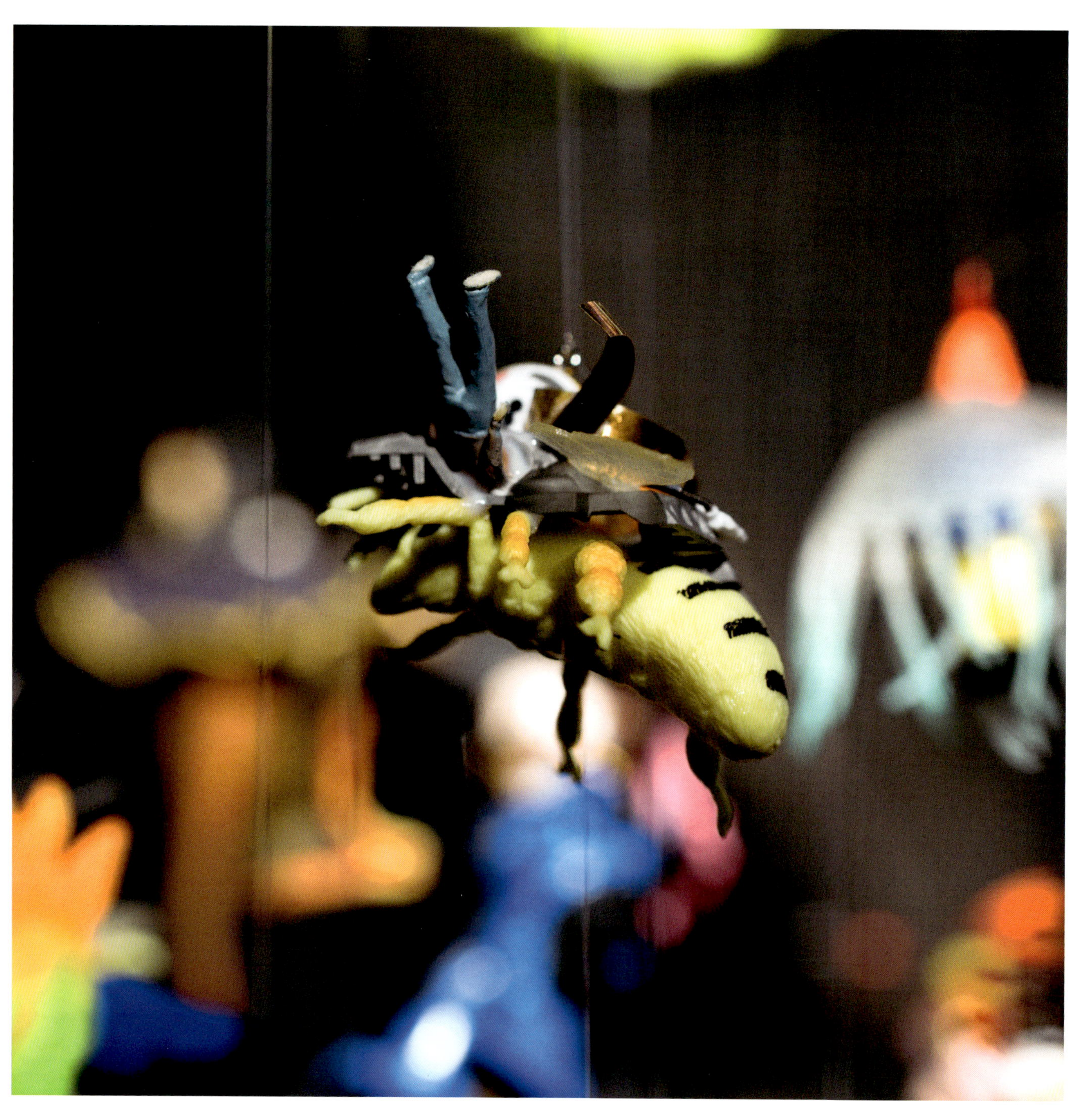

Sterben der Götter, Details

Passing of the Gods, details

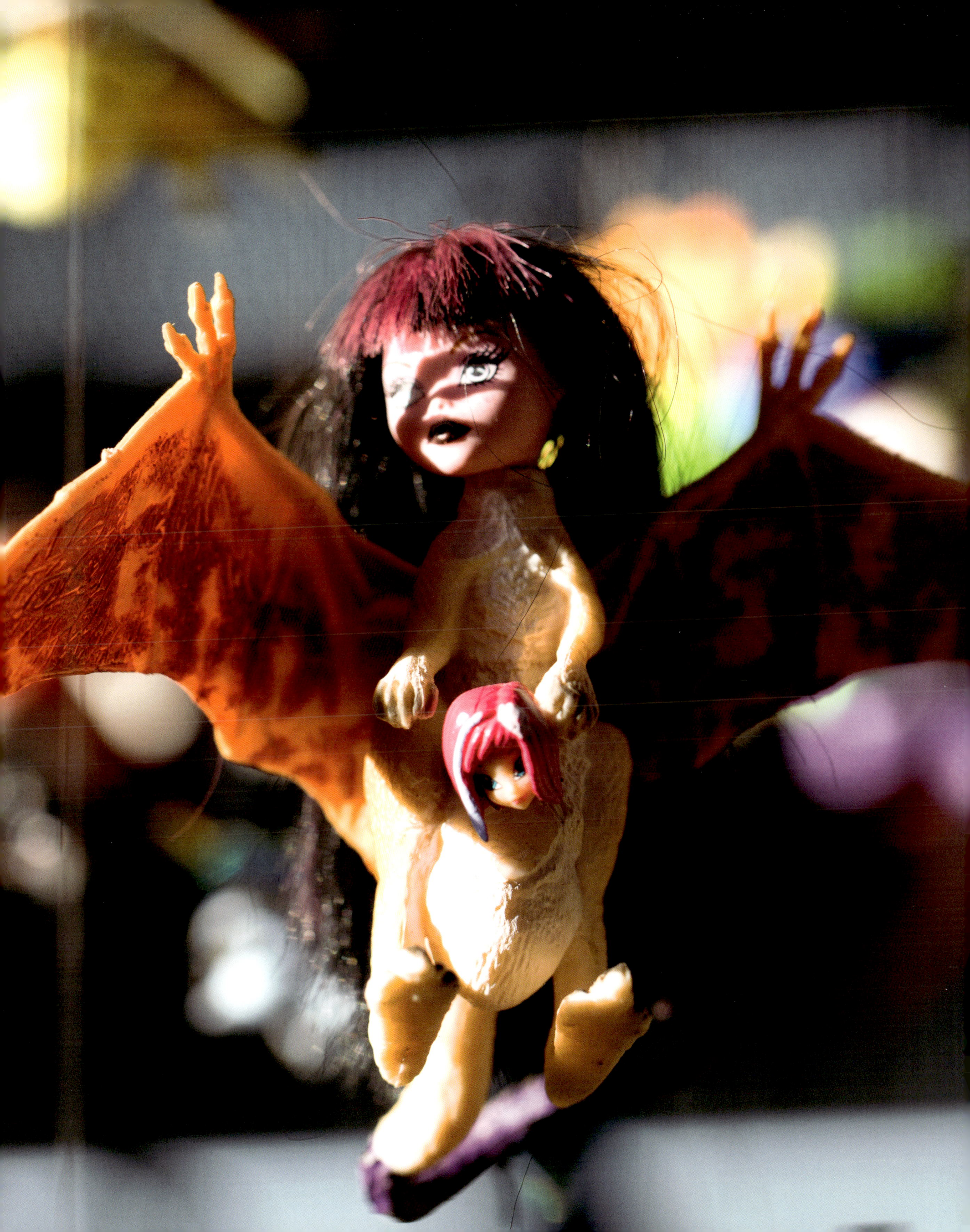

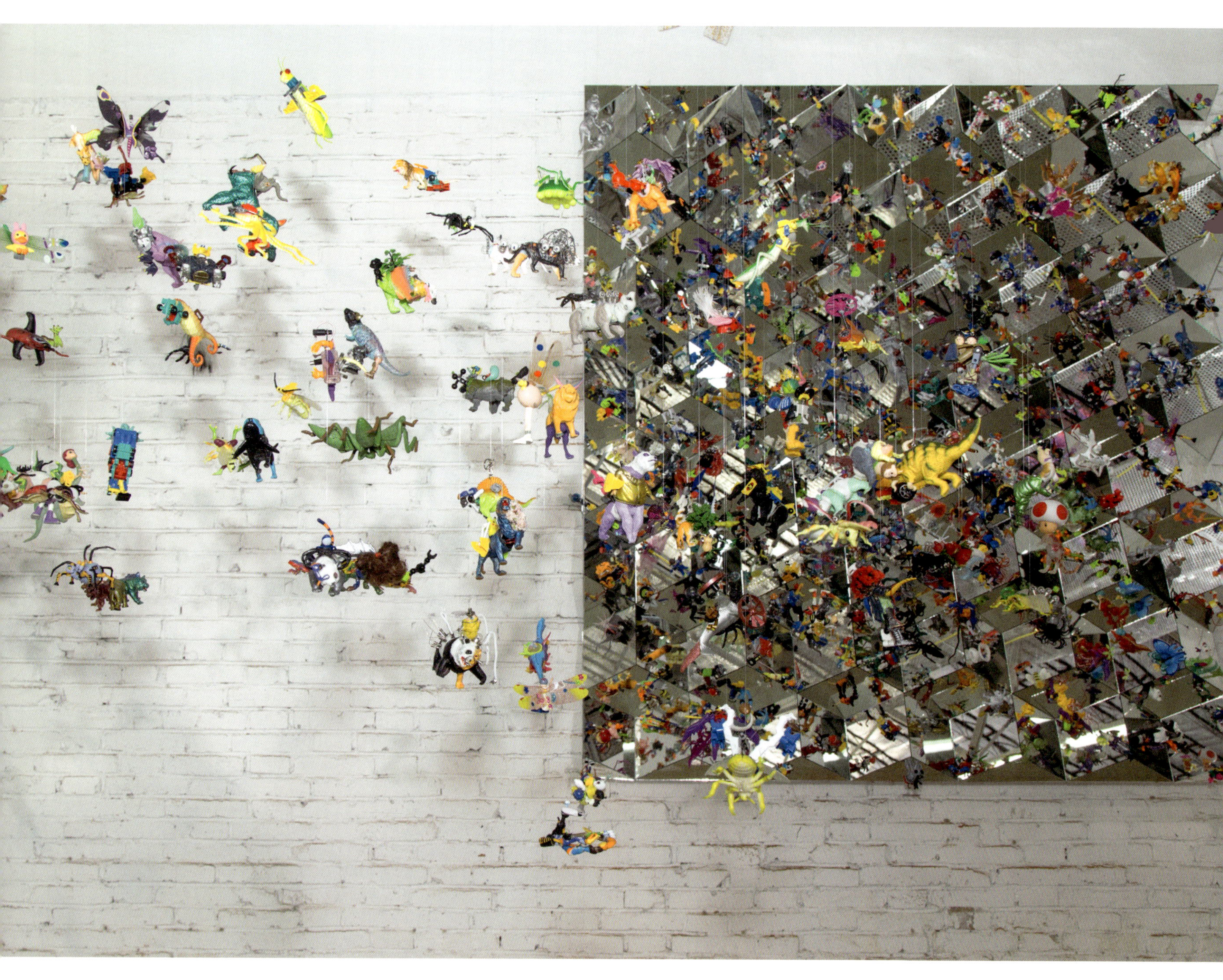

Sterben der Götter, Detail

Passing of the Gods, detail

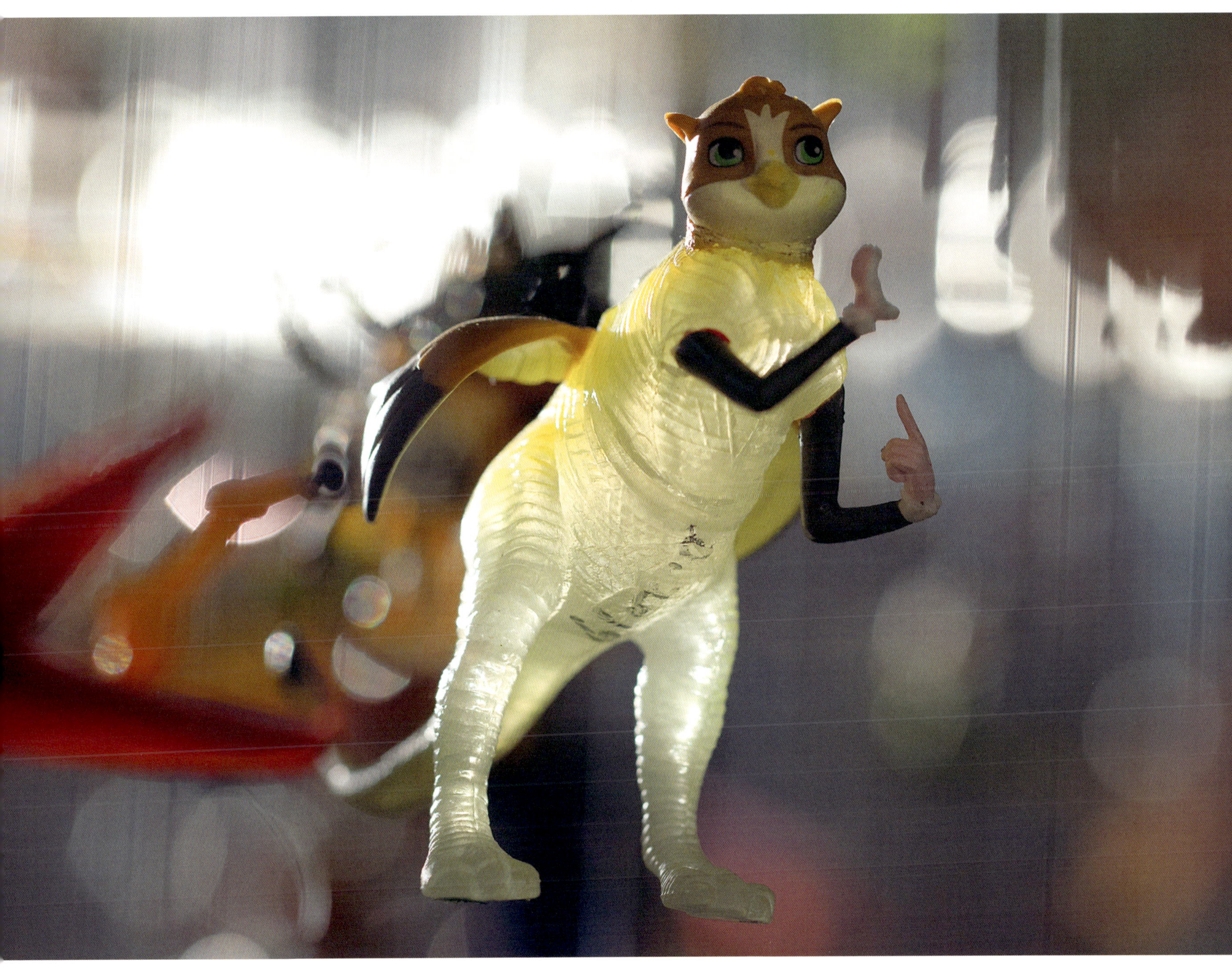

Sterben der Götter, Detail

Passing of the Gods, detail

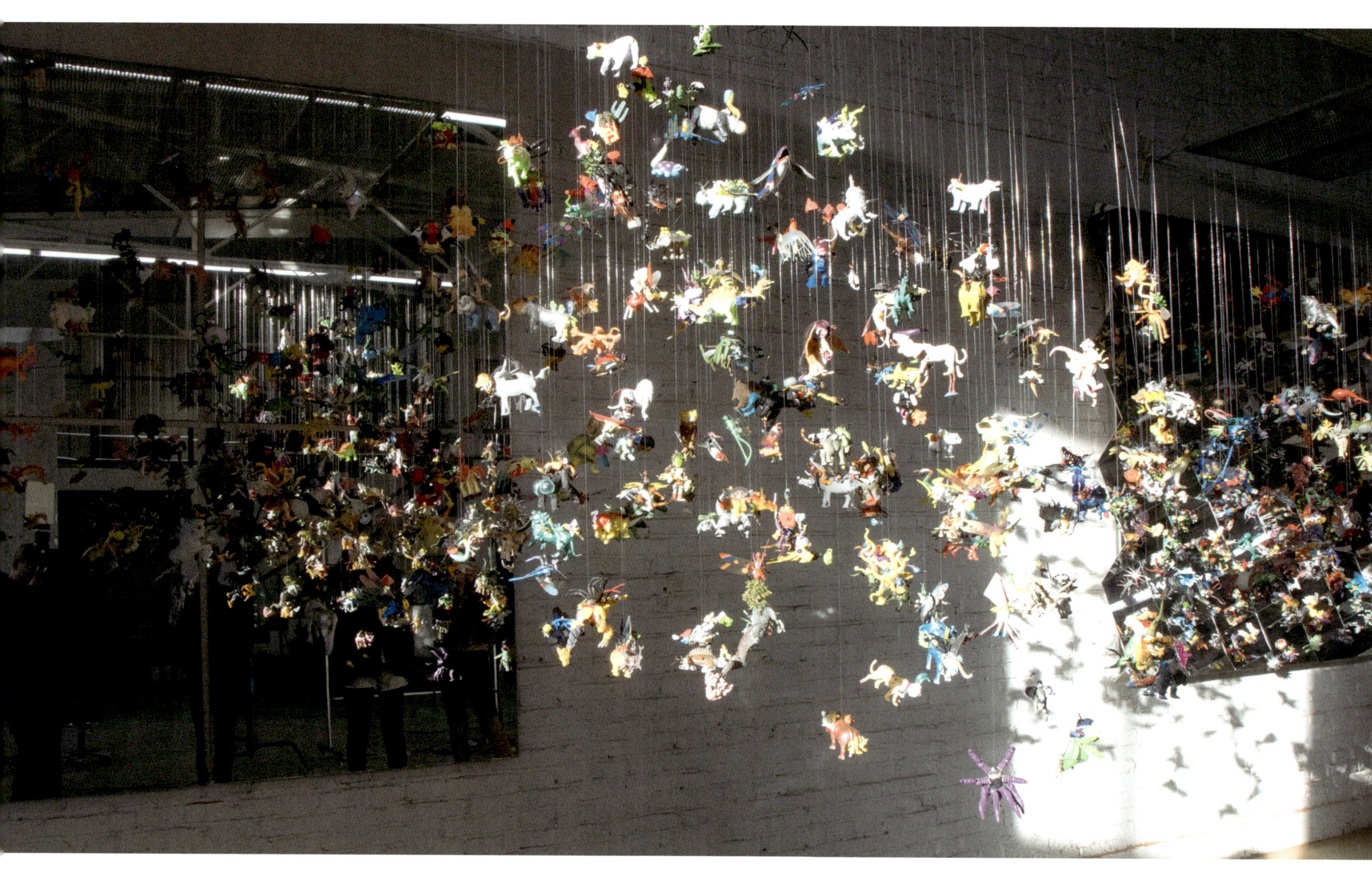

Sterben der Götter, Detail

Passing of the Gods, detail

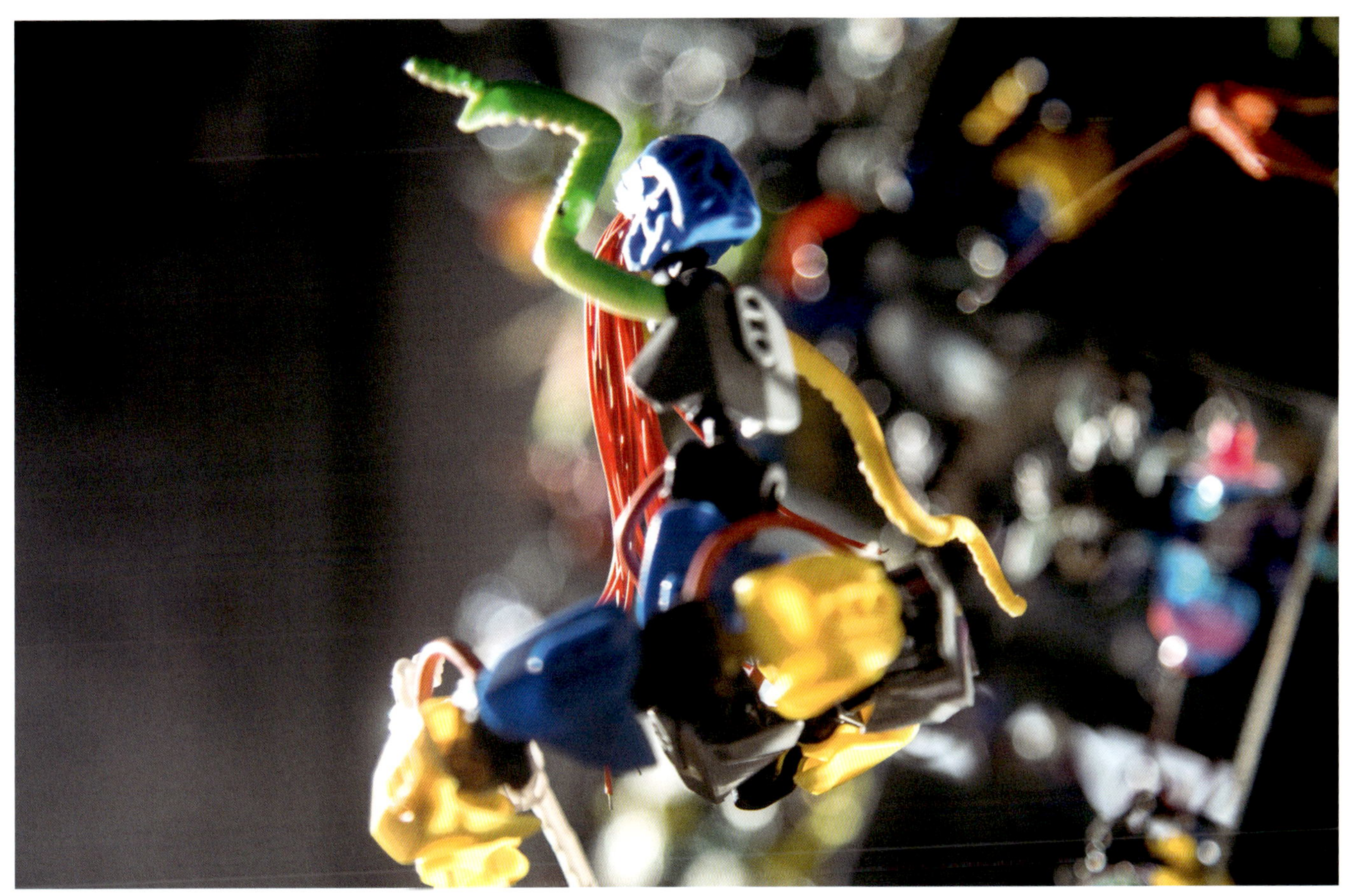

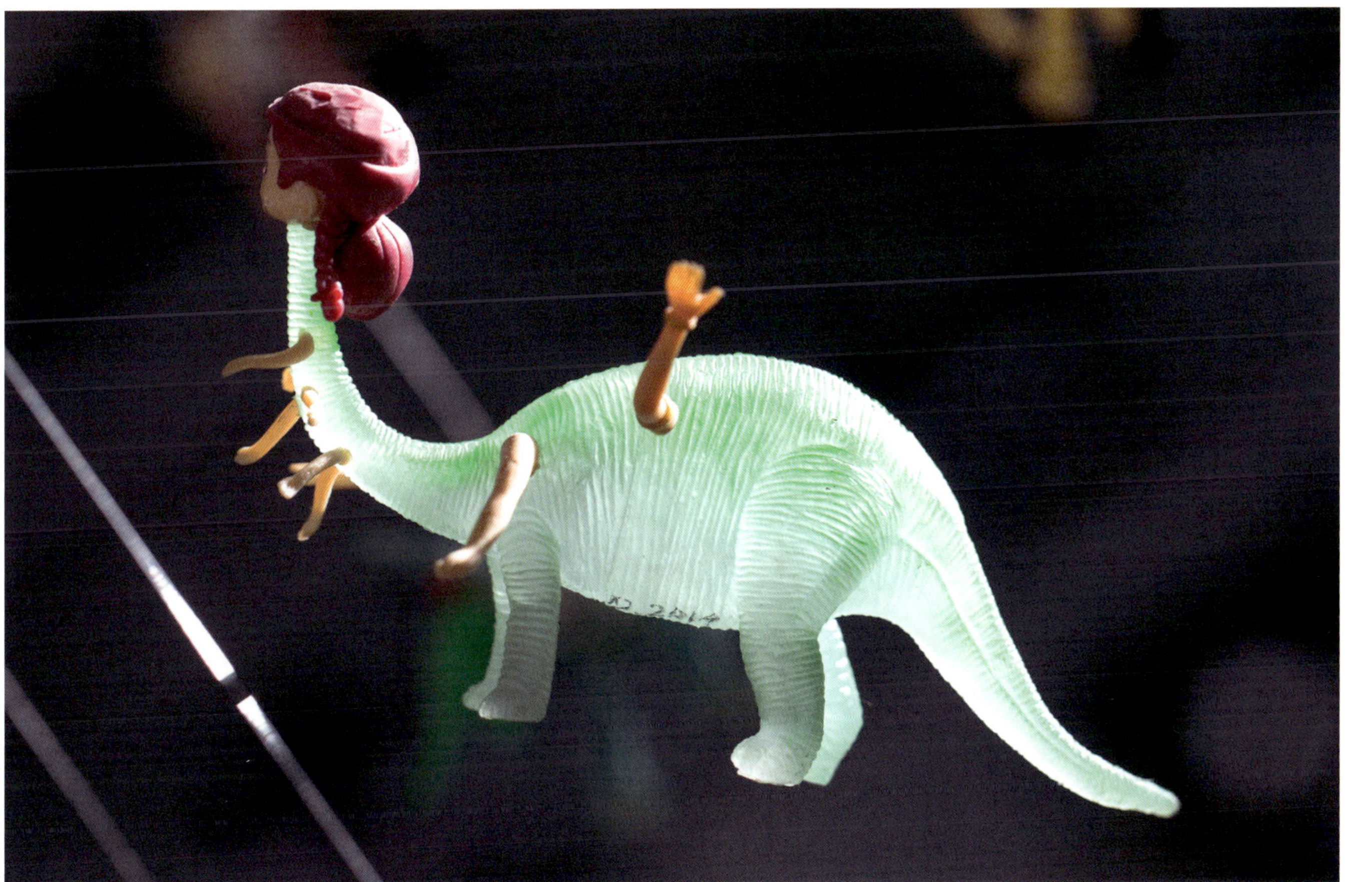

Sterben der Götter, Details

Passing of the Gods, details

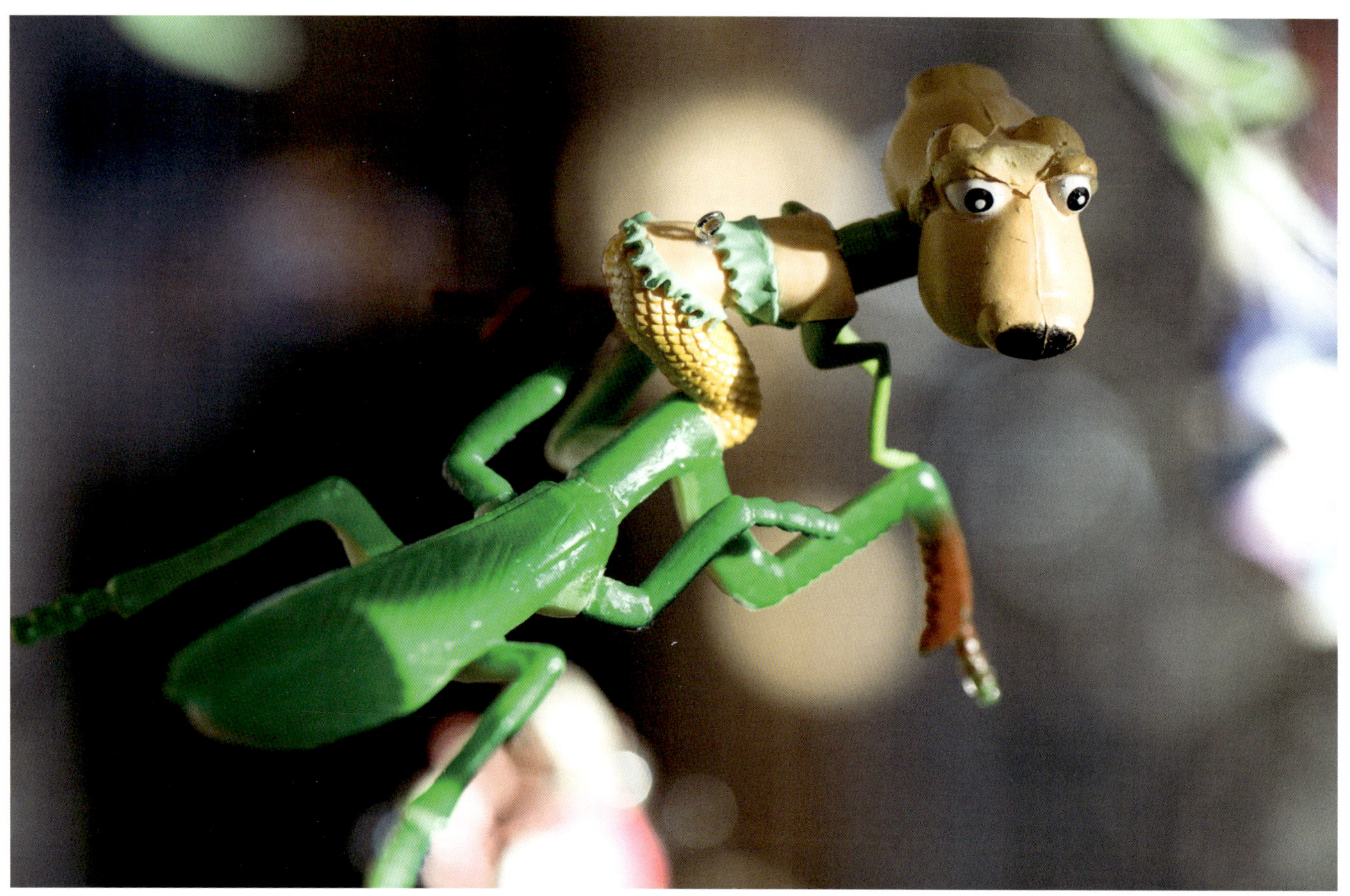

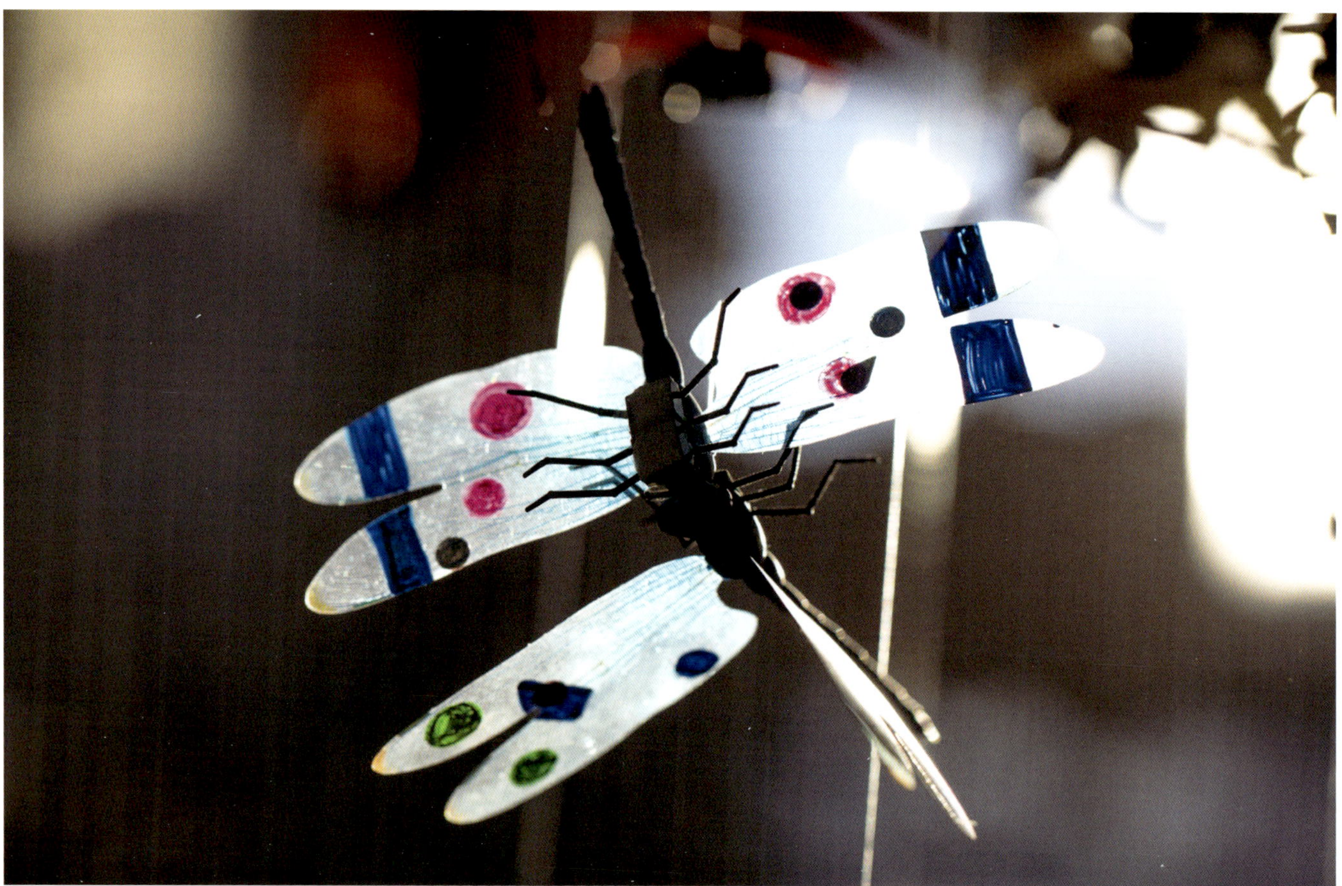

Sterben der Götter, Details

Passing of the Gods, details

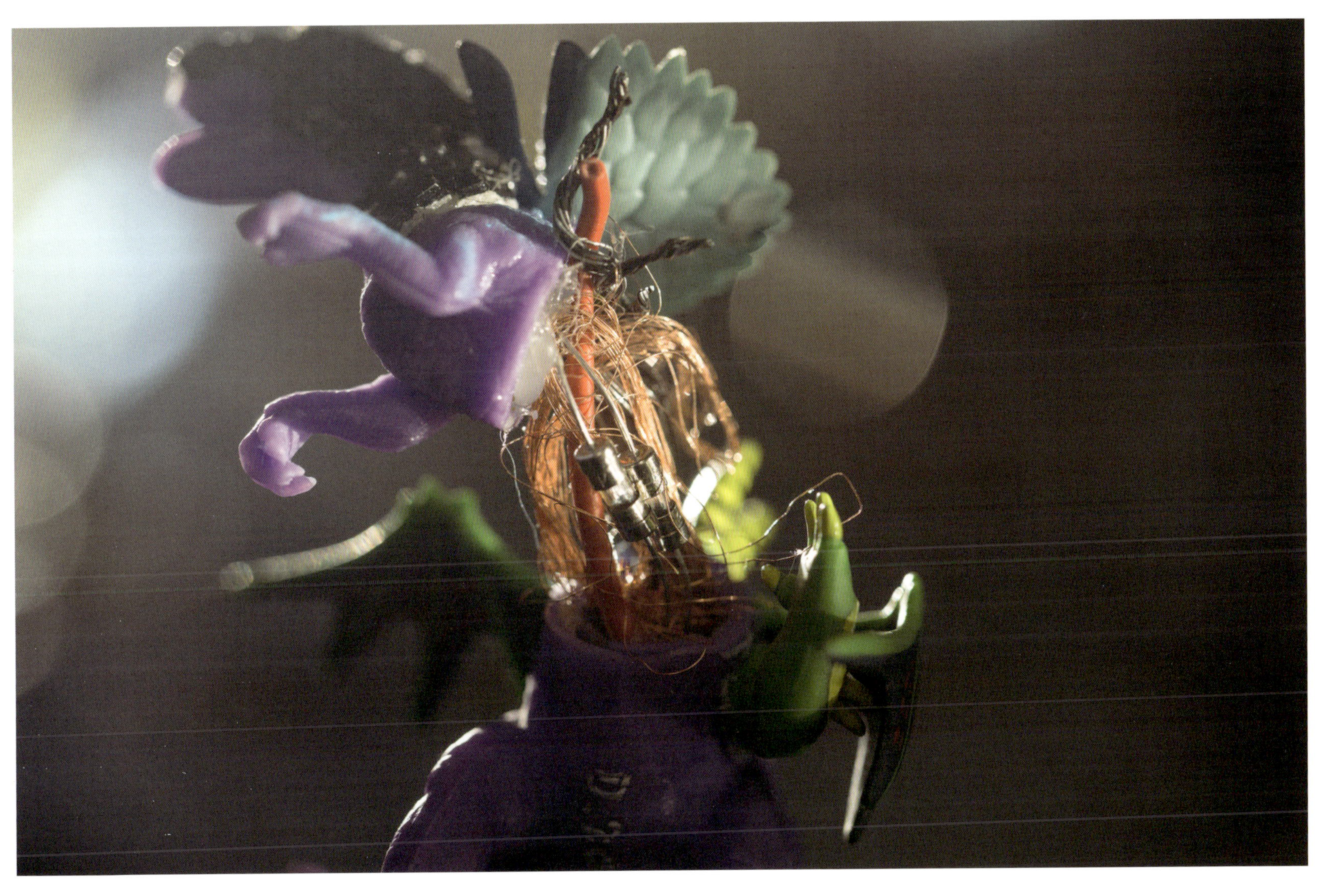

Sterben der Götter, **Detail**

Passing of the Gods, **detail**

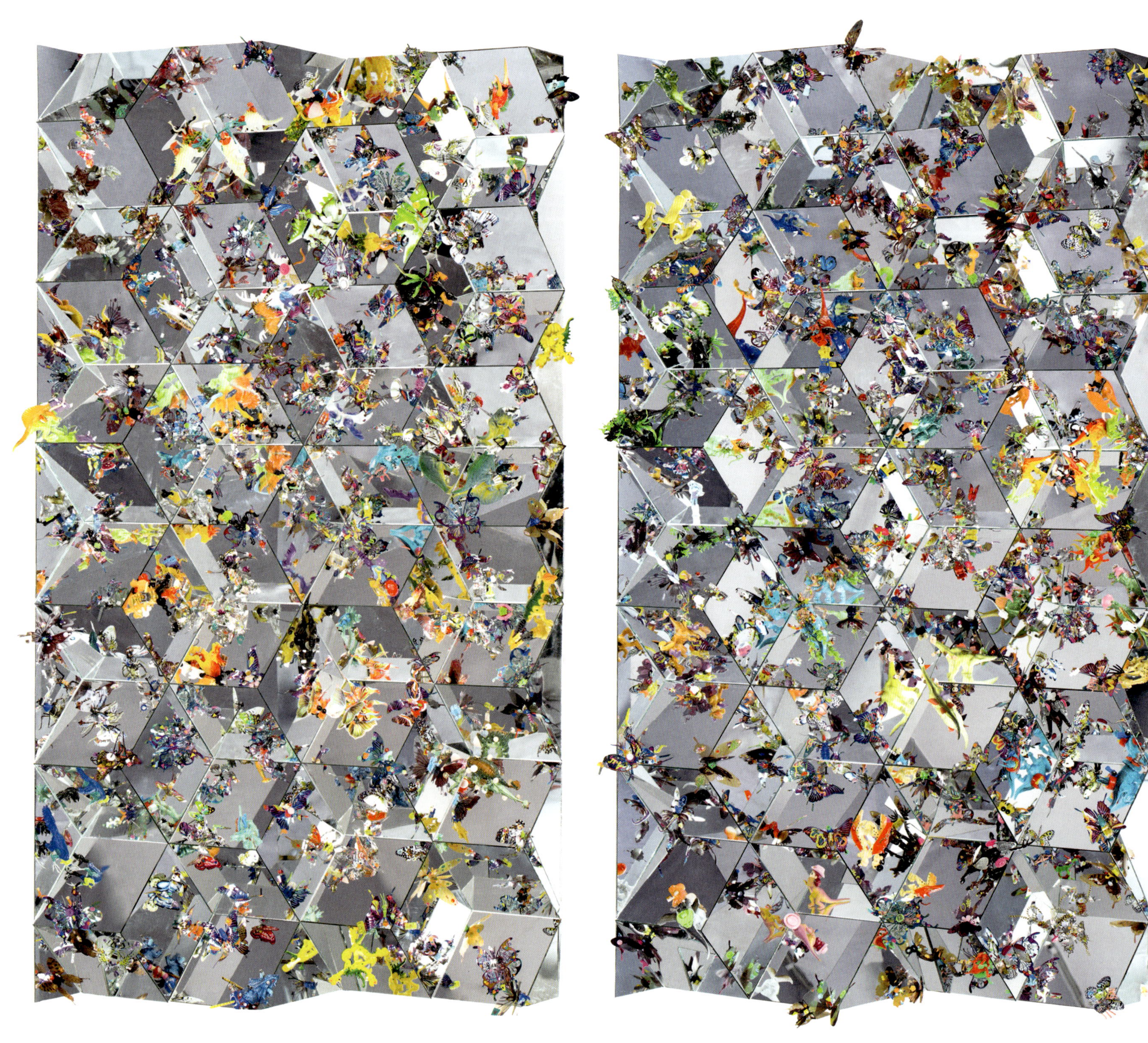

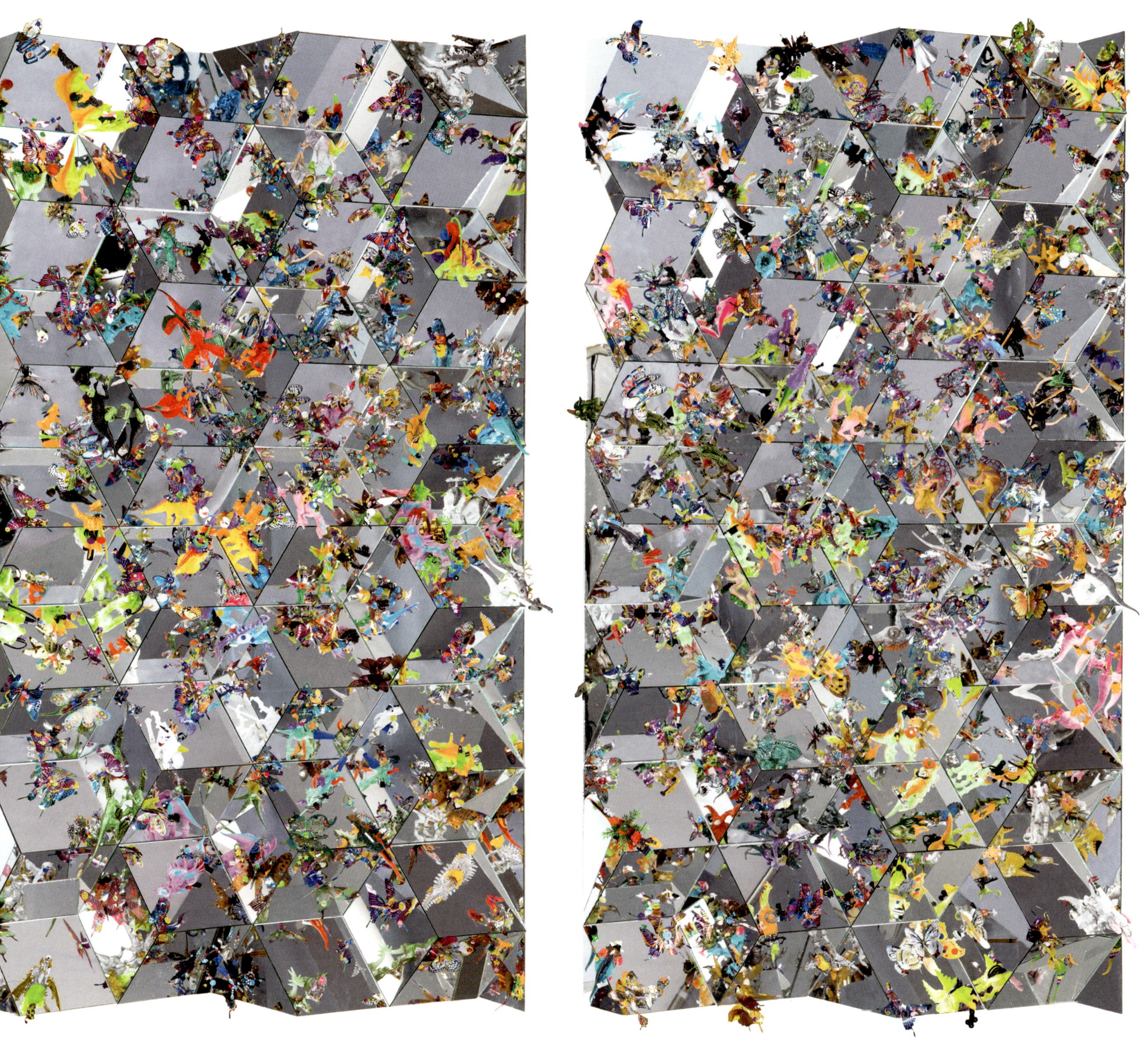

Schmetterlinge erobern den Garten der Dinosaurier, 2019
Aluminiumblech, Spiegelglas, verändertes Spielzeug,
Acrylfarbe, Emailfarbe
100 × 180 × 30 cm

Butterflies Conquer the Dinosaurs' Garden, 2019
Aluminium sheet, glass mirror, modified toys,
acrylic paint, enamel paint
100 × 180 × 30 cm

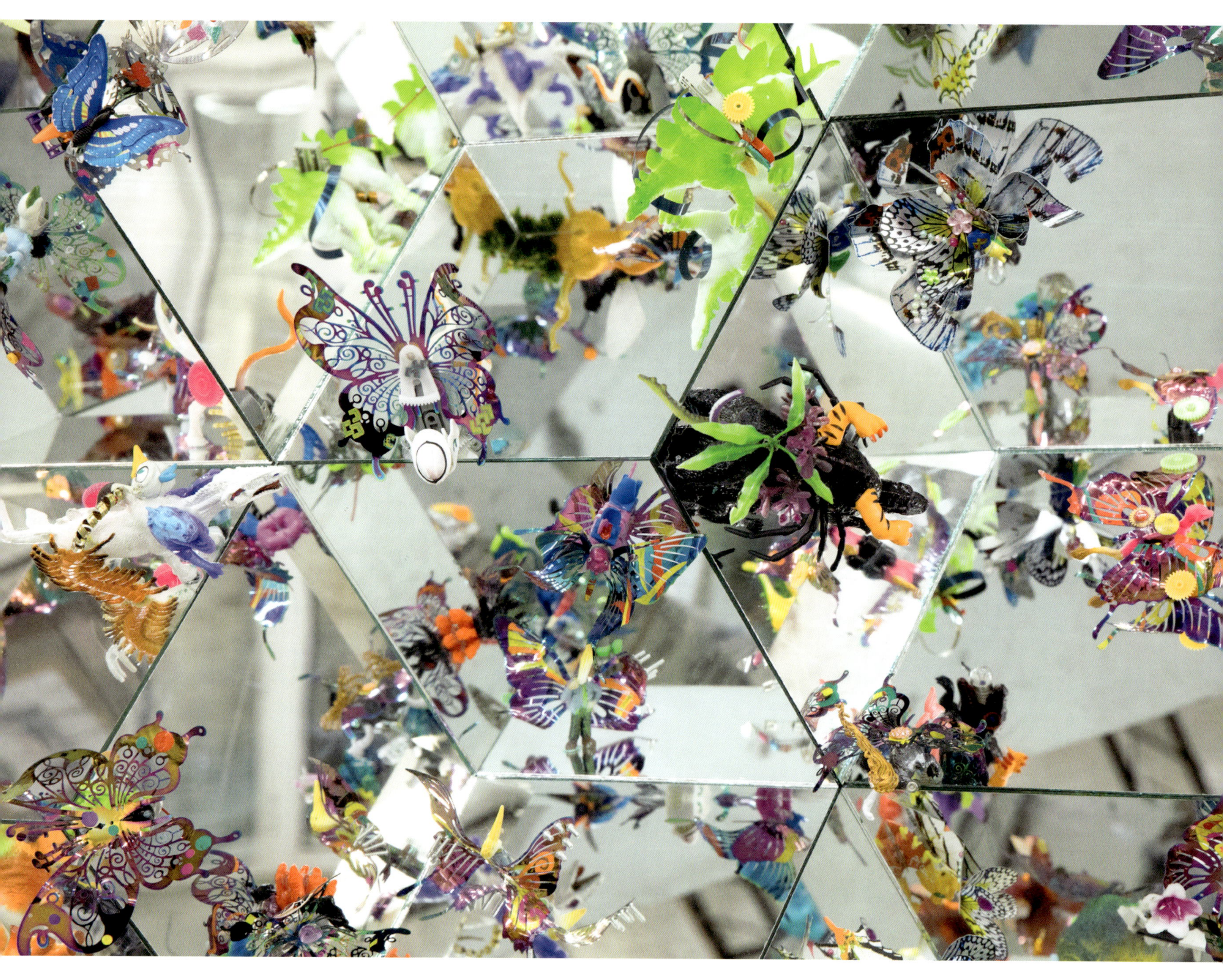

Schmetterlinge erobern den Garten der Dinosaurier, Detail

Butterflies Conquer the Dinosaurs' Garden, detail

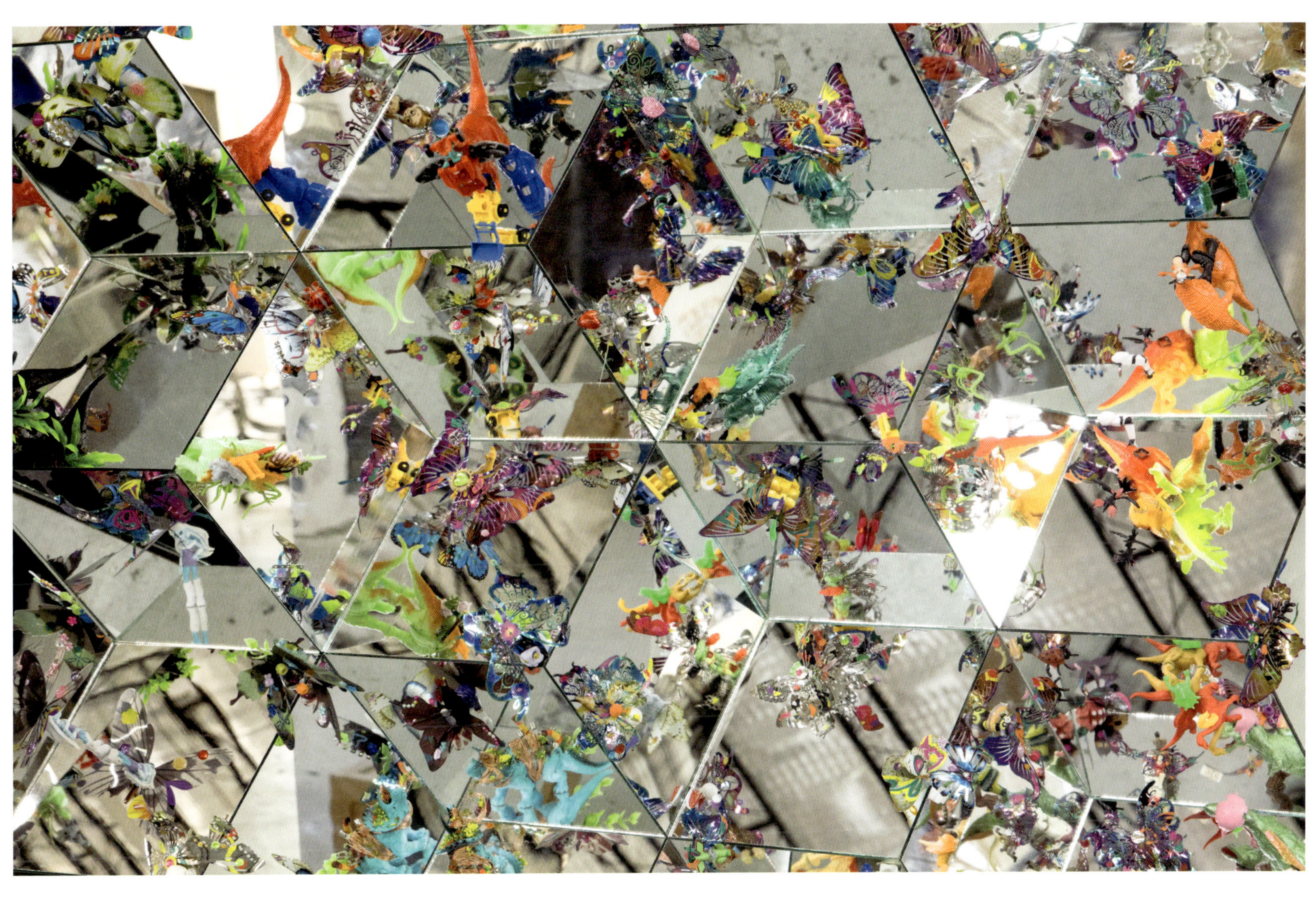

Schmetterlinge erobern den Garten der Dinosaurier, Detail

Butterflies Conquer the Dinosaurs' Garden, detail

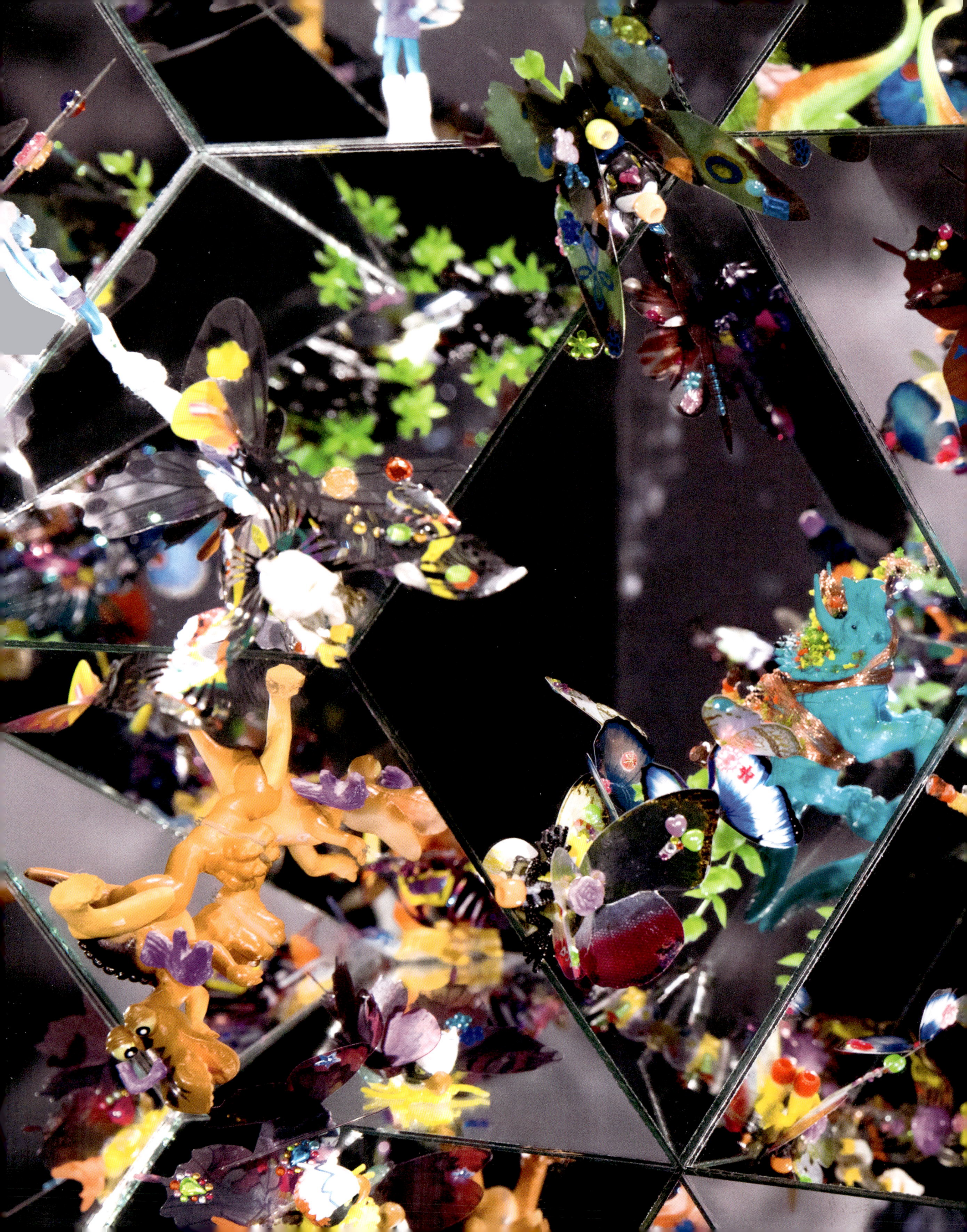

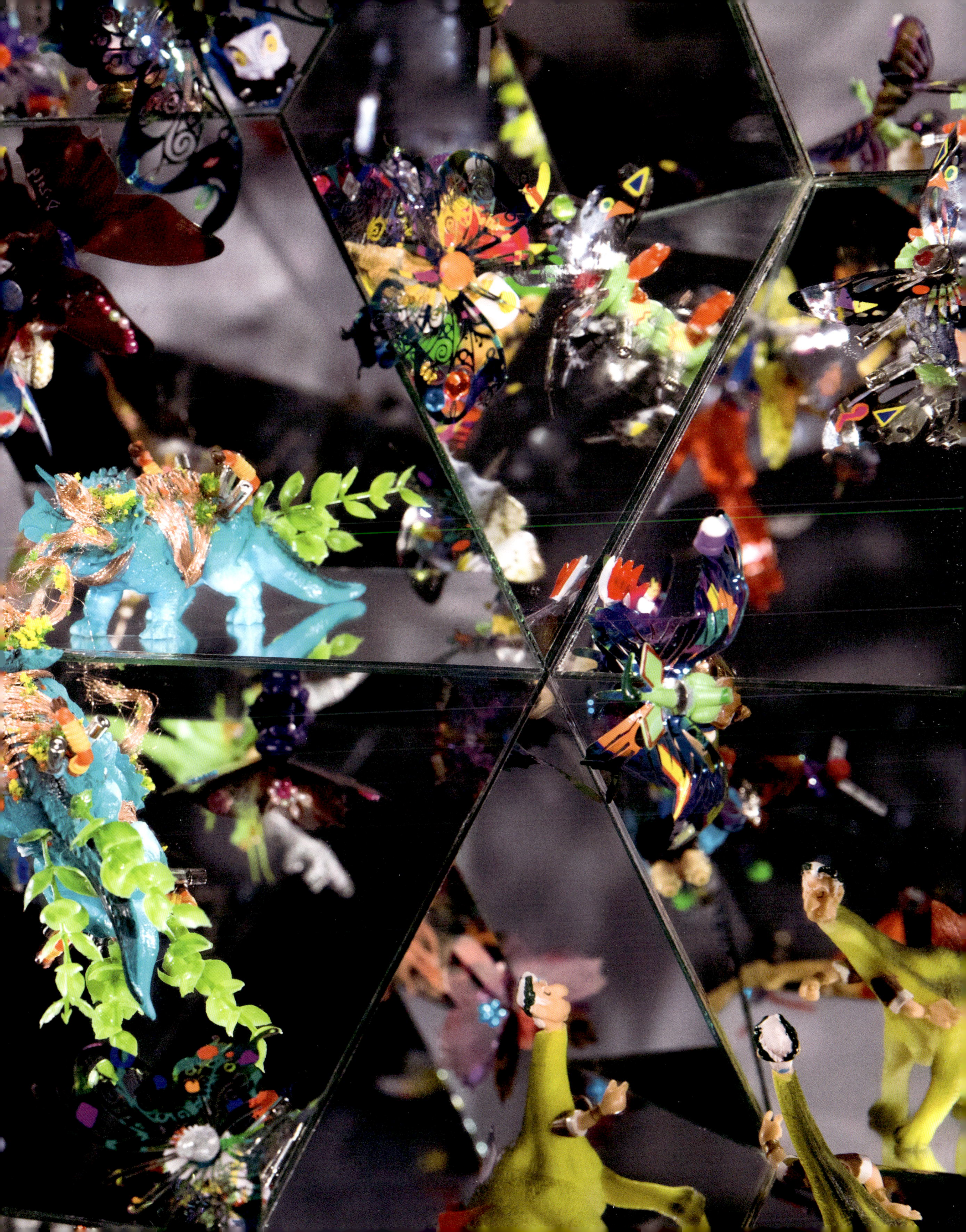

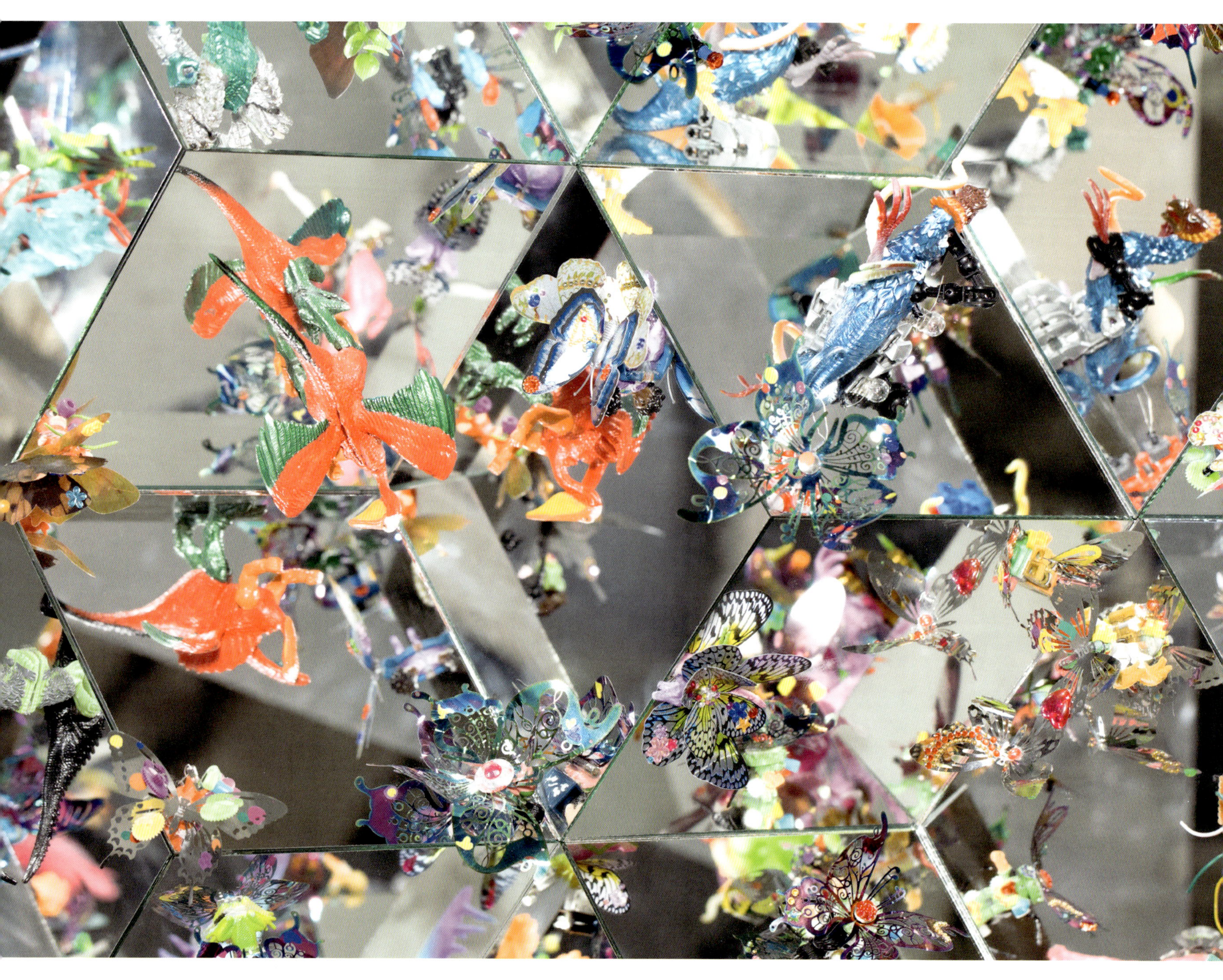

Schmetterlinge erobern den Garten der Dinosaurier, Detail

Butterflies Conquer the Dinosaurs' Garden, detail

Vorherige Seiten:
Schmetterlinge erobern den Garten der Dinosaurier, Detail

Previous pages:
Butterflies Conquer the Dinosaurs' Garden, detail

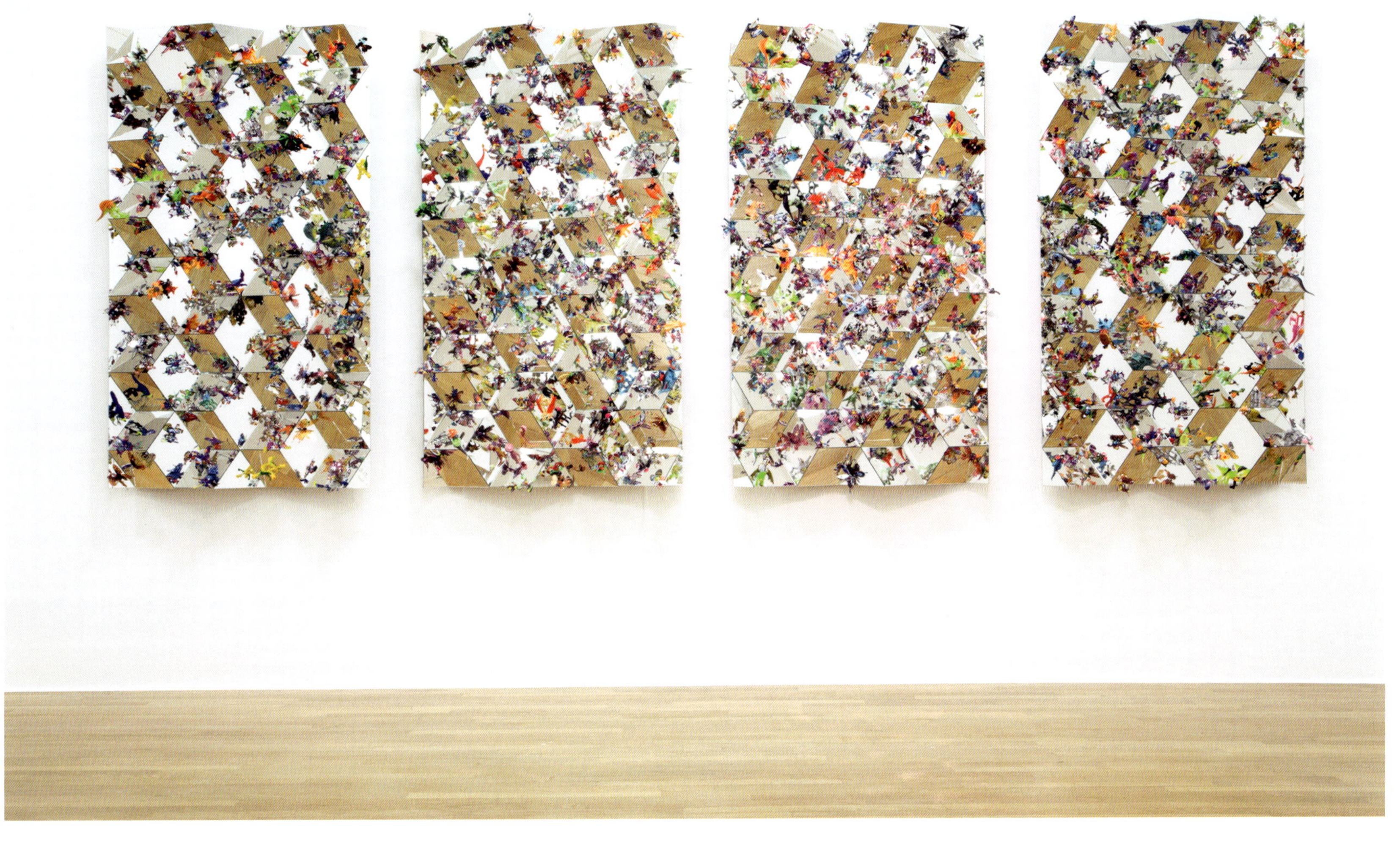

Schmetterlinge erobern den Garten der Dinosaurier, Ansicht der Installation im Ludwig Museum, Koblenz, 2019

Butterflies Conquer the Dinosaurs' Garden, view of the installation in the Ludwig Museum, Koblenz, 2019

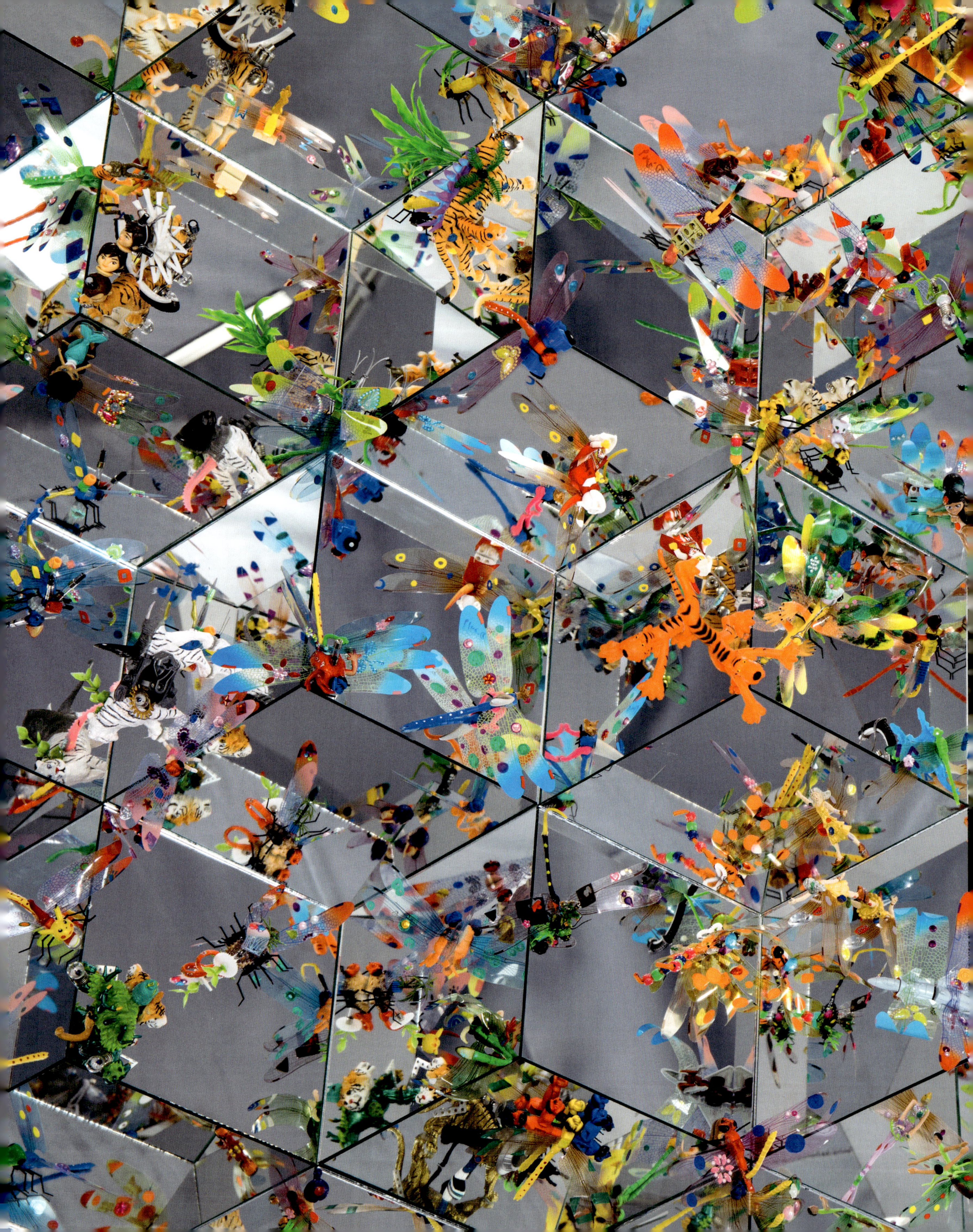

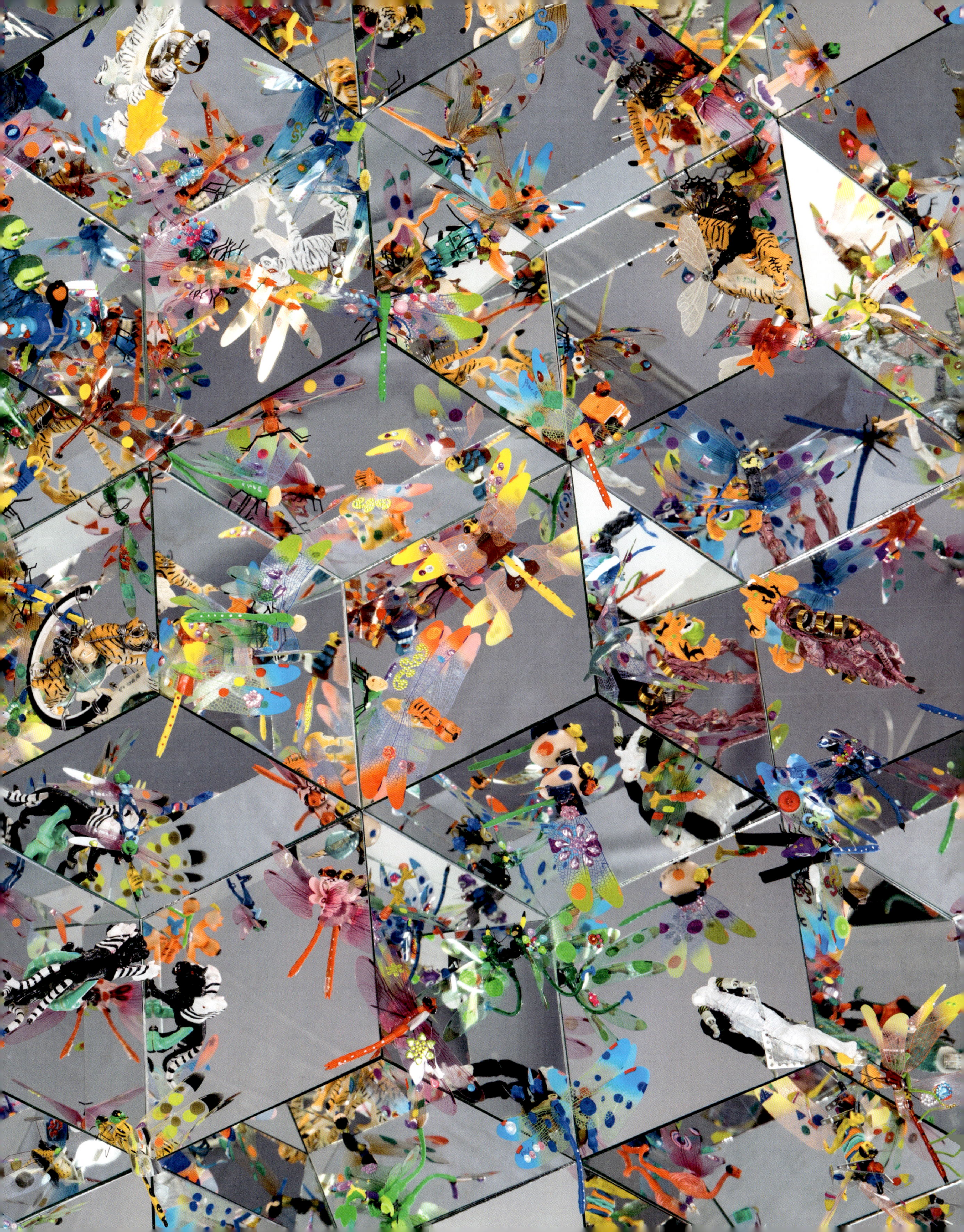

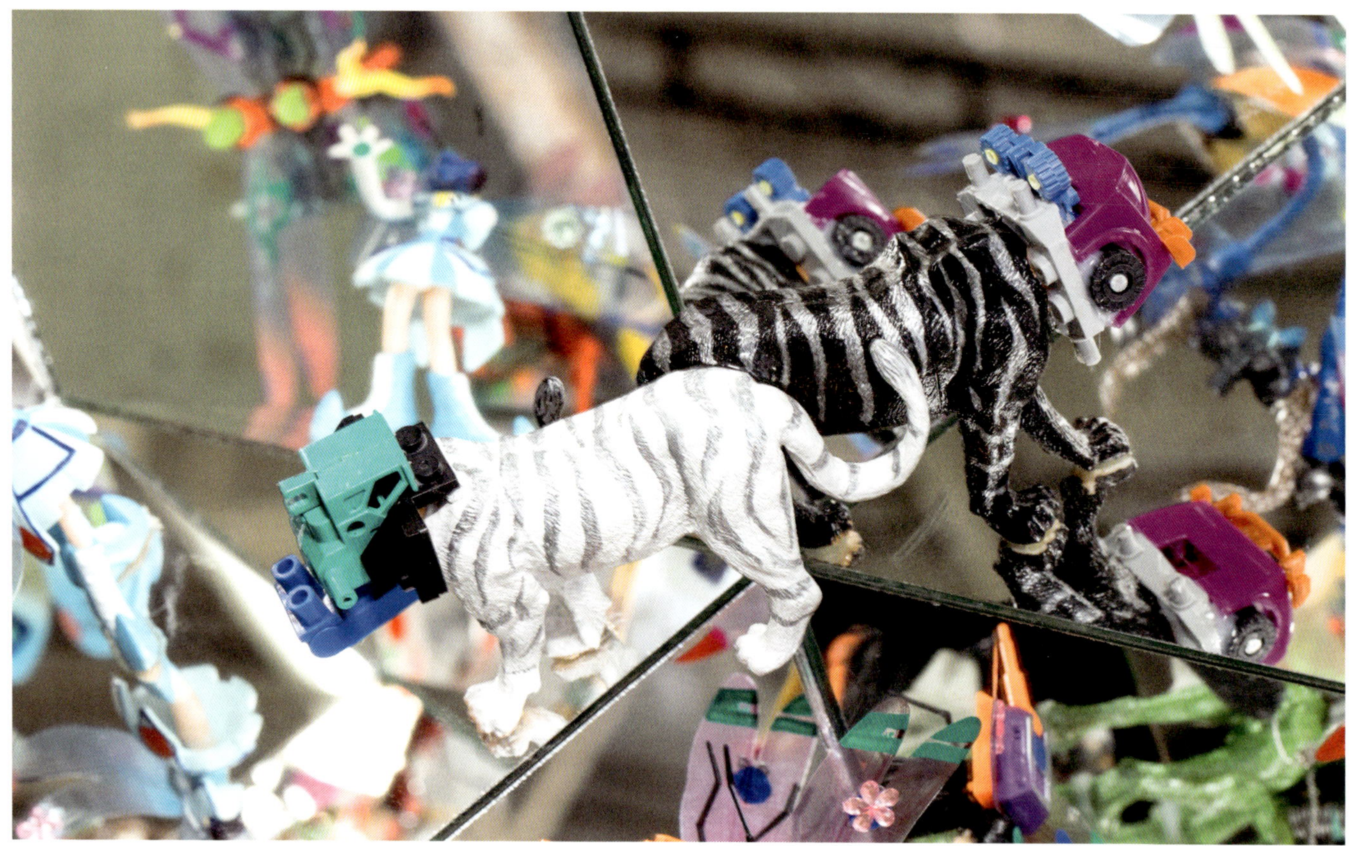

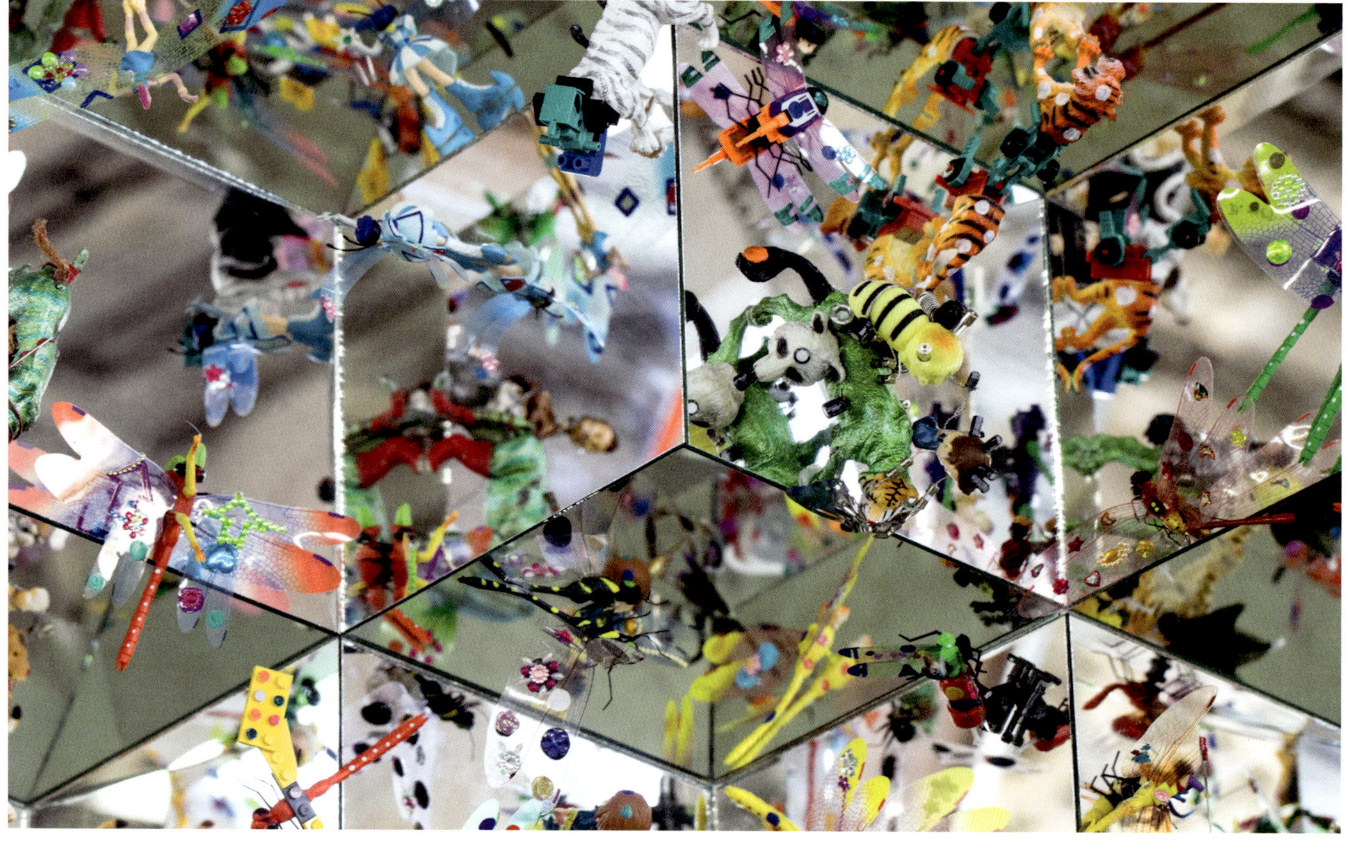

Libellen erobern den Garten der Tiger Nr.1, Details

Dragonflies Conquer the Tigers' Garden No. 1, details

Vorherige Seiten:
Libellen erobern den Garten der Tiger Nr.2, Detail

Previous pages:
Dragonflies Conquer the Tigers' Garden No. 2, detail

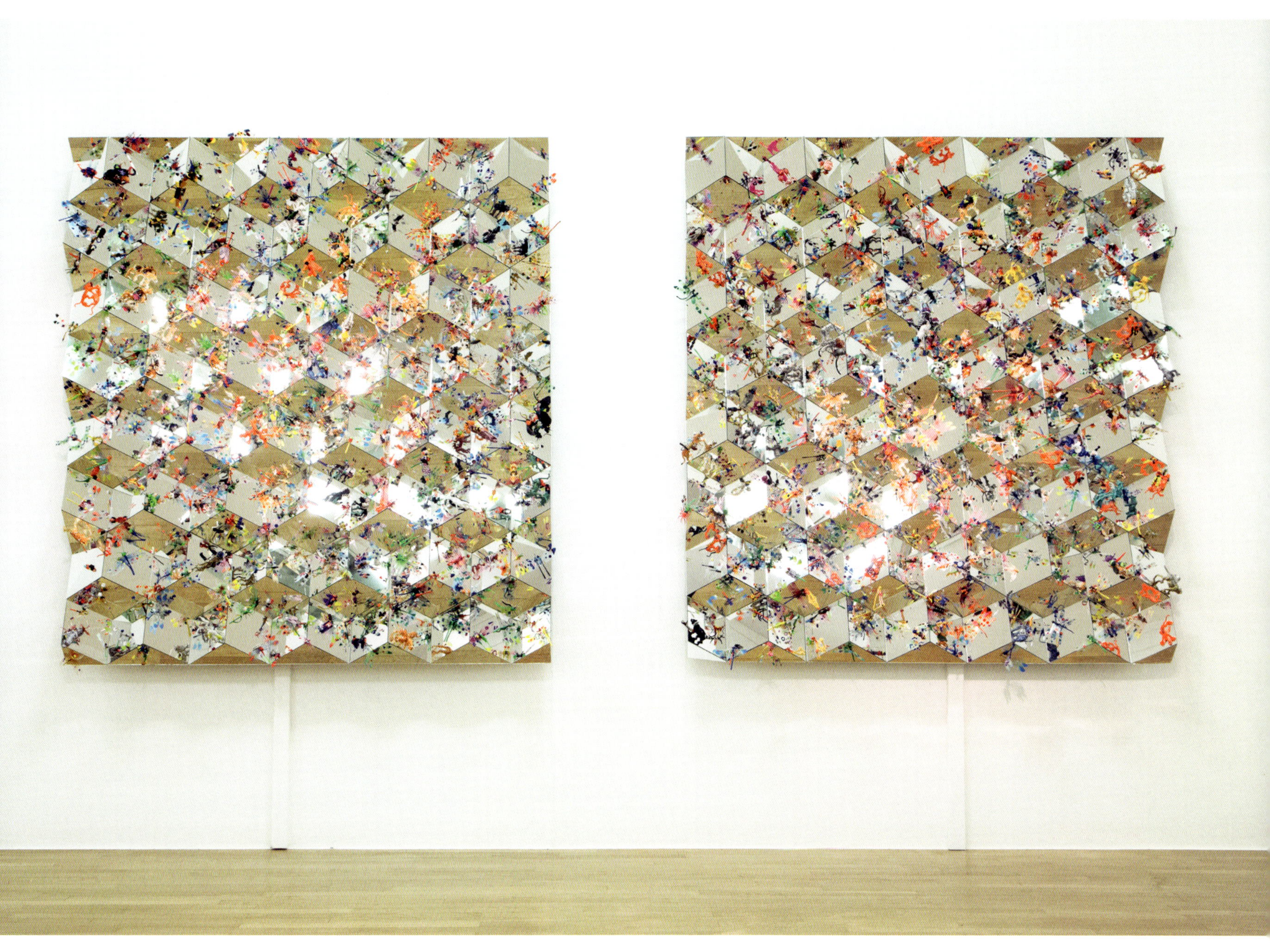

Libellen erobern den Garten der Tiger Nr.2, Ansicht der Installation im Ludwig Museum, Koblenz, 2019

Dragonflies Conquer the Tigers' Garden No. 2, view of the installation in the Ludwig Museum, Koblenz, 2019

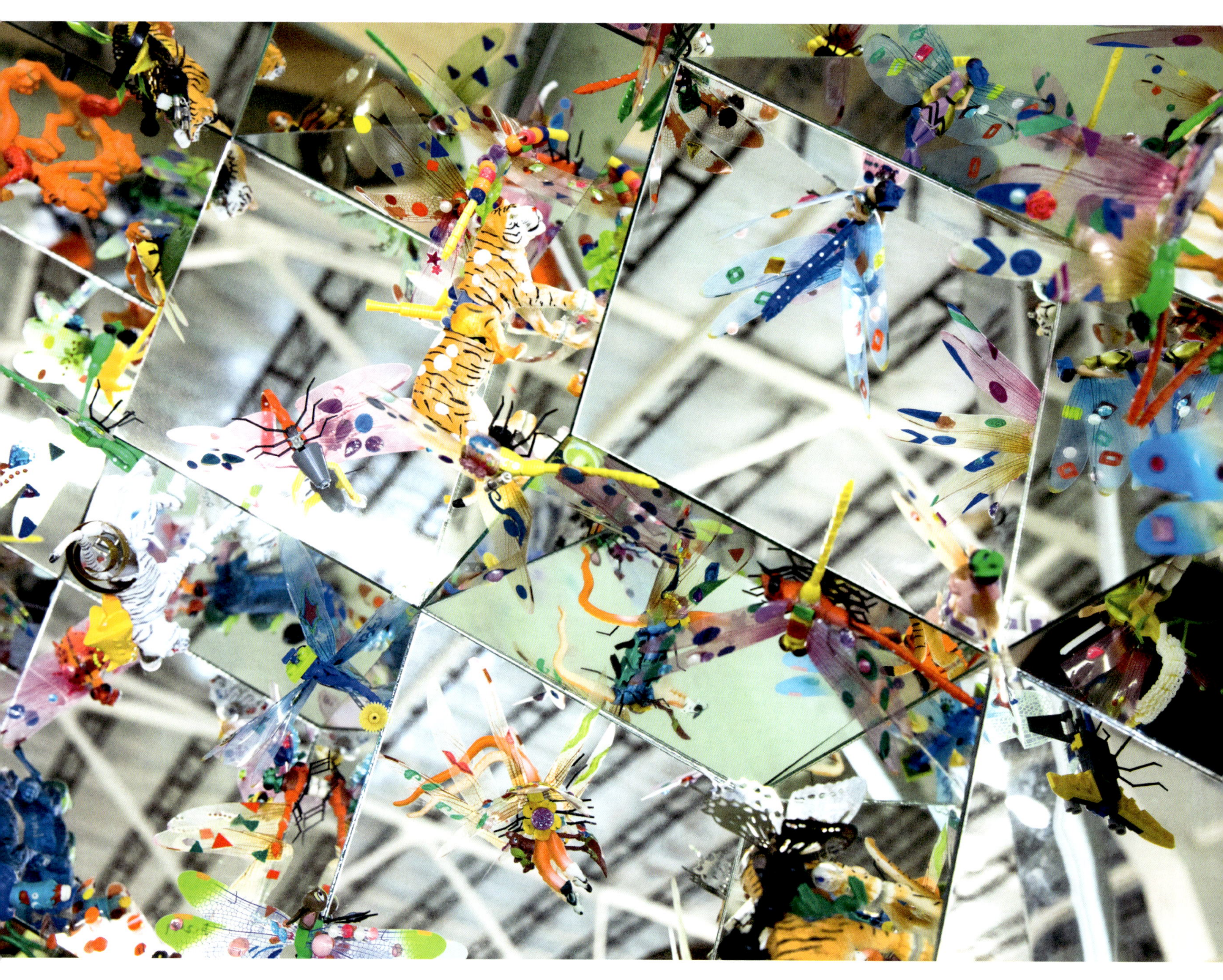

Libellen erobern den Garten der Tiger Nr.2, Detail

Dragonflies Conquer the Tigers' Garden No. 2, detail

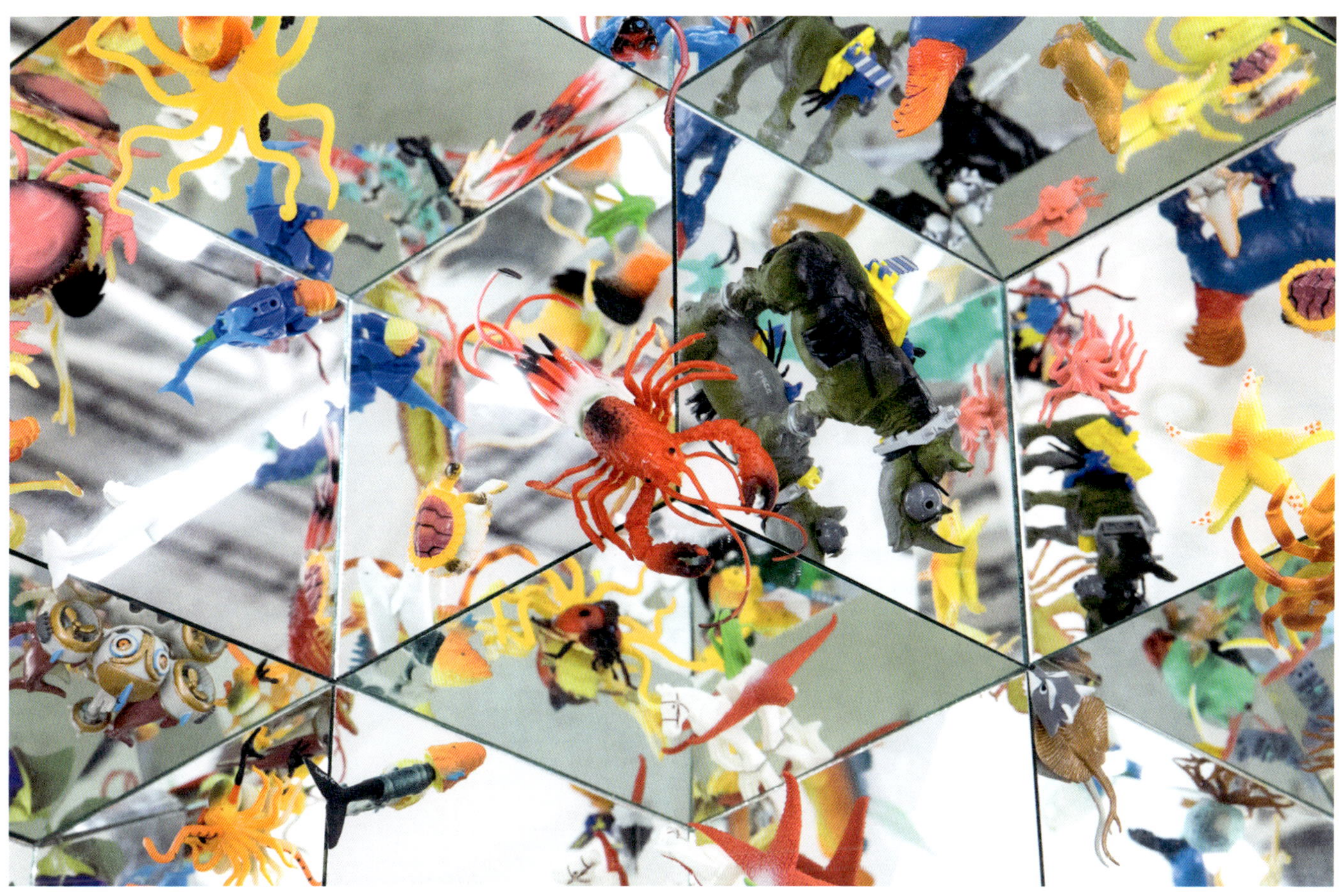

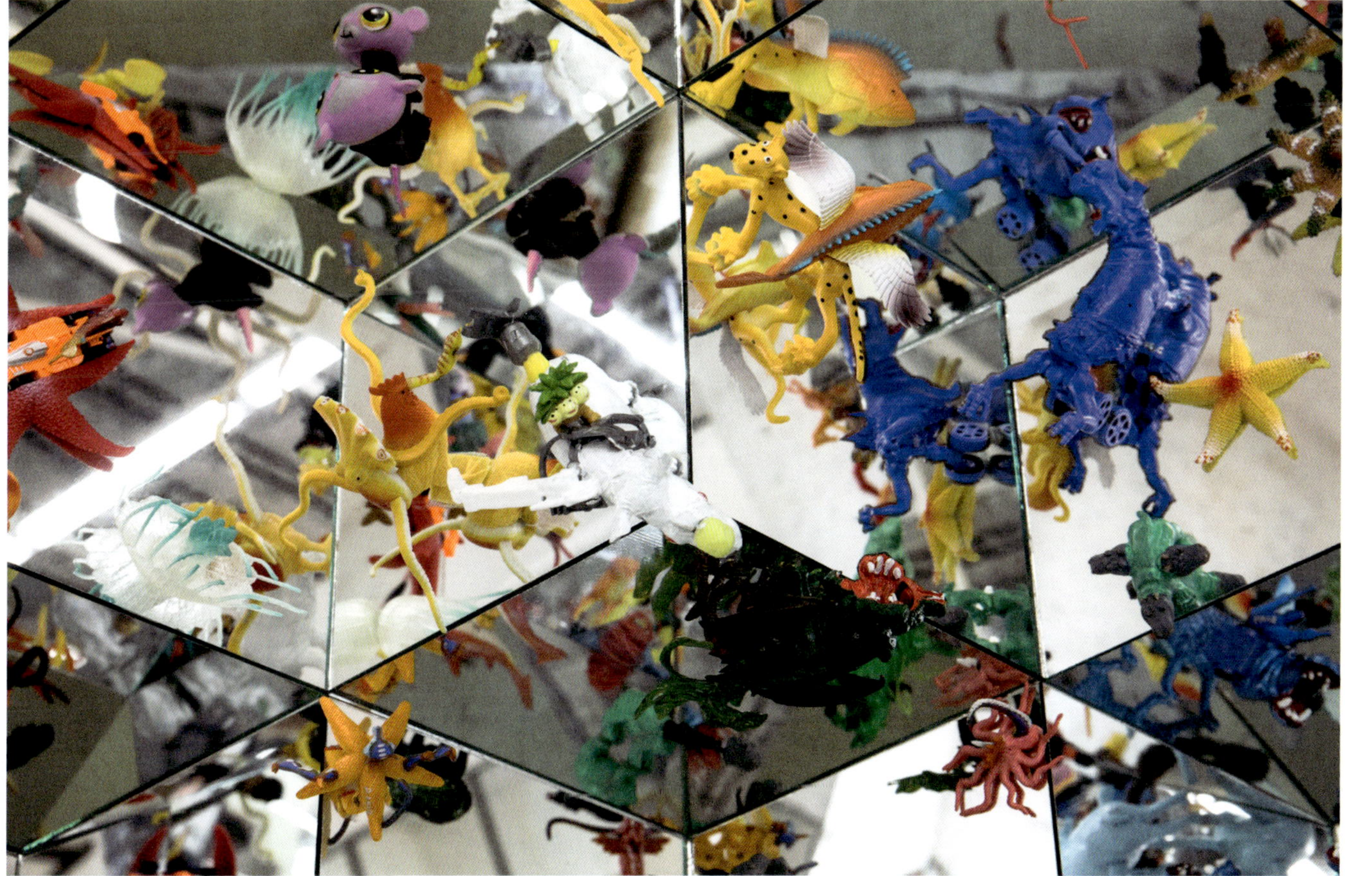

Meerestiere erobern den Garten der Flusspferde, Details

Sea Creatures Conquer the Hippos' Garden, details

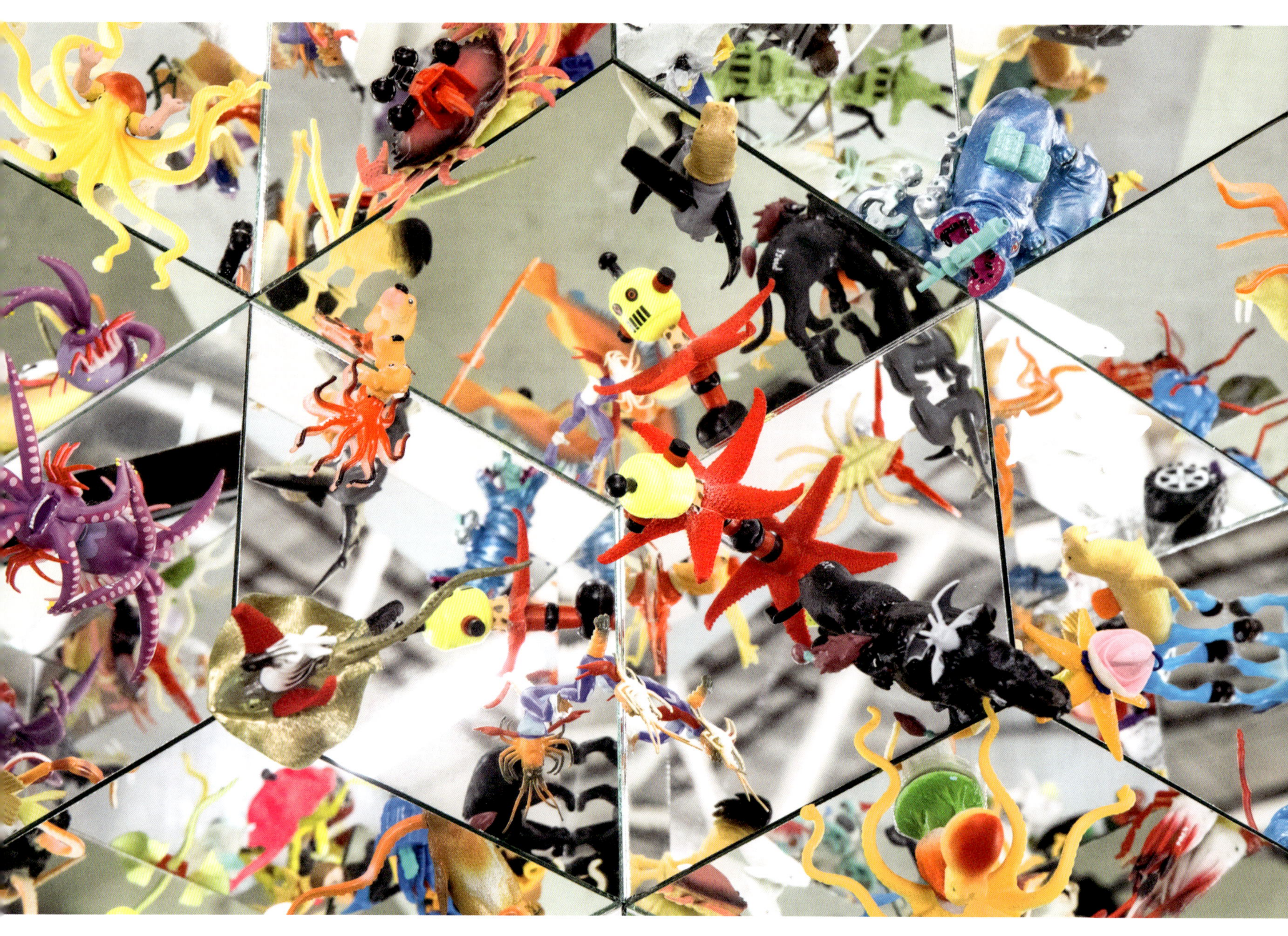

Meerestiere erobern den Garten der Flusspferde, Details

Sea Creatures Conquer the Hippos' Garden, details

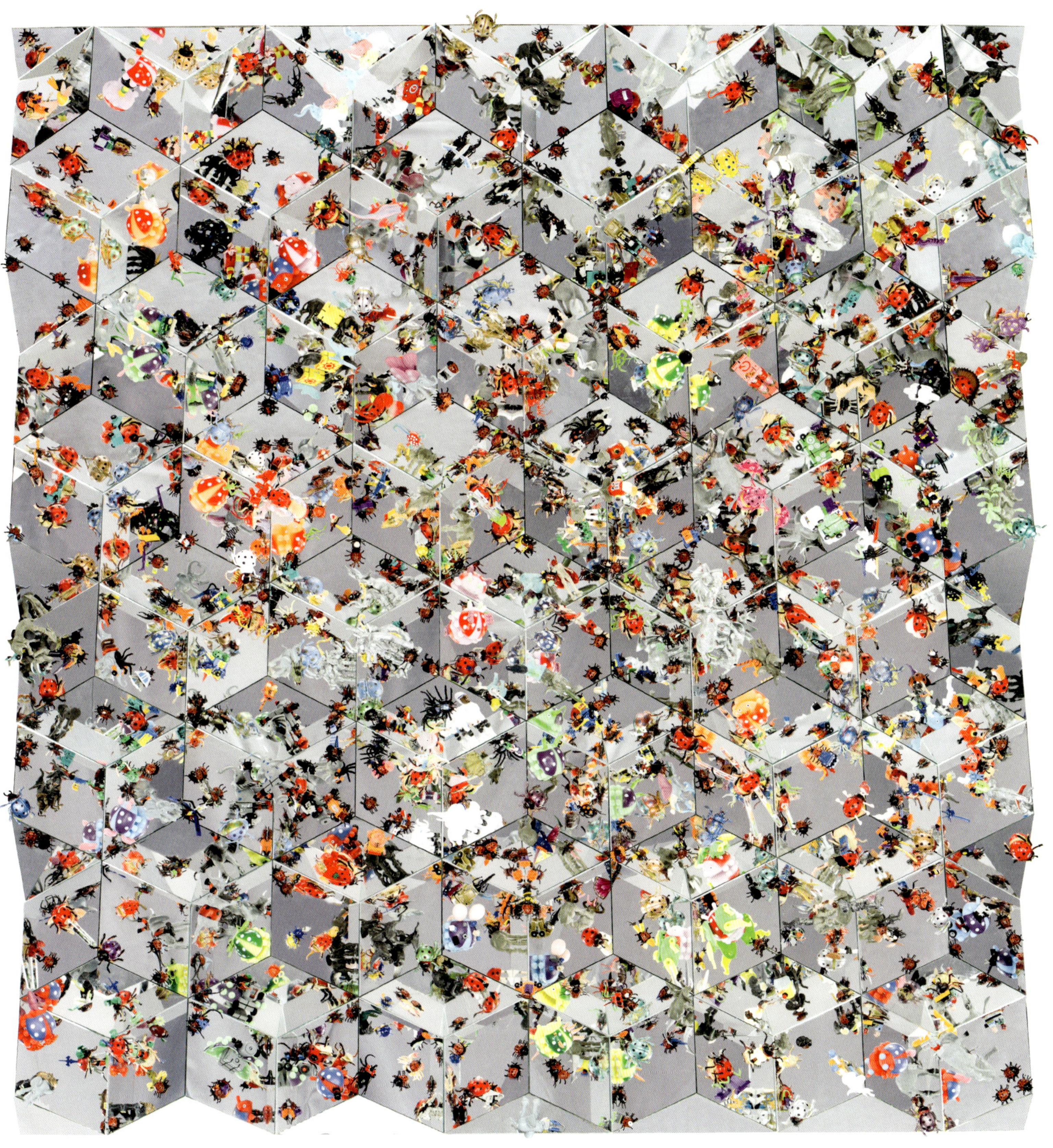

Käfer erobern den Garten der Elefanten, 2019
Aluminiumblech, Spiegelglas, verändertes Spielzeug, Acrylfarbe, Emailfarbe
200 × 180 × 30 cm

Beetles Conquer the Elephants' Garden, 2019
Aluminium sheet, glass mirror, modified toys, acrylic paint, enamel paint
200 × 180 × 30 cm

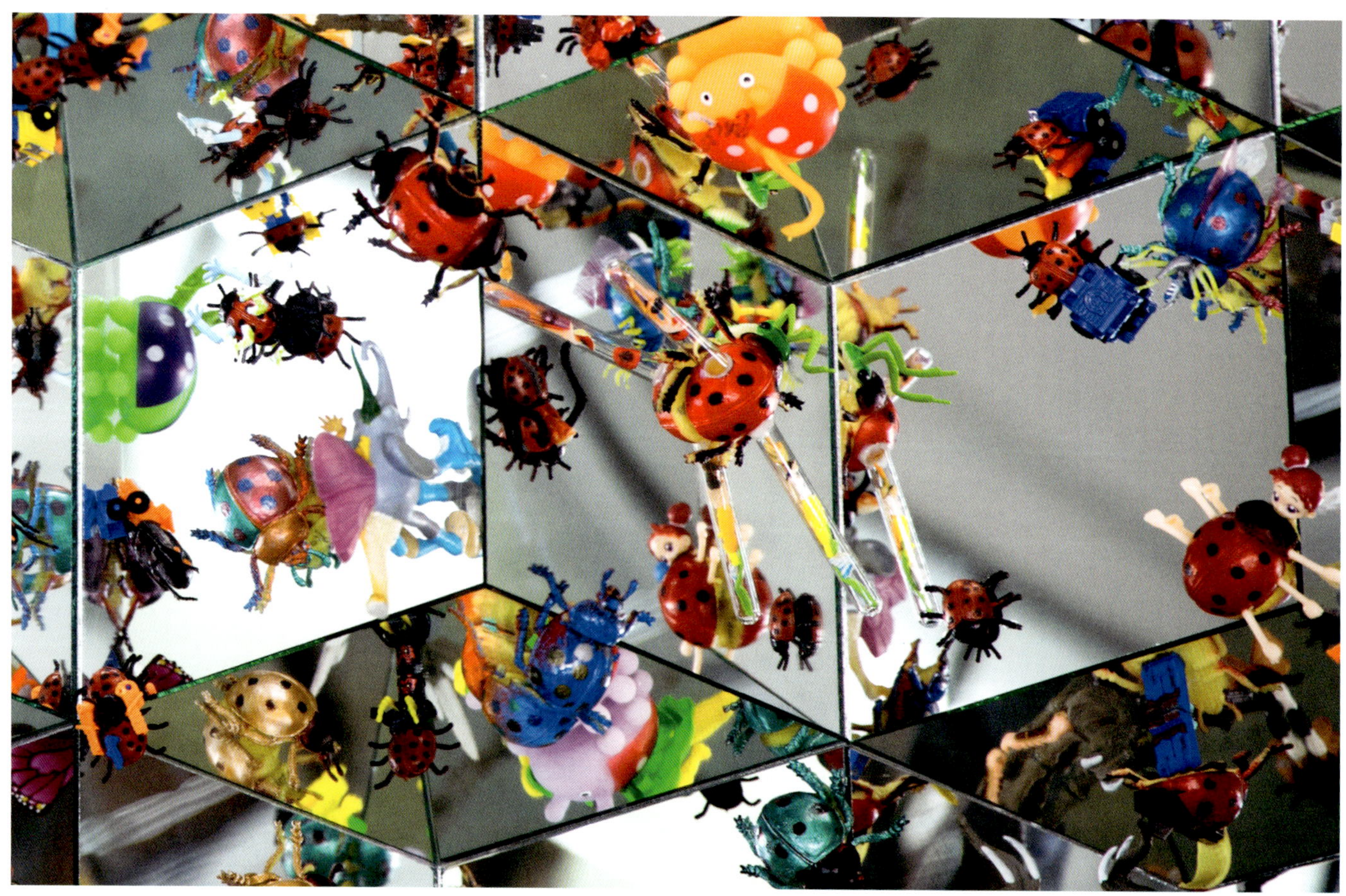

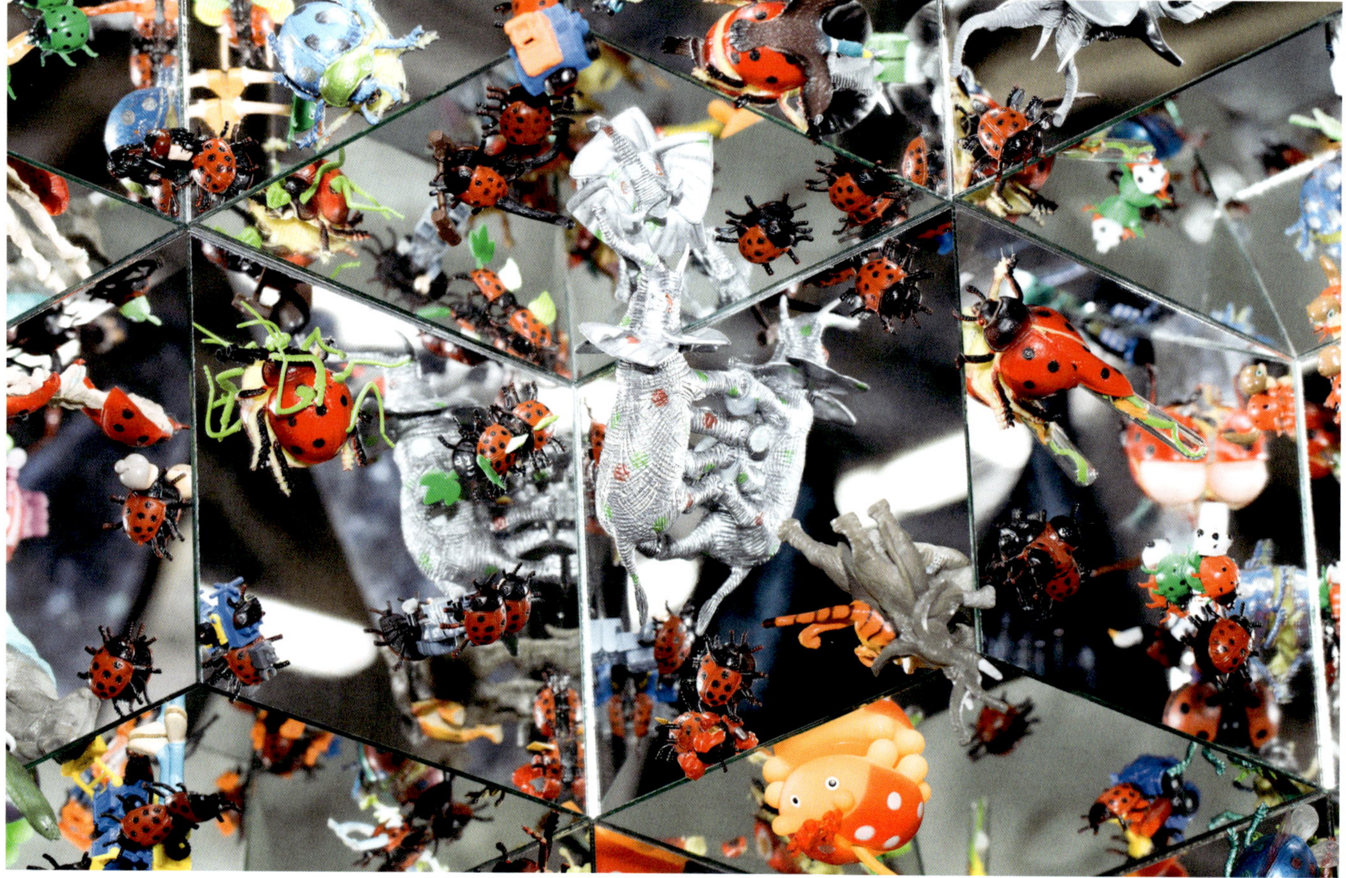

Käfer erobern den Garten der Elefanten, Details

Beetles Conquer the Elephants' Garden, details

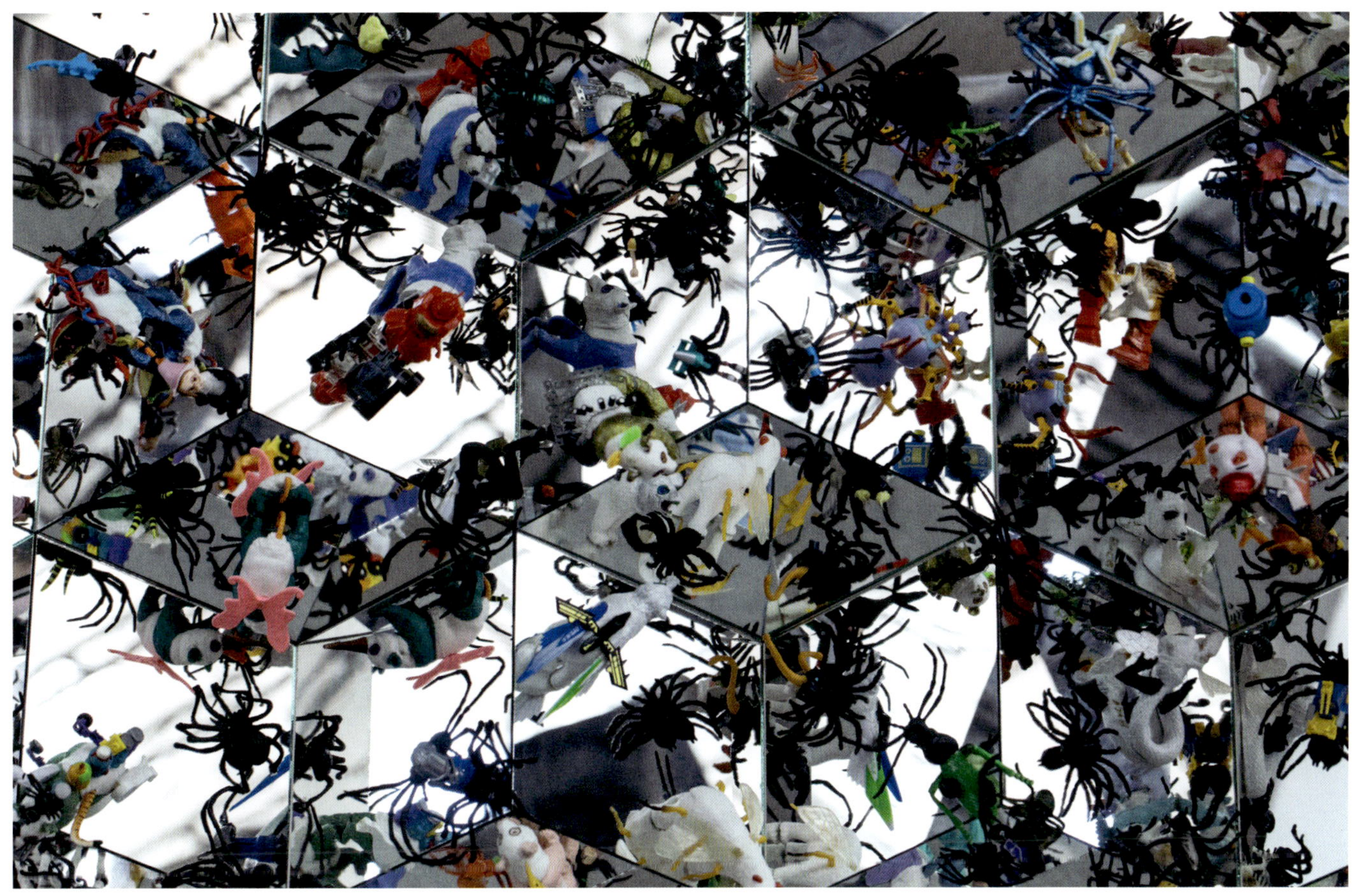

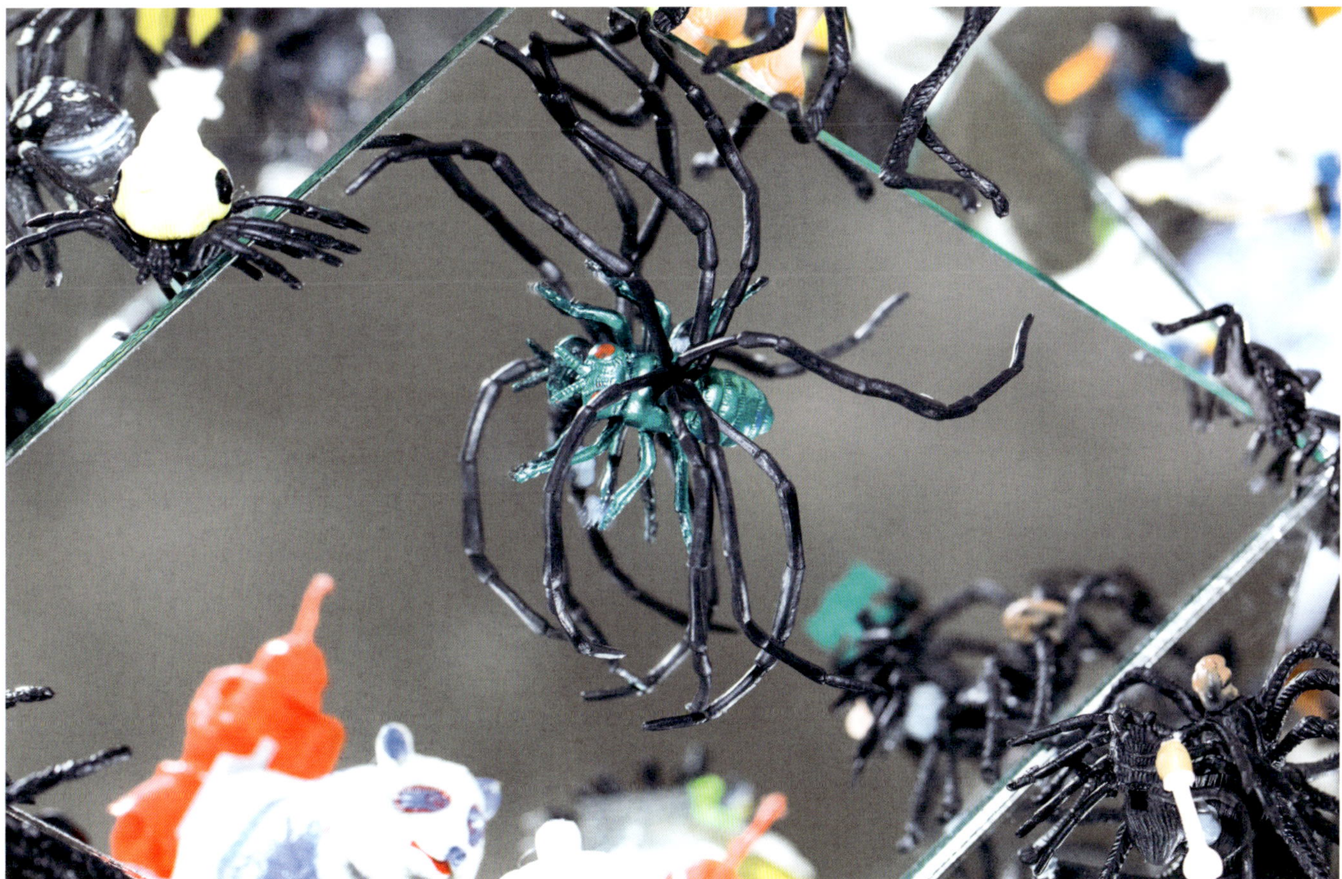

Spinnen erobern den Garten der Pandas, Details

Spiders Conquer the Pandas' Garden, details

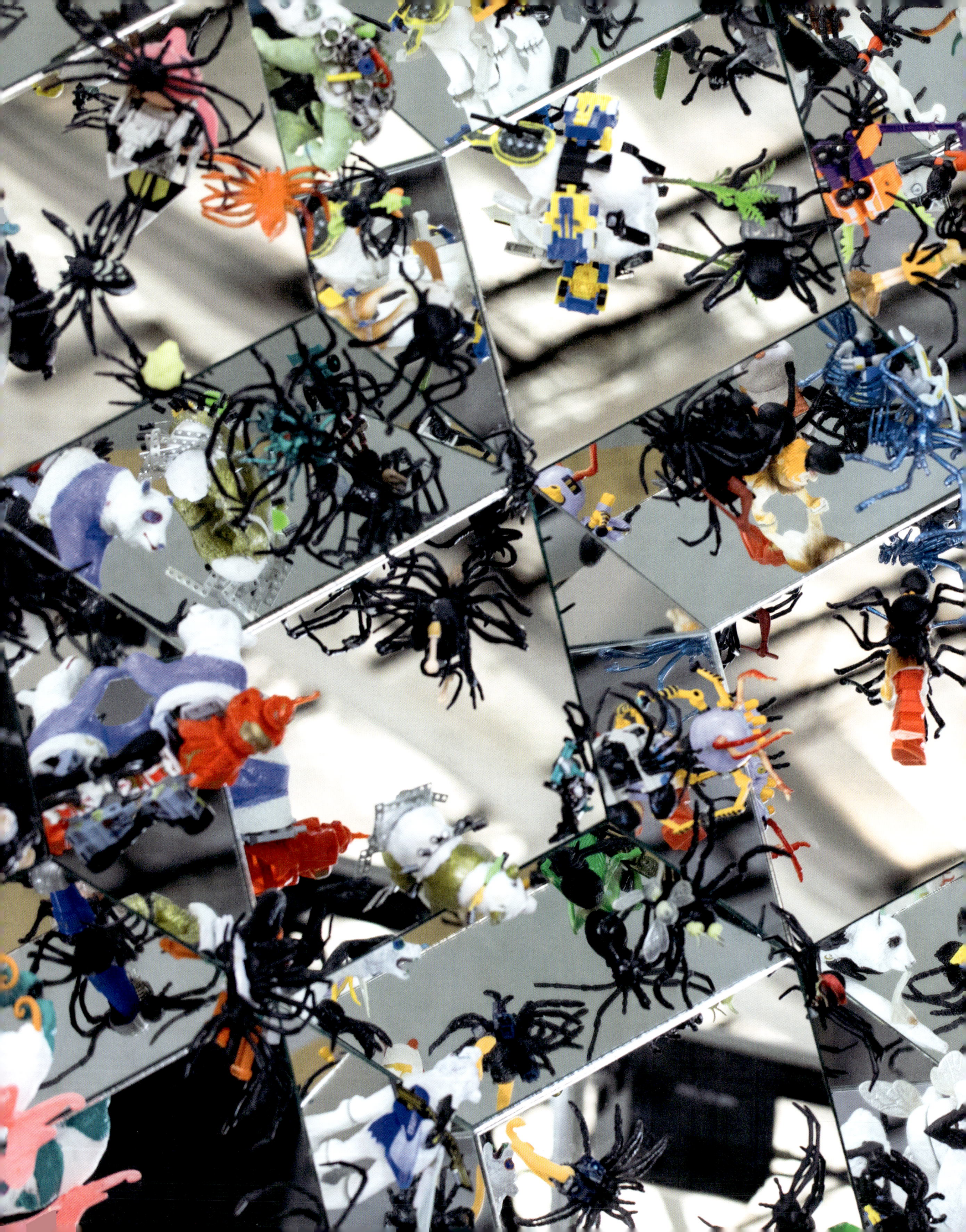

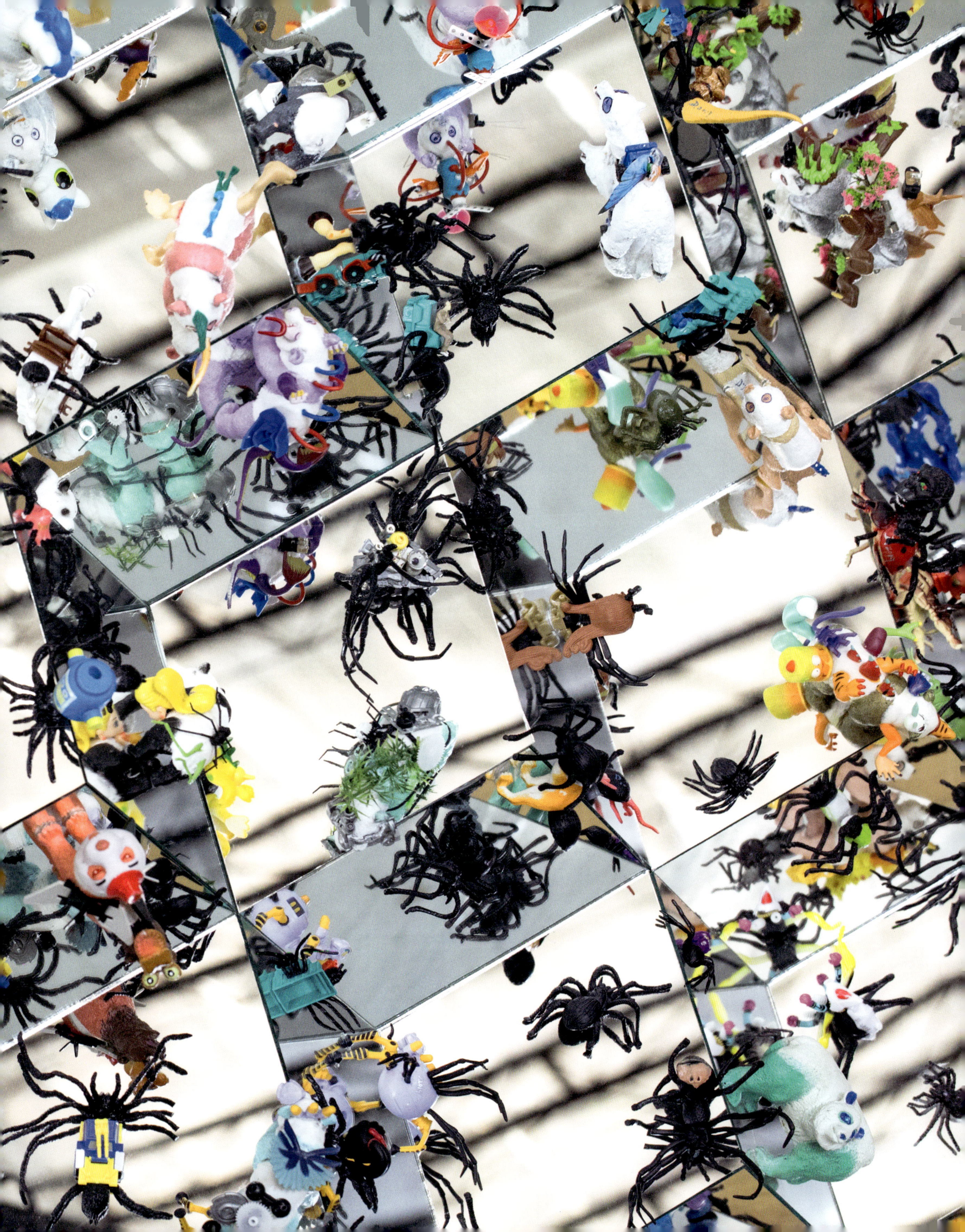

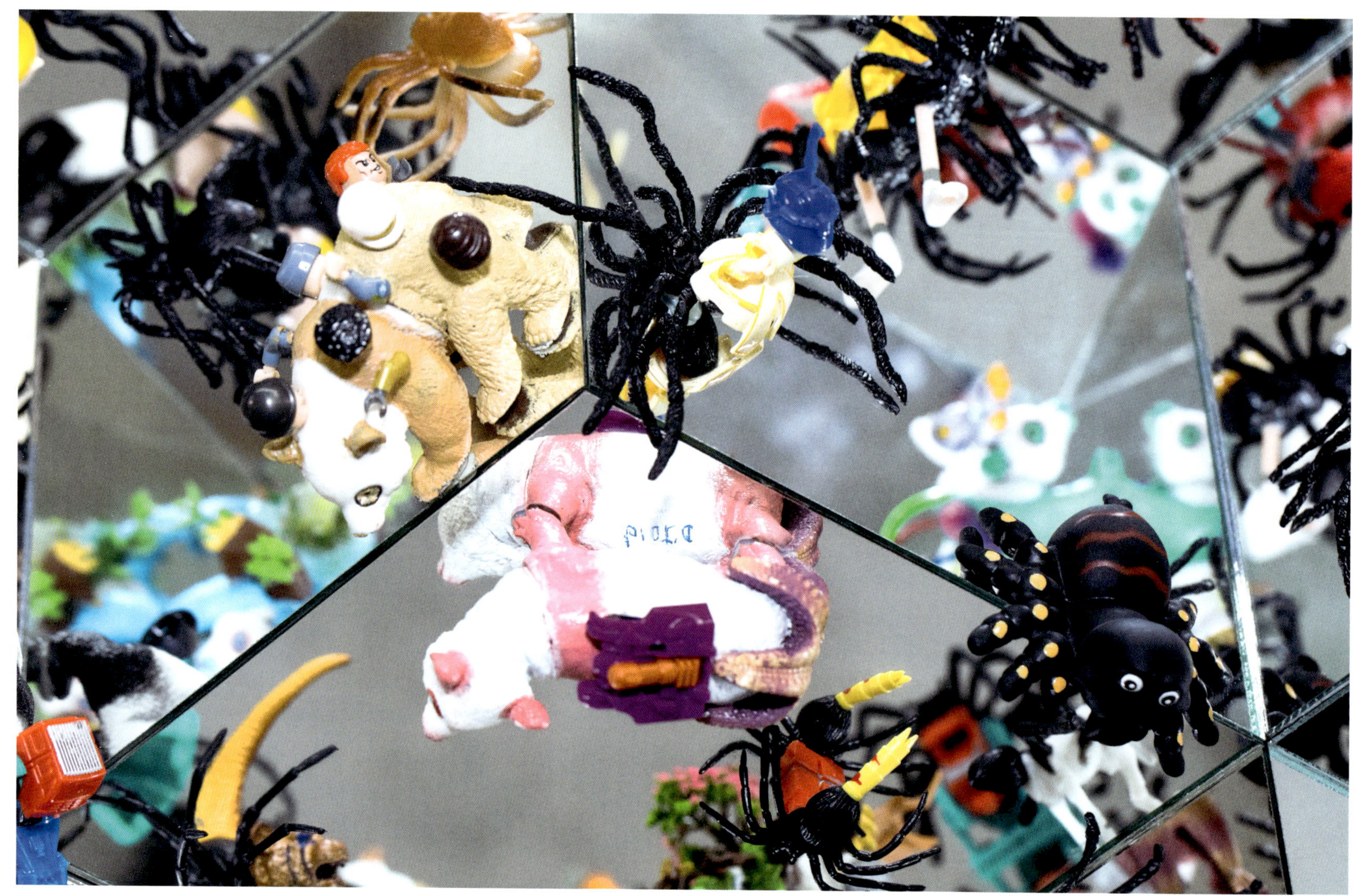

Spinnen erobern den Garten der Pandas, Details

Spiders Conquer the Pandas' Garden, details

Rechts:
Gottesanbeterinnen erobern den Garten der Löwen, 2019
Aluminiumblech, Spiegelglas, verändertes Spielzeug,
Acrylfarbe, Emailfarbe
200 × 180 × 30 cm

Right:
Mantises Conquer the Lions' Garden, 2019
Aluminium sheet, glass mirror, modified toys,
acrylic paint, enamel paint
200 × 180 × 30 cm

Vorherige Seiten:
Spinnen erobern den Garten der Pandas, Detail

Previous pages:
Spiders Conquer the Pandas' Garden, detail

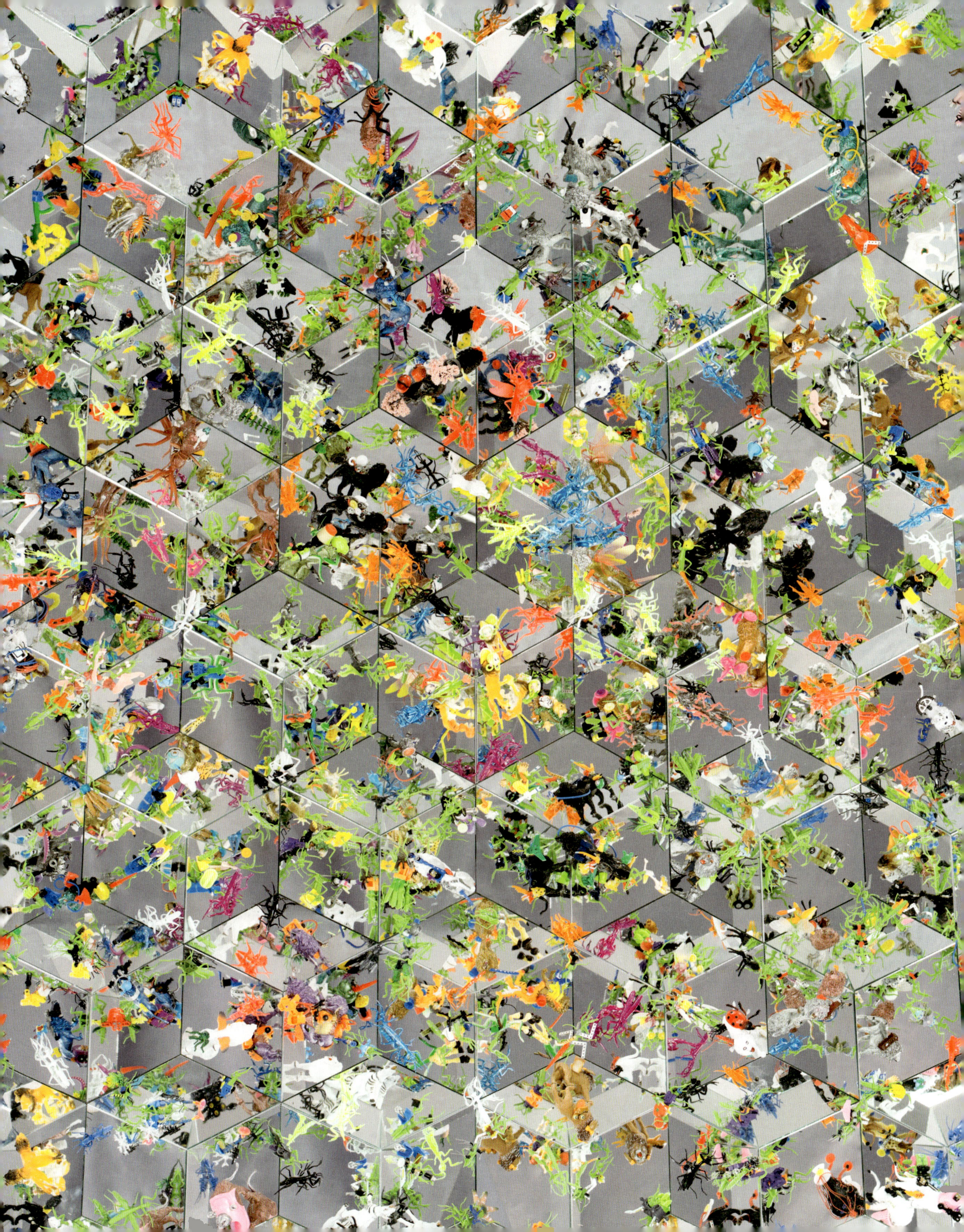

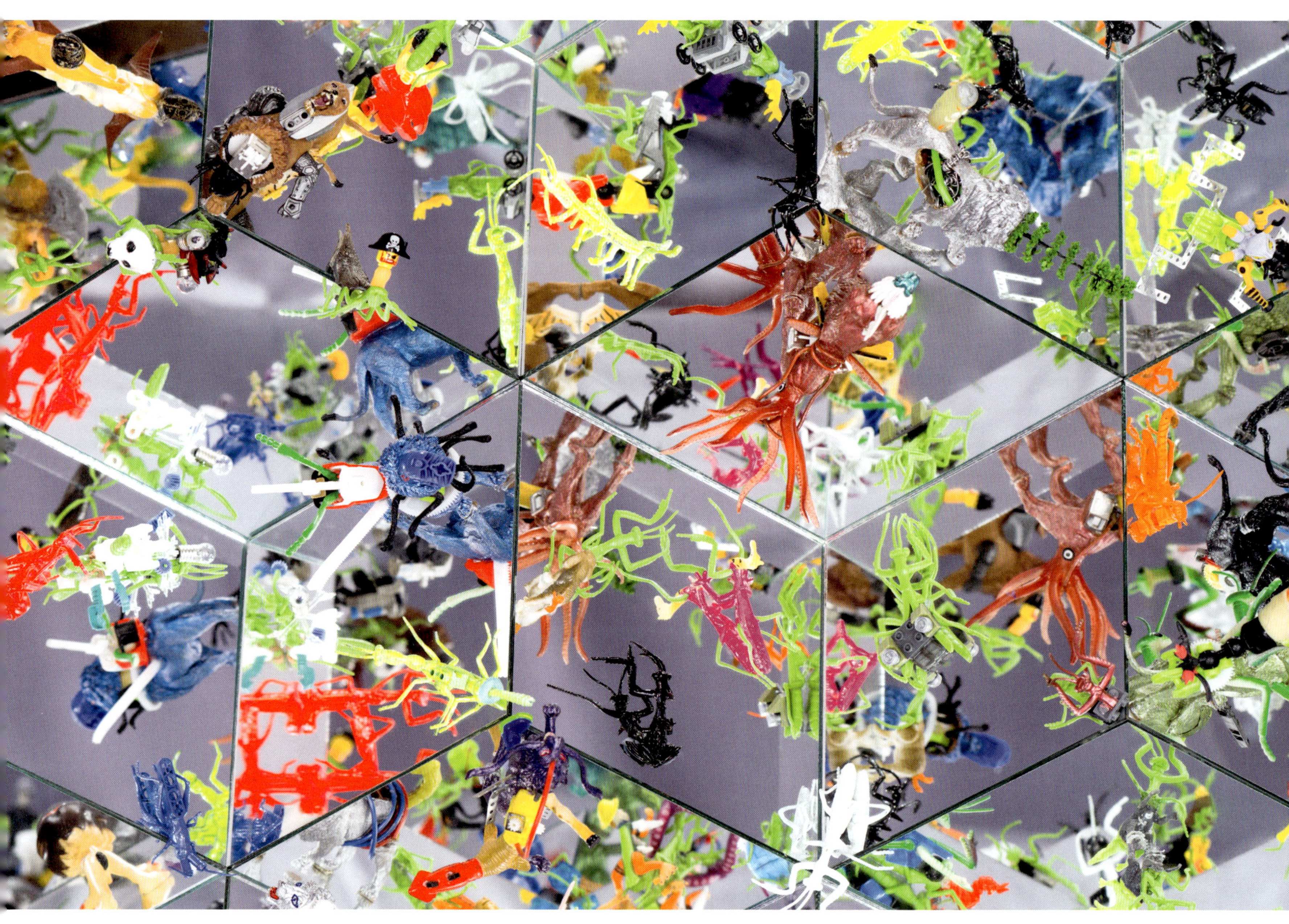

Gottesanbeterinnen erobern den Garten der Löwen, Detail

Mantises Conquer the Lions' Garden, detail

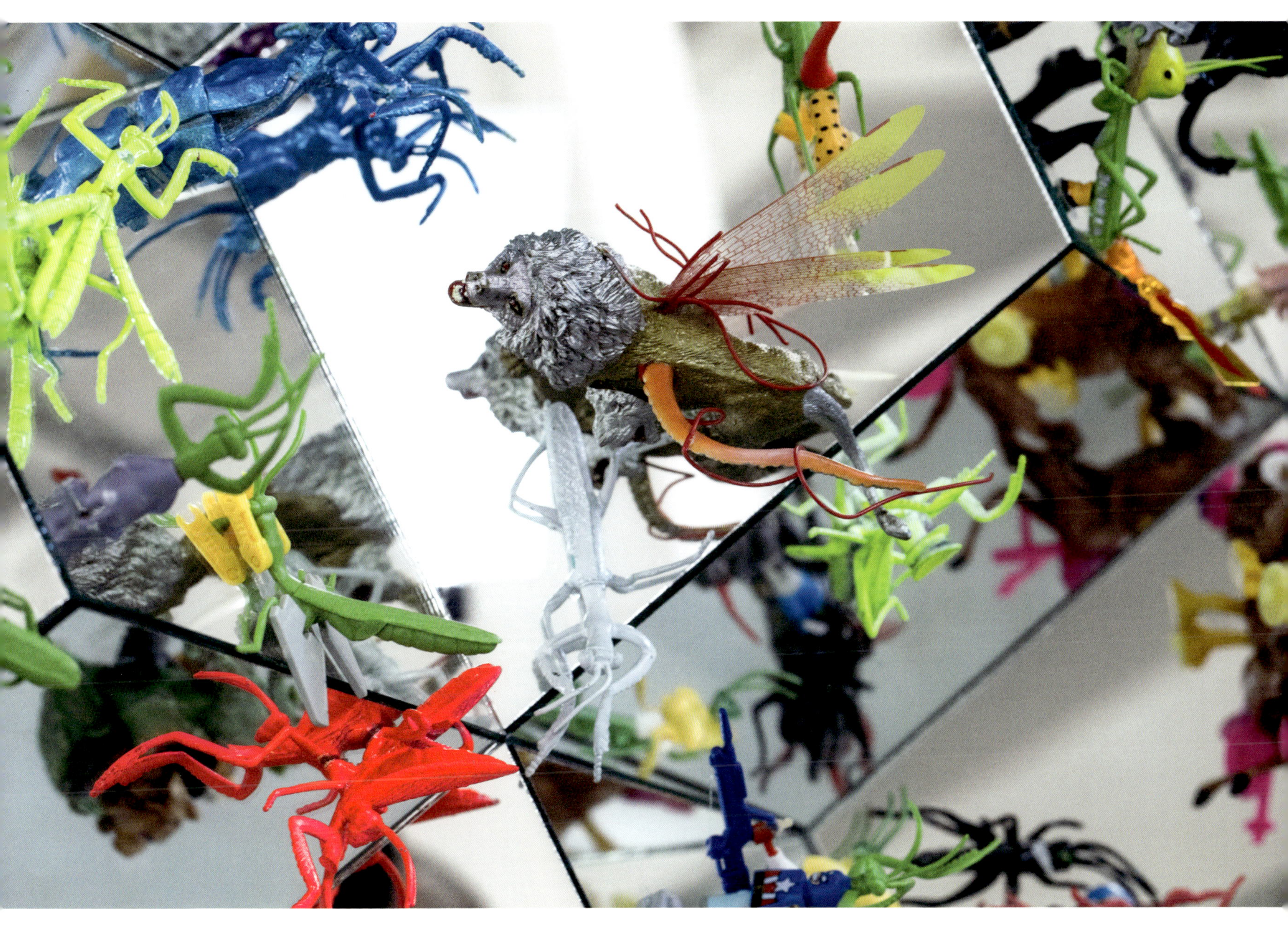

Gottesanbeterinnen erobern den Garten der Löwen, Detail

Mantises Conquer the Lions' Garden, detail

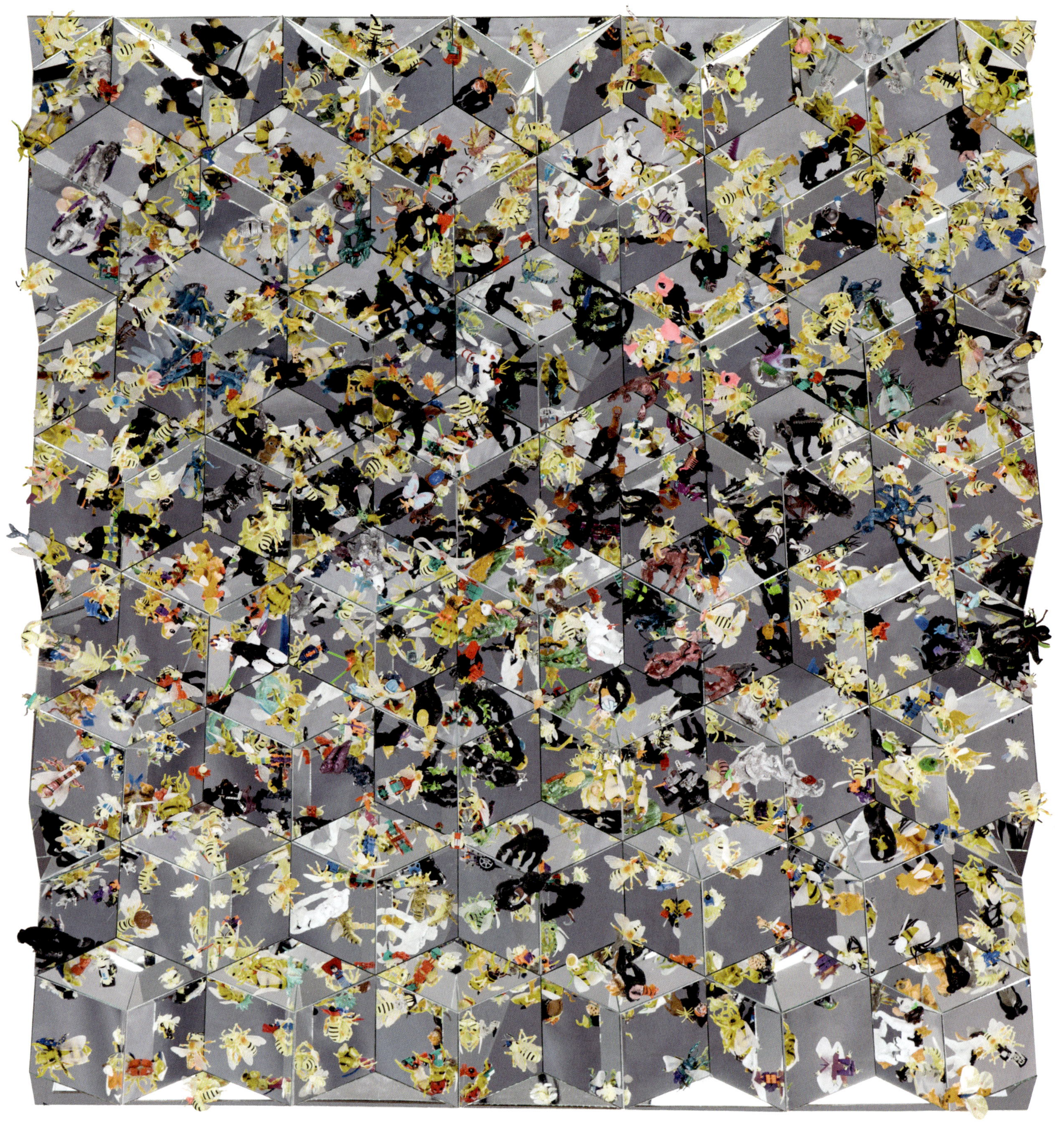

Bienen erobern den Garten der Orang-Utans, 2019
Aluminiumblech, Spiegelglas, verändertes Spielzeug, Acrylfarbe, Emailfarbe
200 × 180 × 30 cm

Bees Conquer the Orangutans' Garden, 2019
Aluminium sheet, glass mirror, modified toys, acrylic paint, enamel paint
200 × 180 × 30 cm

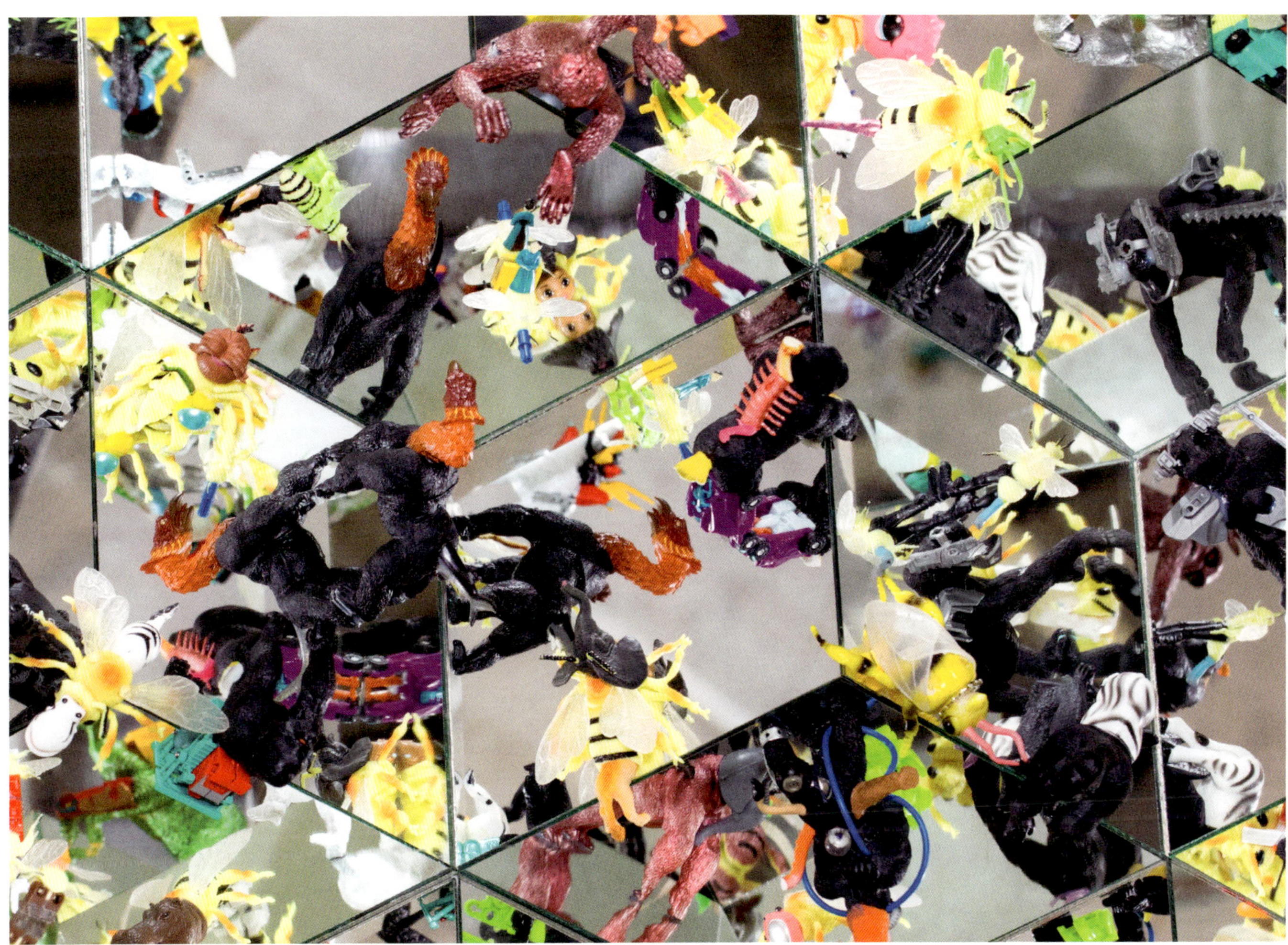

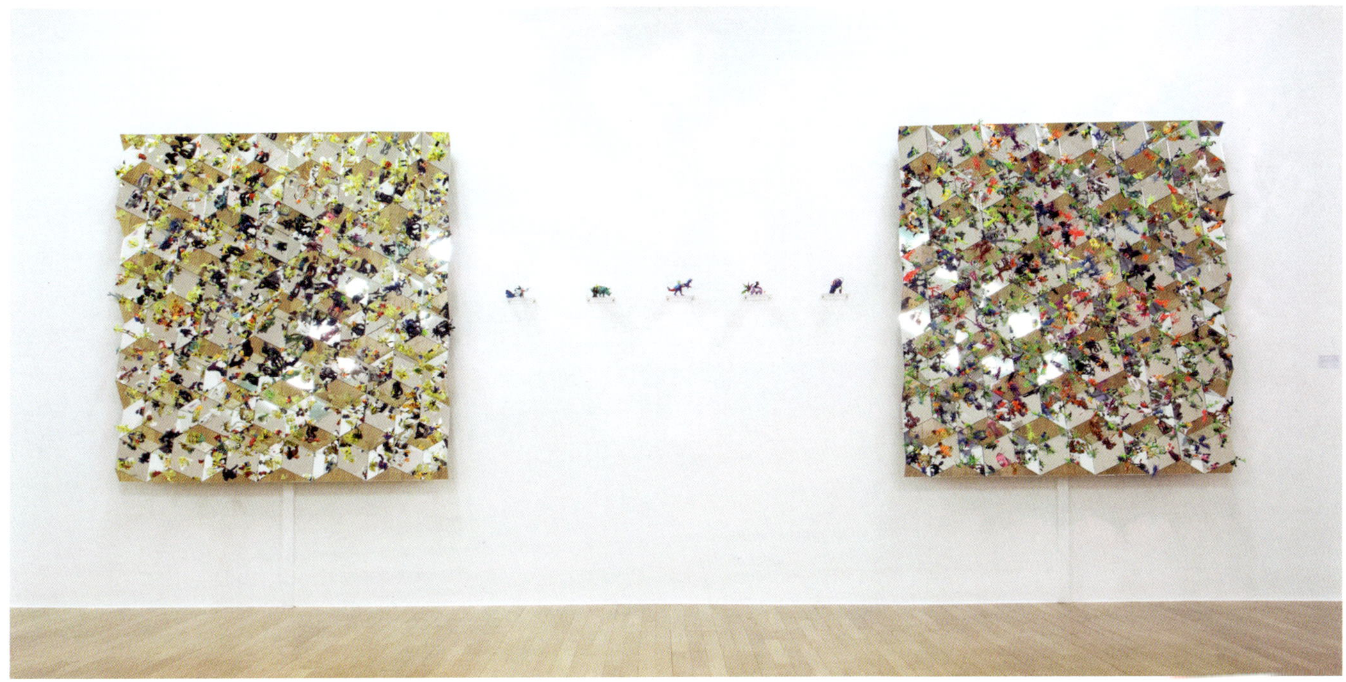

Oben:
Bienen erobern den Garten der Orang-Utans, **Detail**

Above:
***Bees Conquer the Orangutans' Garden*, detail**

Unten:
***Bienen erobern den Garten der Orang-Utans*, Ansicht der Installation im Ludwig Museum, Koblenz, 2019**

Below:
***Bees Conquer the Orangutans' Garden*, view of the installation in the Ludwig Museum, Koblenz, 2019**

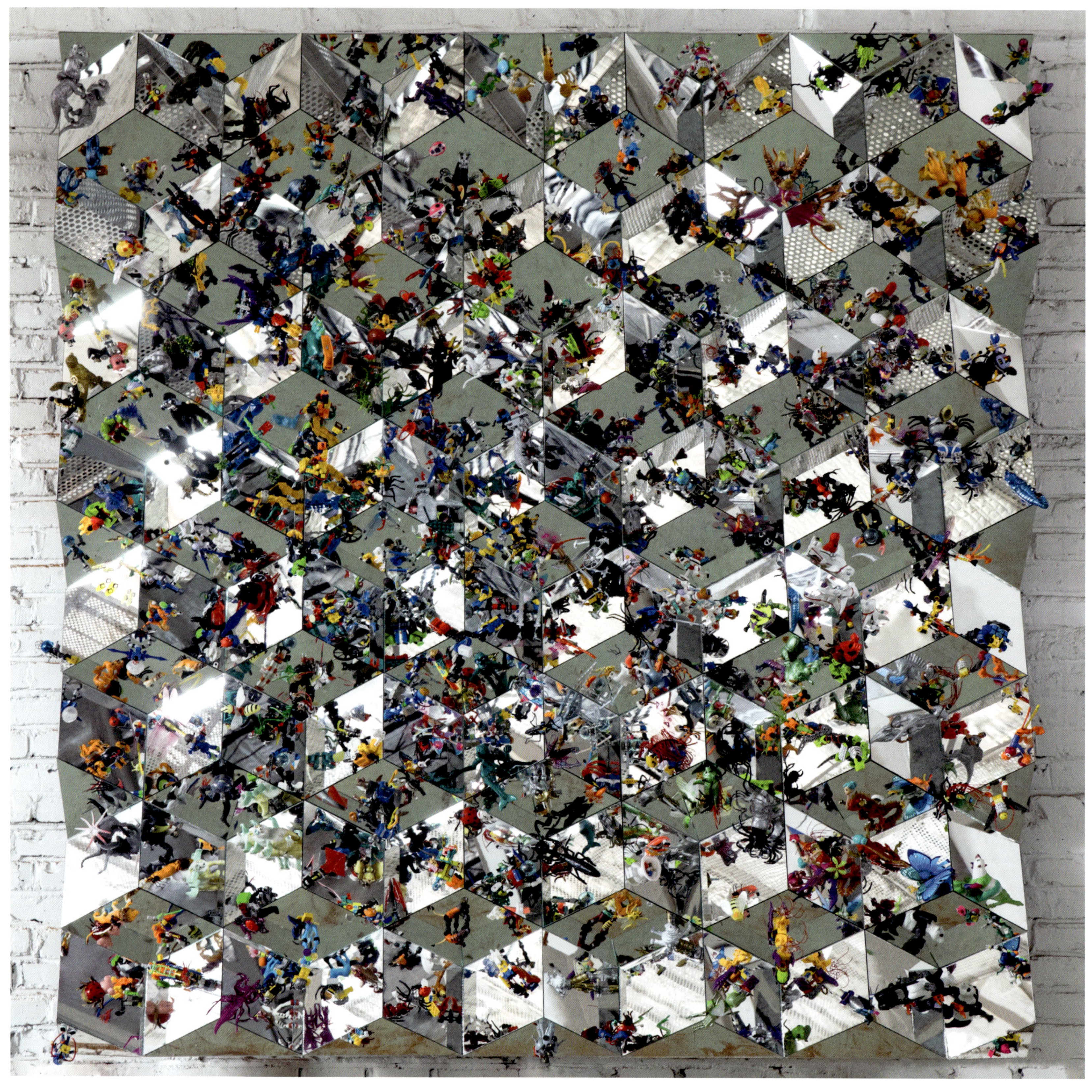

Götter erobern den Garten der Roboter, 2019
Aluminiumblech, Spiegelglas, verändertes Spielzeug, Acrylfarbe, Emailfarbe
200 × 180 × 30 cm

Gods Conquer the Robots' Garden, 2019
Aluminium sheet, glass mirror, modified toys, acrylic paint, enamel paint
200 × 180 × 30 cm

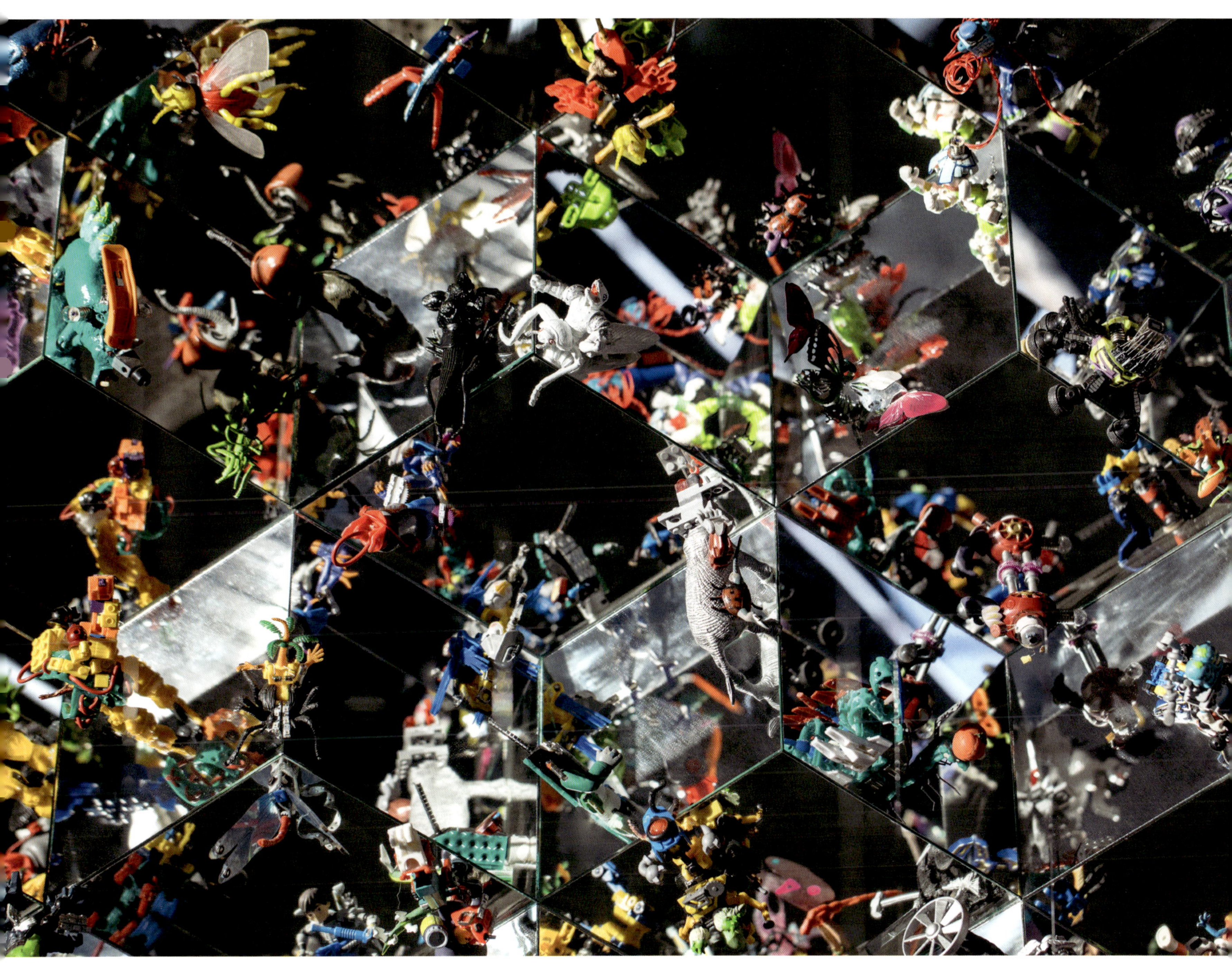

Götter erobern den Garten der Roboter, Detail

Gods Conquer the Robots' Garden, detail

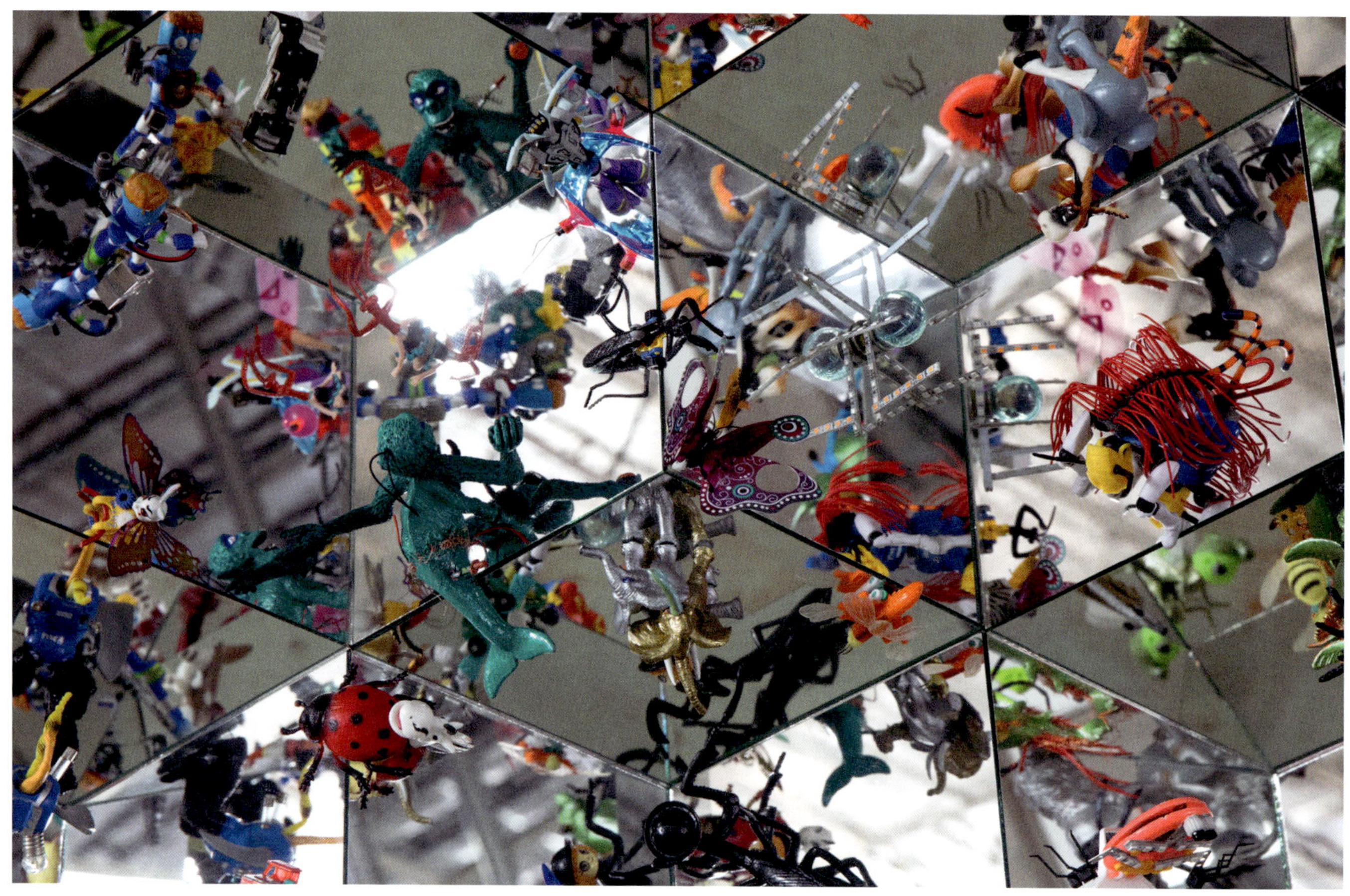

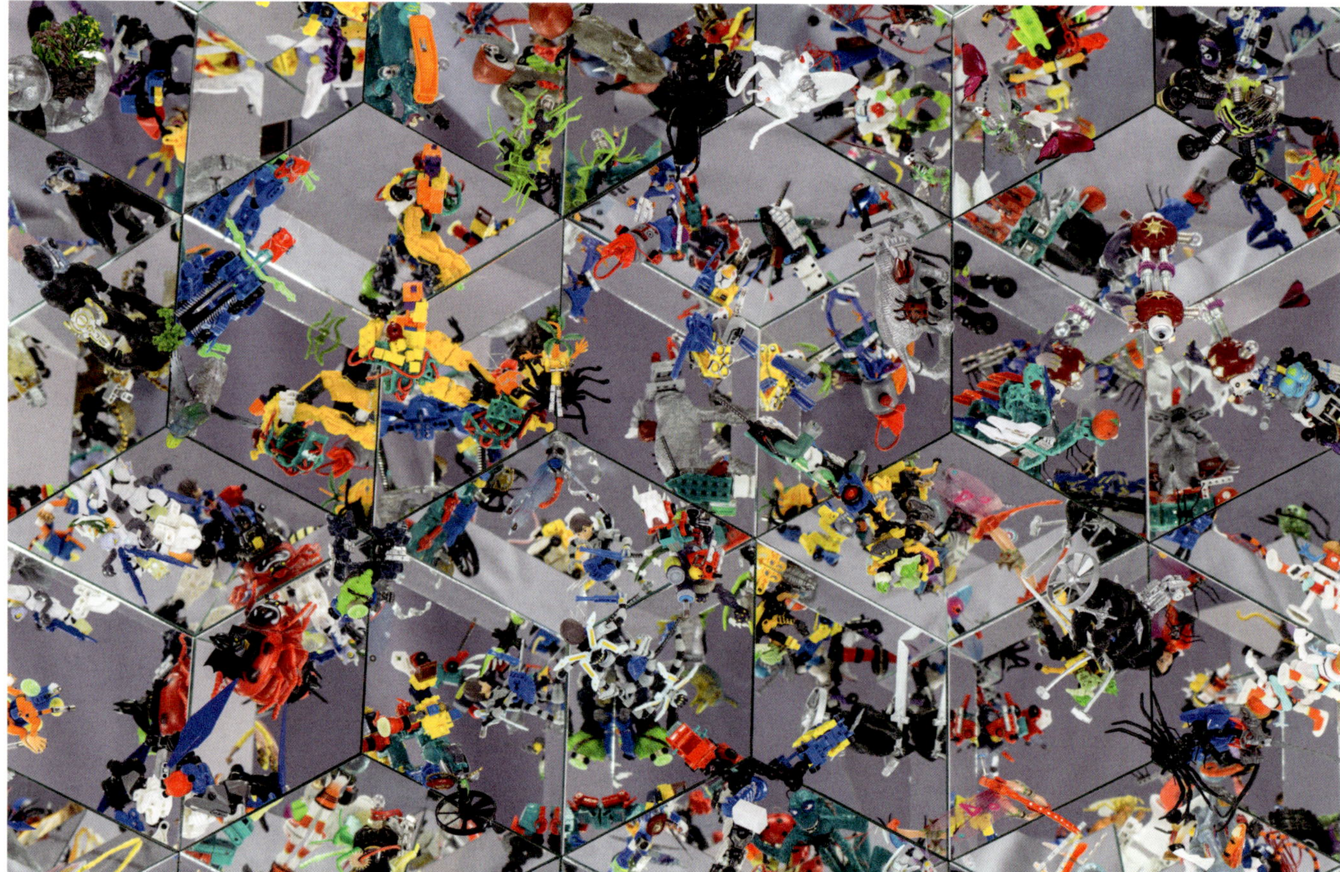

Götter erobern den Garten der Roboter, Details

Gods Conquer the Robots' Garden, details

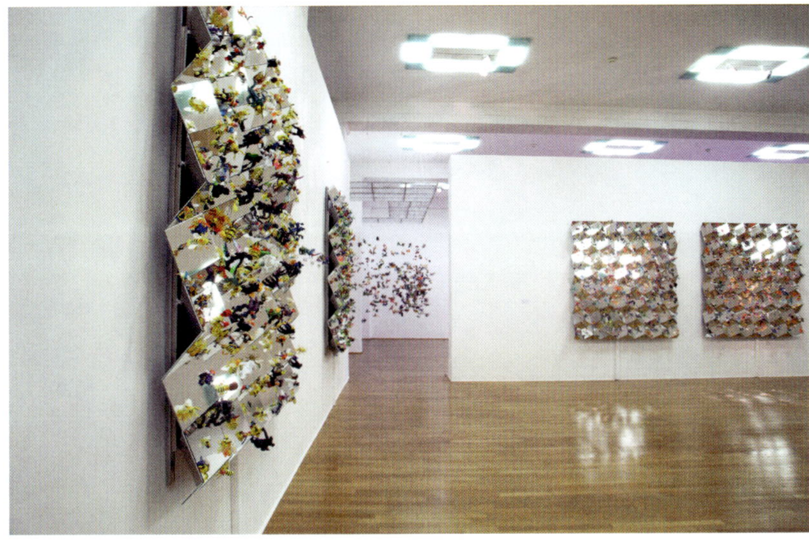
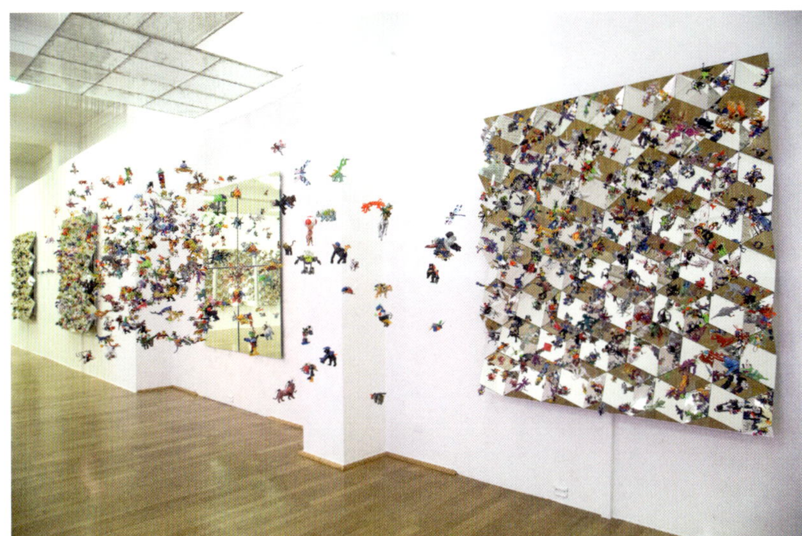
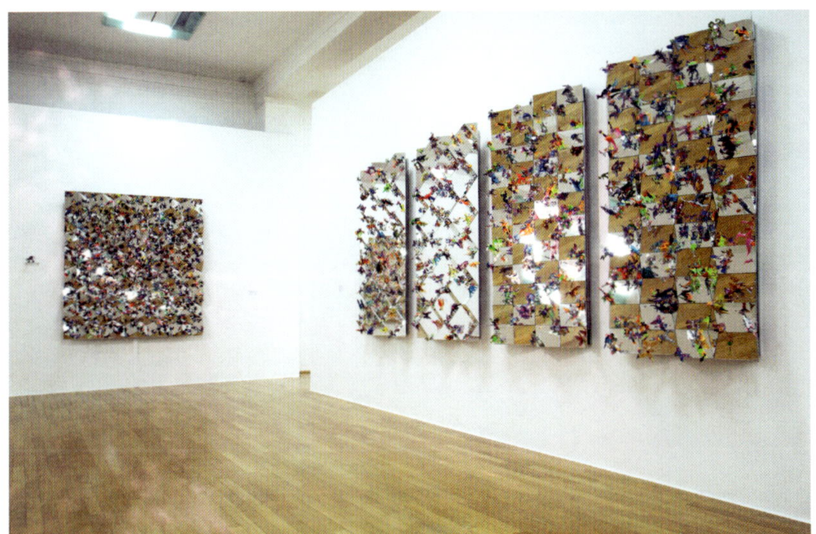
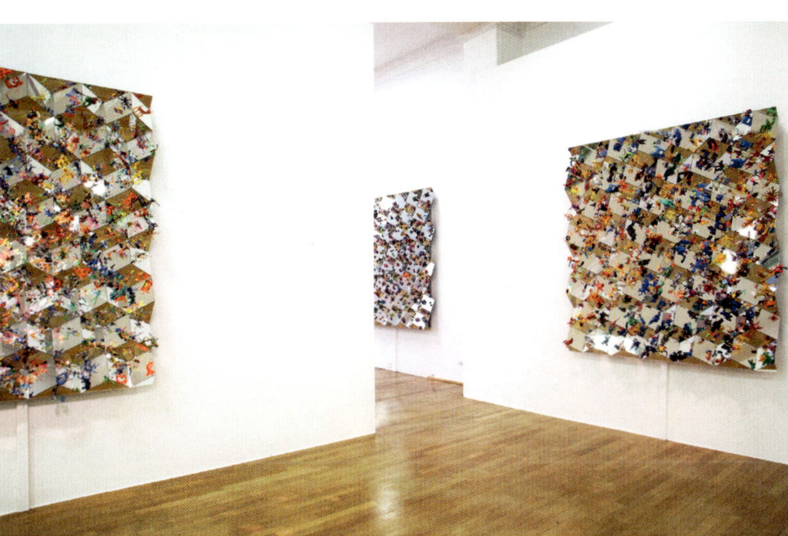

Götter erobern den Garten der Roboter, Ansicht der Installation im Ludwig Museum, Koblenz, 2019

Gods Conquer the Robots' Garden, view of the installation in the Ludwig Museum, Koblenz, 2019

Die Götter der neuen Arten

The Gods of New Species

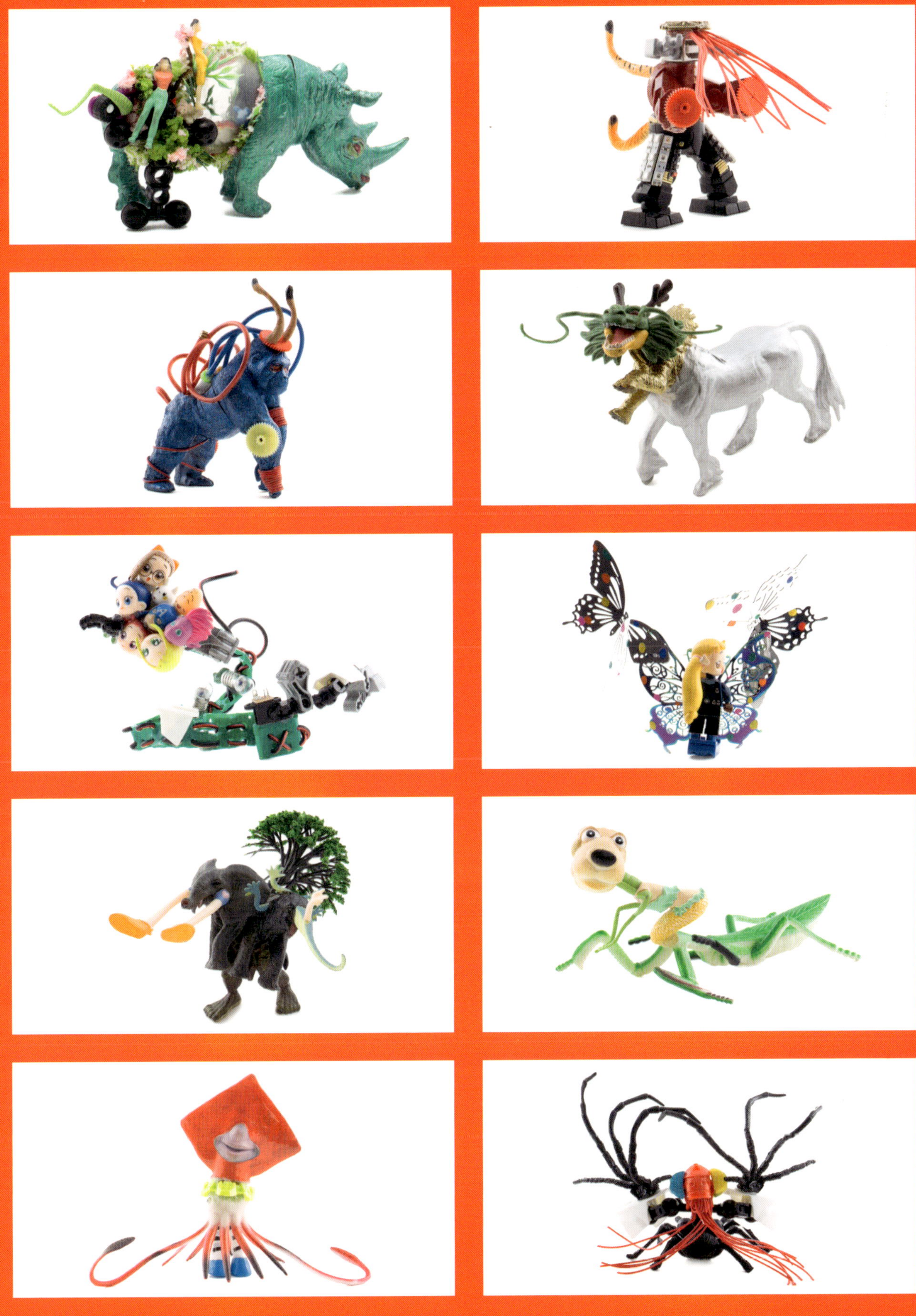

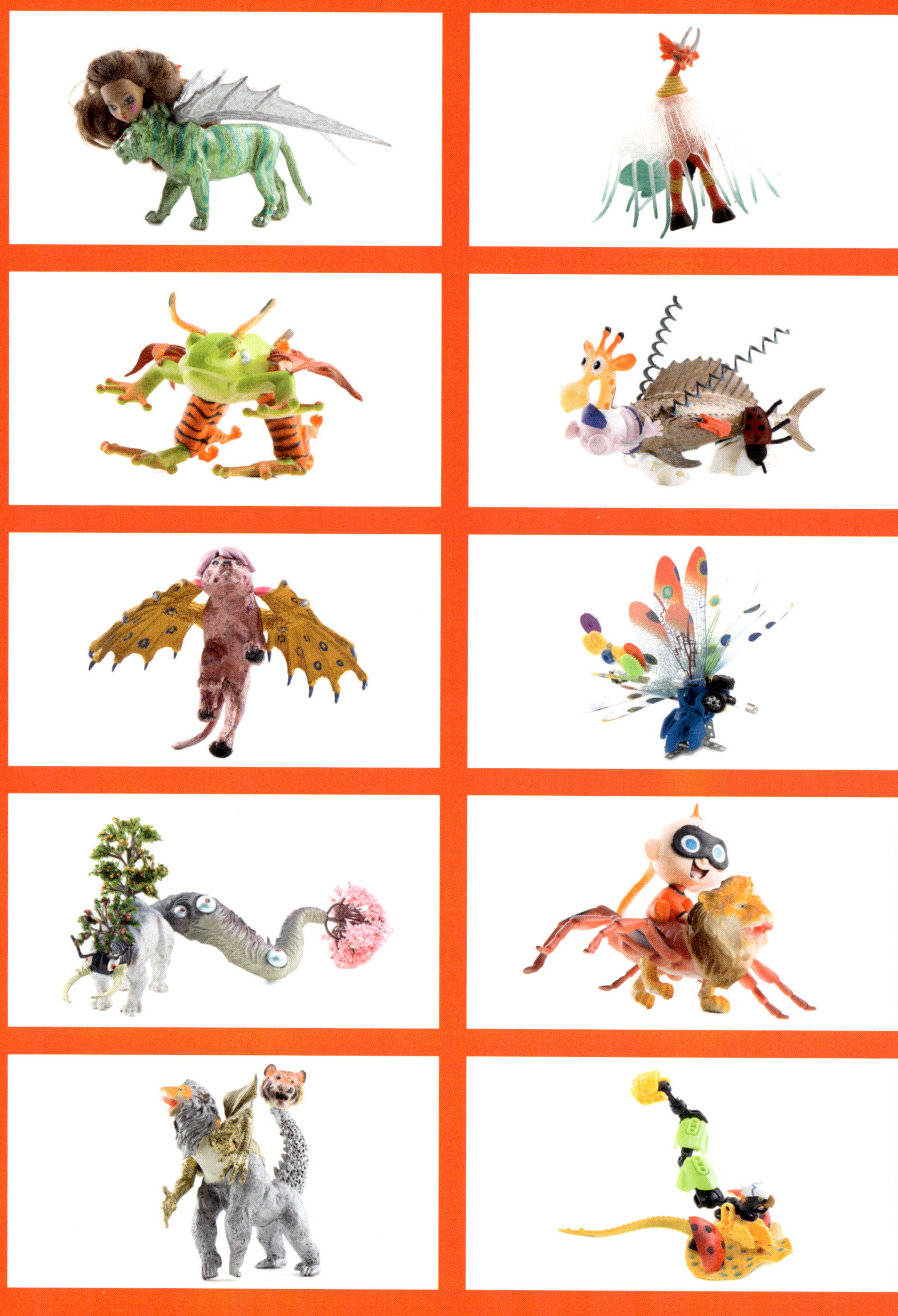

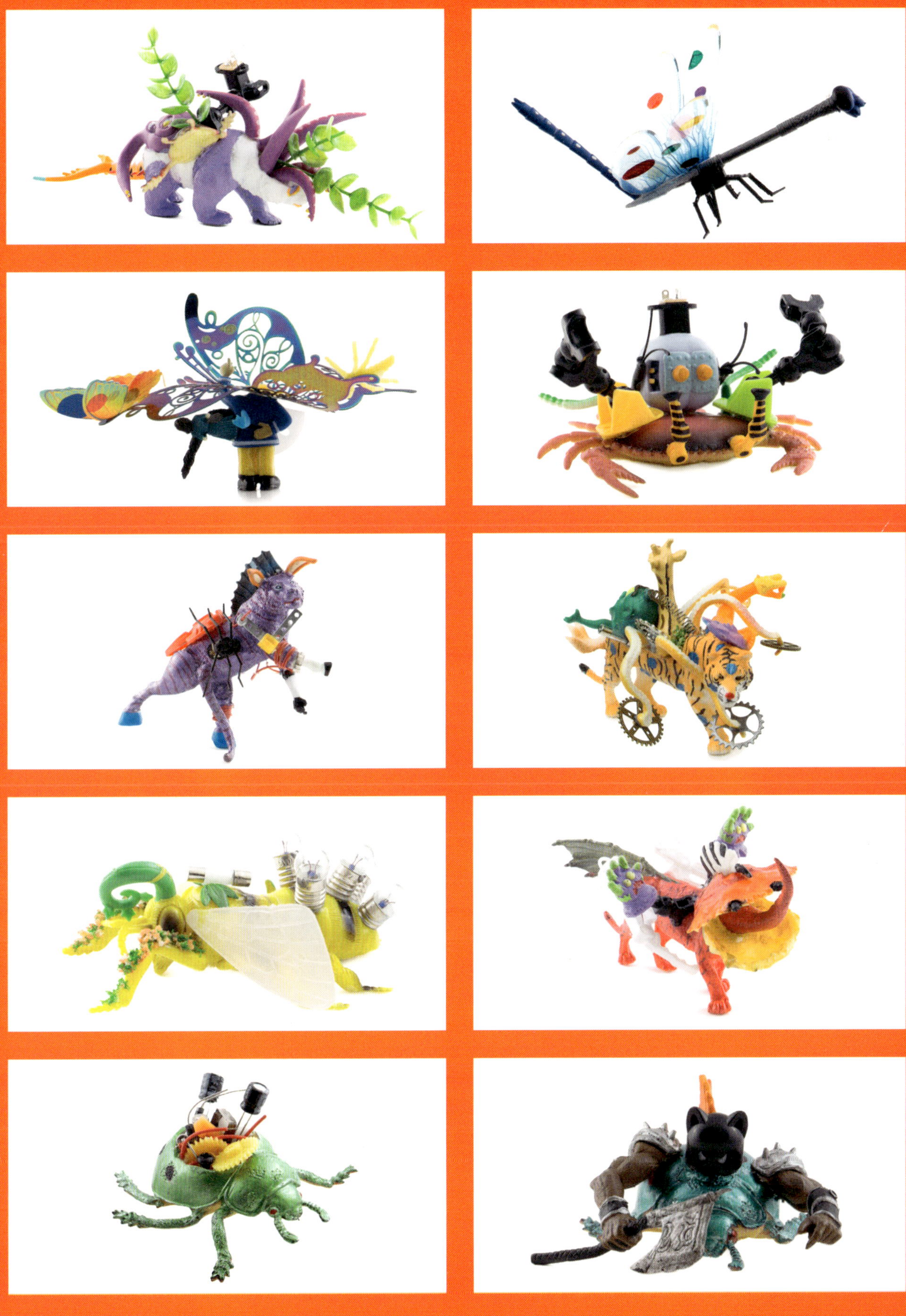

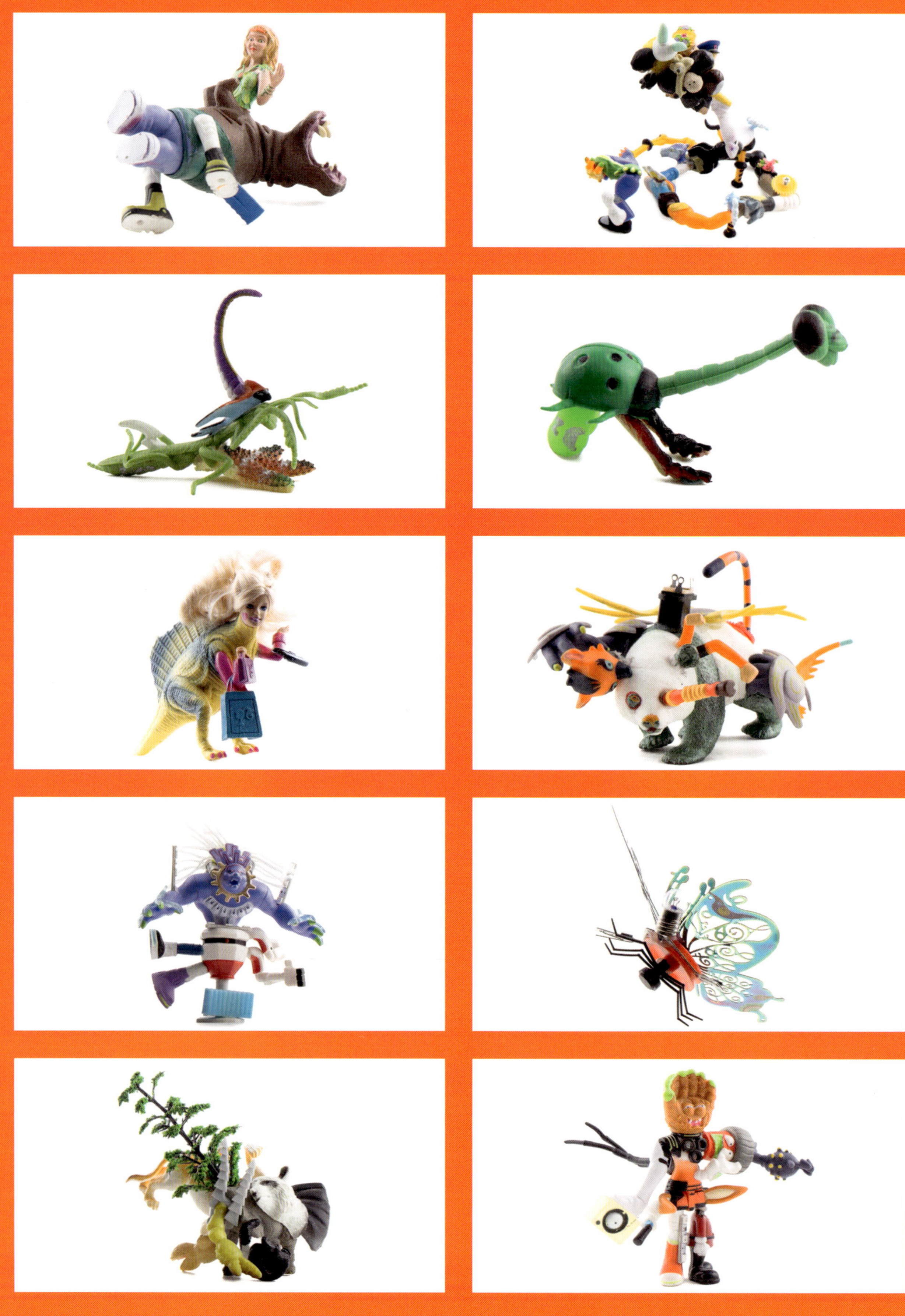

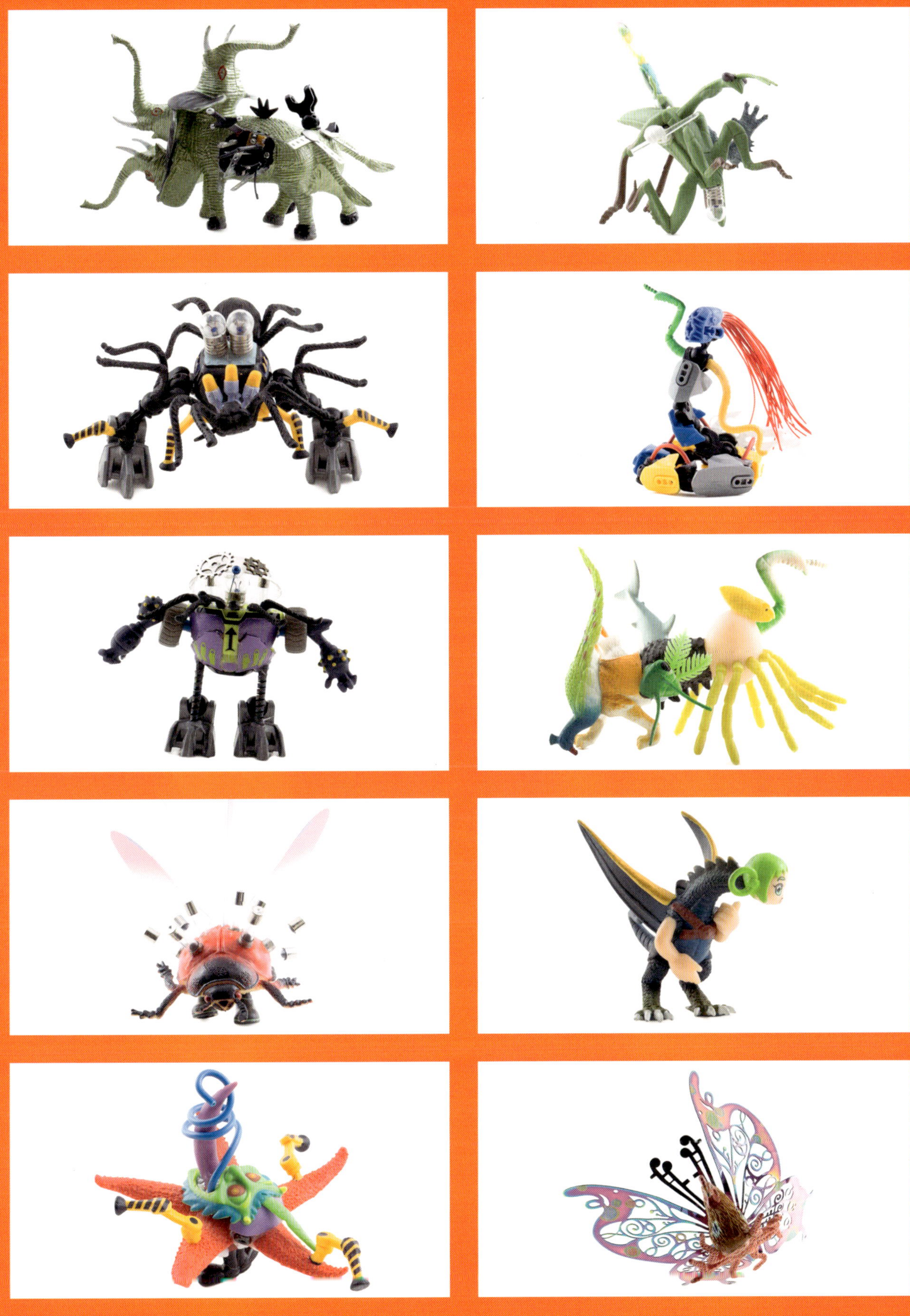

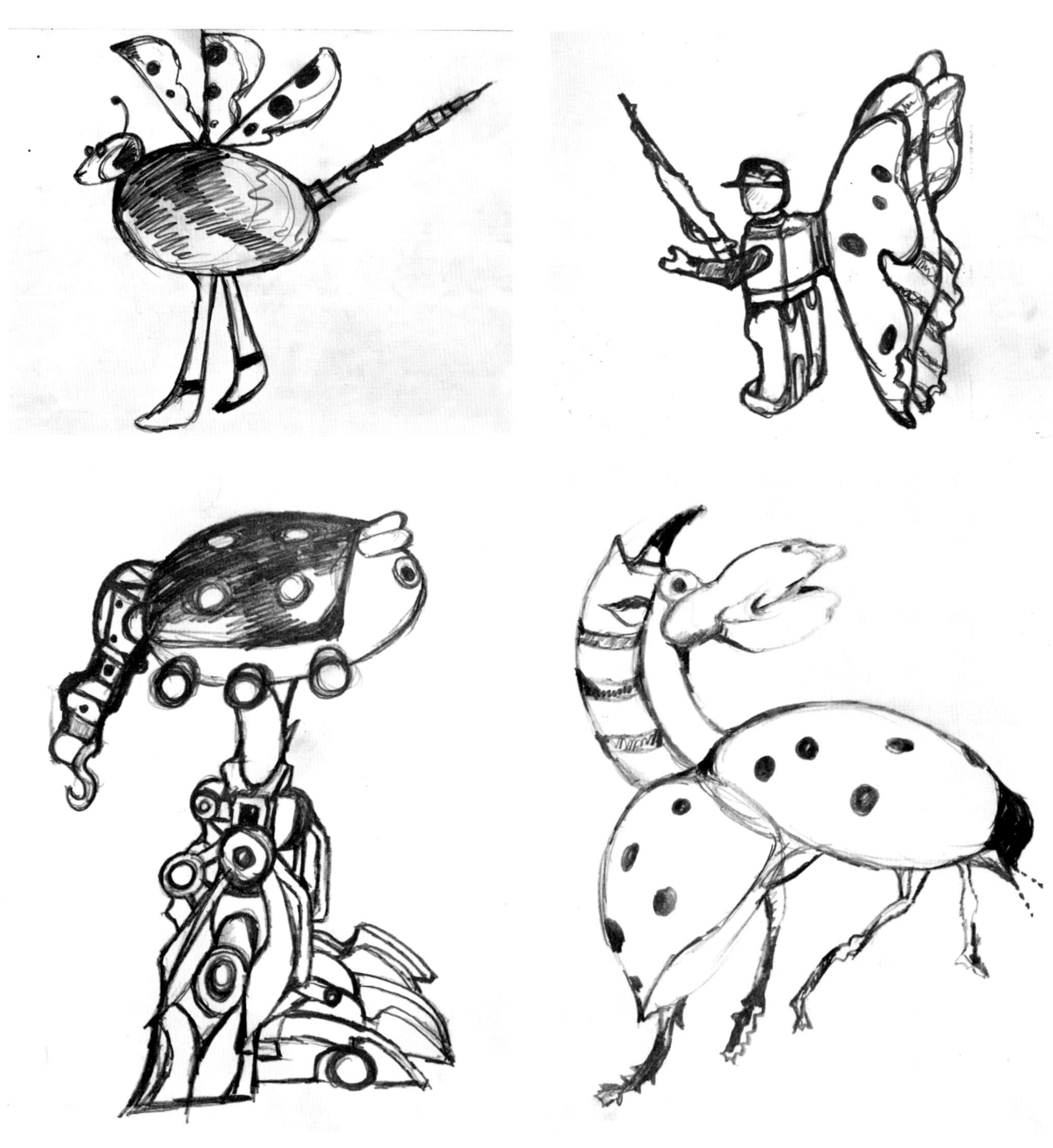

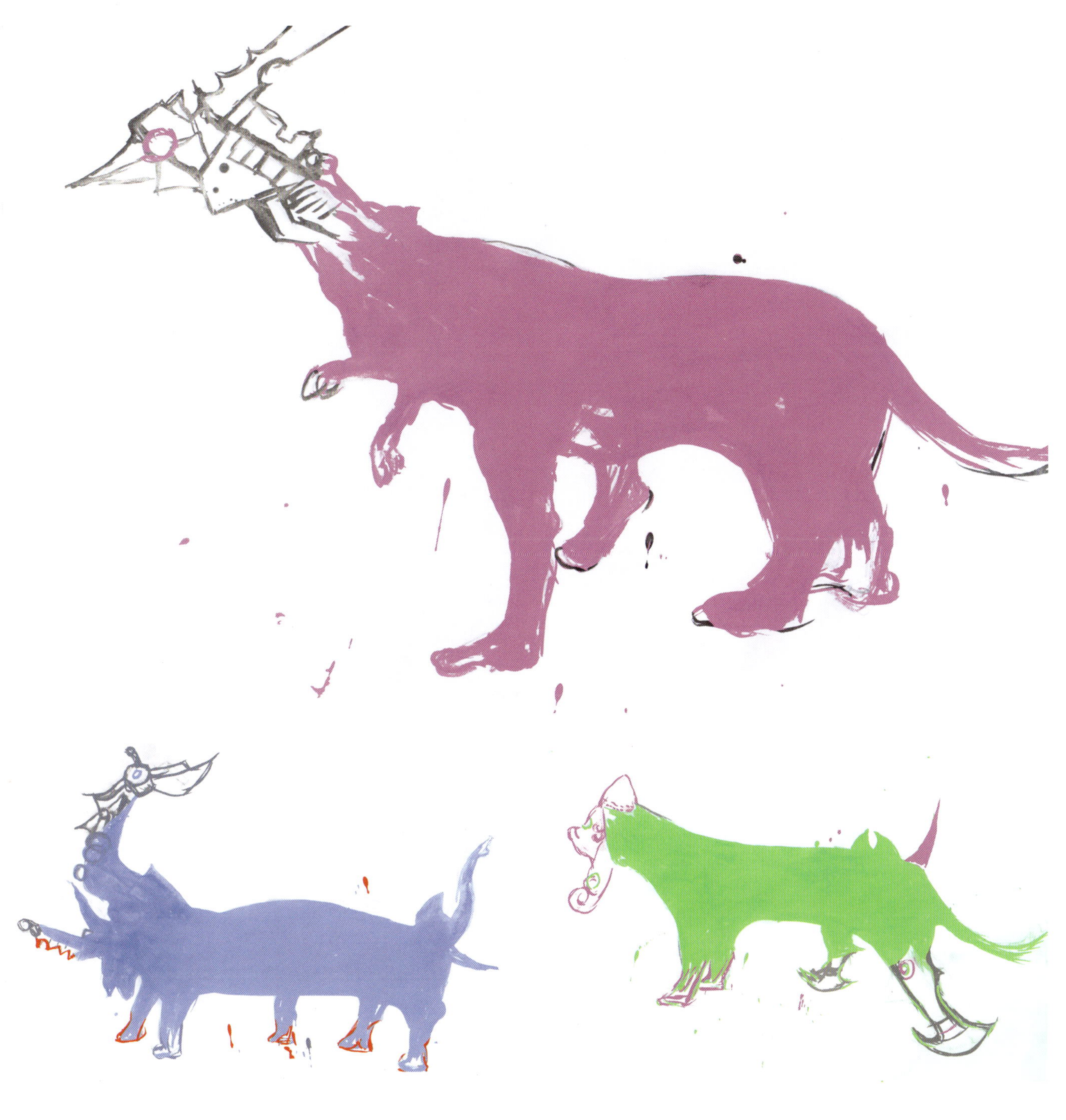

Die Götter der neuen Arten, 2019
Mixed Media
21 x 29.7 cm

The Gods of New Species, 2019
Mixed media
21 x 29.7 cm

Erwartungen und Nachsinnen im Zeitalter der Neugenese: Kontext, Struktur und Bedeutung von Deng Guoyuans *New Species* Serie

Wang Duanting

Gentechnik und Künstliche Intelligenz zählen zweifellos zu den größten Herausforderungen, mit denen sich die moderne Gesellschaft konfrontiert sieht. Grund dafür ist, dass diese beiden Technologien nicht nur einen maßgeblichen Einfluss auf das menschliche Leben ausüben, sondern auch das Schicksal der Weltzivilisationen mitbestimmen werden.

Seit ihrer Entstehung in den 1970er-Jahren hat sich die Gentechnik rapide weiterentwickelt und bahnbrechende Ergebnisse hervorgebracht. Diese Technologie, die die Krankheits- und Insektenresistenz und ertragreiche Pflanzensorten in die Landwirtschaft einführte, und neue Medikamente und Behandlungstechniken hervorbrachte, trägt somit zum Kampf gegen Hunger und Krankheiten bei. Die Gentechnik wurde jedoch von Beginn an von der Gesellschaft hinterfragt und die Menschen diskutieren über die Sicherheit von gentechnisch veränderten Lebensmitteln. Die Geburt des geklonten Schafs Dolly 1997 schlug hohe Wellen unter Wissenschaftlern, Politikern und in religiösen Kreisen, und löste eine langanhaltende Debatte über Gentechnologie und Ethik aus. Als 2018 das erste genetisch veränderte Baby auf die Welt kam, war die ethische Grenze erreicht worden und starker Widerstand erhob sich in der gesamten Gesellschaft und in der internationalen Wissenschaftsgemeinde. Stephen William Hawking äußerte sich hierzu folgendermaßen: „Das Gesetz kann Menschen daran hindern, Gene zu verändern, aber die Menschheit kann der Versuchung nicht widerstehen".

Als ein Zweig der Computerwissenschaften, kann die Künstliche Intelligenz menschliche intellektuelle Aktivitäten nachahmen, über die individuelle Erinnerung hinausgehen und komplexe Kalkulationen durchführen, sodass menschliche Aufgaben schneller und effizienter ausgeführt werden können. Diese Technologie wurde seit ihrem Auftreten in den 1970er-Jahren zunehmend auf verschiedenen Gebieten der menschlichen Gesellschaft angewandt, und begann nach und nach die menschliche Arbeit

The Expectation and Rumination in the Era of Re-Genesis: The Context, Grammar and Significance of Deng Guoyuan's *New Species* Series

Wang Duanting

Undoubtedly, gene engineering and artificial intelligence are among the most popular topics in modern society. This is because the above two technologies are exerting significant influence on human lives, or will change the direction of the civilizations in the world.

Since its born in 1970s, the gene engineering has developed rapidly, with great achievements. This technology not only brings disease and insect tolerance and high-yield crops to agriculture, but also provides new medicine and treatments techniques to medical science, contributing to the fight against hunger and disease. But the gene engineering has been questioned by the public since the beginning, and people have been arguing about the safety of genetically modified foods. The birth of the cloned Dolly in 1997 caused strong repercussions in the scientific, political, and religious circles in the world, and led to a long-standing discussion on genetic technology and ethics. The genetically edited baby was given birth in 2018, which has touched the bottom line of human ethics, and has been strongly resisted by the entire society and the international scientific community. Stephen William Hawking said, "the law can prohibit humans from editing genes, but humanity cannot resist the temptation."

As a branch of computer science, artificial intelligence can simulate human intellectual activities and have the ability to go beyond the individual's memory and perform complex calculations, so that people's work can be completed more quickly and efficiently. This technology has been more and more widely applied to various fields of human society since its appearance in the 1970s, and it has become more and more popular to replace human labour. In 1997, IBM's Deep Blue computer defeated chess master Kasparov; in 2016, Google's artificial intelligence AlphaGo defeated South Korea's World Go Champion Lee Sedol; in 2017, Sophia, a simulation robot manufactured by the Hanson Robotics, was able to talk freely with humans

zu ersetzen. 1997 forderte der Schachcomputer Deep Blu von IBM den Schachweltmeister Kasparow heraus. 2016 forderte Googles künstliche Intelligenz AlphaGo den südkoreanischen Go-Weltmeister Lee Sedol heraus. 2017 gelang es Sophia, einem von Hanson Robotics produzierten humanoiden Roboter, frei mit Menschen zu sprechen und eine Rede zu halten. Sophia erhielt sogar die Staatsbürgerschaft vonseiten der saudisch-arabischen Regierung. Sie war hiermit der erste Roboter weltweit, dem eine Staatsbürgerschaft zugestanden wurde. Im Februar 2019 lancierten die chinesische Xinhua News Agency und die Sogou Company den „weltweit ersten weiblichen KI-Nachrichtensprecher". Dann tauchten die Sexroboter auf. Jetzt kommen die Roboter als Partner… Daraus ist ersichtlich, inwieweit sich die Intelligenz von Robotern rasant verbessert und ihr Potenzial grenzenlos ist. Aus all diesen Fakten geht hervor, dass viele Arbeitsplätze zunehmend durch intelligente Roboter ersetzt werden, und dass sich die der Arbeit inhärente soziale Verteilung grundlegend verändert.

Ich nenne das Zeitalter der Gentechnik und Künstlichen Intelligenz „Das Zeitalter der Neugenese". Es besteht kein Zweifel daran, dass die mit der Gentechnik und Künstlichen Intelligenz verbundenen Ergebnisse die tiefgreifendsten Umbrüchen seit der biblischen Erschaffung von Himmel und Erde darstellen. Wir werden uns bewusst, dass der Mensch durch die Gentechnik eine gottähnliche Schöpferkraft erlangt und noch nie dagewesene Arten in die Welt eingeführt hat. Die Künstliche Intelligenz hat eine neue Form von Leben hervorgebracht, das „siliciumdioxidbasierte" Leben. Diese Art von Leben entwickelt sich mit rapider Geschwindigkeit weiter und ist dabei, das „kohlenstoffbasierte Leben" zu verdrängen und die Welt zu beherrschen. Sind Gentechnik und Künstliche Intelligenz für die Menschen Segen oder Fluch? Sind sie wirklich die „Büchse der Pandora", die geöffnet wurde?

In einem seiner Vorträge legt Yuval Noah Harari, der Autor des Buches *Homo Deus: Eine Geschichte von Morgen* dar, „dass ein Risiko der neuen Technologien darin liegt, dass einige Menschen zu Übermenschen aufsteigen, während andere Menschen, aller Voraussicht nach der Großteil, zu einer neuen wertlosen Klasse degradiert wird. Die Revolutionen des 21. Jahrhunderts könnten folglich eine neue überflüssige Klasse hervorbringen, Millionen, sogar Milliarden von Menschen ohne jeden ökonomischen Wert und politische Macht, da sie nichts besser machen können als die Computer, Roboter und KI. Das ist vielleicht das drängendste soziale, politische und ökonomische Thema des 21. Jahrhundert."

Als Künstler verfolgt Deng Guoyuan die Entwicklung der Gentechnik und Künstlichen Intelligenz sowie die unbekannten Auswirkungen dieser neuen Technologien mit großem Interesse. Seine neuen Werke geben seine Vorstellungswelt in einer zeitgenössischen Kunstsprache wieder und umfassen Arbeiten, die auf einer Vielzahl von künstlerischen Ausdrucksformen beruhen („ausklappbare Spiegelinstallation", „Neoninstallation mit Edelstahlplatten" und „Neonskulptur"), sowie fünf Werkserien (*Der Garten der Götter*, *Loreleys Garten*, *Die Götter der neuen Arten*, *Das Sterben der Götter*, *Offenbarung*). Der allgemeine Werktitel von „einklappbare Spiegelinstallation" ist *Der Garten der Götter* mit acht Arbeiten: *Schmetterlinge erobern den Garten der Dinosaurier*, *Libellen erobern den Garten der Tiger*, *Gottesanbeterinnen erobern den Garten der Löwen*, *Käfer erobern den Garten der Elefanten*, *Bienen erobern den Garten*

and deliver a speech. She was even granted the citizenship by the Saudi Arabian government. She becomes the first intelligent robot to obtain citizenship in the world; in February 2019, China's Xinhua News Agency and Sogou Company jointly launched the "world's first artificial intelligence female anchor;" the sex robots have emerged, the robot partners are coming to us... All of these show that the intelligence of robots is improving by leaps and bounds, and its potential is limitless. Objective facts also tell us that more and more occupations are being replaced by intelligent robots, and the inherent social division of labour will be completely changed.

I call the era of gene engineering and artificial intelligence "the era of re-genesis." There is no doubt that the results of gene engineering and artificial intelligence are the biggest changes in the world since the creation of the heavens and the earth according to the Bible. We have noticed that, through the gene engineering, human beings have acquired God-like creativity and brought unprecedented new species to the world. Artificial intelligence has created a new life form, namely "silica-based life." This kind of life is rapidly evolving, and has a tendency to replace the "carbon-based life" and even dominate the world. For humans, is gene engineering and artificial intelligence a blessing or a curse? Are they really the "Pandora's box" that was opened?

In a speech, Yuval Noah Harari, the author of the book *Homo Deus: A Brief History of Tomorrow* told us, "one danger than the new technologies pose is that while some people will be upgraded to being super humans, other people, maybe even the most of the people in the world will become part of the new useless class. The revolutions of the 21st century might create a new useless class, millions, even billions of people with no economic value and no political power, because they can't do anything better than computers and robots and AI. This may be the biggest social, political and economic question of 21st century."

As an artist, Deng Guoyuan pays close attention to the development of gene engineering and artificial intelligence, as well as unknown consequence of these new technologies. His new artworks are unique expression of his focus through contemporary artistic language. These artworks are a range of works made up of a variety of artistic form (folding mirror installation, stainless steel plate neon installation and neon sculpture) and five series works (*The Gardens of the Gods, Loreley's Garden, The Gods of New Species, Passing of the Gods, Revelation*). The general title of the folding mirror installation is *The Gardens of the Gods*, which includes eight works: *Butterflies Conquer the Dinosaurs' Garden, Dragonflies Conquer the Tigers' Garden, Mantises Conquer the Lions' Garden, Beetles Conquer the Elephants' Garden, Bees Conquer the Orangutans' Garden, Spiders Conquer the Pandas' Garden, Sea Creatures Conquer the Hippos' Garden*, and *Gods Conquer the Robots' Garden*. Among them, the *Butterflies Conquer the Dinosaurs' Garden* is a tetraptych, while the *Dragonflies Conquer the Tigers' Garden* is diptych. The neon sculpture is called the *Loreley's Garden*, which is made up of ten different geometric stone blocks and four metamorphosed animals, namely butterfly, dinosaur, dragonfly, and dragon horse. The *Revelation* is made up of two stainless steel plate neon installations and an artwork titled *Passing of the Gods*. On the stainless-steel plates, the artist wrote

der Orang-Utans, *Spinnen erobern den Garten der Pandas*, *Meerestiere erobern den Garten der Flusspferde* und *Die Götter erobern den Garten der Roboter. Schmetterlinge erobern den Garten der Dinosaurier* besteht aus vier Teilen, während *Libellen erobern den Garten der Tiger* ein Diptychon ist. Die „Neonskulptur" trägt den Werktitel *Loreleys Garten.* Der Garten setzt sich aus zehn verschiedenen Steinblöcken und vier metamorphosierten Tieren zusammen, und zwar Schmetterling, Dinosaurier, Libelle und Drachenpferd. Offenbarung besteht hingegen aus zwei „Edelstahlplatten-Neoninstallationen" und einer Arbeit namens *Das Sterben der Götter.* Der Künstler hat die Edelstahlplatten mit einigen Wörtern auf Englisch – Gene Engineering, Gene Mutation, DNA Recombination, Evolution, Artificial Intelligence und Virtual Reality – zusammen mit Neonlichtern versehen. Diese Begriffe sind die Schlüsselwörter der Werkserie. Die Tiere in diesen Arbeiten haben nichts mit denen der realen Welt gemeinsam. Sie stellen vielmehr Dekonstruktionen und Neukombinationen einer Vielzahl von Spielzeugmodellen von Tieren und Pflanzen dar. Genauer gesagt handelt es sich um neue Tiere, die aus den Körperteilen verschiedener Kreaturen realisiert sind. Jede „einklappbare Spiegelinstallation" umfasst an die 300 Kreaturen, die gesamte Werkserie über 4.000. Neben Insekten und Bestien zählen zu den Bestandteilen dieser bizarren Tiere Puppen, Spielzeugautos, Spielzeugflugzeuge, Spielzeugroboter, Transformatoren, Legosteine, LED, Glühbirnen, Schraubkappen, Getriebe und elektronische Komponenten. Die bizarren Tieren nehmen demzufolge surrealistische Züge an, die aus der Vorstellungswelt des Künstlers entstehen. Auch die Materialien der Arbeit unterliegen dem Zufallsprinzip. Ich nenne diese Werkserie *Neue Arten*.

Die Gentechnik und die Künstliche Intelligenz haben Guoyuan dazu inspiriert, bizarre Tiere zu erschaffen. Den realistischen Hintergrund von Guoyuans *Neue Arten* Serie bildet somit das „neue Schöpfungszeitalter", das mit der Gentechnik und Künstlichen Intelligenz einhergeht. Darüber hinaus wurde Guoyuan aber auch von der alten chinesischen Mythologie, insbesondere dem literarischen Werk *Klassiker der Berge und Meere* angeregt. Guoyuan unternimmt anhand dieser neuen Arbeiten den Versuch, ihren historischen Kontext miteinander zu verknüpfen und weitere Beziehungen zwischen ihnen auszuloten. Die *Neue Arten* Serie ist zusammenfassend gesagt eine spirituelle Reflexion über Guoyuans künstlerische Annäherung an dieses neue Zeitalter der technologischen Innovation und ihre Errungenschaften.

Guoyuan ist ein offener Künstler, der auch einige Zeit in Europa verbrachte. Er löst nicht nur die Grenzen zwischen der künstlerischen Sprache auf, sondern verwendet auch eine Vielzahl von künstlerischen Mitteln für seinen Schaffensprozess. Darüber hinaus geht er über ein auf den lokalen Kontext begrenztes Bewusstsein hinaus und setzt sich mit universellen Belangen auseinander. Seit dem 21. Jahrhundert widmet er sich zunehmend der Installationskunst und präsentierte in diesem Zusammenhang die *Metamatically Birth* Serie (2009-2017) und die *Noahs Garten* Serie (2015-2017), welche mit der Umwelt verbundene Themen aufgreifen. Die *Neue Arten* Serie beweist, dass Guoyuan ein neues Niveau in seinem künstlerischen Schaffen bezüglich künstlerische Techniken und Themen erreicht hat.

Es ist allseits bekannt, dass die Installationskunst eine antikünstlerische und antiästhetische Form der Konzeptkunst ist, die ursprünglich auf Marcel Duchamp zu-

down some English terms – gene engineering, gene mutation, DNA recombination, evolution, artificial intelligence and virtual reality – with neon lights. These are the key words of this series. Animals in these artworks are not the same with the ones in reality. They are, in fact, deconstruction and recombination of a variety of toy models of animals and plants. More precisely, they are new animals made up of body parts of varieties of creatures. Each of the "folding mirror installation" involves nearly 300 creatures, and the whole series includes more than 4000 creatures. Besides insects and beasts, the components of these bizarre animals include dolls, toy cars, toy airplanes, toy robots, transformers, Legos, LED, light bulbs, screw caps, gears, and electronic components. Therefore, these bizarre animals incorporate surrealistic characteristics – they are not real animals, but creatures on the basis of the artist's imagination; even the materials of the artwork are randomness. I nominate this series of works as *New Species* series.

Undoubtedly, the results of gene engineering and artificial intelligence have inspired Deng Guoyuan to create these bizarre animals. That is to say, the "new creation era" brought by the gene engineering and artificial intelligence is the realistic background of Deng Guoyuan's *New Species* series. In addition, the ancient Chinese mythology of *The Classic of Mountains and Seas* also inspired Deng Guoyuan, and made this set of contemporary artworks with the function of connecting the historical context, and build further relationship between them. In any case, the *New Species* series is a spiritual reflection of Deng Guoyuan's artistic approach to this unprecedented era of technological innovation and its new things.

Deng Guoyuan is an artist with an open mind. This artistic quality is related to his experience of living in Europe. He not only breaks the boundaries between artistic language, but also use a variety of artistic means to create. Moreover, he transcends the narrow local consciousness and regards the universal concern of all mankind as his own creative theme. Since the 21st century, he has been increasingly devoted to installation art, and has launched the *Mathematically Birth* series (2009-2017) and the *Noah's Garden* series (2015-2017), which are excellent installations with the theme of ecological environment. In terms of artistic techniques and artistic themes, the *New Species* series marks that Deng Guoyuan's art has reached a new height.

It is known that the installation art is an anti-artistic and anti-aesthetic conceptual art originally created by Marcel Duchamp. However, according to a basic law of the development of Western art – the negation of negation – today's installation art has become a post-conceptualist art. Post-conceptual installation art has four characteristics. First, the installation art has changed from anti-art to a new art style, which is a formal and aesthetic style. Second, the function of installation art has changed from critical to narrative. Like traditional art styles such as painting and sculpture, it can also present any subject matter and theme, and even being lyric. Third, the installation has combined with the sculpture. The "sculpturization" of the installation and the "installationization" of the sculpture become obvious and common. Fourth, the relationship between the installation works and the space for displaying becomes inseparable. Artists often create works based on specific spaces. They

rückgeht. Gemäß den Prinzipien der westlichen Kunstentwicklung – die Negation der Negation – gilt die zeitgenössische Installationskunst als postkonzeptuelle Kunst. Die postkonzeptuelle Installationskunst kennzeichnet sich durch vier Eigenschaften. Erstens hat sich die Installationskunst von einer Antikunst hin zu einem neuen Kunststil entwickelt, der sich als formal und ästhetisch definieren lässt. Zweitens liegt die Funktion der Installationskunst nicht mehr in der kritischen Beurteilung, sondern in der Narration. Analog zu traditionellen Kunstgattungen wie Malerei und Skulptur kann die Installationskunst jeden Gegenstand behandeln und sogar lyrische Züge annehmen. Drittens wurde die Installationskunst mit der Skulptur verbunden, wobei es ein gängiges Vorgehen war, dass der Installation „skulpturale" und der „Skulptur" installative Eigenschaften verliehen wurden. Viertens bilden die installativen Arbeiten und der Raum in denen diese ausgestellt werden eine unzertrennbare Einheit. Künstler/innen realisieren des Öfteren Arbeiten, die auf spezifische, ihre Größe und Ausrichtung determinierende Räume abgestimmt sind, berücksichtigen aber auch die lokale Geografie, die Geschichte und das kulturelle Umfeld als integrativen Bestandteil.

Guoyuans *Neue Arten* Serie weist alle Merkmale auf, die den Postkonzeptualismus ausmachen. Die Tiere sind das Ergebnis eines Prozesses der Aneignung und des Re-engineerings von Ready-Mades. Durch die Verwendung von Glasspiegeln, Edelstahlplatten, Neonlichtern und LED-Lampen erhalten die Arbeiten eine starke visuelle Wirkkraft. Insbesondere aufgrund der reflektierenden Glasspiegel vermitteln die seltsam anmutenden Tiere den Eindruck, dass die Monsterwesen überhandnehmen. Dank der Vielzahl von bizarren, aber schönen Tierformen, hat die gesamte Installation eine suggestive visuelle Ästhetik, die vor allem Kinder anspricht.

Im Allgemeinen finden in Installationen, die von chinesischen Künstler/innen realisiert werden, organische Materialien und manuelle Techniken Verwendung, darunter Fasern, Stoffe, Papier, Holz und Bambus, während industrielle Materialien und Techniken wie Metall, Glas und Plastik in geringerem Maße zum Einsatz kommen. Auf akustische und optische Mittel wird hingegen kaum zurückgegriffen. Neben ökonomischen Aspekten ist die Herausbildung jeder dieser Eigenschaften eng mit der Produktion, dem Lebensstil und den kulturellen Traditionen der ländlichen Bevölkerung verknüpft. Meiner Meinung nach kann man in der Vorliebe chinesischer Installationskünstler/innen für pflanzliche Materialien und Handwerkskunst ein Spiegelbild von der chinesischen bäuerliche Zivilisation im zeitgenössischen Kunstschaffen sehen. Pflanzliche Materialien und manuelle Arbeiten sind die Produkte der Landwirtschaft und des Lebensstils der bäuerlichen Zivilisation, zu der die Chinesen natürlicherweise neigen. Chinesen lehnen die industrielle Produktion und den mit Metall und Maschinen assoziierten Lebensstil instinktiv ab. Im Gegensatz hierzu verwendet Guoyuan für die *Neue Arten* Serie (und die vorausgehende *Noahs Garten* Serie) zeitgenössische industrielle Materialien (insbesondere lichtelektrische Mittel), die sich nicht nur im zeitgenössischen China durch ihren einmaligen Charakter auszeichnen.

Darüber hinaus nimmt Guoyuan für den Produktionsprozess seiner *Neue Arten* Serie dieselbe Strategie der zeitgenössischen internationalen Kunstwelt an. Das heißt, der Künstler bietet Kreativität an, und wird von technischem Personal unterstützt. Die Produktion der gesamten Arbeit glich der Operation einer Heeresgruppe. In fünf Mo-

determine the size and orientation of works on the basis of space. Even local geography, history and cultural environment have been considered by the artists, and become constituent of the work.

Deng Guoyuan's *New Species* series fully embody the characteristics of post-conceptualism. All the animals in the works are the products of the appropriation and re-engineering of ready-mades. The use of glass mirrors, stainless steel plates, neon lights and LED lights give the work a strong visual impact. In particular, due to the reflective function of the glass mirror, the large number of bizarre animals present the illusion that monsters are overwhelming and swarming. Due to the large number of the bizarre but tidy animal shapes, the entire installation has a fascinating visual aesthetic, especially for children.

It is worth mentioning that in the installations created by Chinese artists, organic materials and hand-made techniques, such as fibre, cloth, paper, wood and bamboo, are widely used; but industrial materials and techniques, such as metal, glass and plastic, are less used; the application of acoustic and optical media is rare. In addition to funding, the formation of such feature is closely related to the production, living habits and cultural traditions of Chinese agricultural civilization. In my opinion, the preference of Chinese installation artists for vegetal materials and craftsmanship is a reflection of Chinese agricultural civilization in contemporary art creation. Vegetal materials and manual labour are the products of farming and lifestyle of the agricultural civilization, which are the indigenous preferences of Chinese people. The Chinese have an instinctive rejection towards industrial production and lifestyle produced by metal materials and machinery. In contrast, Deng Guoyuan's *New Species* series (and the previous *Noah's Garden* series) use contemporary industrial materials (especially photoelectric media), which are outstanding and precious in contemporary China and the global world.

In addition, the production method of Deng Guoyuan's *New Species* series also adopts the strategy of the international contemporary art world. That is, the artist proposes creativity, and is assisted by technical personnel. The production of the whole work took the form of military operations. In five months, more than 30 people participated in the production. It shows that it is a vast work.

The animals in Deng Guoyuan's *New Species* series are both new species brought about by gene engineering and artificial intelligence, and surreal gods created by himself. The artist has placed his expectation that the new technology will benefit human beings on these creatures. They also contain the anxiety and fear of the artist, because new technology may threaten human society. As part of the artwork, Deng Guoyuan conducted numerous social surveys on gene engineering and artificial intelligence. He invited people from all walks of life, including his friends, mayors, district heads, academicians, scientists, bank presidents, entrepreneurs and artists, to write down their views on gene engineering and artificial intelligence. Most of them hold a negative attitude. Such an investigation not only enhanced his passion for creation, but also enriched and deepened his understanding of new technologies.

naten waren über 30 Personen in den Produktionsprozess involviert, und das zeigt die Ausmaße dieses Werks.

Die von Guoyuan für die *Neue Arten* Serie realisierten Tiere stellen sowohl durch Gentechnik und Künstliche Intelligenz hervorgebrachte neue Arten als auch surreale, von ihm erschaffene Wesen dar, wobei sich der Künstler erhofft, dass die neue Technologie den Menschen mithilfe dieser Kreaturen zugutekommt. Diese teilen auch die Sorgen und Ängste des Künstlers, da die neuen Technologien eine Bedrohung für die Gesellschaft darstellen können. Als integrativer Bestandteil der Arbeit führte Guoyuan mehrere Umfragen zur Gentechnik und Künstlichen Intelligenz durch. Hierzu forderte er Personen aus allen Gesellschaftsschichten, darunter Freunde/innen, Bürgermeister/innen, Bezirksverwalter/innen, Akademiker/innen, Wissenschaftler/innen, Bankpräsident/innen, Unternehmer/innen und Künstler/innen dazu auf, ihre Gedanken zur Gentechnik und Künstlichen Intelligenz niederzuschreiben. Viele von ihnen sind diesen Technologien gegenüber negativ eingestellt. Diese Studie regte nicht nur Guoyuans künstlerischen Schaffensprozess an, sondern half ihm auch dabei, seine Kenntnisse über die neuen Technologien zu vertiefen.

Die Geschichte lehrt uns, dass die Menschen, wenn sie von unbekannten Kräften bedroht werden oder das Verhältnis zwischen Mensch und Natur aus dem Gleichgewicht gerät, ihre Probleme durch Mythenbildung zu lösen versuchen. Die griechische und römische Mythologie entstand auf diese Weise, und auch die alte chinesische Mythologie, die den *Klassiker der Berge und Meere* hervorbrachte, wurde in einem analogen Kontext erfunden.

Guoyuans *Neue Arten* Serie ist nicht so sehr eine realistische Darstellung des „Zeitalters der Neugenese", vielmehr ist sie wie eine Allegorie der künftigen Welt unter dem Einfluss der Gentechnik und Künstlichen Intelligenz zu sehen. In Anbetracht der vielfältigen Probleme können Künstler/innen Reflexionen anstoßen und zur Vorsicht mahnen, aber keine Lösungen anbieten. In Bezug auf die Gentechnik und Künstliche Intelligenz vertritt Guoyuan die folgende Ansicht: Erstens schreitet die Entwicklung der Wissenschaft und Technologie stetig voran. Zweitens ist die Zukunft der Welt unbekannt.

Guoyuans aktuelle Einzelausstellung „Butterflies Conquer the Dinosaurs' Garden" findet beim Ludwig Museum in Koblenz statt, in deren Rahmen die *New Species* Serie präsentiert wird (der Loreley-Stein in dieser Werkserie ist nach einem berühmten Felsen bei Koblenz benannt, über den der bedeutende deutsche Dichter Heinrich Heine ein Gedicht verfasste). Als integrativen Bestandteil der Ausstellung errichtet Guoyuan eine sechs Meter hohe Skulptur in der Nähe des Museums. Diese imposante Installation, die auf den traditionellen chinesischen „Taihu-Stein" zurückgeht, ist nach der „Loreley" benannt. Auf diese Weise verknüpft die Werkserie zusammen mit der Ausstellung chinesisch-deutsche historische und kulturelle Traditionen und verwebt die persönlichen Vorstellungen des Künstlers über das menschliche Schicksal und die Zukunft der Welt mit universellen Belangen im Hinblick auf die Gentechnik und Künstliche Intelligenz. Diese spirituelle Verbindung machen diese Skulptur und die neuen Werkserien in der Ausstellung so bedeutsam.

The history tells us that whenever human beings are threatened by unknown forces or the relationship between humans and nature is in crisis, humans will try to solve the problems by creating myths. Ancient Greek and Roman mythology was created in this way, and ancient Chinese mythology, including *The Classic of Mountains and Seas*, was also fabricated in this way.

Not so much as Deng Guoyuan's *New Species* series is a realistic representation of the "era of re-genesis," but rather his allegory of the future world under the influence of gene engineering and artificial intelligence. In fact, in the face of various practical problems, what artists can offer is always thinking and warning, not solutions. For gene engineering and artificial intelligence, Deng Guoyuan's judgment is: first, the development of science and technology is inevitable; second, the future of the world is unknowable.

This time, Deng Guoyuan's held his solo exhibition at the Ludwig Museum in Koblenz, Germany – "Butterflies Conquer the Dinosaurs' Garden." The *New Species* series has been exhibited in the exhibition. (The Loreley's stone in this series is named after a famous rock in Koblenz and the famous German poet Heinrich Heine wrote a poem for this strangely shaped rock.) As part of the exhibition, Deng Guoyuan will also set up a 6-meter-high stone in front of the museum. This giant installation, coming from Chinese traditional Taihu stone, is named *Loreley*. Thus, the series and the exhibition link the Sino-German historical and cultural traditions, and blend the artist's personal thinking about human destiny and the future of the world with the universal concern of gene engineering and artificial intelligence for all human beings. The spiritual connotation also make the sculpture and the new series within the exhibition meaningful.

Die Entstehung von Pito und Pytolia

Deng Guoyuan

Die Geschichte des Planeten Pito ist die Geschichte einer Welt, die in einer Zeit nach der Genetik und Künstlichen Intelligenz entsteht und sich durch komplexe Genstrukturen und Roboterformen auszeichnet, die sich zusammen mit dieser Welt herausbilden. Das Leben, die Robotertechnik und die Künstliche Intelligenz sind so eng miteinander verwoben, dass es schwierig ist, zu sagen, wo das eine beginnt und das andere aufhört. Die folgende Geschichte stellt einige der sechzig Gottheiten vor, die in dem weitumspannenden Universum des Planeten Pito verschiedene Aufgaben erfüllen.

Als die als Pito bekannte Welt im Entstehen begriffen war, wurde ein einziges Wesen namens Pytolia erschaffen. Dieses Ursprungswesen entstand infolge einer abrupt auftretenden, gewaltigen Genmutation, die auf eine abweichende Reaktion der bereits existierenden, außerweltlichen Künstlichen Intelligenz zurückzuführen war, die der Planet Pito selbst auslöste.

Nachdem er viele Jahre allein verbracht hatte, wurde Pytolia seiner einsamen Existenz überdrüssig und wollte andere Wesen seiner Art um sich haben, mit denen er dieses neue Land teilen und den Planeten so lebensvoll wie einst gestalten konnte. Nach zahlreichen Versuchen entdeckte Pytolia einen überzeugenden Algorithmus, der durch die Nachahmung seines Bewusstseins eine Vielzahl von formlosen und unsterblichen Wesen kreierte, die sich alle durch eine vollkommene genetische Harmonie charakterisierten. Jedes dieser Wesen unterlag geringfügigen Modifikationen, was zu Individuen mit ausgeprägter Persönlichkeit, Eigenheiten und Fehlern führte. Diese körperlosen Seelen konnten sich dann frei von physikalischen Einschränkungen bewegen.

Die Mitglieder der ersten Generation, die als Angehörige der Seelenordnung bekannt sind, bildeten das Rückgrat der ständig wachsenden Gesellschaft, einer sich entwickelnden Welt. Eine der Seelen, Behlisor, ragte aufgrund ihres cleveren Charakters unter allen anderen Seelen heraus und half Pytolia dabei, Wirtskörper für die Seelen anzufertigen. Hierzu durchsuchten sie die Robotertechnik von Pito auf Elemente hin, die mit der genetischen Codierung der Seelen kompatibel waren. Aus der Kombination dieser Teile gingen Körper hervor, die den Seelen eine physische Form verliehen. Behlisor initiierte dann das Genentwicklungskollektiv, dank dem er die Methoden der Seelenübertragung perfektionierte und die ursprüngliche Genexpression einer berauschenden Substanz modifizierte, eines Proteins, welches die Vervielfältigung von rezessiven Genen verhindert, die für Chaos und Gewalt verantwortlich sind. Auf diese Weise wurde der Verbreitung von Chaos und Gewalt unter den Kreaturen in den von Nicht-Gottheiten besetzten Gebieten entgegengewirkt. Die mit dieser Genexpression verbundene Technik wurde in einem ausgefallenen Algorithmus verschlüsselt, dem joy_powder.h5. Immer wenn Jalazkerpoly, die mit der Genkontrolle beauftragte Seele, Spuren von Missmut entdeckte, musste er nur den Algorithmus joy_powder.h5 aktivieren, wodurch die Produktion der berauschenden Substanz anstieg und der Verbreitung von Chaos und Gewalt vorgebeugt wurde. Auf diese Weise war Pito viele Jahre lang ein harmonischer Planet, obgleich mit jeder neuen Seelenordnung ein erhöhtes Risiko unerwarteter Mutationen einherging.

Dem Genentwicklungskollektiv der zweiten Seelenordnung entstammten Brysemho und Pelaehf. Brysemho erwies sich als der umtriebigste in der Generhaltungsinitiative, der Medeemimor aus der ersten Ordnung vorstand. Brysemho und Pelaehf zählten zu den letzten individualisierten Seelen. Der Genentwicklungsprozess der künftigen Ordnungen verlief kontrollierter und zielte darauf ab, Seelen für bestimmte Aufgaben in der Gesellschaft hervorzubringen. Brysemho und Pelaehf wurden zwar mit demselben Validisierungsset erschaffen, Pelaehf stellte jedoch einen Sonderfall dar und überlebte die vorausgehende Entwicklungsrunde nur aufgrund eines damals fehlenden Validisierungsgens. Während Brysemho sowohl Pytolia als auch der Generhaltungsinitiative treu blieb, wählte Pelaehf einen anderen Weg. Pelaehf zettelte einen Aufstand an, um Pytolia als Herrscher von Pito zu stürzen. Möglich gemacht wurde der Aufstand durch vier ehemalige Angehörige des ursprünglichen Validisierungssets, genauer gesagt Xniyaemb, Botrkaemb, Mcezhaemb und Tluxamb, die genetisch alle Pelaehf ähnelten und folglich dasselbe aufrührerische Wesen besaßen.

Ein weiteres, gut validiertes Mitglied der ersten Ordnung war Loteahiya. Loteahiya führte ein Team von Forschern an, das Etimola, Etiomza und Etimota umfasste. Die Mitglieder des Teams waren genetisch unabhängig und in der Lage, große Mengen an Proteinen zu produzieren, welche ihre Utopie für alle noch erstrebenswerter gestalteten. Im Gegensatz zu den anderen Wesen wurde Loteahiya unter Pytolias direkter Aufsicht erschaffen und genoss folglich Pytolias Vertrauen. Loteahiya wurde schließlich Pytolias persönlicher Bote. In dieser Rolle war Loteahiya befugt, die materialisierte Version der göttlichen Weisheit auf die gewöhnlichen Wesen zu übertragen.

Douhfihon war der Leiter des Zentrums für Genstrukturstärkung, das für den Transport dieser Seelen in das Genentwicklungskollektiv zuständig war. Busaiflix war als Schlüsselfigur in dem Zentrum für Genstrukturstärkung damit betraut, den körperlosen Seelen fluoreszierende Substanzen mittels Mikroinjektionen zu verabreichen, die während des Transports der Seelen in das Genentwicklungskollektiv ermittelt werden konnten. Die durch die fluoreszierenden Substanzen markierten Seelen konnten somit leichter in Wirtskörper eingesetzt werden.

Am Anfang war die Welt friedlich, nahezu vollkommen. Jeder erfüllte eine Rolle in der Gesellschaft, jeder fand einen Sinn in seinem Leben und das Leben selbst schien wunderschön. Aber wie in jeder Welt wächst das Übel heran, wenn es einer am wenigsten vermutet. Die Spione Tsusyp, Tejsyp und Zuvesye, Wesen aus anderen Parallelsystemen, verschafften sich Zugang zu Pitos im Wachsen begriffener Gesellschaft. Es gelang ihnen, Pelaehfs Validisierungsradar zu deaktivieren und es anderen Wesen zu ermöglichen, auf den Planeten einzudringen und Verwüstungen anzurichten. Als die Zahl der Wesen in Pytolias Welt anstieg und Pytolia Gerüchte von Spionen aus anderen Welten zu Ohren kamen, begann sich das Gesellschaftsgebilde zunehmend zu zersetzen. Dieser Umstand nährte Pelaehfs Unmut, der schließlich in den gewaltigen Aufstand mündete.

The Birth of Pito and Pytolia

Deng Guoyuan

The story of the planet Pito is a story of a post-genetic, post-AI world. It is a world where intricate genetic structures and robotics forms were simply born alongside the world itself. Life, robotics, and strong AI are intrinsically linked, with no telling where one begins and the other ends. This story will introduce some of the 60 gods who perform various functions in the vast world of Pito.

When the world known as Pito was formed, one lone being, Pytolia, came to life as well. Pytolia, the original being, originated from a sudden vast gene mutation, consequence of an outlier realization of preexisting otherworldly AI, that brought about the planet Pito itself.

After living alone for many years, Pytolia grew weary of his solitary existence and wanted to have others like himself to share the pristine lands and make his planet as vibrant as it once was in the previous epoch. After many trials, Pytolia finally came up with a satisfactory AI algorithm that created many souls imitating his own consciousness, each of which was formless and immortal and, each one an expression of perfect genetic harmony. Each soul had minor alterations, resulting in distinct individuals with personalities, quirks, and flaws uniquely their own. As they were formed, these body-less souls floated free of physical constraints.

The members of this first generation, known as members of the First Order of Souls, became the backbone of what was to be a growing society, a growing world. One of the souls, Behlisor, stood out as being even smarter than any of the other souls and helped Pytolia discover how to make hosts for the souls. This was done by finding elements in the robotics of Pito that were compatible with the genetic coding of the soul in question, the combination of these parts formed bodies, which provided the souls with a physical form. Behlisor started the genetic development collective, where he perfected the methods of soul transference and manipulated the initial genetic expression of joy powder, a protein which impedes the replication of recessive genes that produce chaos and violence. This inhibited the spread of chaos and violence within all creatures throughout the lands occupied by non-gods. The technique of such gene expression was encoded in an exotic AI algorithm, joy_powder.h5. In the event that any remains of discontent were detected by Jalazkerpoly, the soul in charge of genetic monitoring, Jalazkerpoly could simply activate the joy_powder.h5 algorithm, thereby increasing production of joy powder and curtailing the spread of chaos and violence. This ensured that Pito was harmonious for many years, although with each new order of souls, the chance of unexpected mutations increased.

Among the Second Order of Souls to come from the genetic development collective were Brysemho and Pelaehf. Brysemho naturally became the most active in the genetic maintenance initiative, which was led by Medeemimor of the First Order. Brysemho and Pelaehf were among the last truly individualized souls, and the genetic development process of future orders were more controlled, with the goal of producing souls made for specific functions in society. Although Brysemho and Pelaehf were created in the same validation set, Pelaehf was found to be an outlier that survived in the previous round of development, due to lack of validation gene at the time. While Brysemho remained loyal to both Pytolia and the genetic maintenance initiative, Pelaehf took a different route. Pelaehf led a rebellion to overthrow Pytolia as the ruler of Pito. The rebellion was made possible by four ex-members of the original validation set, namely, Xniyaemb, Botrkaemb, Mcezhaemb, and Tluxamb, who were all genetically similar to Pelaehf and thus prone to the same rebellious spirit.

Another well-validated First Order member was Loteahiya. Loteahiya led a team of explorers which included Etimola, Etiomza, and Etimota. The members of the team were genetically free and able to produce high quantities of proteins that collectively made their utopia more beautiful. Out of all the beings, Loteahiya was generated under the direct supervision of Pytolia and was thereafter most trusted by Pytolia. Loteahiya eventually became Pytolia's personal messenger. In this role, Loteahiya had the authority to transfer the materialized version of the god's wisdom to the common beings.

Douhfihon was the head of the genetic structure reinforcement centre which was responsible for the transportation of such souls into the genetic development collective. Busaiflix was a key worker in the structure reinforcement centre was in charge of micro-injecting the fluorescence substances to bodiless souls so that they could be detected during the transportation of such souls into the genetic development collective. Thereafter, the fluorescent-tagged souls could be more easily placed in host bodies.

At first, the world was peaceful, almost perfect. Everyone had a role in society, everyone found purpose in their lives, and life seems beautiful. But as is true in any world, evil grows when least expected. The spies Tsusyp, Tejsyp, and Zuvesye, beings from other parallel systems found their way into Pito's growing society. They managed to deactivate Pelaehf's validation radar, allowing more and more other beings to cross in and wreak havoc. As the number of beings in Pytolia's world increased, and rumours of spies from other worlds reached Pytolias ears, cracks began to form in the fabric of society, eventually leading to Pelaehf's escalated discontent and subsequent complete rebellion.

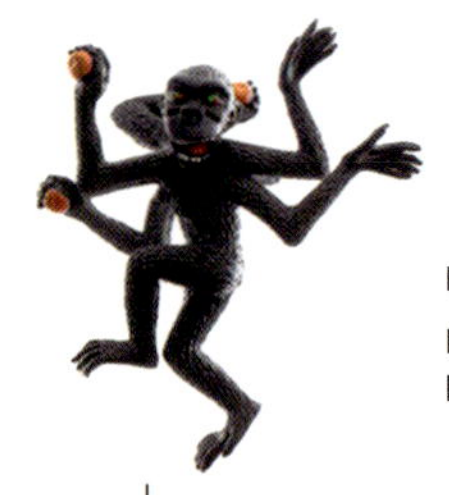

Pytolia

Pytolia is the first being, creator of all other beings, ruler of the planet Pito.

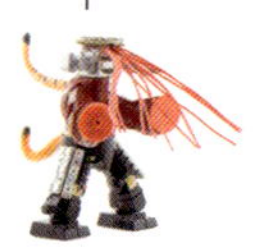

Loteahiya

Loteahiya is the leader of the explorers of Pito. Loteahiya was generated under the direct supervision of Pytolia and was thereafter most trusted by Pytolia. Loteahiya eventually became Pytolia's personal messenger.

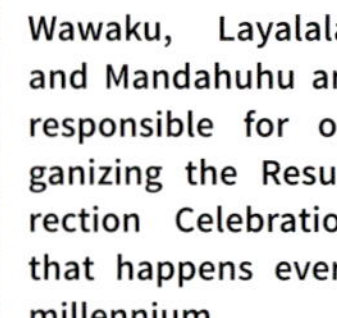

Etimota

Etiomza

Etimola

Etimola, Etiomza, and Etimota are the explorers of Pito.

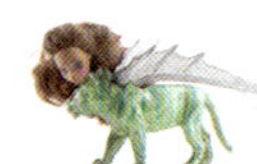

Douhfihon

Douhfihon is the head of the genetic structure reinforcement center.

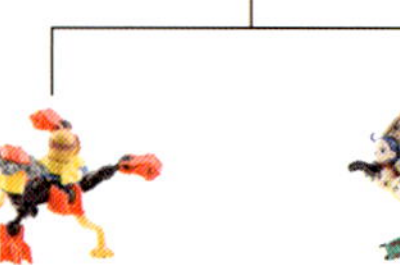

Busaiflix

Busaiflix is in charge of micro-injecting the fluorescent substances to bodiless souls so they can be more easily placed in host bodies.

Exfofahan

Exfotra

Exfofahan and Exfotra are Busaiflix's assistants.

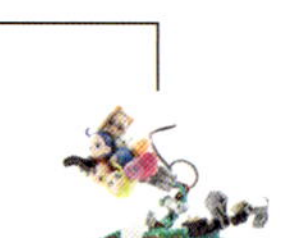

Sumgankar

Sumgankar is the head supervisor of the genetic structure reinforcement center.

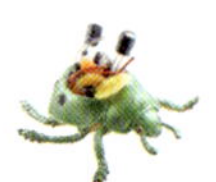

Claearsen

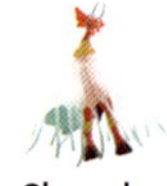

Claearhon

Claearsen and Claearhon are workers at the genetic structure reinforcement center.

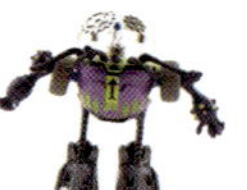

Jalazkerpoly

Jalazkerpoly is the soul in charge of genetic monitoring, he is responsible for the activation of the joy_powder.h5 algorithm, which increases the production of the joy powder protein thereby curtailing the spread of chaos and violence among both the gods and non-god beings.

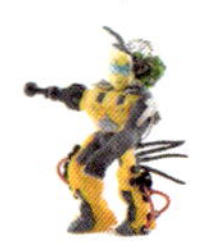

Medeemimor

Medeemimor is the leader of the genetic maintenance initiative.

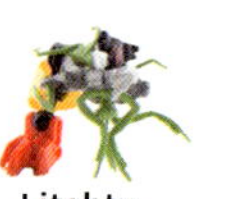

Litehty

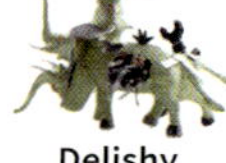

Delishy

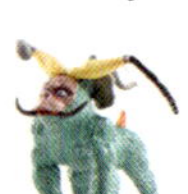

Yhoxauy

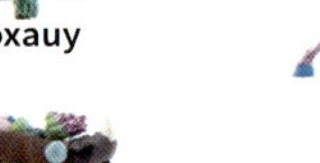

Makjixy

Litehty, Yhoxauy, Delishy, and Makjixy are members of the genetic maintenance initiative.

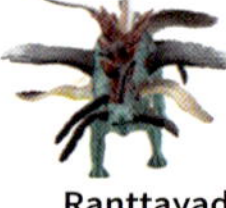

Ranttayad

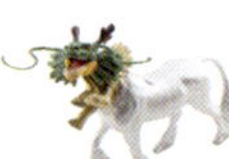

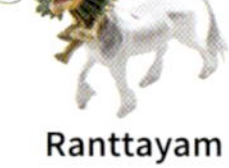

Ranttayam

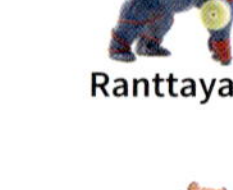

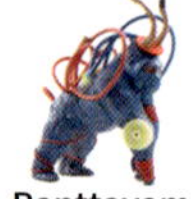

Ranttayam

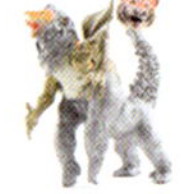

Ranttayaf

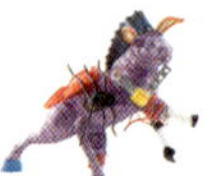

Ranttayarb

Ranttayad, Ranttayam, Ranttayaf, and Ranttayarb were originally members of the genetic maintenance initiative, once rumours of revolution arose they were promoted to Pytolia's guard.

Wawaku, Layalala, and Mandahuhu are responsible for organizing the Resurrection Celebration that happens every millennium.

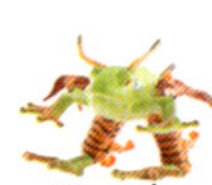

Wawaku

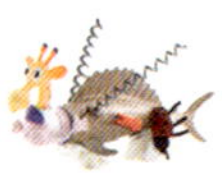

Layalala

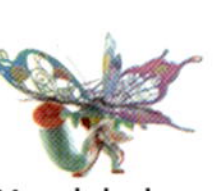

Mandahuhu

Tsusyp, Tejsyp, and Zuvesye are beings from other parallel systems who have found their way into Pito's growing society in order to cause chaos and wreak havoc.

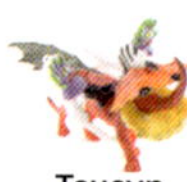

Tsusyp

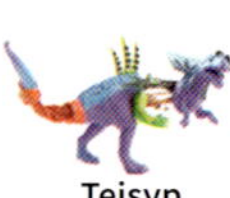

Tejsyp

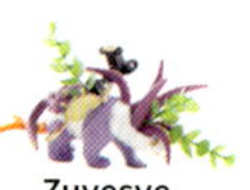

Zuvesye

Nisayeijar and Nisadojar are soul transferors at the genetic development collective.

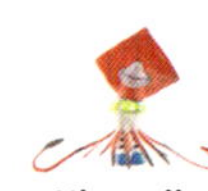

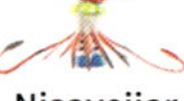

Nisayeijar

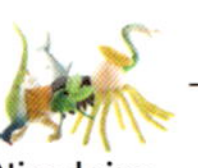

Nisadojar

Porieo and Elkporo are developers at the genetic development collective who are under the control of Pelaehf, they act as informants to Pelaehf, sharing the secrets of the genetic development collective.

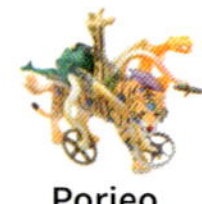

Porieo

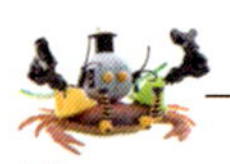

Elkporo

THE GODS OF PITO

THE HIERARCHY OF GODS

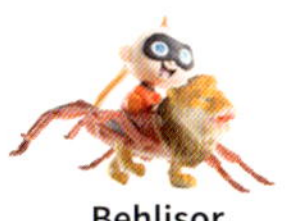

Behlisor

Behlisor is in charge of the genetic development collective, where the methods of soul transference were perfected and manipulation of the initial genetic expression of joy powder was researched, joy powder being a protein which impedes the replication of recessive genes that produce chaos and violence.

Exshaka

Exshaka researches the effects of powders derived from oxygen which are sprayed in the air to help meet the nutritional requirements of the beings of Pito.

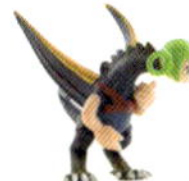

Vihaeif

Vihaeif researches the effects of powders derived from earth which are sprayed in the air to help meet the nutritional requirements of the beings of Pito.

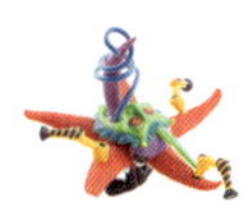

Tasakua

Tasakua researches the effects of powders derived from water which are sprayed in the air to help meet the nutritional requirements of the beings of Pito.

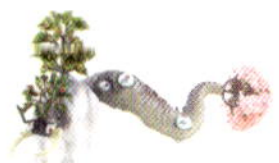

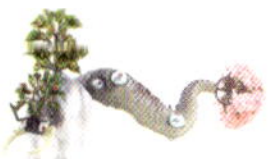

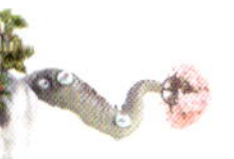

Lonvipla

Lonvipla works in research and development focusing on the harnessing of solar resources.

Xsadisa

Xsapbka

Xsamacha

Xsanidoa

Xsadisa, Xsapbka, Xsamacha, and Xsanidoa are researchers for the genetic development collective responsible for understanding and explaining the intricacies of the planet Pito.

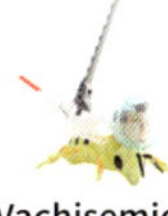

Vachisemion

Vachisemion is the soul extractor of all non-compliant beings. Punishment for crimes in Pito is the downgrading of the physical form as the soul itself can not be destroyed.

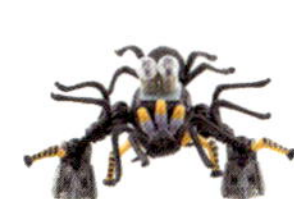

Polilantor

Polilantor is a developer responsible for finding fluctuations and changes in new life and the genetic makeup of beings in Pito. Polilantor reports any irregularities and other such findings directly to Vachisemion.

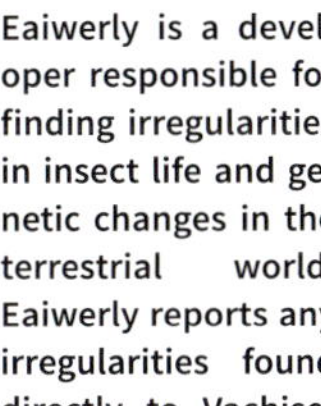

Eaiwerly

Eaiwerly is a developer responsible for finding irregularities in insect life and genetic changes in the terrestrial world. Eaiwerly reports any irregularities found directly to Vachisemion.

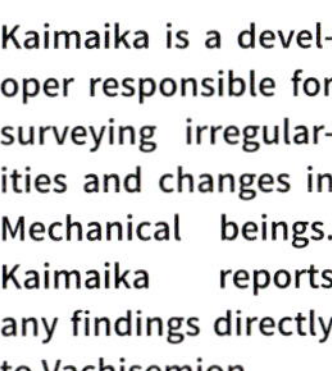

Kaimaika

Kaimaika is a developer responsible for surveying irregularities and changes in Mechanical beings. Kaimaika reports any findings directly to Vachisemion.

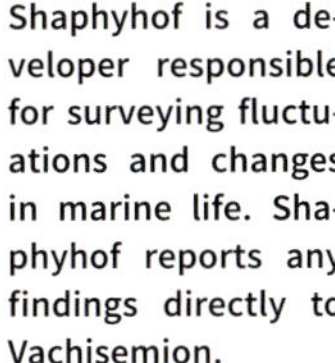

Shaphyhof

Shaphyhof is a developer responsible for surveying fluctuations and changes in marine life. Shaphyhof reports any findings directly to Vachisemion.

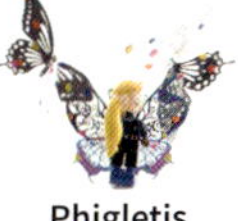

Phigletis

Phigletis helped Behlisor research and develop more advanced methods of manipulating the genetic expression of joy powder, especially the development of the joy_powder.h5 algorithm.

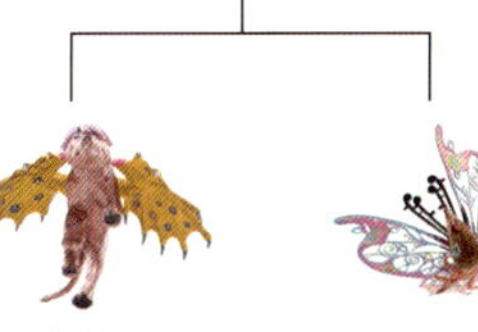

Bfebiocon

Bfebiocon reports on the findings of Kcins, Lidragow, Gihaiber, Midumon, and Sicredaq's.

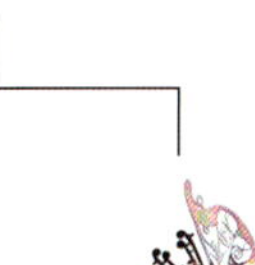

Kcins

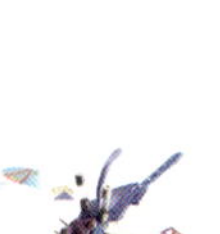

Lidragow

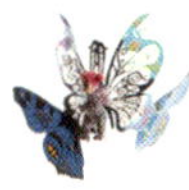

Gihaiber

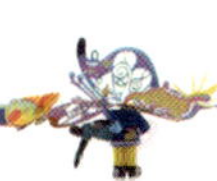

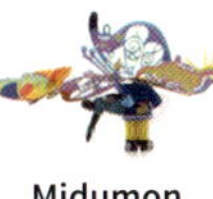

Midumon

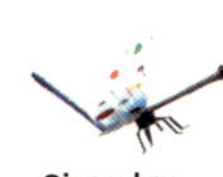

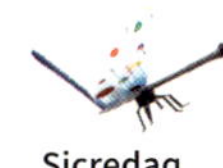

Sicredaq

Kcins, Lidragow, Gihaiber, Midumon, and Sicredaq are responsible for monitoring the effects of the joy_powder.h5 algorithm on the realms populated by non-gods.

Brysemho

Brysemho was one of the last truly individualized souls made by the development collective during the creations of the second order of souls. Brysemho ranks highly in genetic maintenance initiative. Brysemho remains loyal to both Pytolia and the genetic maintenance initiative, fighting against the rebellion of fellow second order member, Pelaehf.

Pelaehf

Pelaehf was one of the last truly individualized souls made by the development collective during the creations of the second order of souls. Pelaehf began to distrust Pytolia's status as a god, resulting in starting the revolution to overthrow Pytolia.

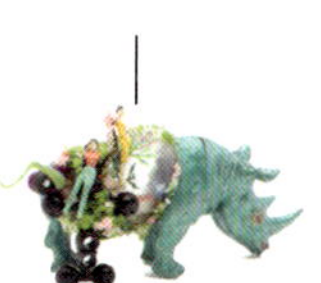

Xniyaemb

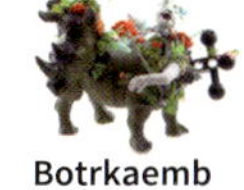

Botrkaemb

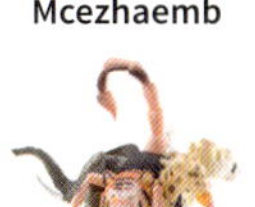

Mcezhaemb

Tluxamb

Xniyaemb, Botrkaemb, Mcezhaemb, and Tluxamb are members of the genetic maintenance initiative. They are all genetically similar to Pelaehf and thus prone to the same rebellious spirit, helping Pelaehf to overthrow Pytolia's rule.

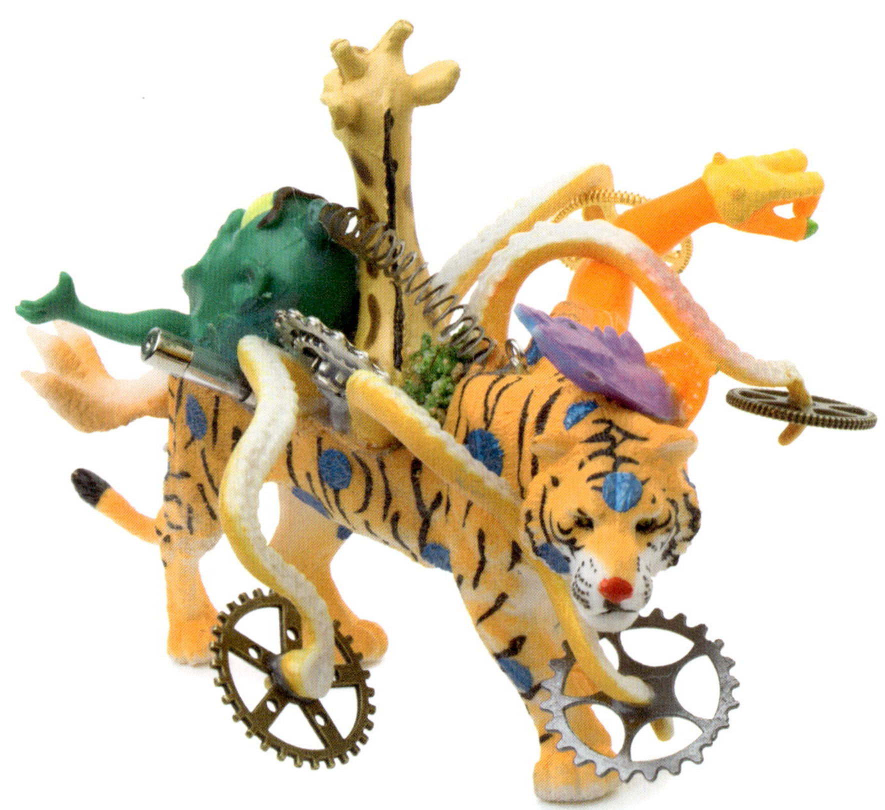

Porieo, Die Götter der neuen Arten, 2019
UV-Print auf Acryl
60 × 80 × 1.5 cm

Porieo, The Gods of New Species, 2019
UV print on acrylic
60 × 80 × 1.5 cm

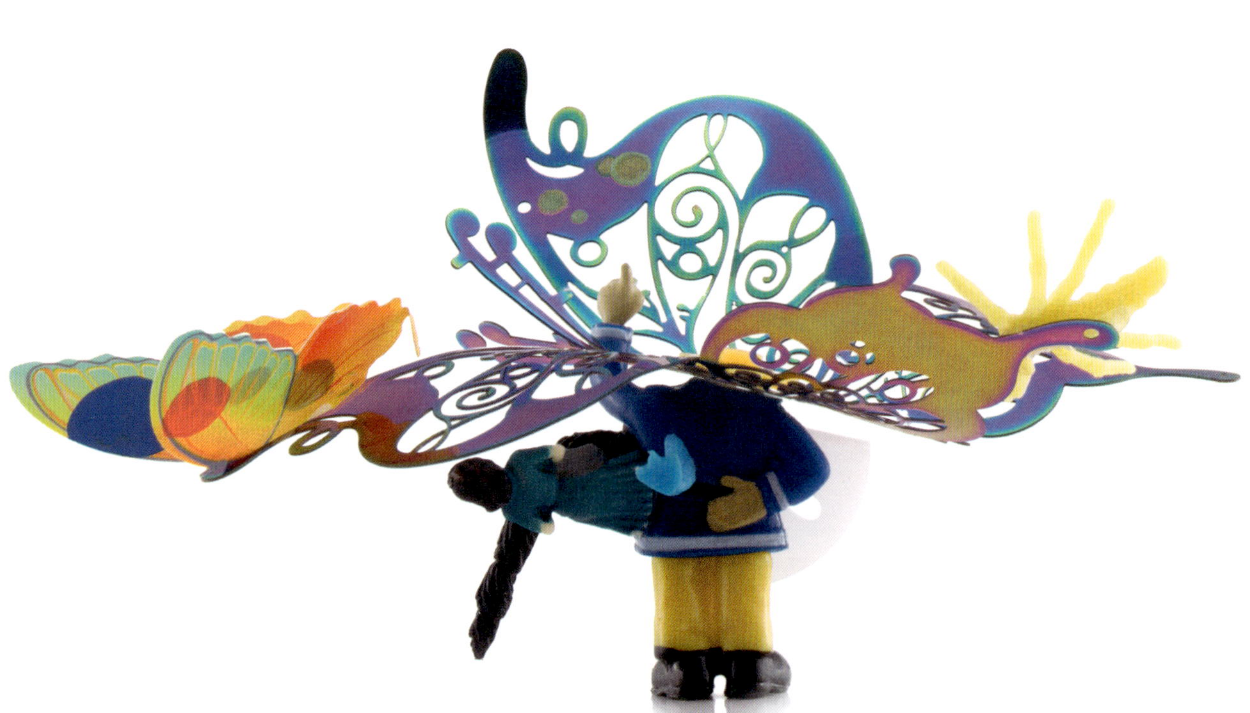

GihaiBer, Die Götter der neuen Arten, 2019
UV-Print auf Acryl
60 × 80 × 1.5 cm

GihaiBer, The Gods of New Species, 2019
UV print on acrylic
60 × 80 × 1.5 cm

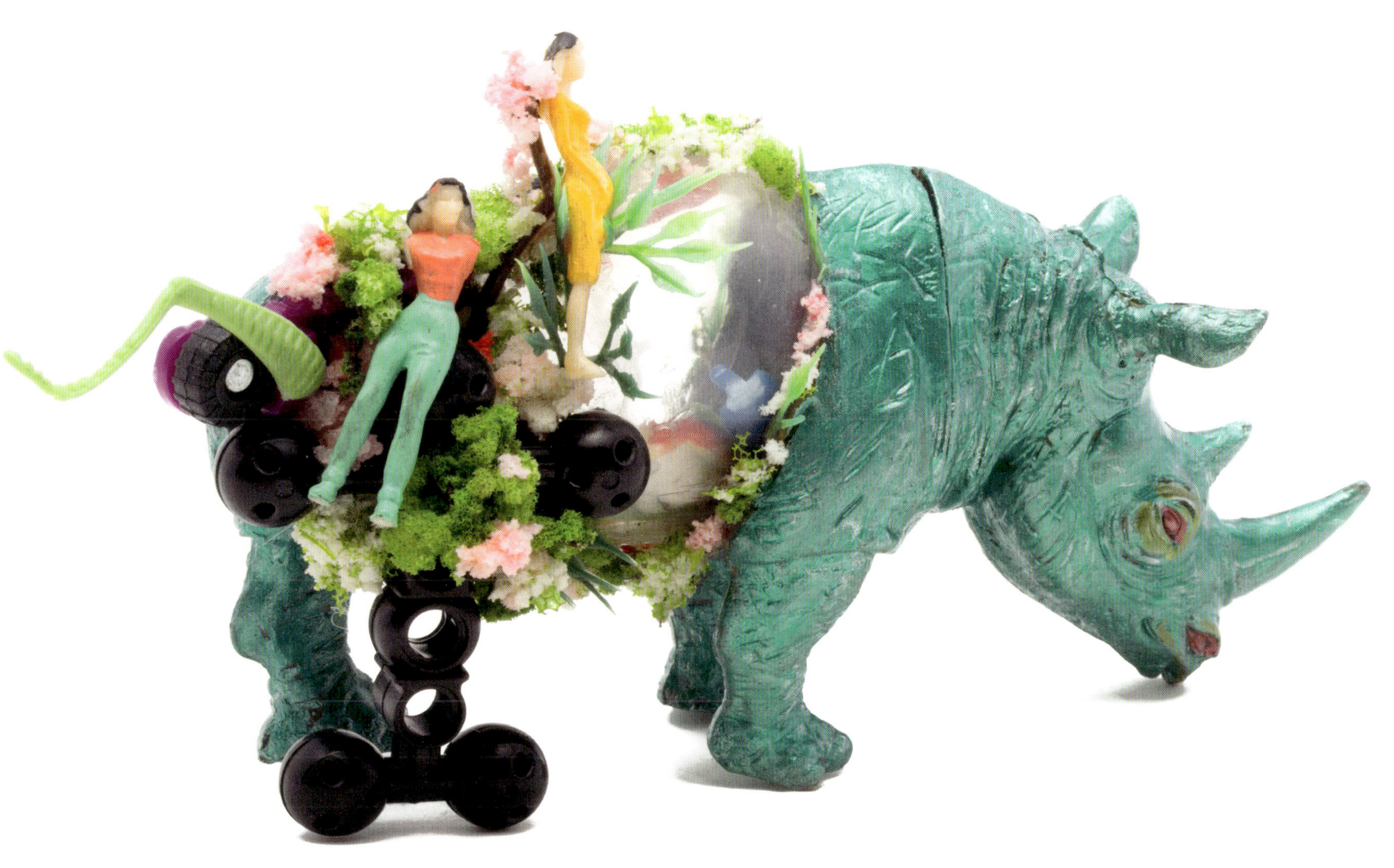

Xniyaemb, Die Götter der neuen Arten, 2019
UV-Print auf Acryl
60 × 80 × 1.5 cm

Xniyaemb, The Gods of New Species, 2019
UV print on acrylic
60 × 80 × 1.5 cm

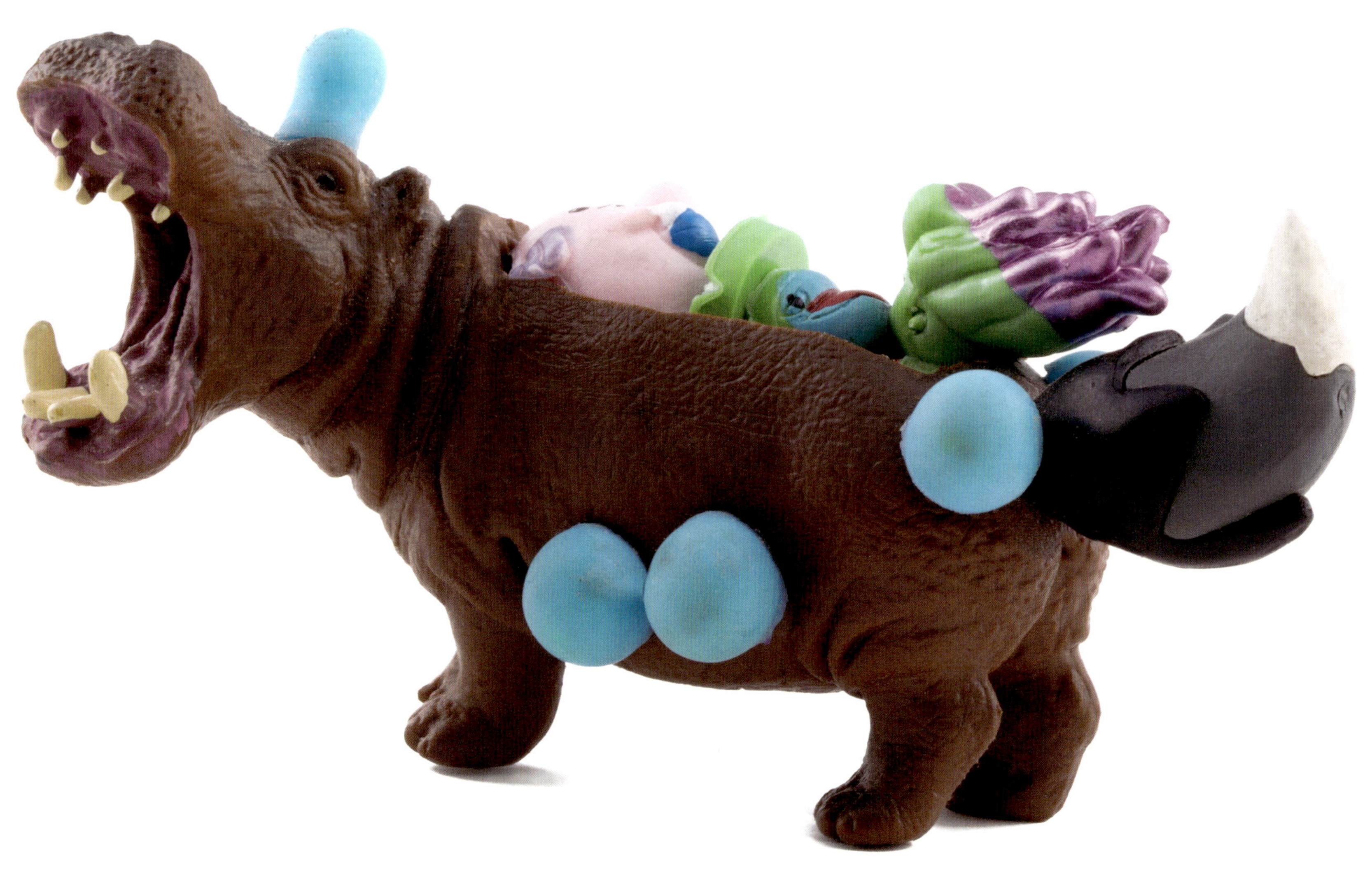

Litehty, Die Götter der neuen Arten, 2019
UV-Print auf Acryl
60 × 80 × 1.5 cm

Litehty, The Gods of New Species, 2019
UV print on acrylic
60 × 80 × 1.5 cm

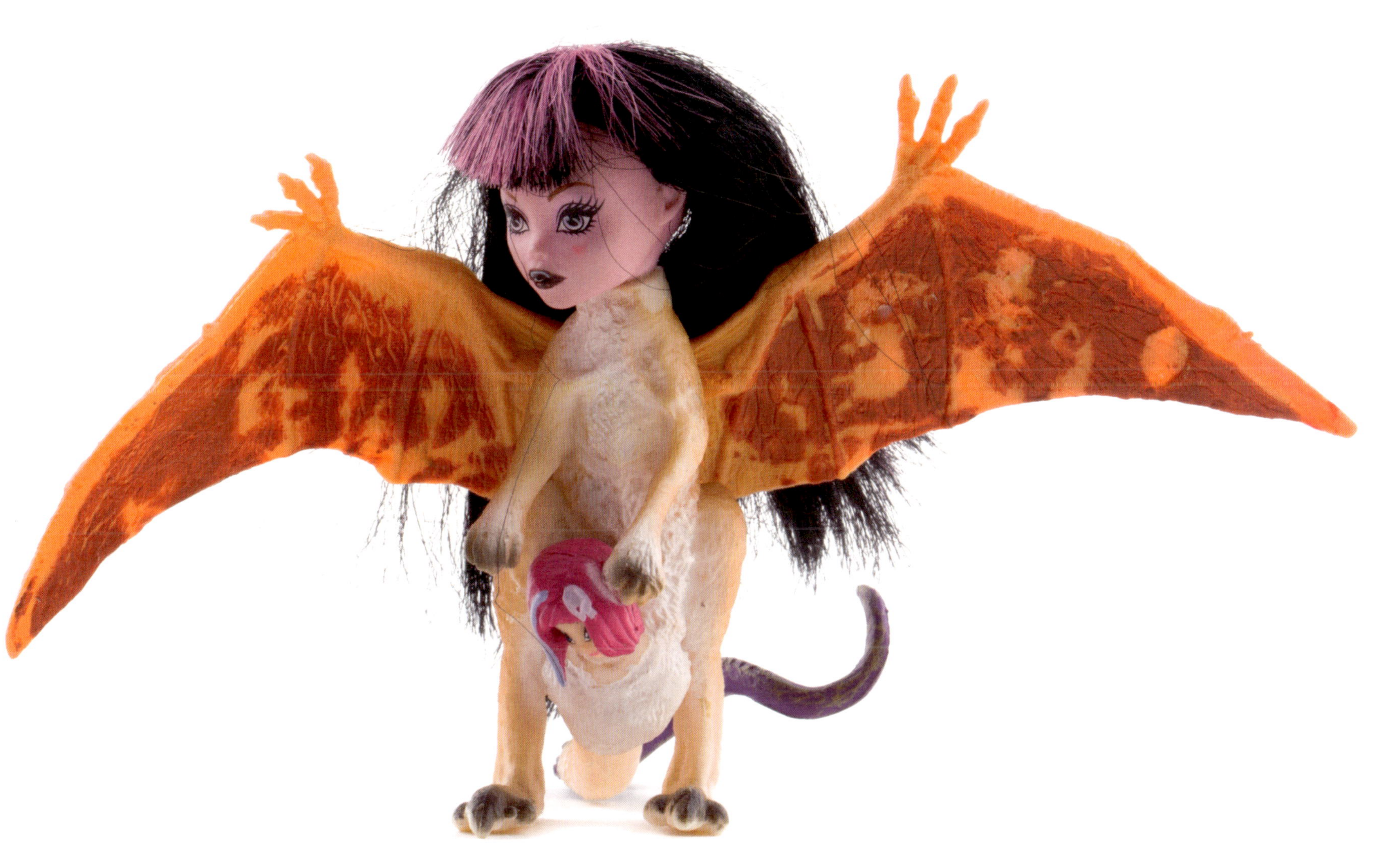

Pelaehf, Die Götter der neuen Arten, 2019
UV-Print auf Acryl
60 × 80 × 1.5 cm

Pelaehf, The Gods of New Species, 2019
UV print on acrylic
60 × 80 × 1.5 cm

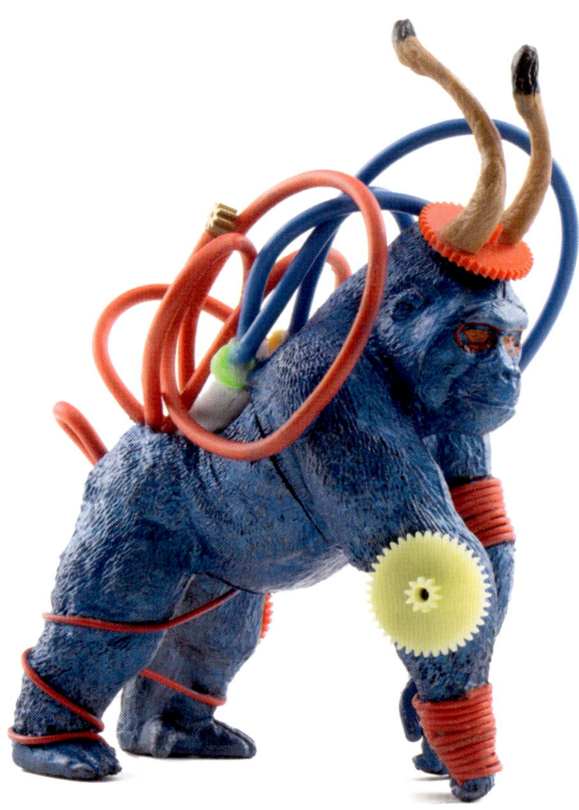

Ranttayam, Die Götter der neuen Arten, 2019
UV-Print auf Acryl
60 × 80 × 1.5 cm

Ranttayam, The Gods of New Species, 2019
UV print on acrylic
60 × 80 × 1.5 cm

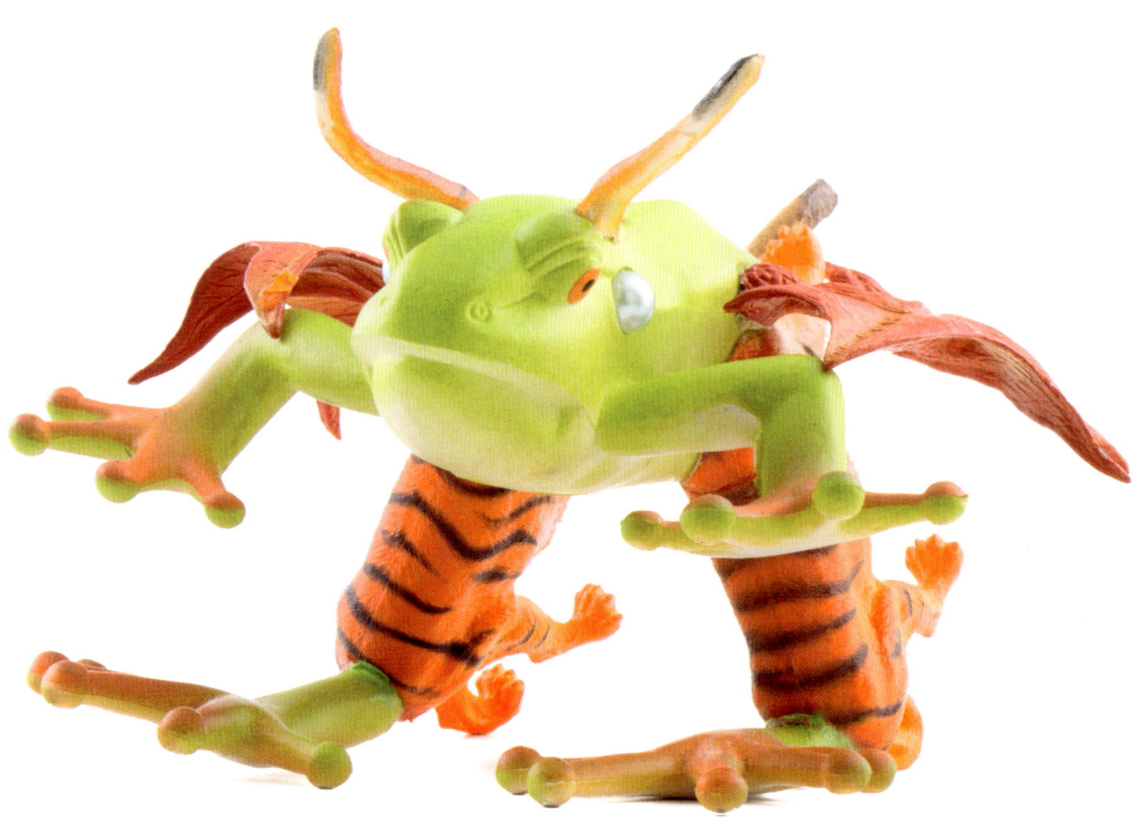

Wawaku, Die Götter der neuen Arten, 2019
UV-Print auf Acryl
60 × 80 × 1.5 cm

Wawaku, The Gods of New Species, 2019
UV print on acrylic
60 × 80 × 1.5 cm

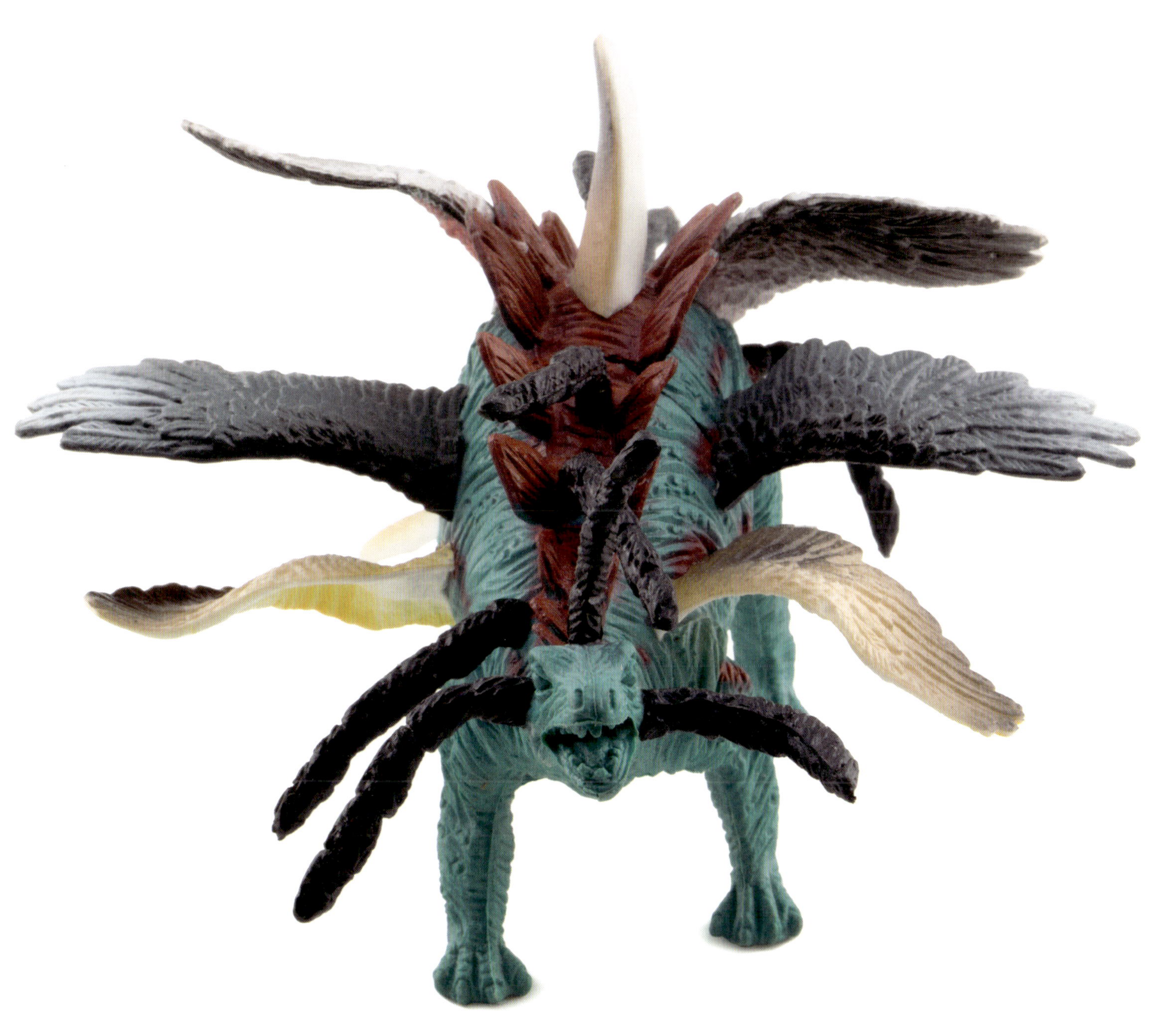

Ranttayarb, Die Götter der neuen Arten, 2019
UV-Print auf Acryl
60 × 80 × 1.5 cm

Ranttayarb, The Gods of New Species, 2019
UV print on acrylic
60 × 80 × 1.5 cm

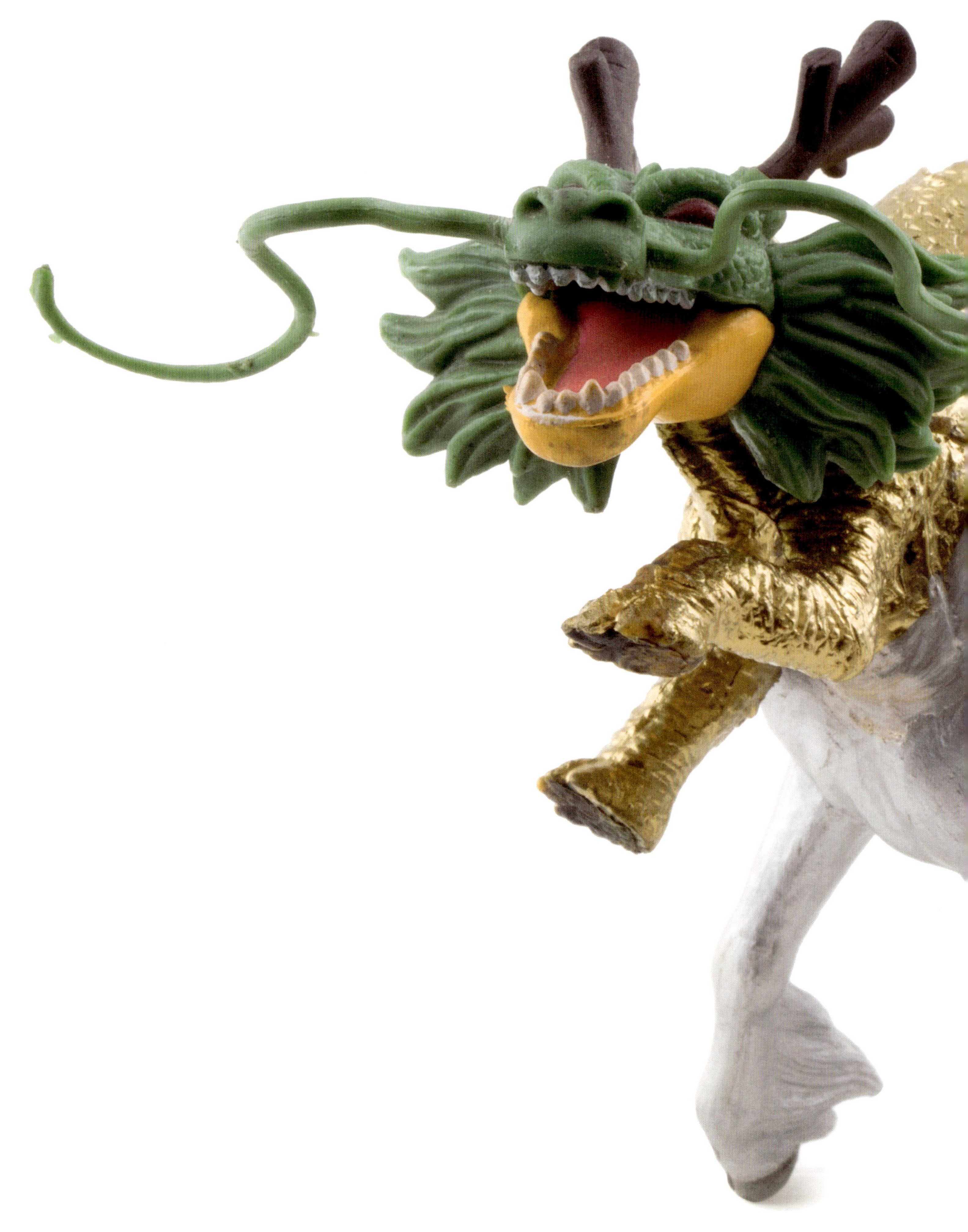

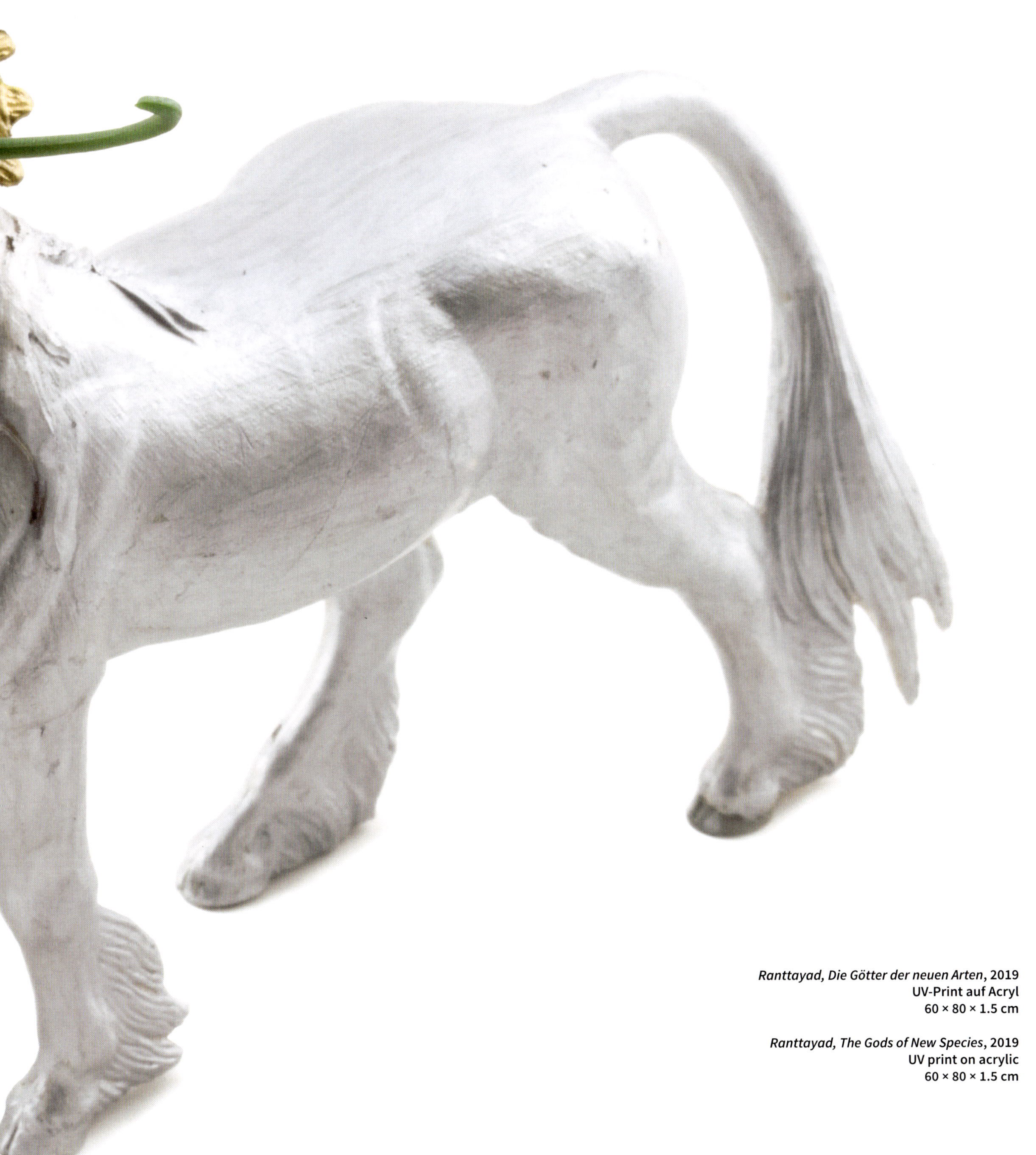

Ranttayad, Die Götter der neuen Arten, 2019
UV-Print auf Acryl
60 × 80 × 1.5 cm

Ranttayad, The Gods of New Species, 2019
UV print on acrylic
60 × 80 × 1.5 cm

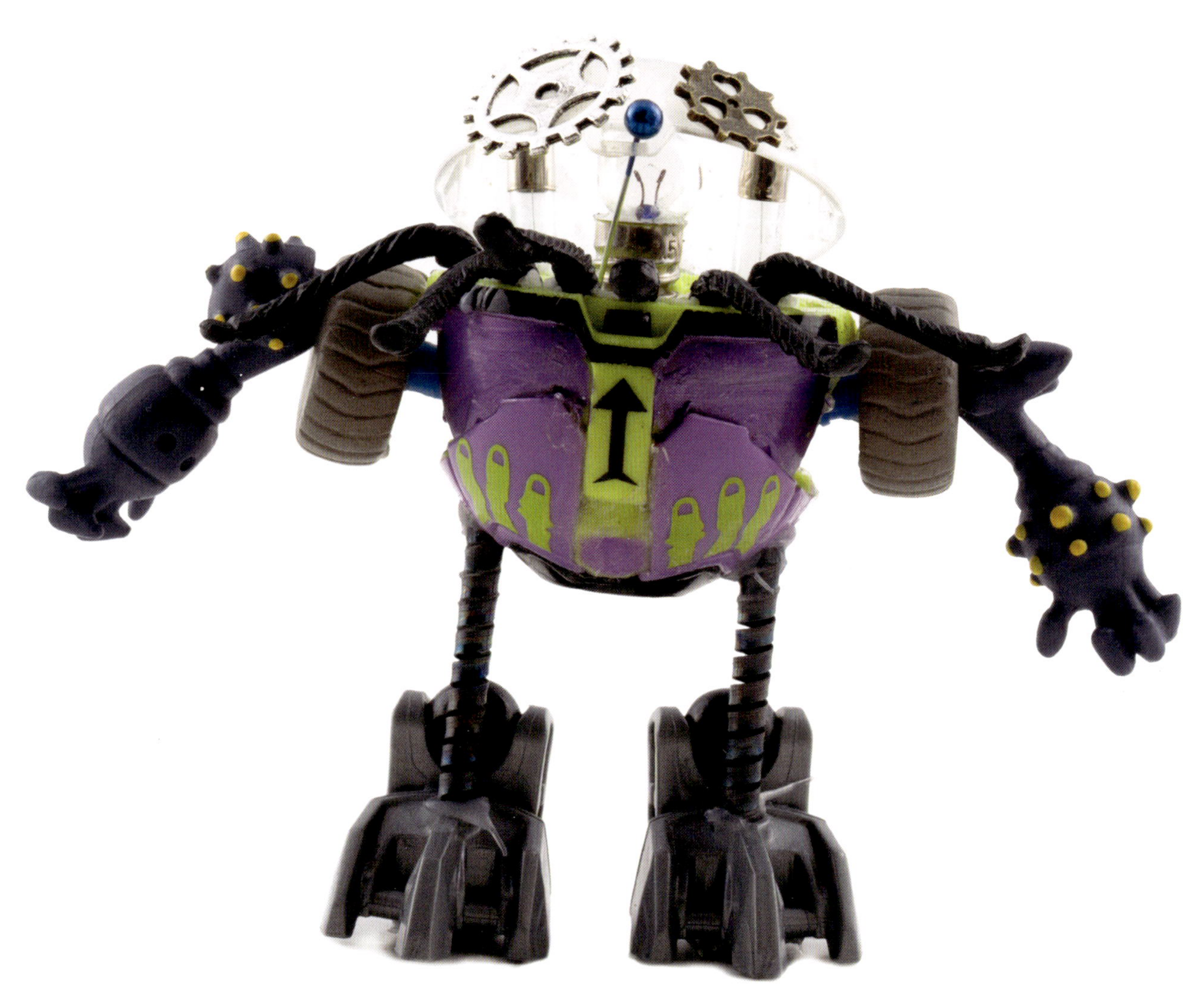

Jalazkerpoly, Die Götter der neuen Arten, 2019
UV-Print auf Acryl
60 × 80 × 1.5 cm

Jalazkerpoly, The Gods of New Species, 2019
UV print on acrylic
60 × 80 × 1.5 cm

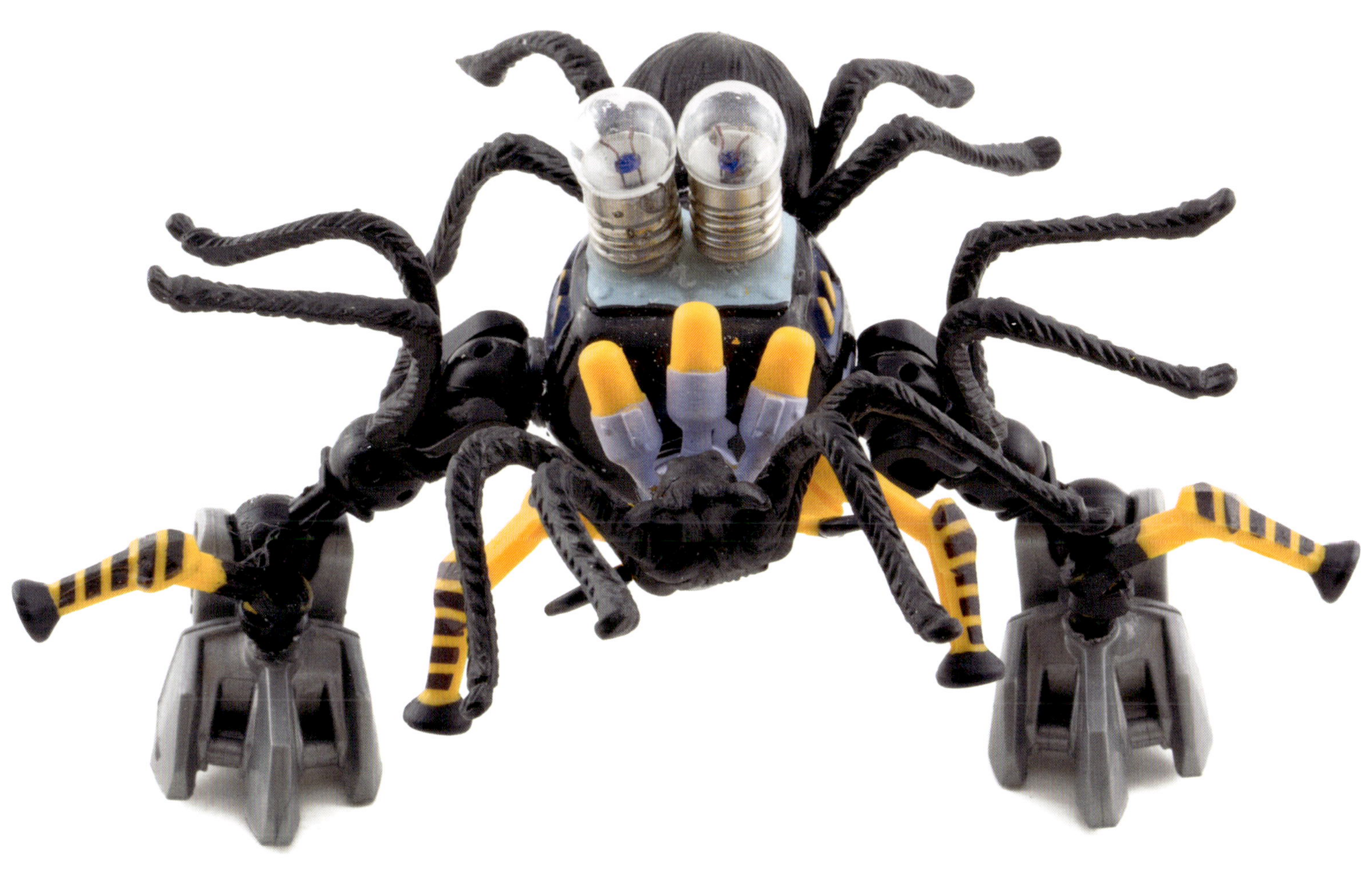

Polilantor, Die Götter der neuen Arten, 2019
UV-Print auf Acryl
60 × 80 × 1.5 cm

Polilantor, The Gods of New Species, 2019
UV print on acrylic
60 × 80 × 1.5 cm

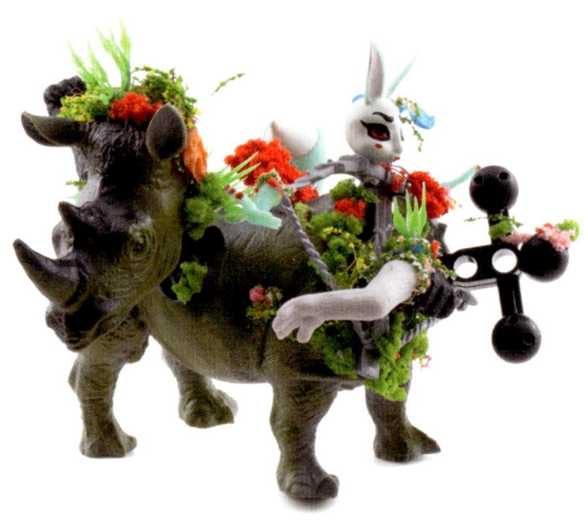

Botrkaemb, Die Götter der neuen Arten, 2019
UV-Print auf Acryl
60 × 80 × 1.5 cm

Botrkaemb, The Gods of New Species, 2019
UV print on acrylic
60 × 80 × 1.5 cm

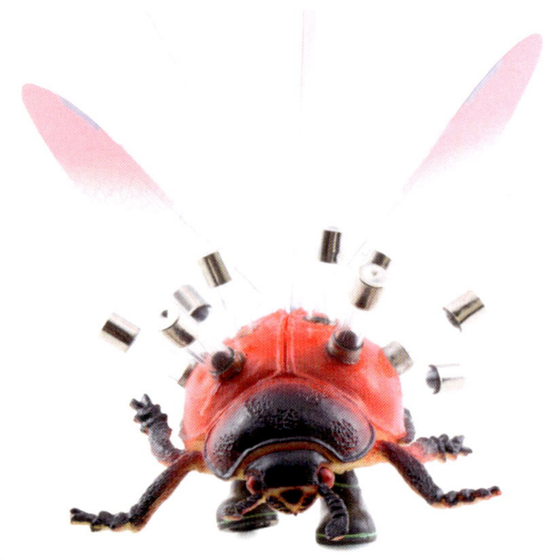

Etimola, Die Götter der neuen Arten, 2019
UV-Print auf Acryl
60 × 80 × 1.5 cm

Etimola, The Gods of New Species, 2019
UV print on acrylic
60 × 80 × 1.5 cm

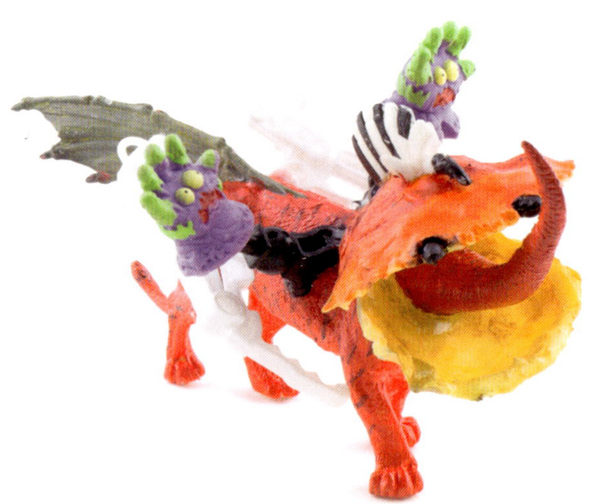

Tsusyp, Die Götter der neuen Arten, 2019
UV-Print auf Acryl
60 × 80 × 1.5 cm

Tsusyp, The Gods of New Species, 2019
UV print on acrylic
60 × 80 × 1.5 cm

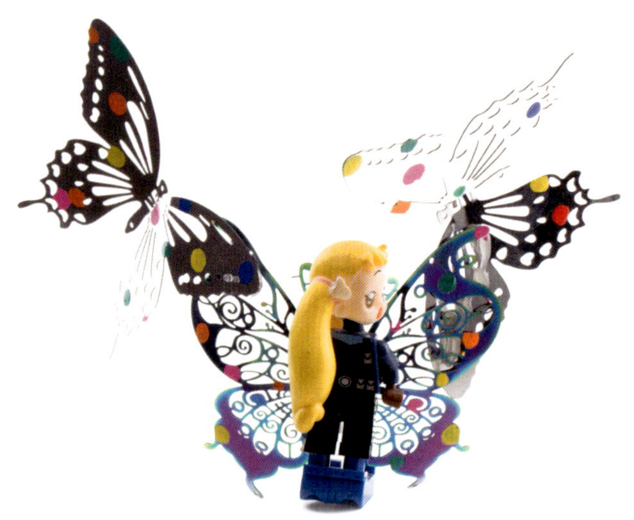

Phigletis, Die Götter der neuen Arten, 2019
UV-Print auf Acryl
60 × 80 × 1.5 cm

Phigletis, The Gods of New Species, 2019
UV print on acrylic
60 × 80 × 1.5 cm

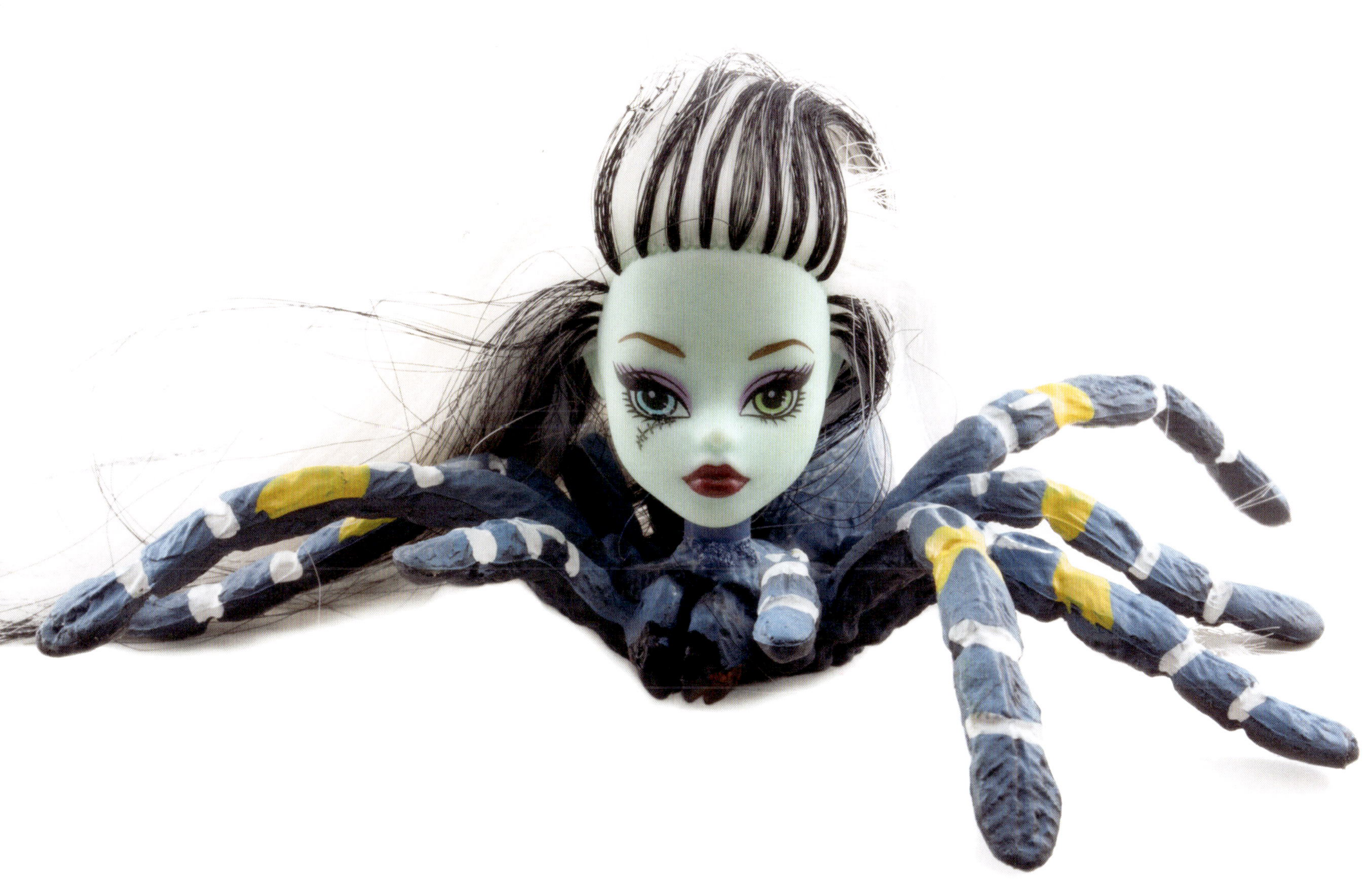

Brysemho, Die Götter der neuen Arten, 2019
UV-Print auf Acryl
60 × 80 × 1.5 cm

Brysemho, The Gods of New Species, 2019
UV print on acrylic
60 × 80 × 1.5 cm

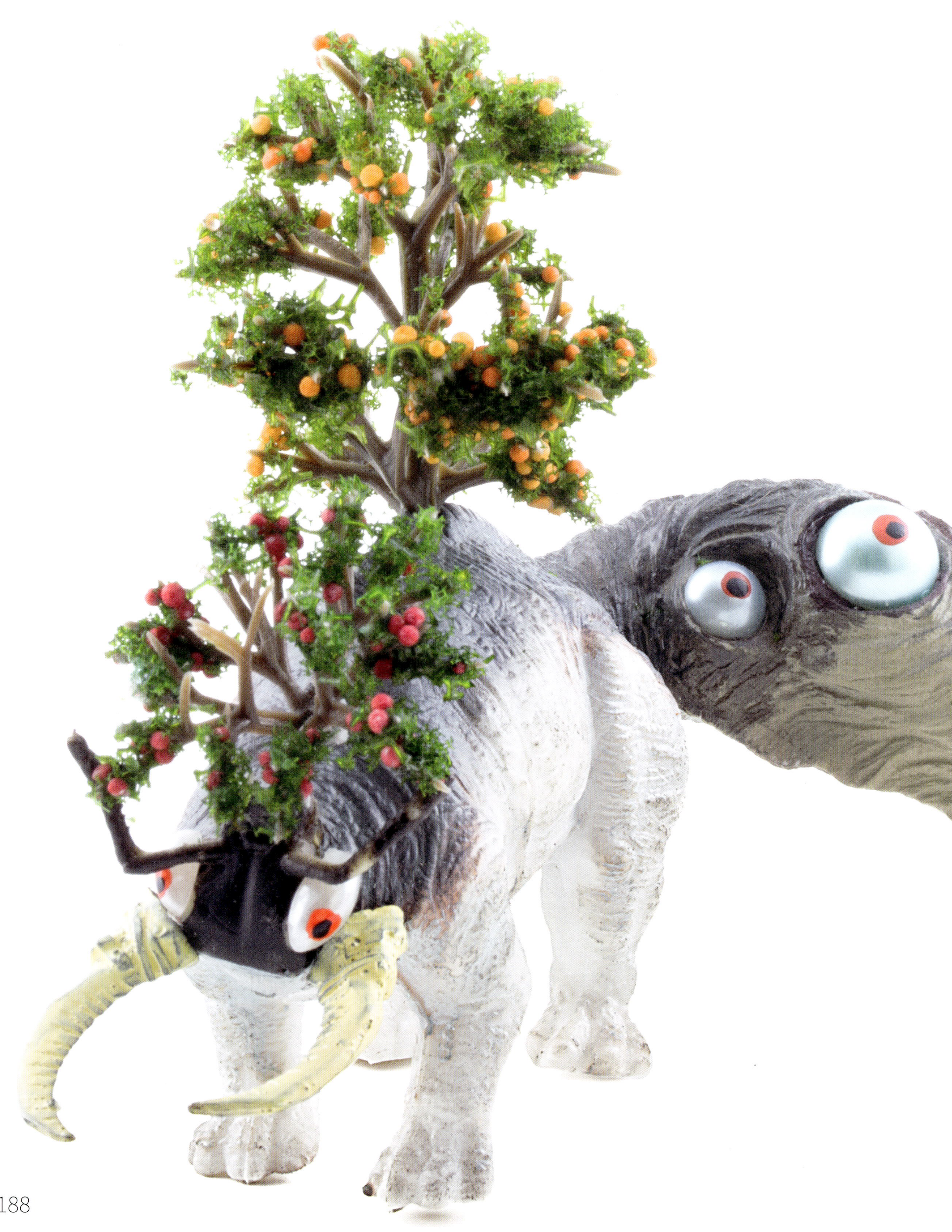

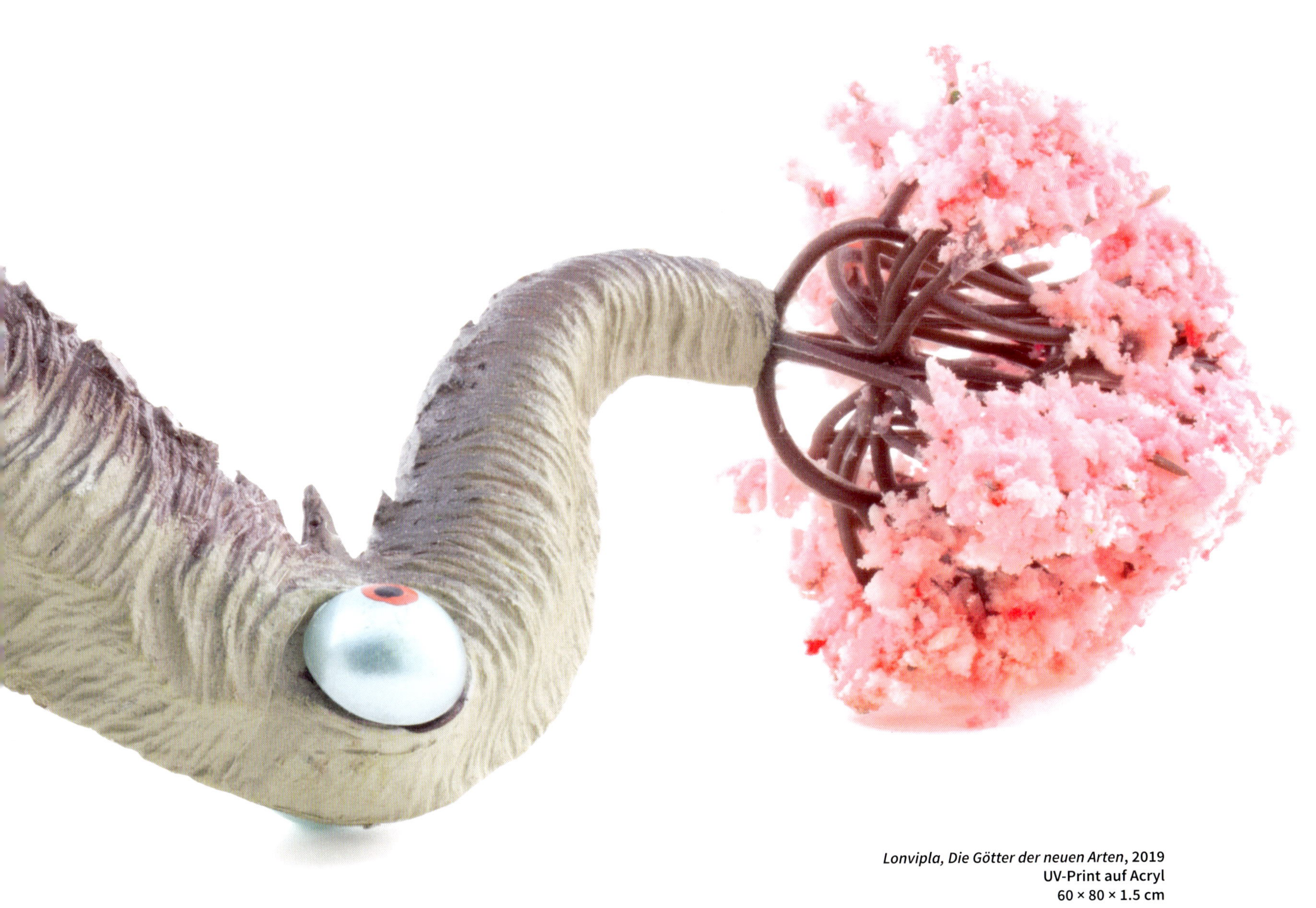

Lonvipla, Die Götter der neuen Arten, 2019
UV-Print auf Acryl
60 × 80 × 1.5 cm

Lonvipla, The Gods of New Species, 2019
UV print on acrylic
60 × 80 × 1.5 cm

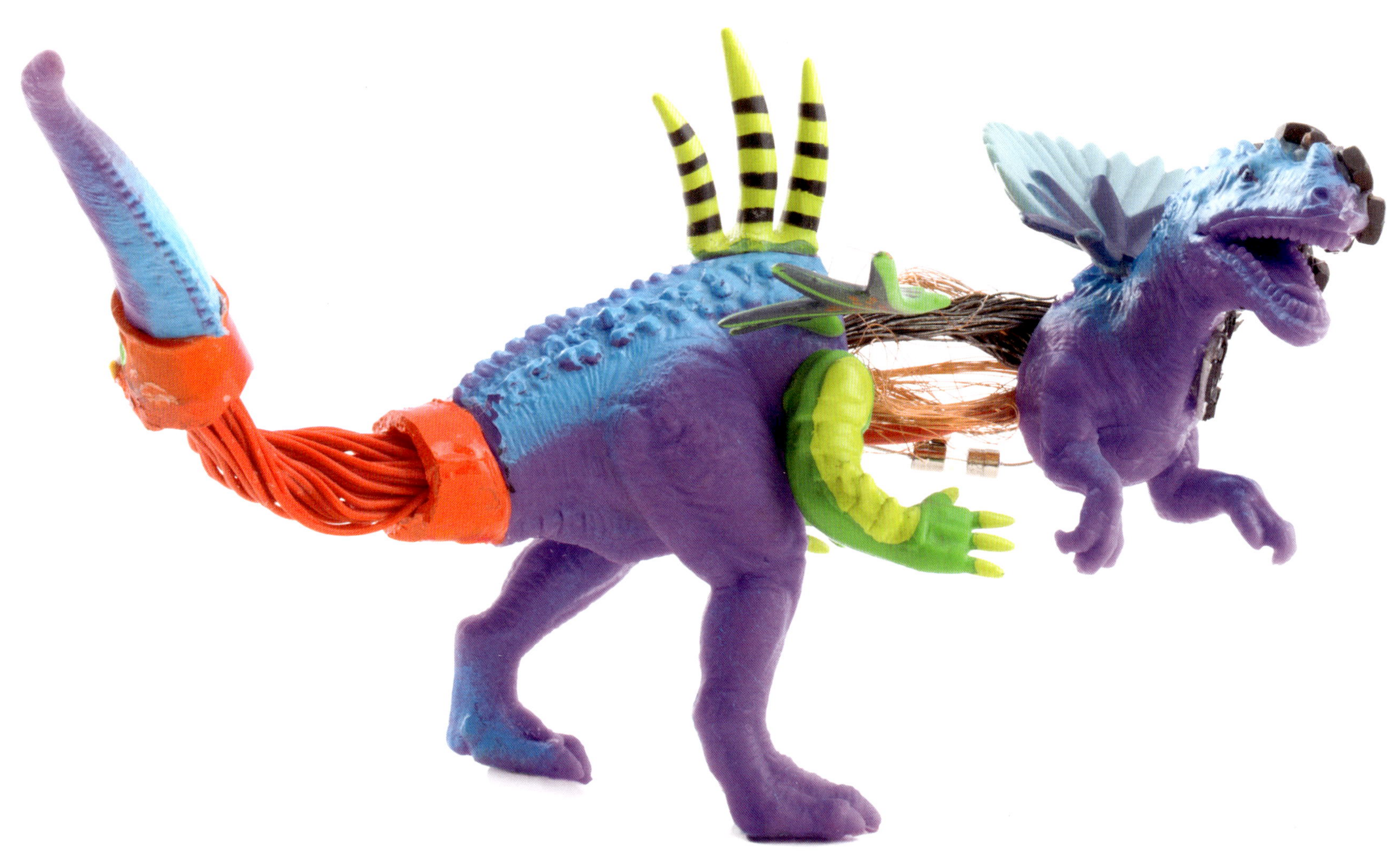

Tejsyp, Die Götter der neuen Arten, 2019
UV-Print auf Acryl
60 × 80 × 1.5 cm

Tejsyp, The Gods of New Species, 2019
UV print on acrylic
60 × 80 × 1.5 cm

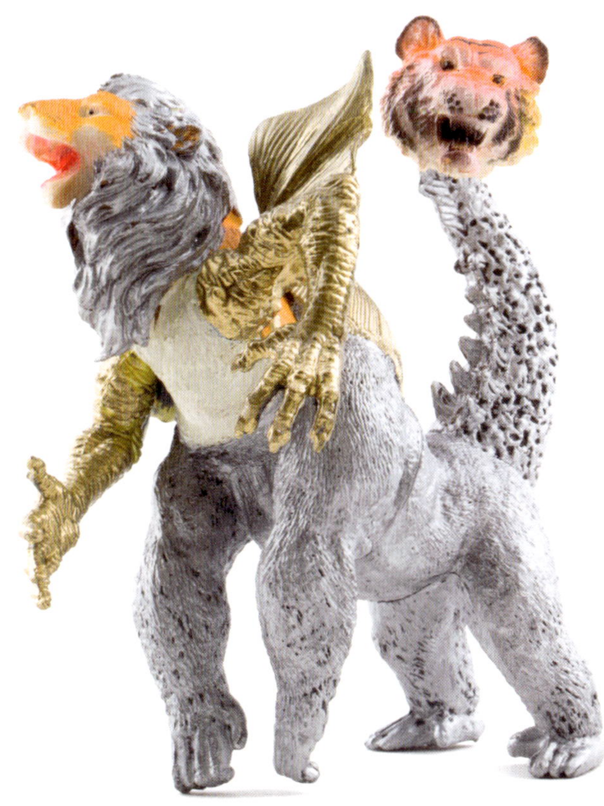

Ranttayaf, Die Götter der neuen Arten, 2019
UV-Print auf Acryl
60 × 80 × 1.5 cm

Ranttayaf, The Gods of New Species, 2019
UV print on acrylic
60 × 80 × 1.5 cm

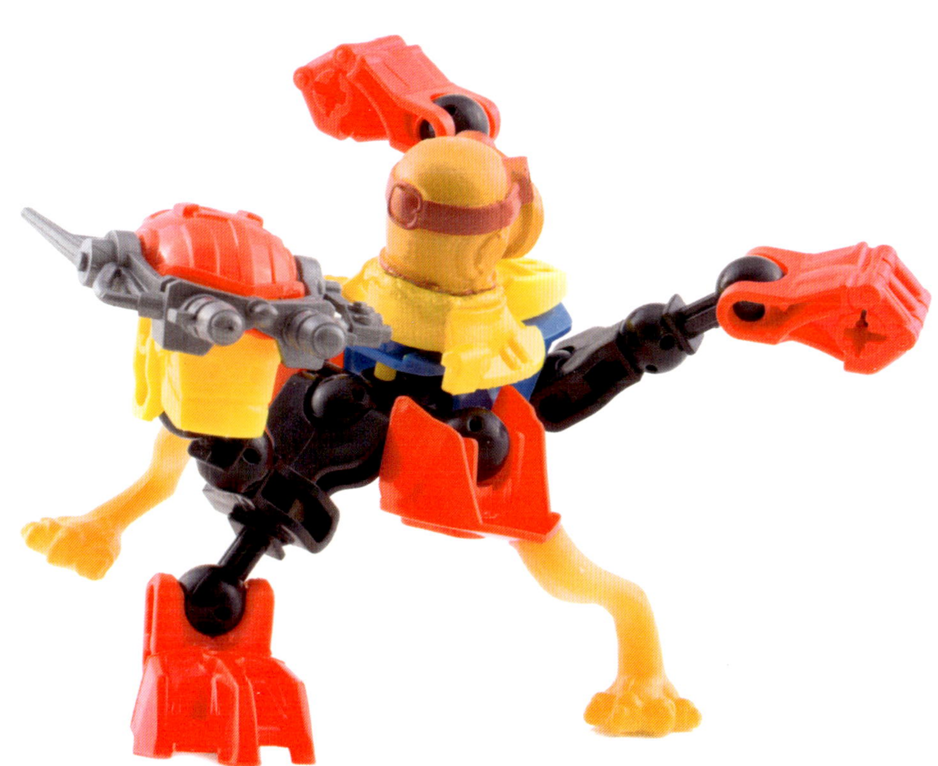

Busaiflix, Die Götter der neuen Arten, 2019
UV-Print auf Acryl
60 × 80 × 1.5 cm

Busaiflix, The Gods of New Species, 2019
UV print on acrylic
60 × 80 × 1.5 cm

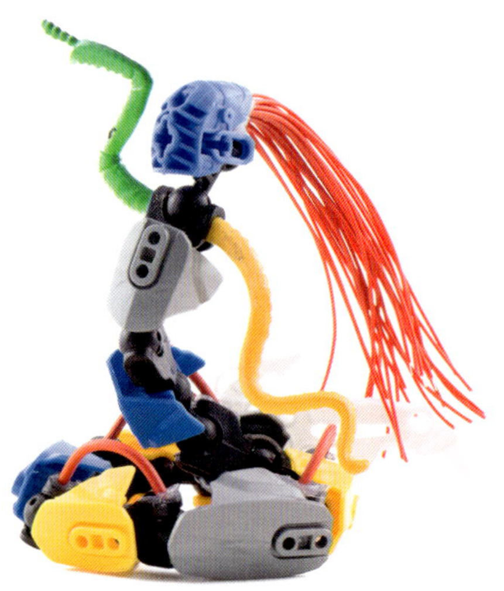

Eaiwerly, Die Götter der neuen Arten, 2019
UV-Print auf Acryl
60 × 80 × 1.5 cm

Eaiwerly, The Gods of New Species, 2019
UV print on acrylic
60 × 80 × 1.5 cm

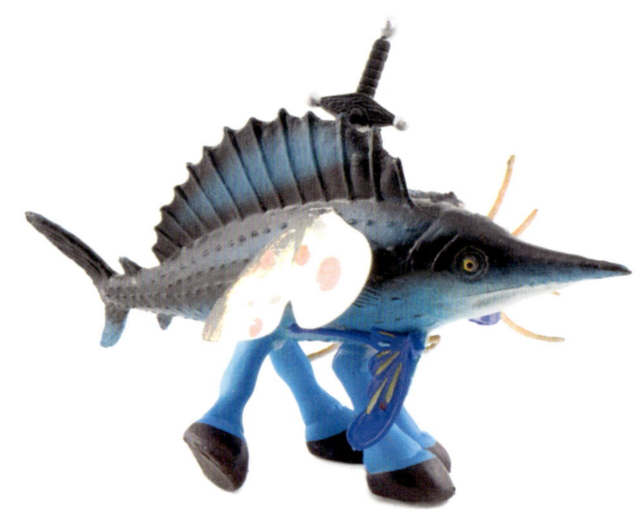

Kaimaika, Die Götter der neuen Arten, 2019
UV-Print auf Acryl
60 × 80 × 1.5 cm

Kaimaika, The Gods of New Species, 2019
UV print on acrylic
60 × 80 × 1.5 cm

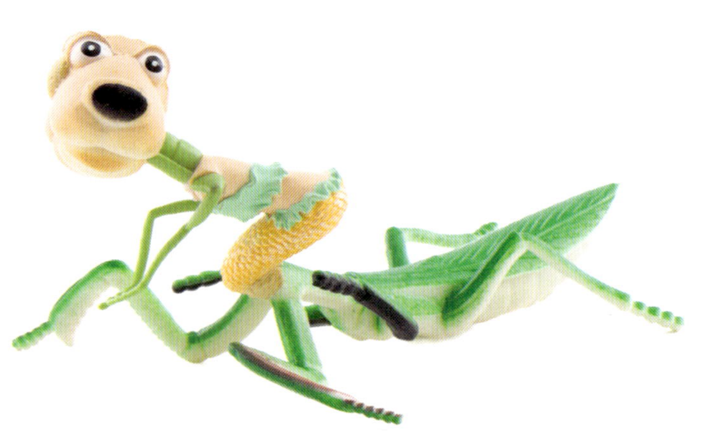

Xsadisa, Die Götter der neuen Arten, 2019
UV-Print auf Acryl
60 × 80 × 1.5 cm

Xsadisa, The Gods of New Species, 2019
UV print on acrylic
60 × 80 × 1.5 cm

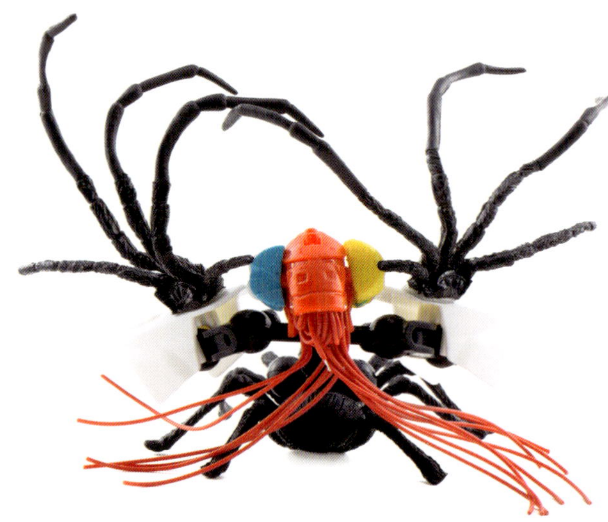

Mcezhaemb, Die Götter der neuen Arten, 2019
UV-Print auf Acryl
60 × 80 × 1.5 cm

Mcezhaemb, The Gods of New Species, 2019
UV print on acrylic
60 × 80 × 1.5 cm

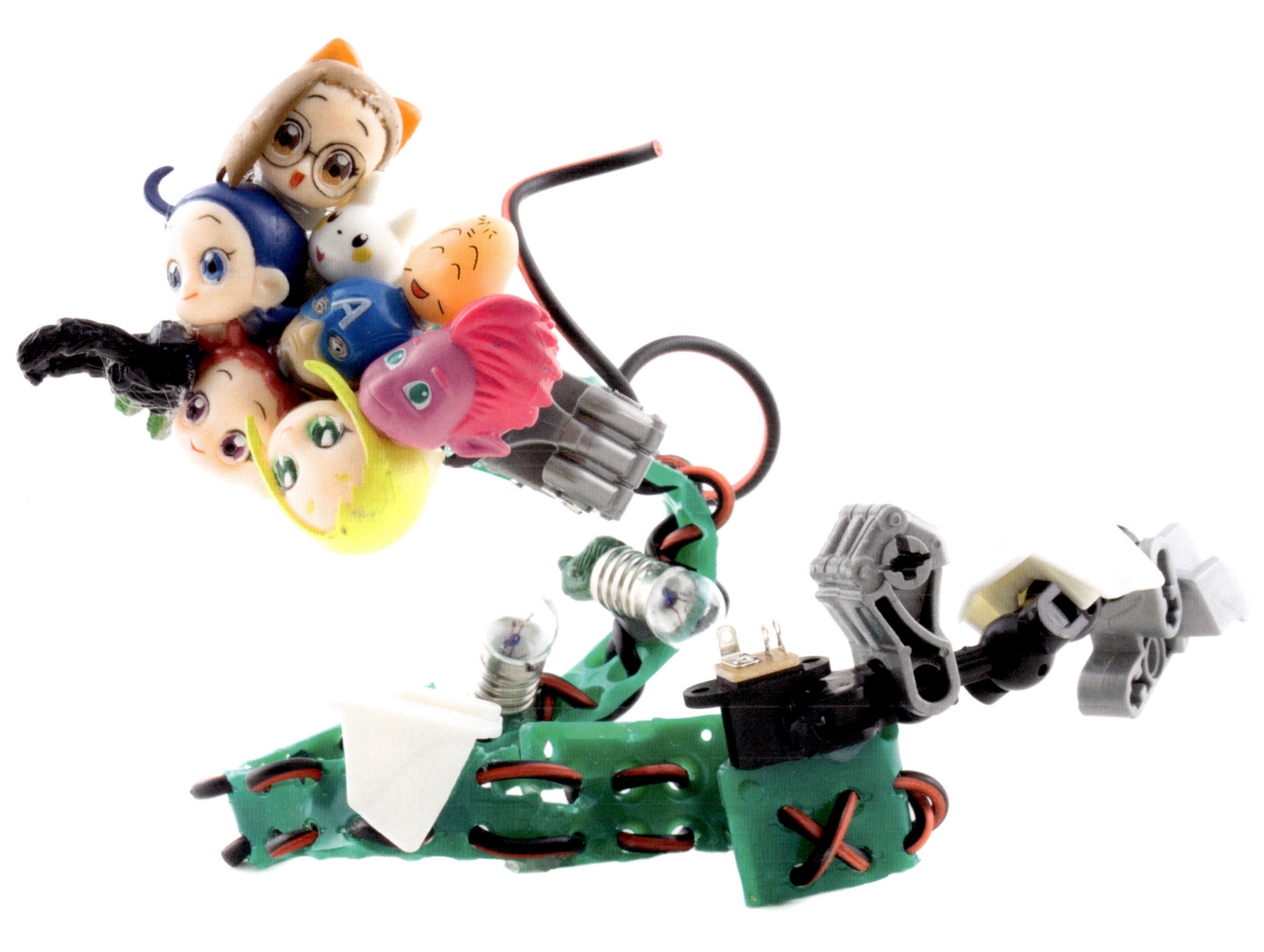

Sumgankar, Die Götter der neuen Arten, 2019
UV-Print auf Acryl
60 × 80 × 1.5 cm

Sumgankar, The Gods of New Species, 2019
UV print on acrylic
60 × 80 × 1.5 cm

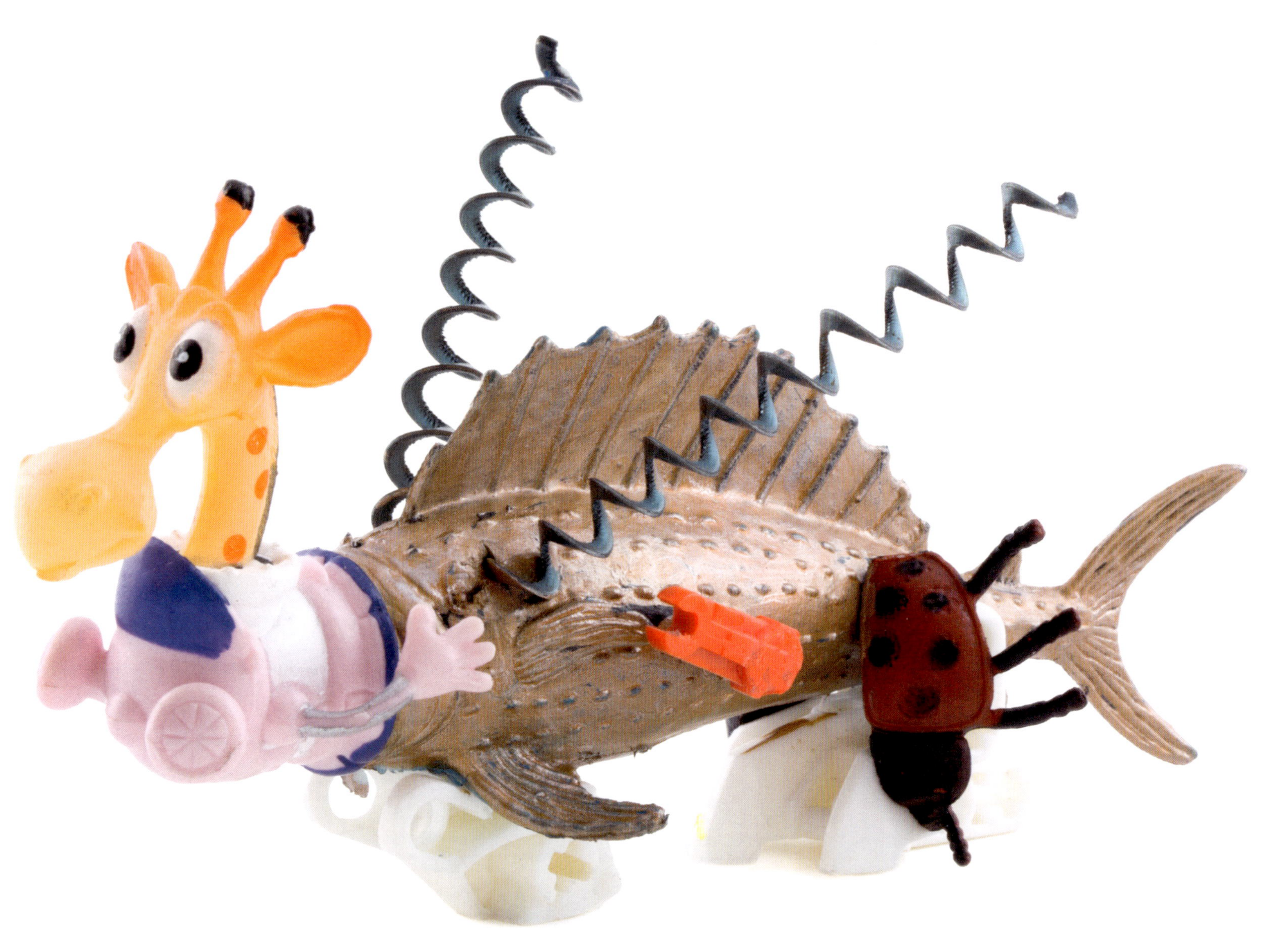

Layalala, Die Götter der neuen Arten, 2019
UV-Print auf Acryl
60 × 80 × 1.5 cm

Layalala, The Gods of New Species, 2019
UV print on acrylic
60 × 80 × 1.5 cm

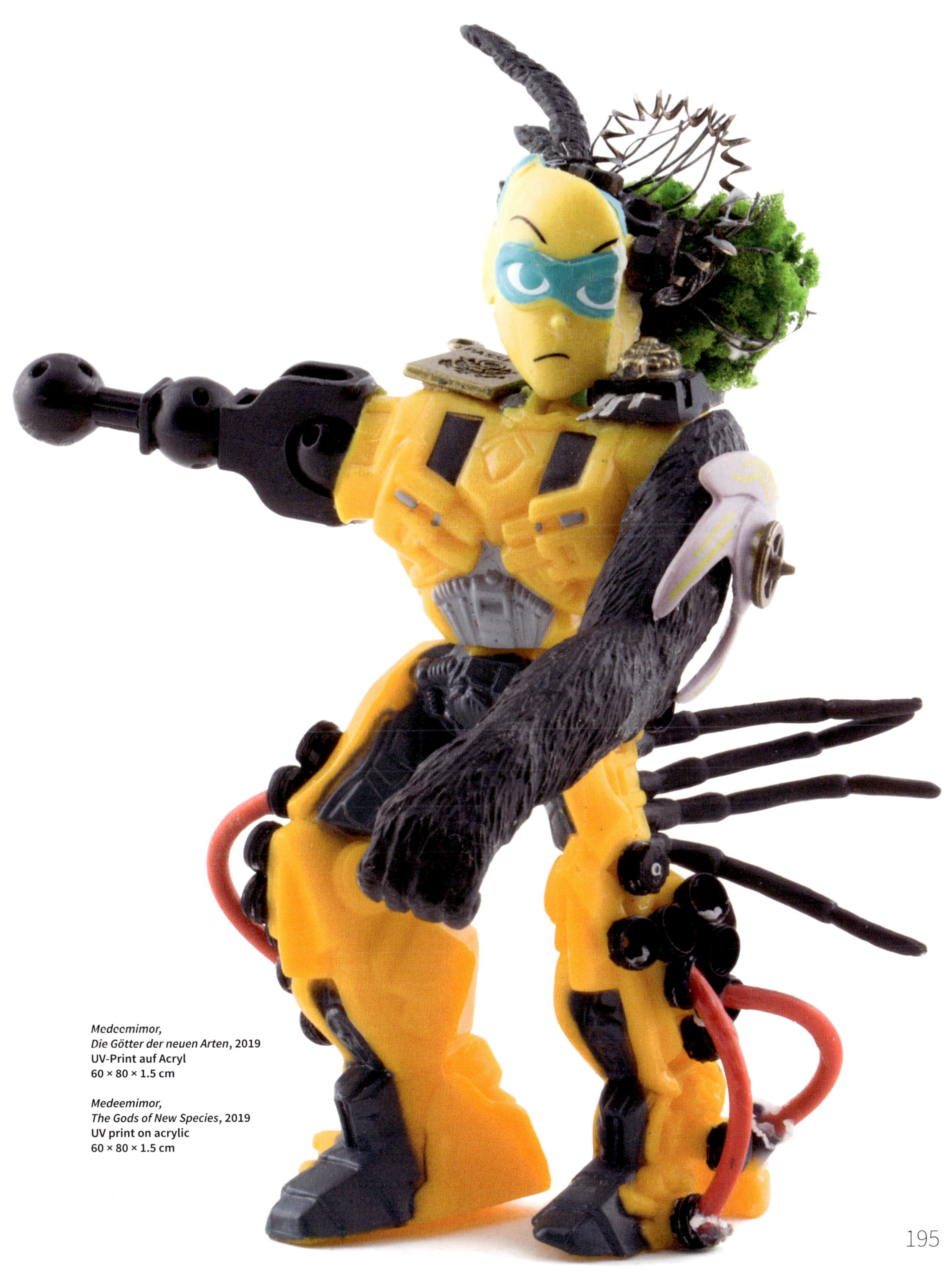

Medeemimor,
Die Götter der neuen Arten, 2019
UV-Print auf Acryl
60 × 80 × 1.5 cm

Medeemimor,
The Gods of New Species, 2019
UV print on acrylic
60 × 80 × 1.5 cm

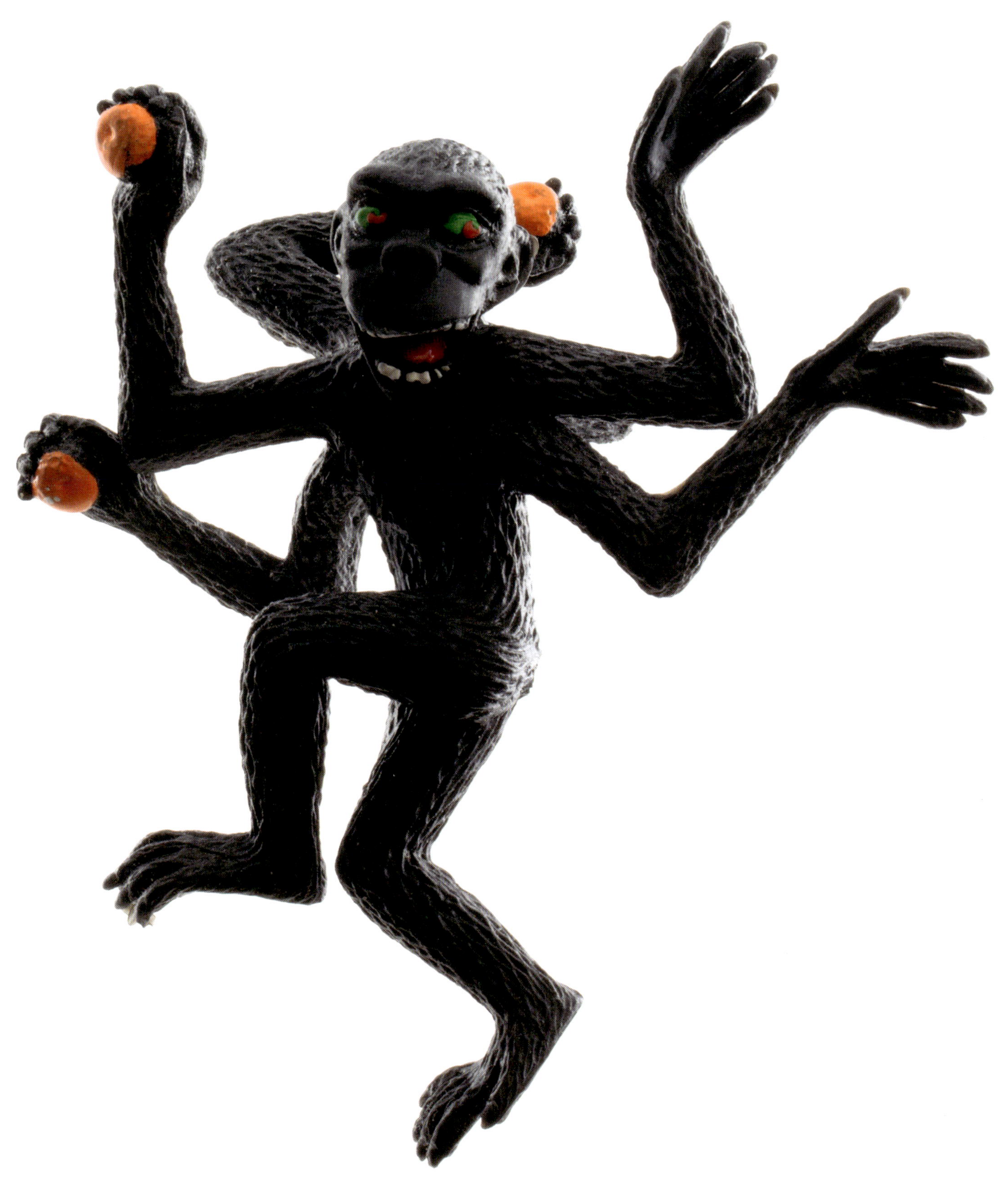

Pytolia, Die Götter der neuen Arten, 2019
UV-Print auf Acryl
60 × 80 × 1.5 cm

Pytolia, The Gods of New Species, 2019
UV print on acrylic
60 × 80 × 1.5 cm

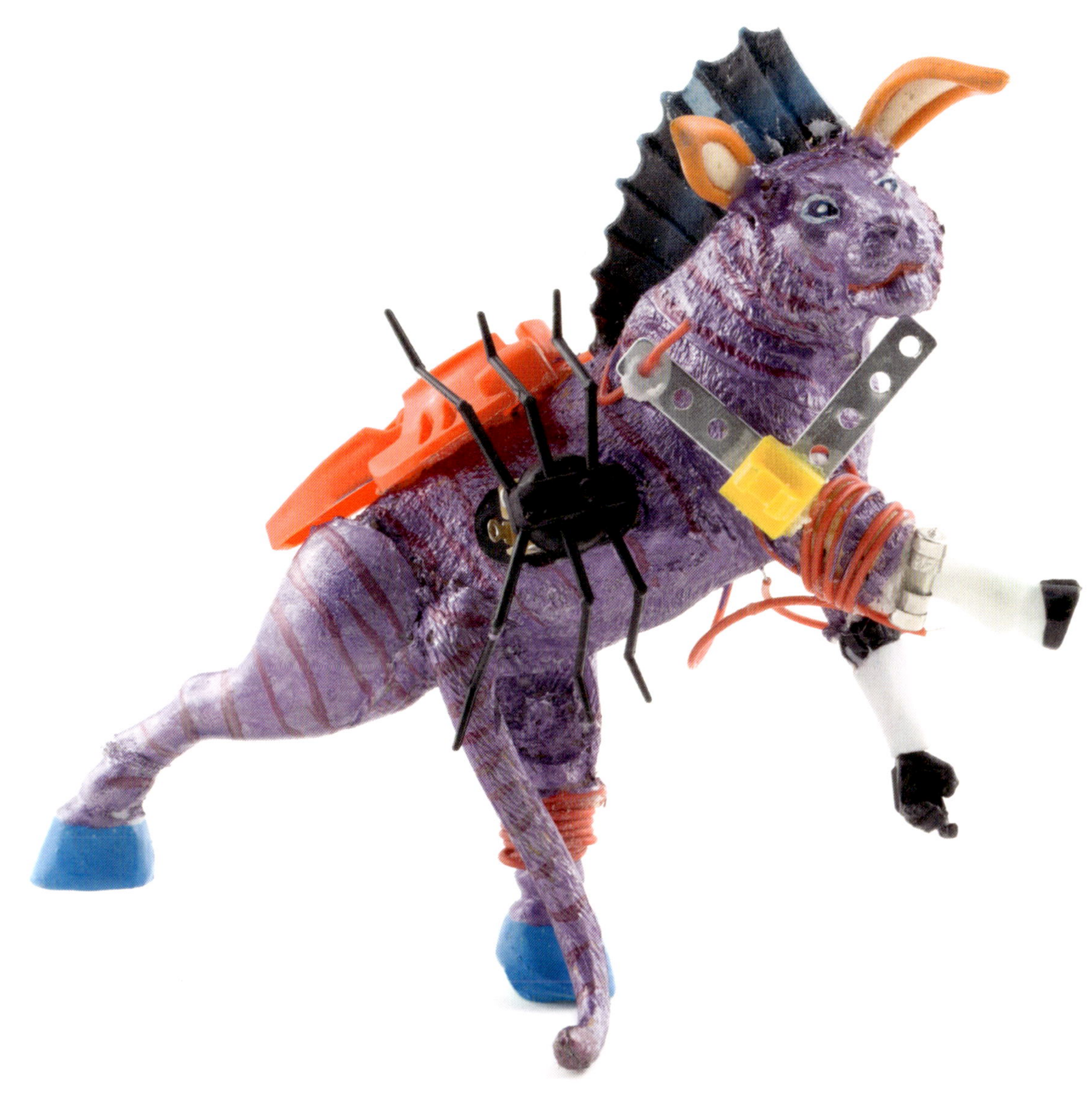

Ranttayarb, Die Götter der neuen Arten, 2019
UV-Print auf Acryl
60 × 80 × 1.5 cm

Ranttayarb, The Gods of New Species, 2019
UV print on acrylic
60 × 80 × 1.5 cm

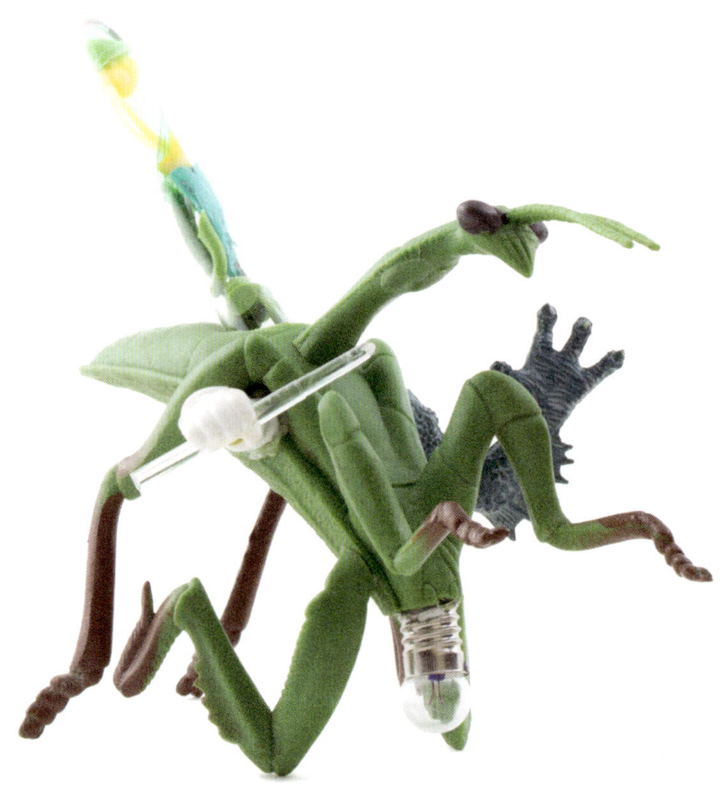

Etiomza, Die Götter der neuen Arten, 2019
UV-Print auf Acryl
60 × 80 × 1.5 cm

Etiomza, The Gods of New Species, 2019
UV print on acrylic
60 × 80 × 1.5 cm

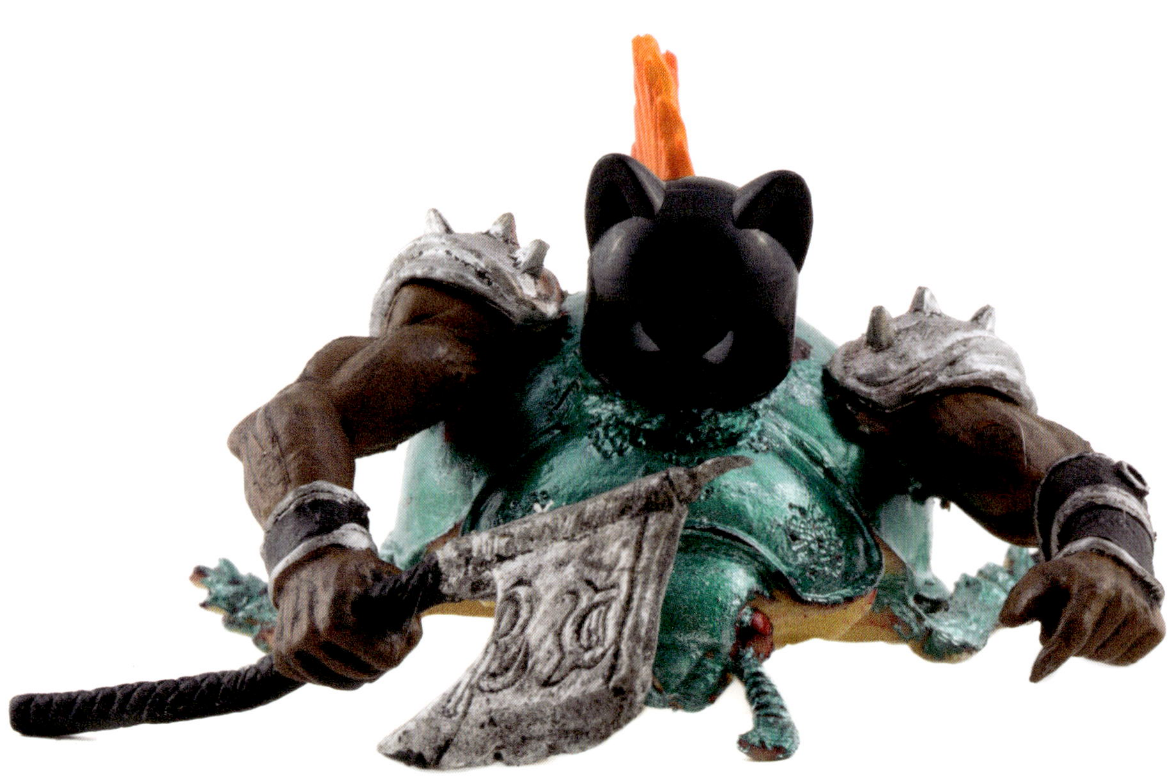

Exfofahan, Die Götter der neuen Arten, 2019
UV-Print auf Acryl
60 × 80 × 1.5 cm

Exfofahan, The Gods of New Species, 2019
UV print on acrylic
60 × 80 × 1.5 cm

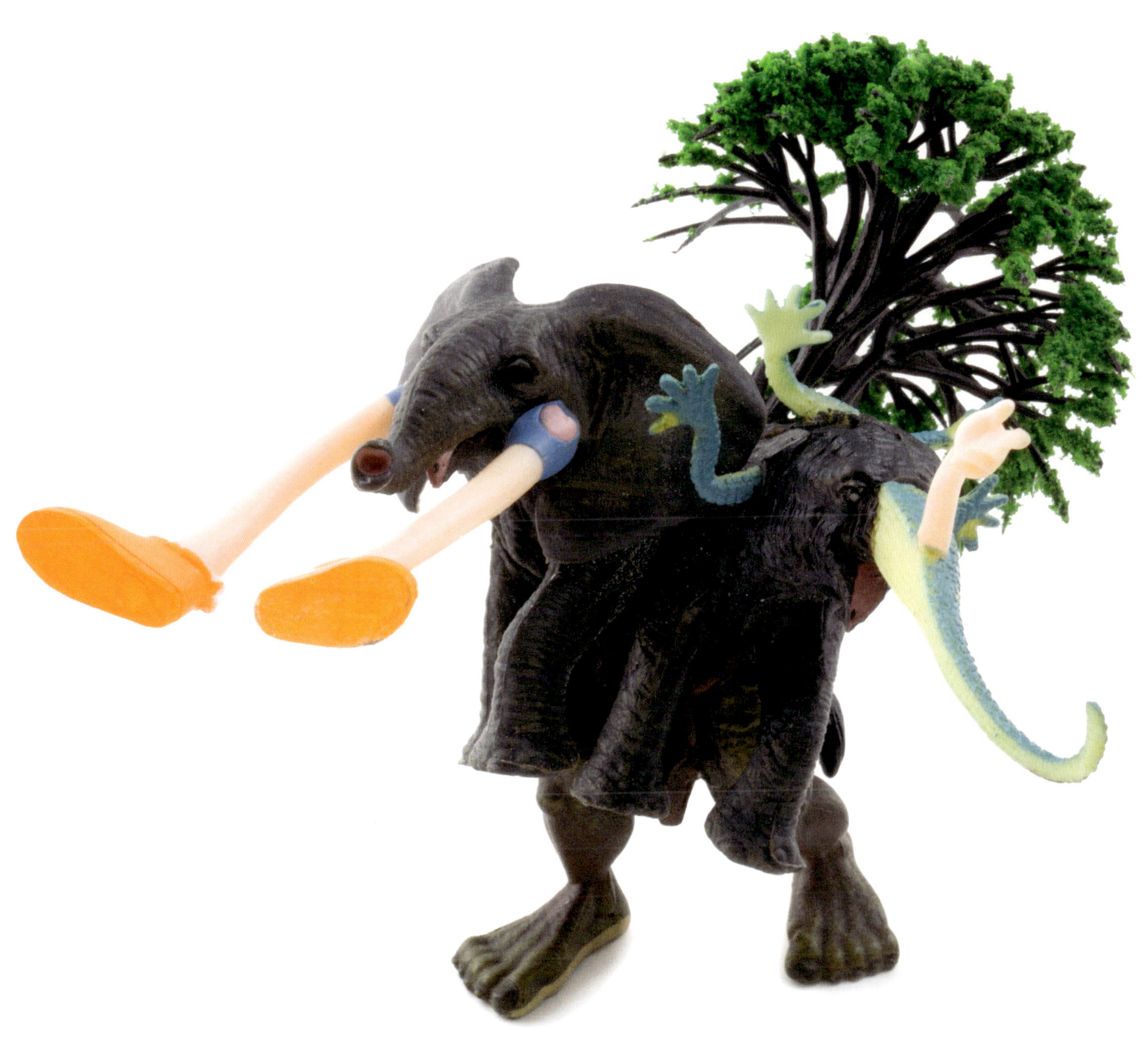

Xsapbka, Die Götter der neuen Arten, 2019
UV-Print auf Acryl
60 × 80 × 1.5 cm

Xsapbka, The Gods of New Species, 2019
UV print on acrylic
60 × 80 × 1.5 cm

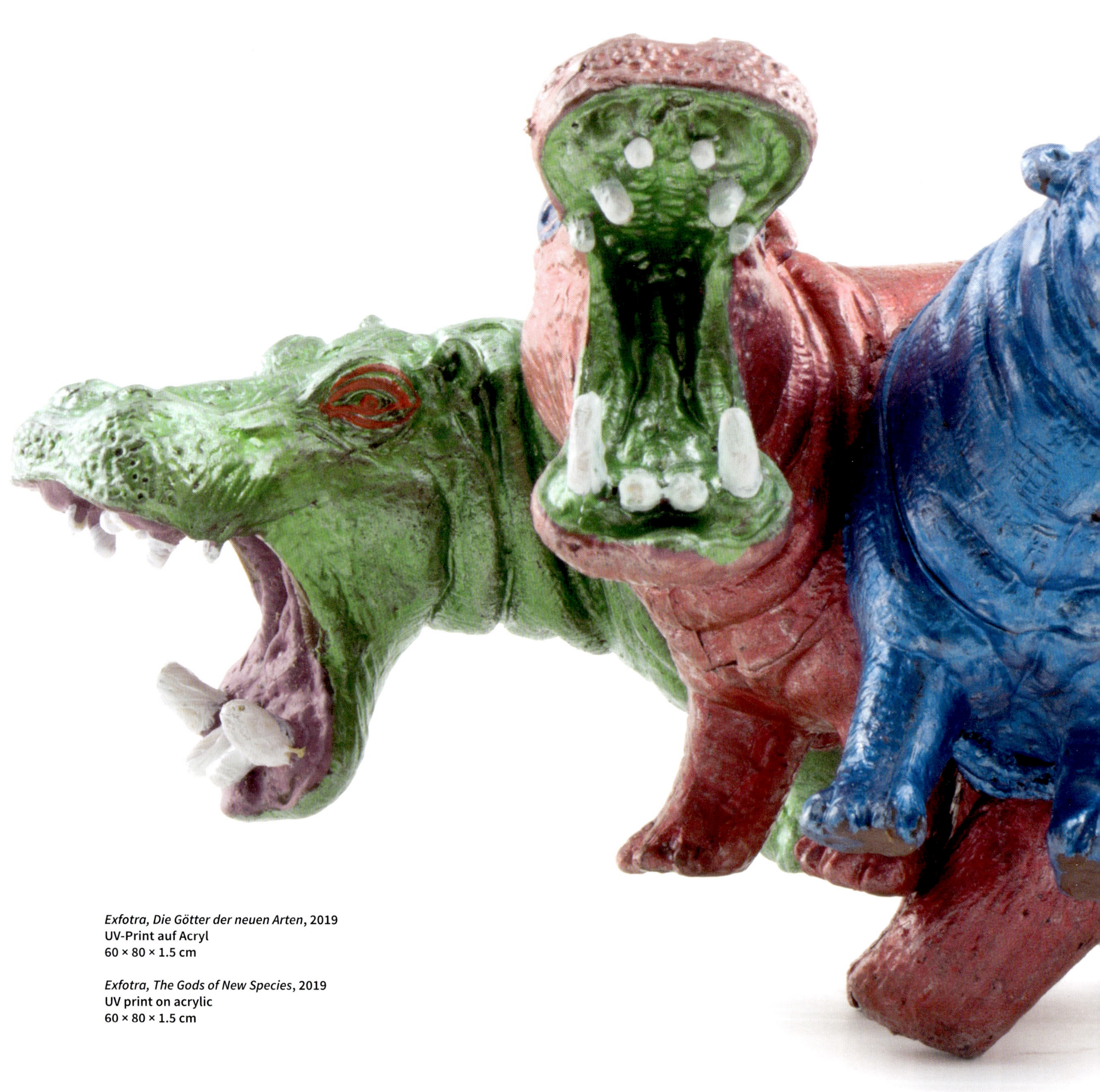

Exfotra, Die Götter der neuen Arten, 2019
UV-Print auf Acryl
60 × 80 × 1.5 cm

Exfotra, The Gods of New Species, 2019
UV print on acrylic
60 × 80 × 1.5 cm

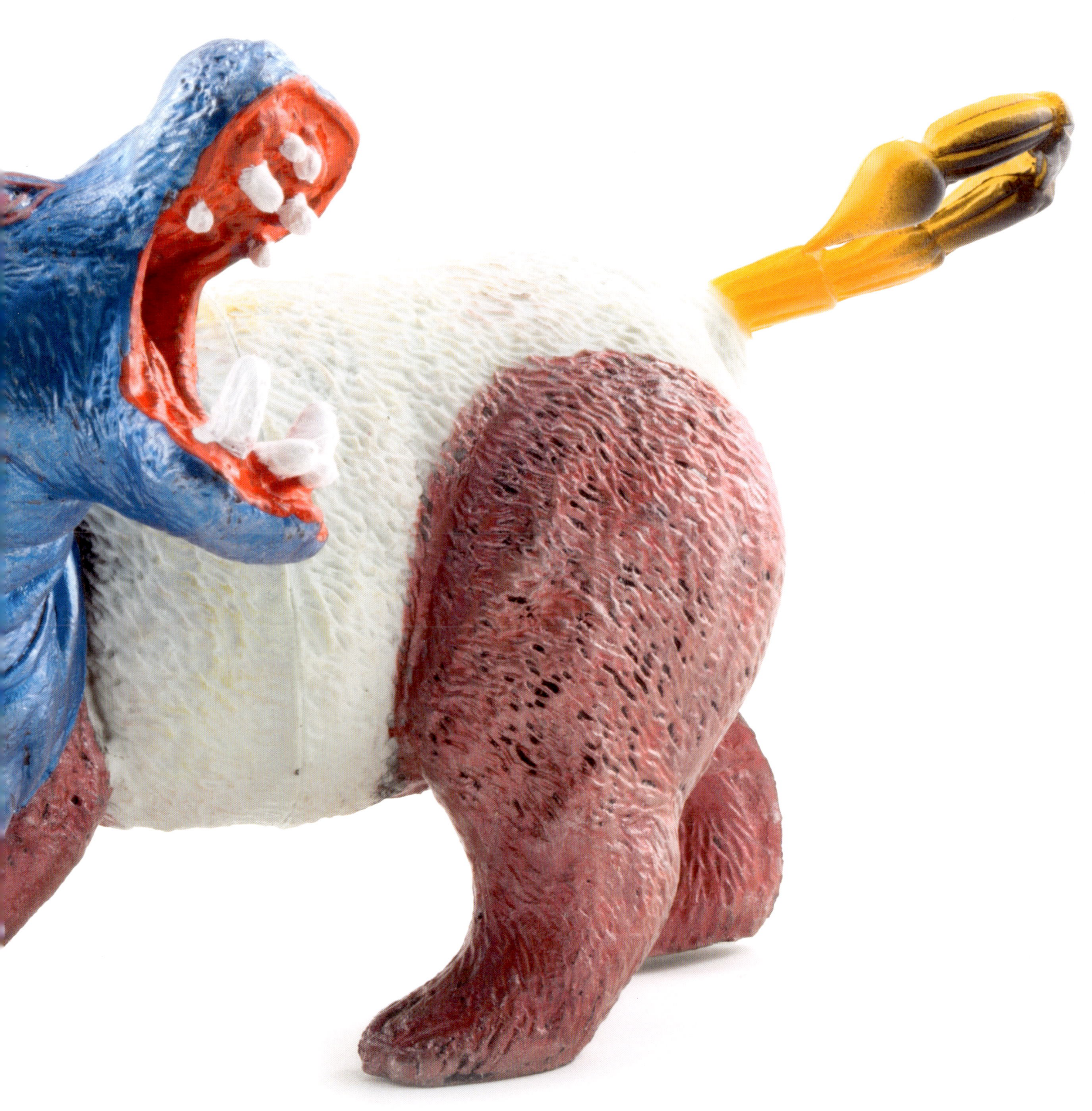

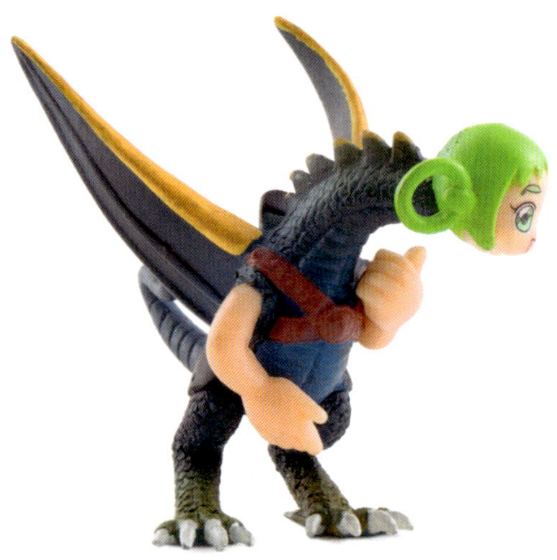

Vihaeif, Die Götter der neuen Arten, 2019
UV-Print auf Acryl
60 × 80 × 1.5 cm

Vihaeif, The Gods of New Species, 2019
UV print on acrylic
60 × 80 × 1.5 cm

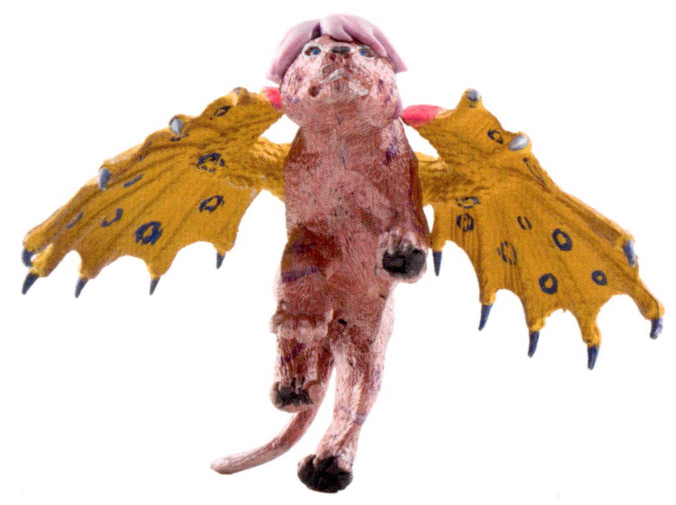

Bfebiocon, Die Götter der neuen Arten, 2019
UV-Print auf Acryl
60 × 80 × 1.5 cm

Bfebiocon, The Gods of New Species, 2019
UV print on acrylic
60 × 80 × 1.5 cm

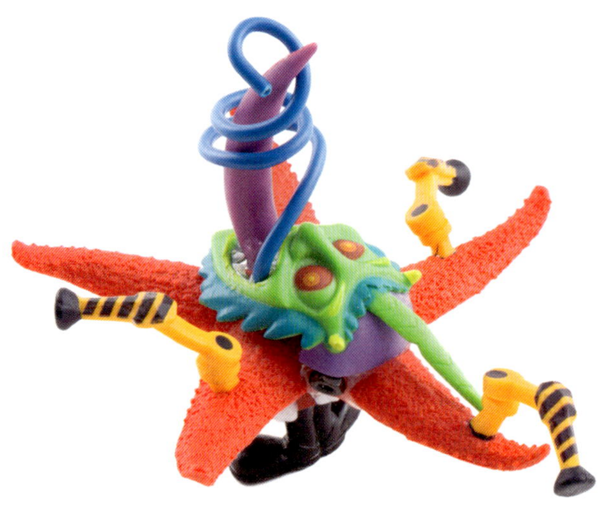

Tasakua, Die Götter der neuen Arten, 2019
UV-Print auf Acryl
60 × 80 × 1.5 cm

Tasakua, The Gods of New Species, 2019
UV print on acrylic
60 × 80 × 1.5 cm

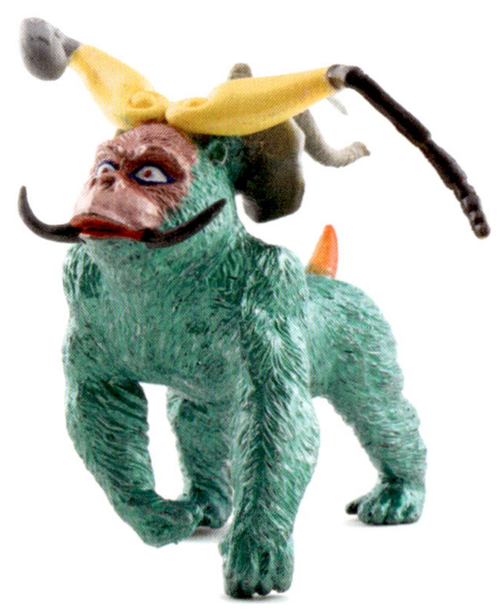

Yhoxauy, Die Götter der neuen Arten, 2019
UV-Print auf Acryl
60 × 80 × 1.5 cm

Yhoxauy, The Gods of New Species, 2019
UV print on acrylic
60 × 80 × 1.5 cm

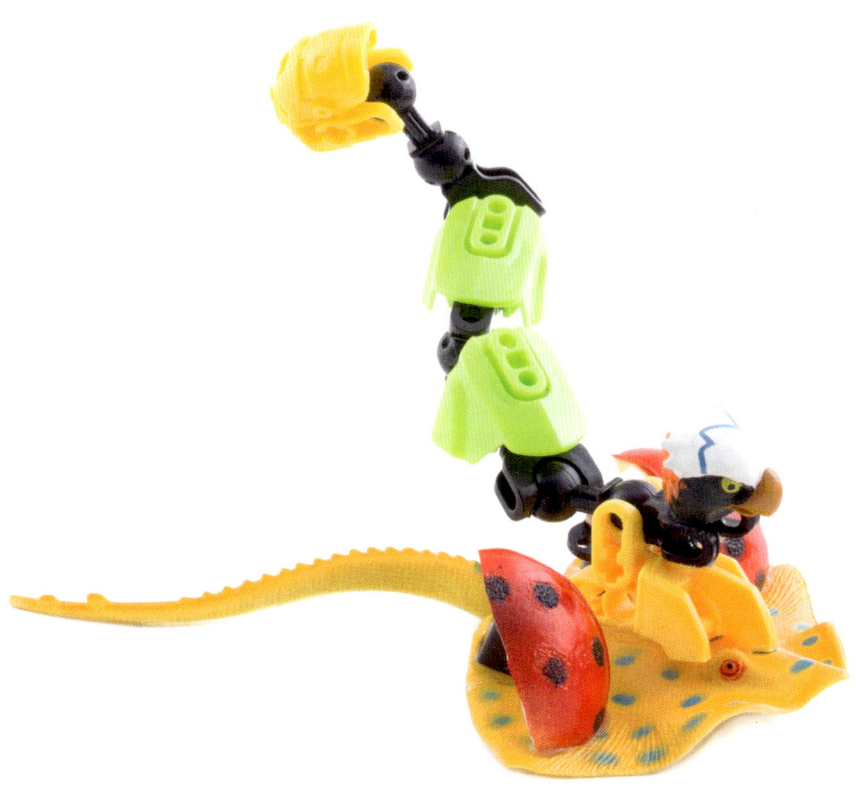

Xsamacha, Die Götter der neuen Arten, 2019
UV-Print auf Acryl
60 × 80 × 1.5 cm

Xsamacha, The Gods of New Species, 2019
UV print on acrylic
60 × 80 × 1.5 cm

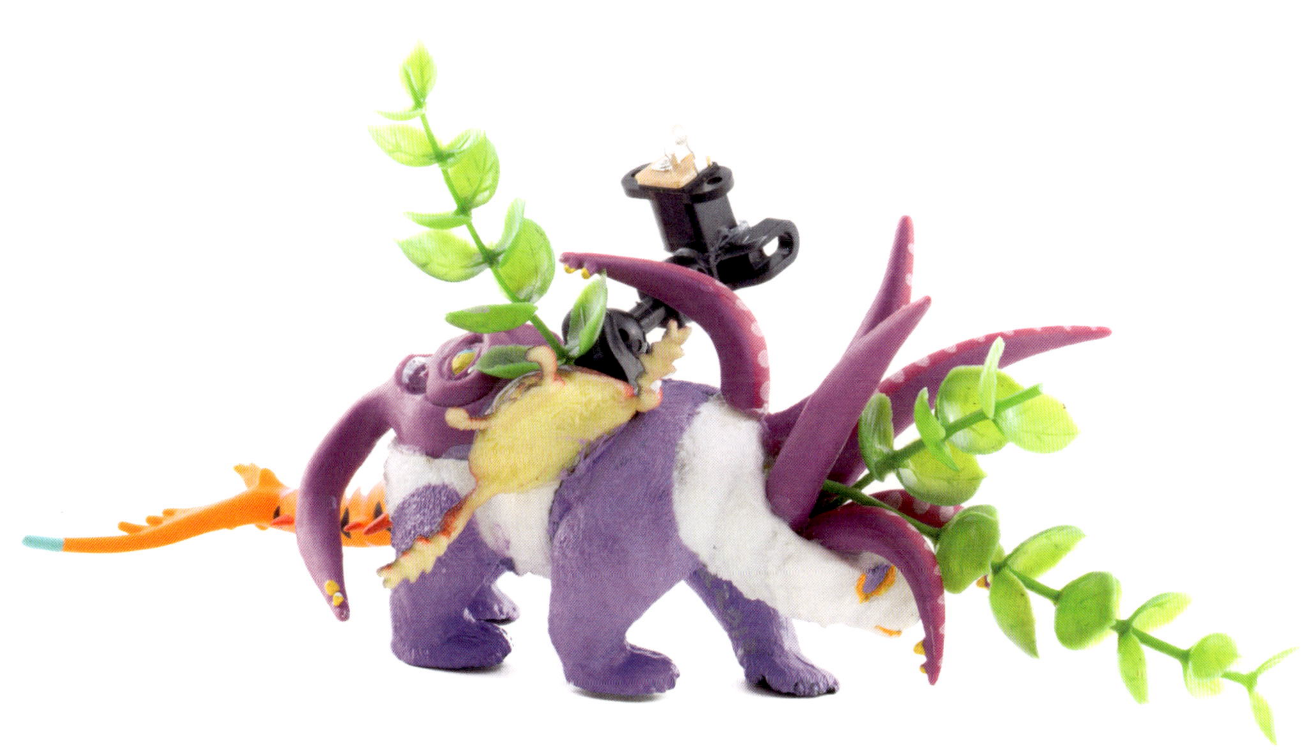

Zuvesye, Die Götter der neuen Arten, 2019
UV-Print auf Acryl
60 × 80 × 1.5 cm

Zuvesye, The Gods of New Species, 2019
UV print on acrylic
60 × 80 × 1.5 cm

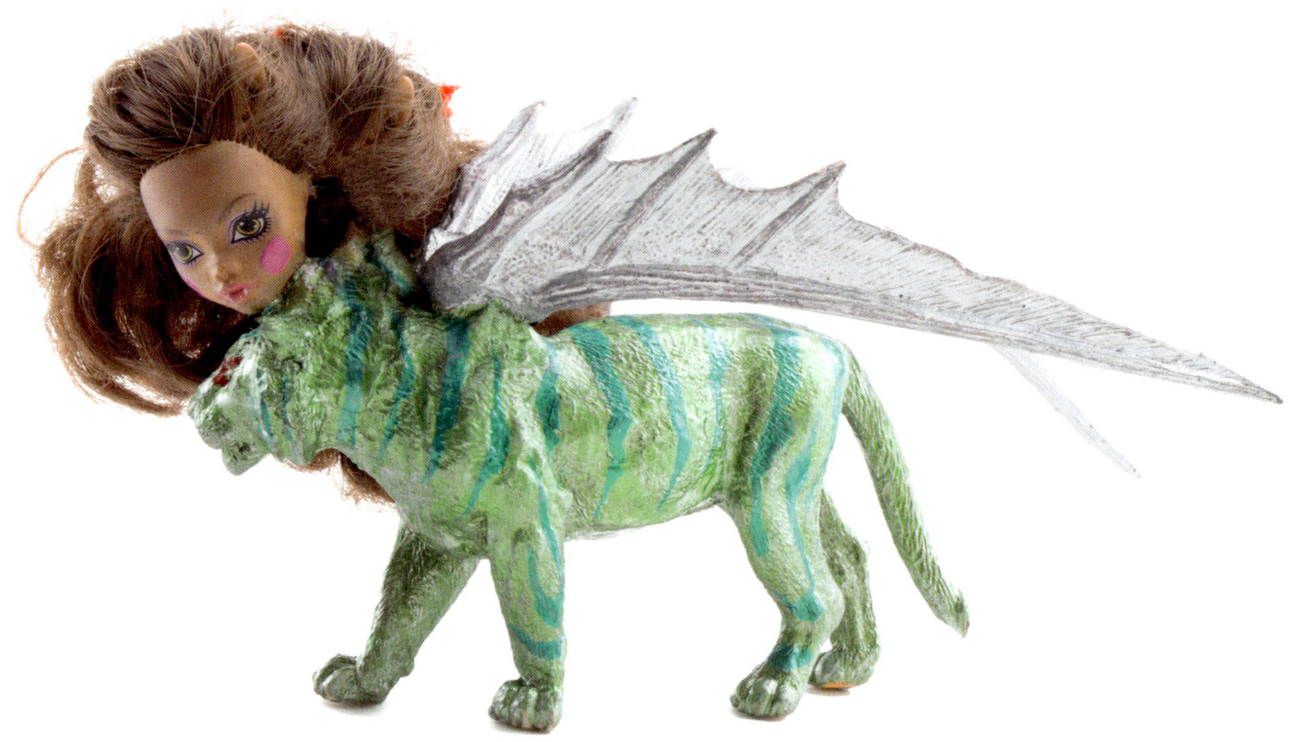

Douhfihon, Die Götter der neuen Arten, 2019
UV-Print auf Acryl
60 × 80 × 1.5 cm

Douhfihon, The Gods of New Species, 2019
UV print on acrylic
60 × 80 × 1.5 cm

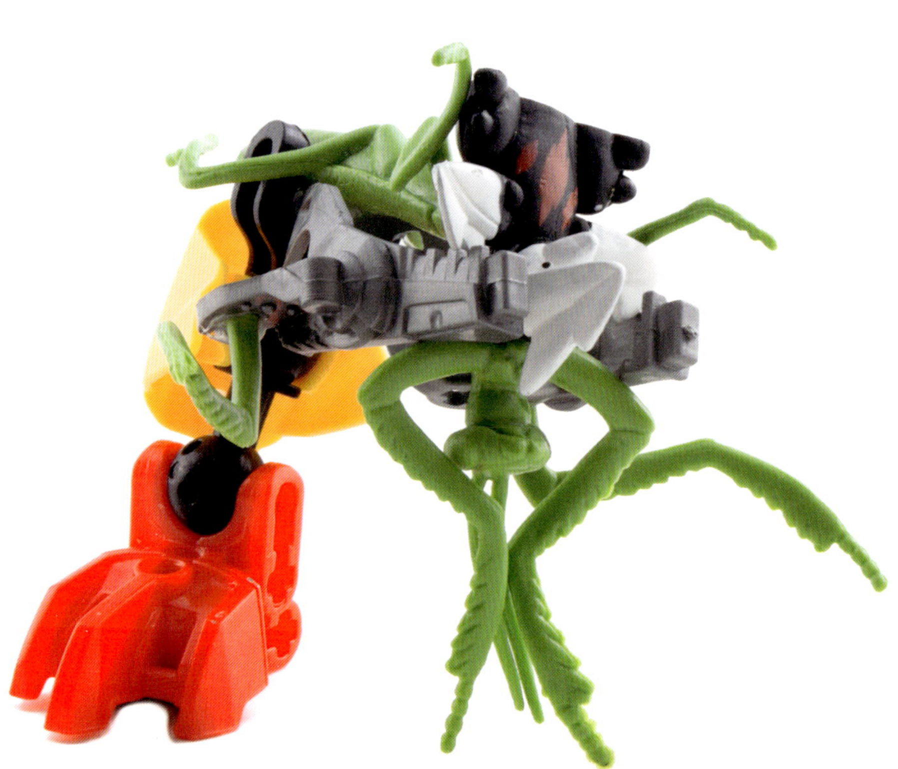

Makjixy, Die Götter der neuen Arten, 2019
UV-Print auf Acryl
60 × 80 × 1.5 cm

Makjixy, The Gods of New Species, 2019
UV print on acrylic
60 × 80 × 1.5 cm

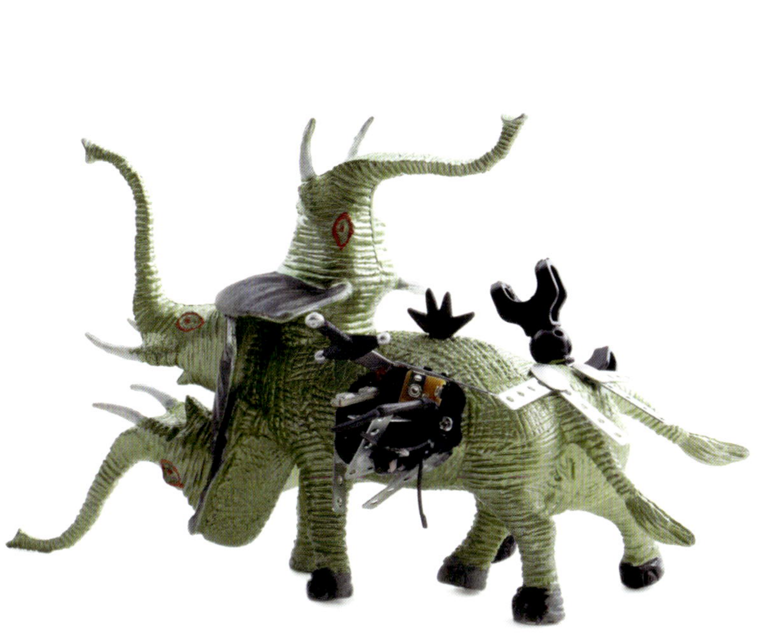

Delishy, Die Götter der neuen Arten, 2019
UV-Print auf Acryl
60 × 80 × 1.5 cm

Delishy, The Gods of New Species, 2019
UV print on acrylic
60 × 80 × 1.5 cm

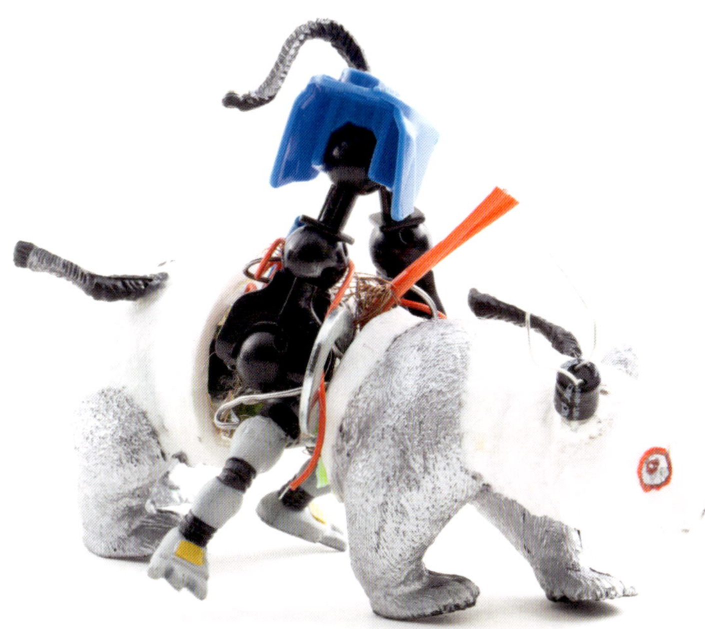

Shaphyhof, Die Götter der neuen Arten, 2019
UV-Print auf Acryl
60 × 80 × 1.5 cm

Shaphyhof, The Gods of New Species, 2019
UV print on acrylic
60 × 80 × 1.5 cm

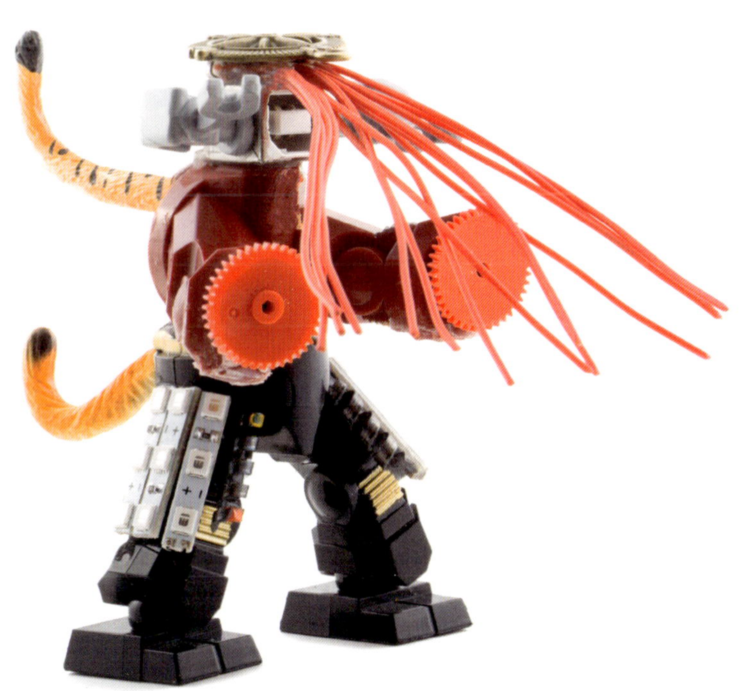

Loteahiya, Die Götter der neuen Arten, 2019
UV-Print auf Acryl
60 × 80 × 1.5 cm

Loteahiya, The Gods of New Species, 2019
UV print on acrylic
60 × 80 × 1.5 cm

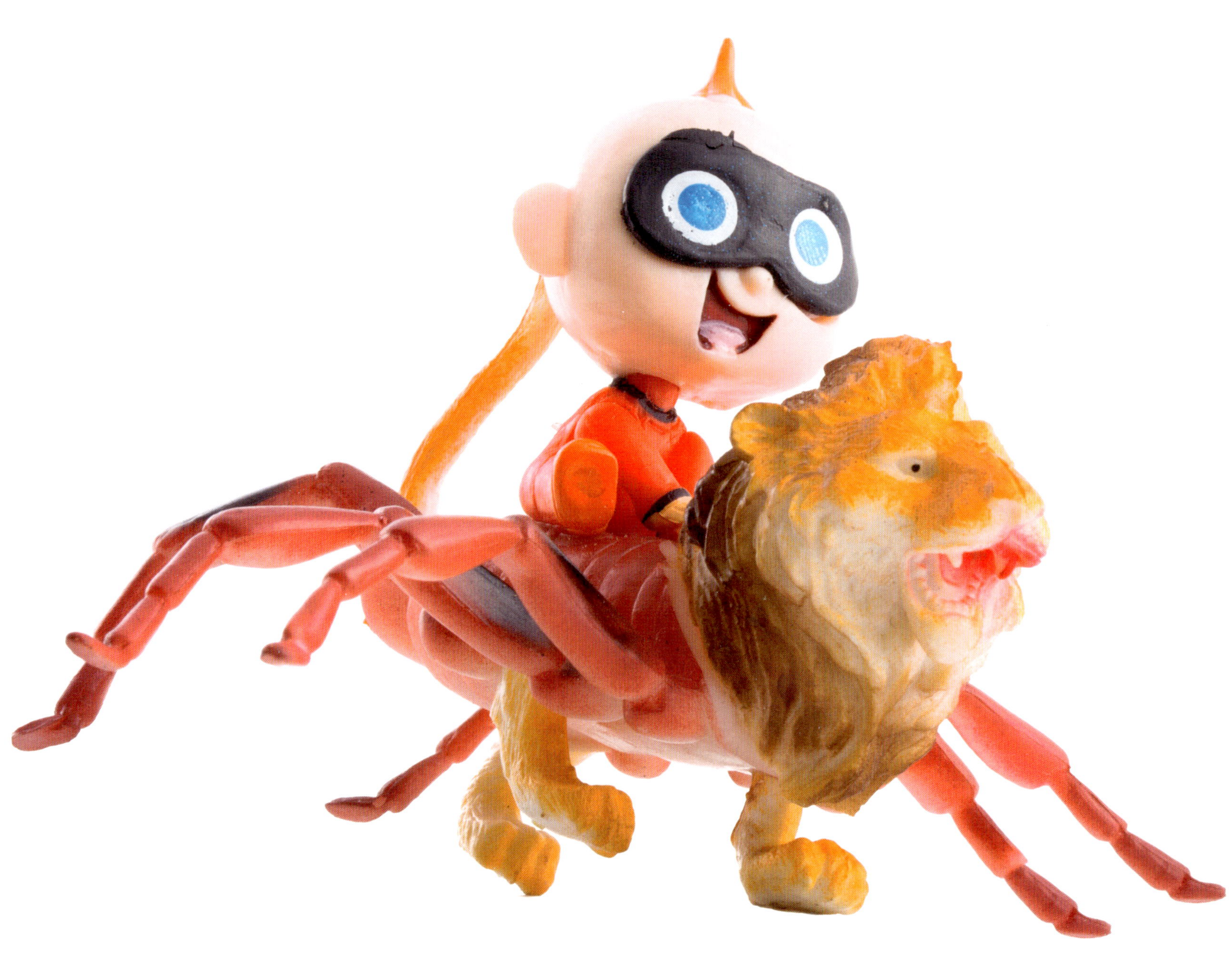

Behlisor, Die Götter der neuen Arten, 2019
UV-Print auf Acryl
60 × 80 × 1.5 cm

Behlisor, The Gods of New Species, 2019
UV print on acrylic
60 × 80 × 1.5 cm

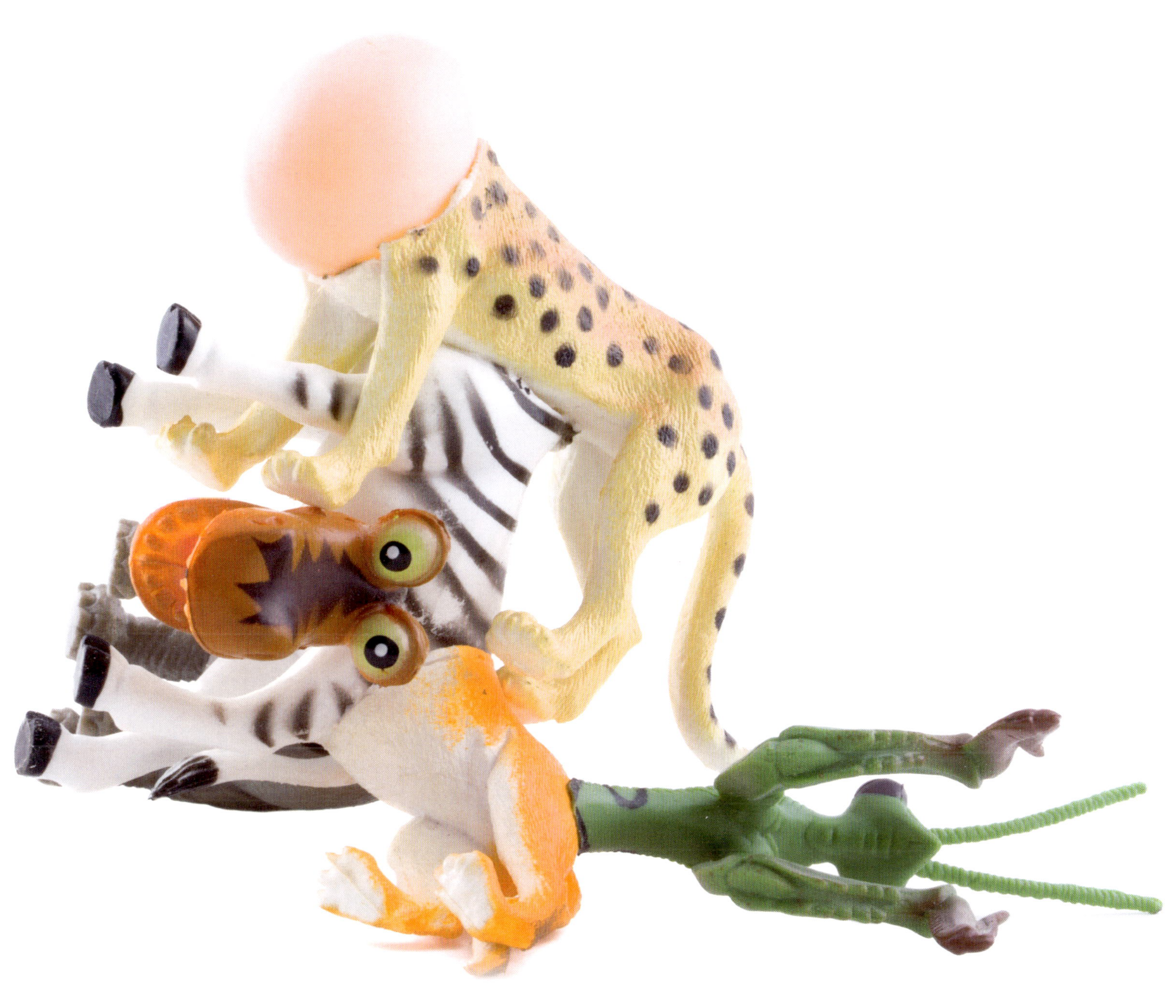

Xsanidoa, Die Götter der neuen Arten, 2019
UV-Print auf Acryl
60 × 80 × 1.5 cm

Xsanidoa, The Gods of New Species, 2019
UV print on acrylic
60 × 80 × 1.5 cm

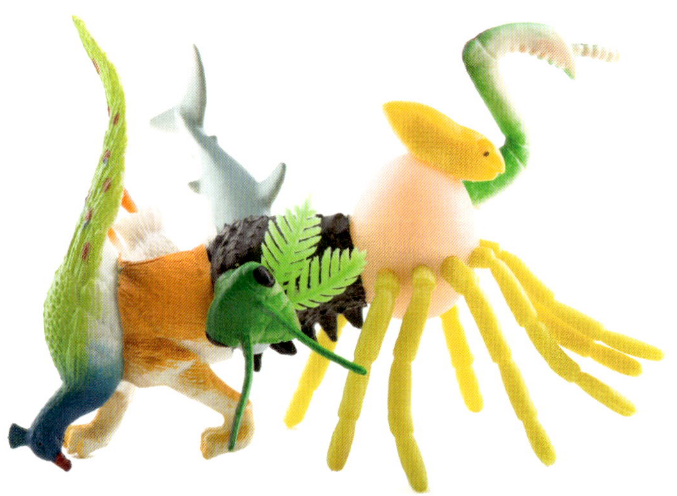

Nisadojar, Die Götter der neuen Arten, 2019
UV-Print auf Acryl
60 × 80 × 1.5 cm

Nisadojar, The Gods of New Species, 2019
UV print on acrylic
60 × 80 × 1.5 cm

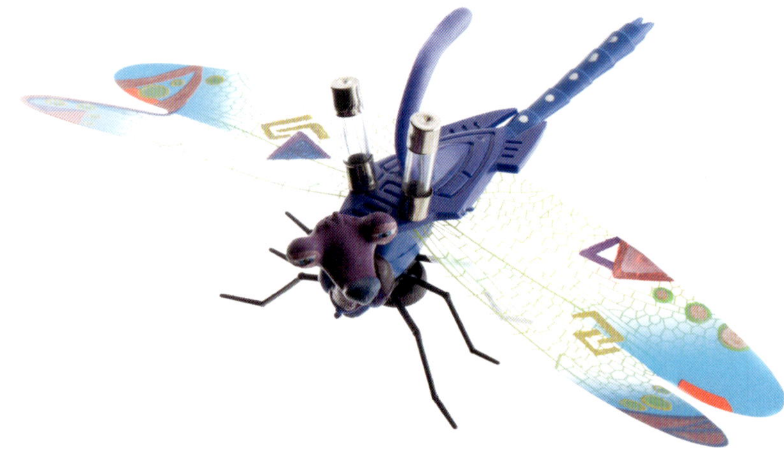

Lidragow, Die Götter der neuen Arten, 2019
UV-Print auf Acryl
60 × 80 × 1.5 cm

Lidragow, The Gods of New Species, 2019
UV print on acrylic
60 × 80 × 1.5 cm

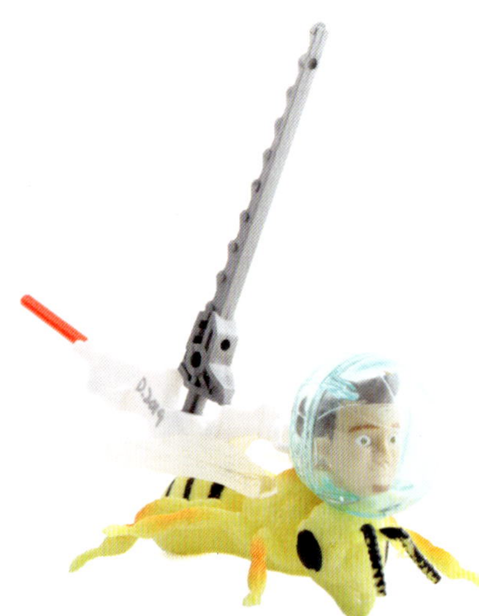

Vachisemion, Die Götter der neuen Arten, 2019
UV-Print auf Acryl
60 × 80 × 1.5 cm

Vachisemion, The Gods of New Species, 2019
UV print on acrylic
60 × 80 × 1.5 cm

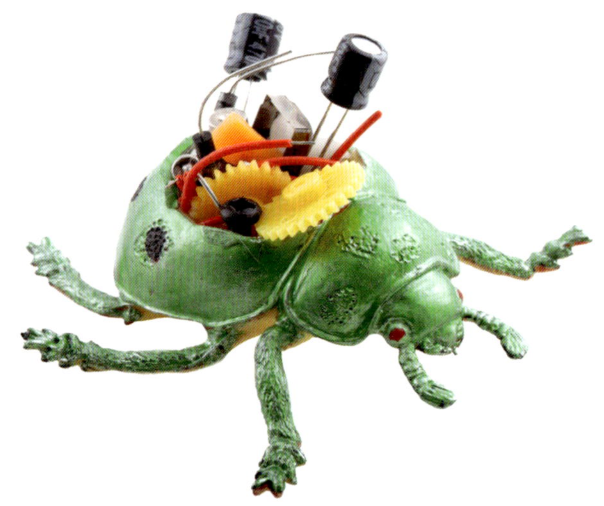

Claearsen, Die Götter der neuen Arten, 2019
UV-Print auf Acryl
60 × 80 × 1.5 cm

Claearsen, The Gods of New Species, 2019
UV print on acrylic
60 × 80 × 1.5 cm

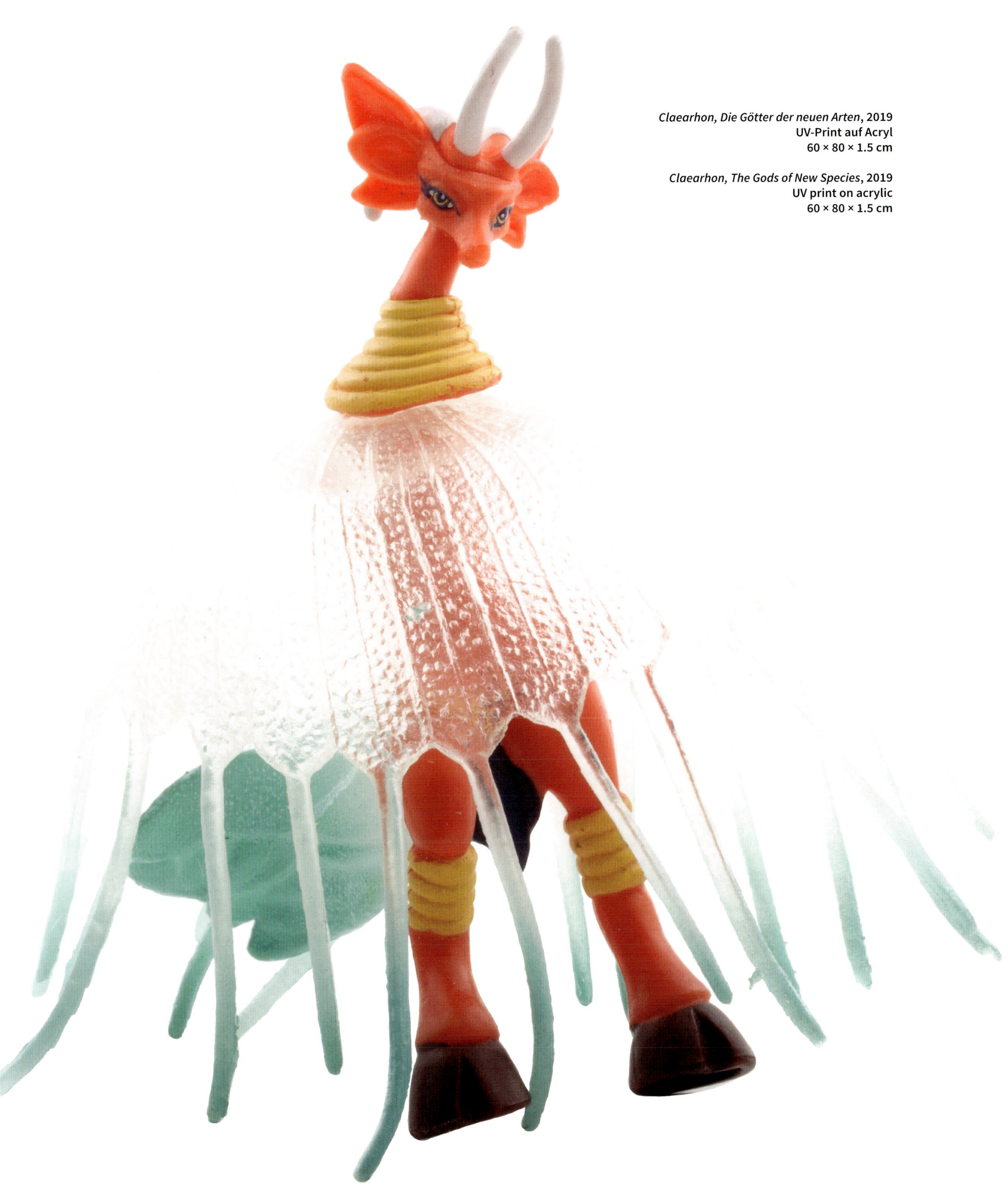

Claearhon, Die Götter der neuen Arten, **2019**
UV-Print auf Acryl
60 × 80 × 1.5 cm

Claearhon, The Gods of New Species, **2019**
UV print on acrylic
60 × 80 × 1.5 cm

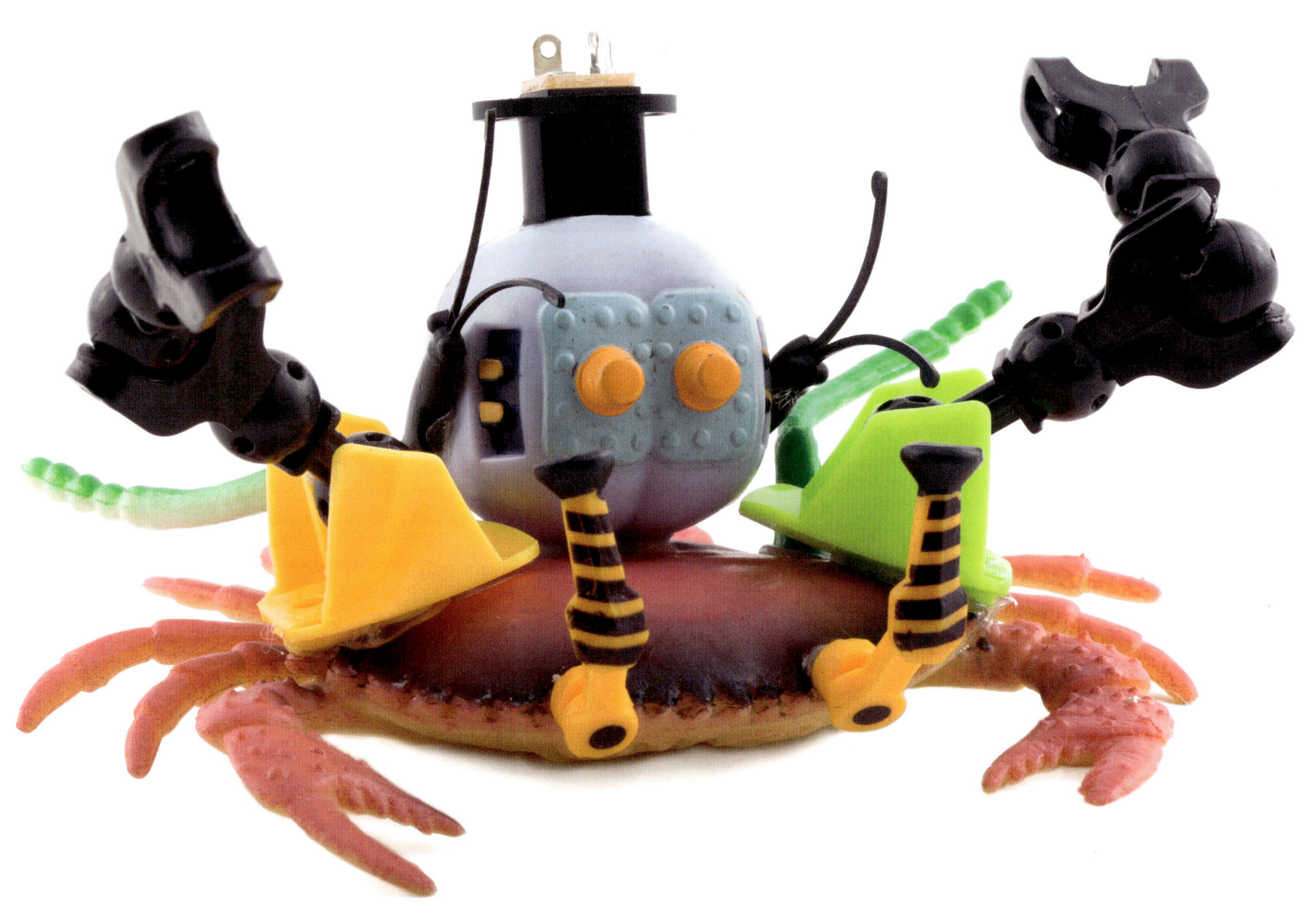

Elkporo, Die Götter der neuen Arten, 2019
UV-Print auf Acryl
60 × 80 × 1.5 cm

Elkporo, The Gods of New Species, 2019
UV print on acrylic
60 × 80 × 1.5 cm

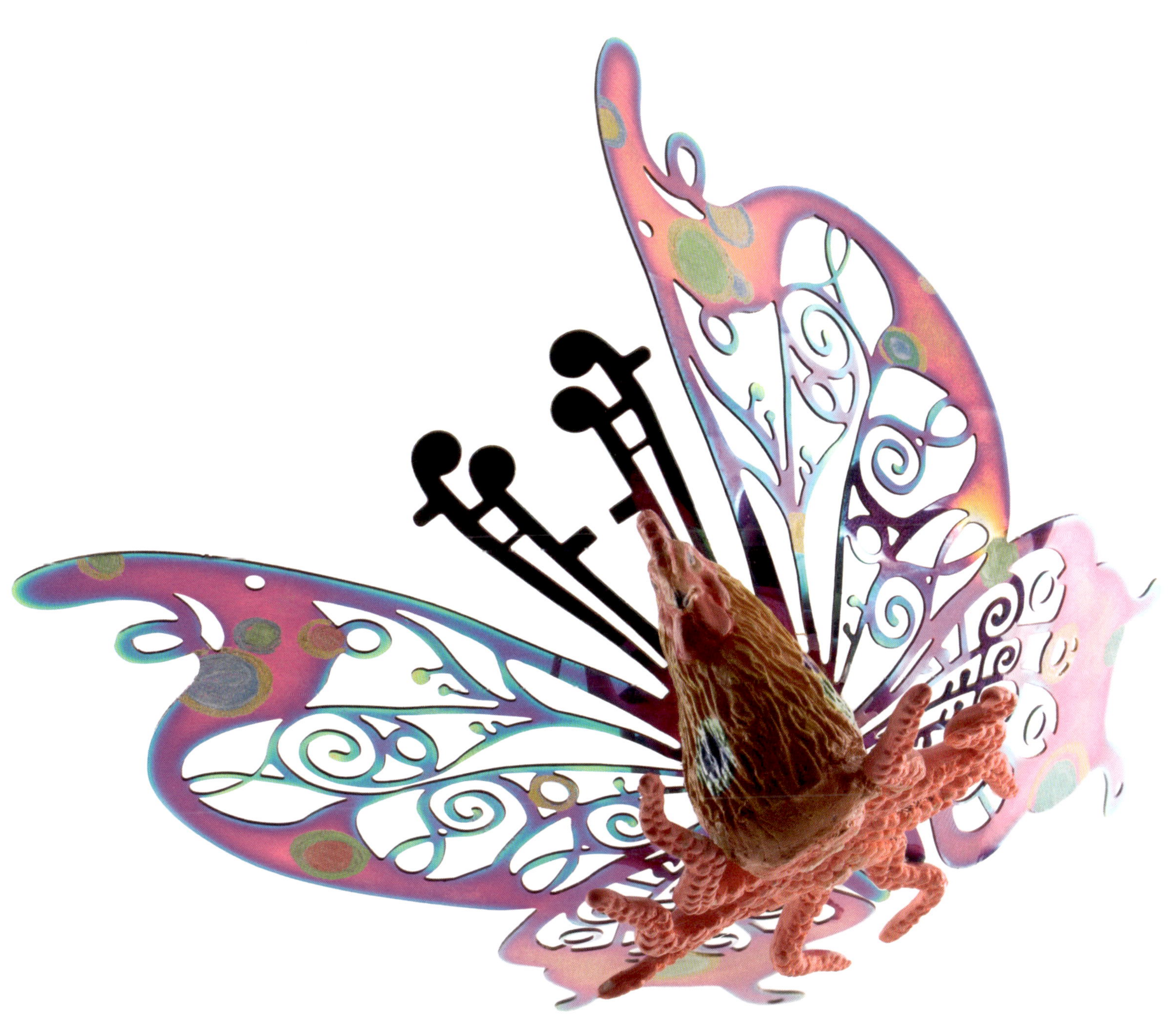

Kcins, Die Götter der neuen Arten, 2019
UV-Print auf Acryl
60 × 80 × 1.5 cm

Kcins, The Gods of New Species, 2019
UV print on acrylic
60 × 80 × 1.5 cm

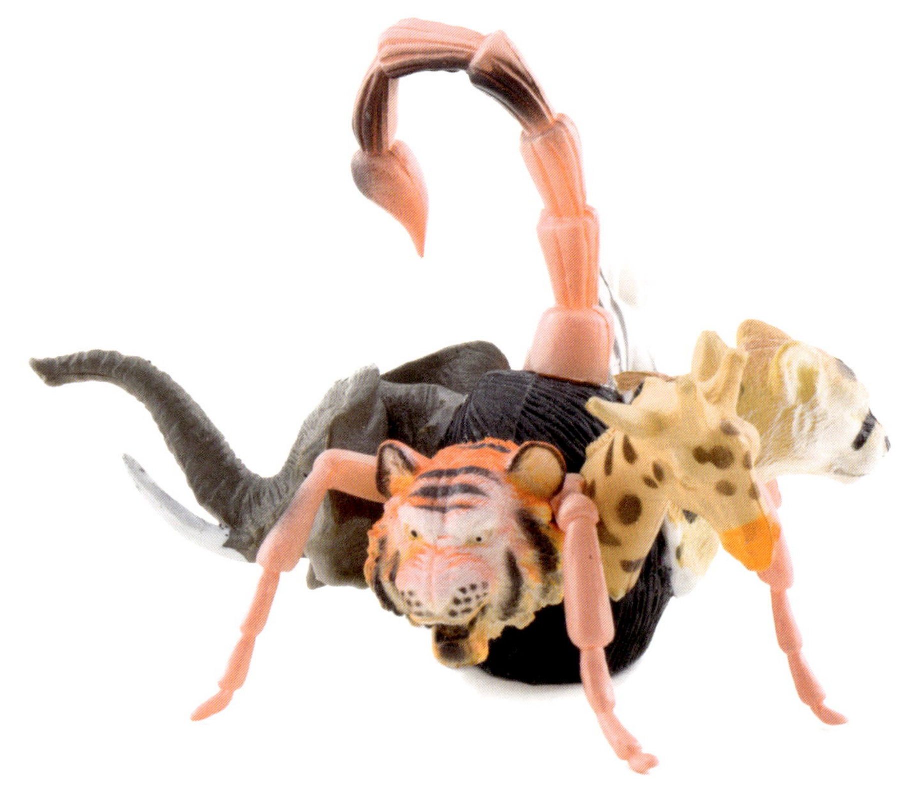

Tluxamb, Die Götter der neuen Arten, 2019
UV-Print auf Acryl
60 × 80 × 1.5 cm

Tluxamb, The Gods of New Species, 2019
UV print on acrylic
60 × 80 × 1.5 cm

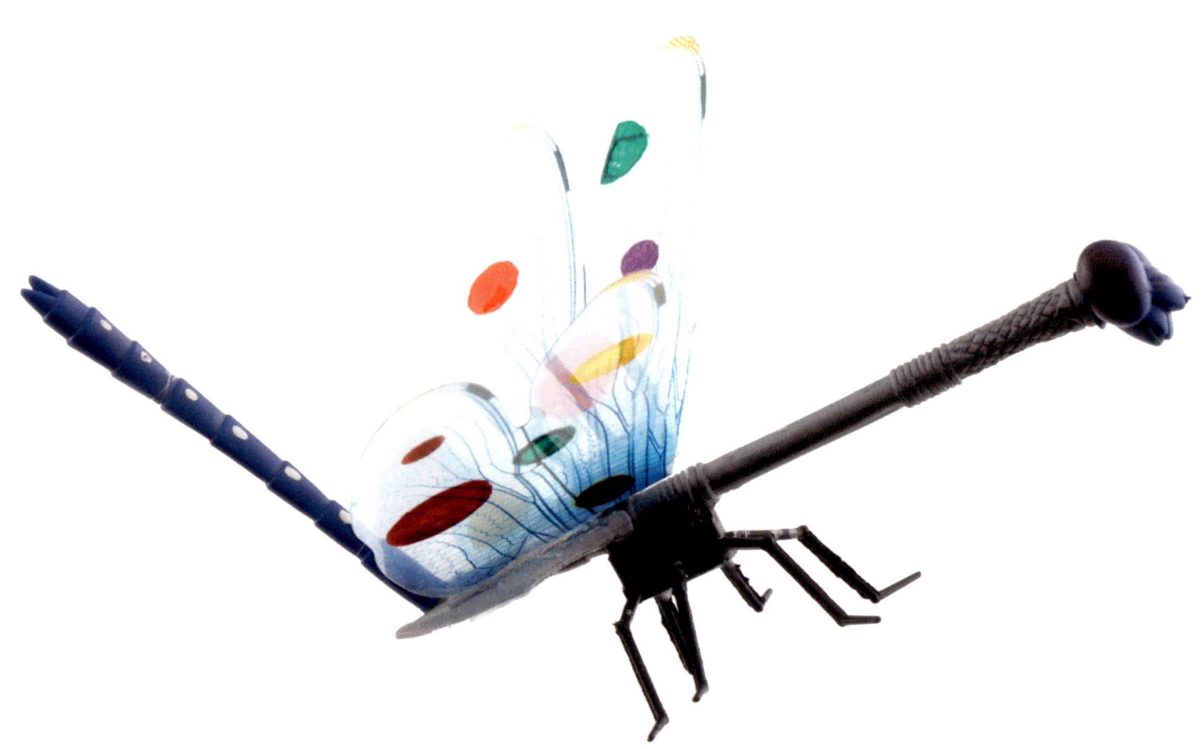

Midumon, Die Götter der neuen Arten, 2019
UV-Print auf Acryl
60 × 80 × 1.5 cm

Midumon, The Gods of New Species, 2019
UV print on acrylic
60 × 80 × 1.5 cm

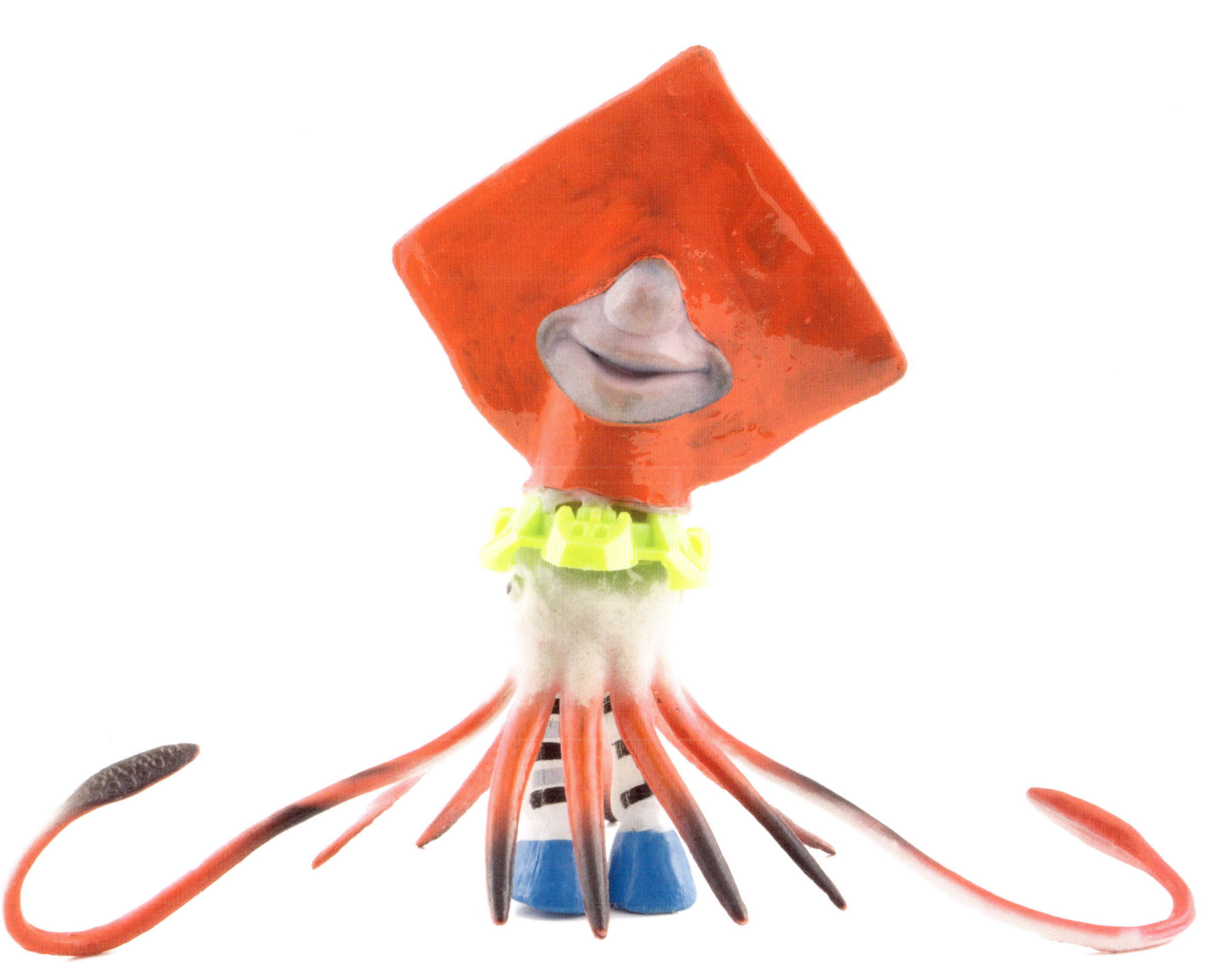

Nisayeijar, Die Götter der neuen Arten, 2019
UV-Print auf Acryl
60 × 80 × 1.5 cm

Nisayeijar, The Gods of New Species, 2019
UV print on acrylic
60 × 80 × 1.5 cm

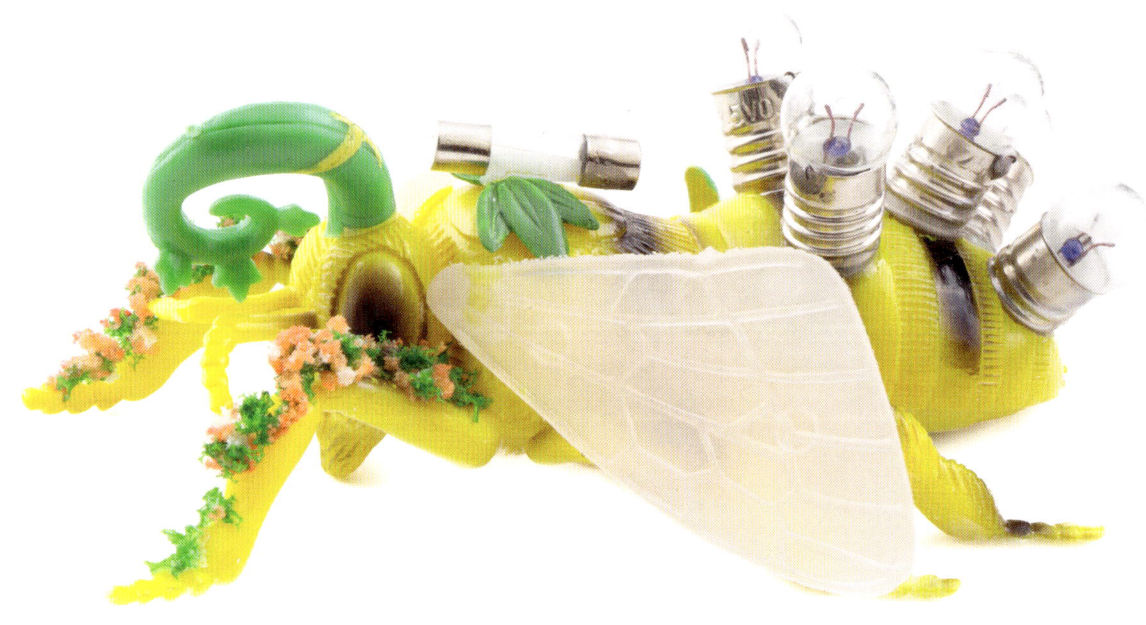

Etimota, Die Götter der neuen Arten, 2019
UV-Print auf Acryl
60 × 80 × 1.5 cm

Etimota, The Gods of New Species, 2019
UV print on acrylic
60 × 80 × 1.5 cm

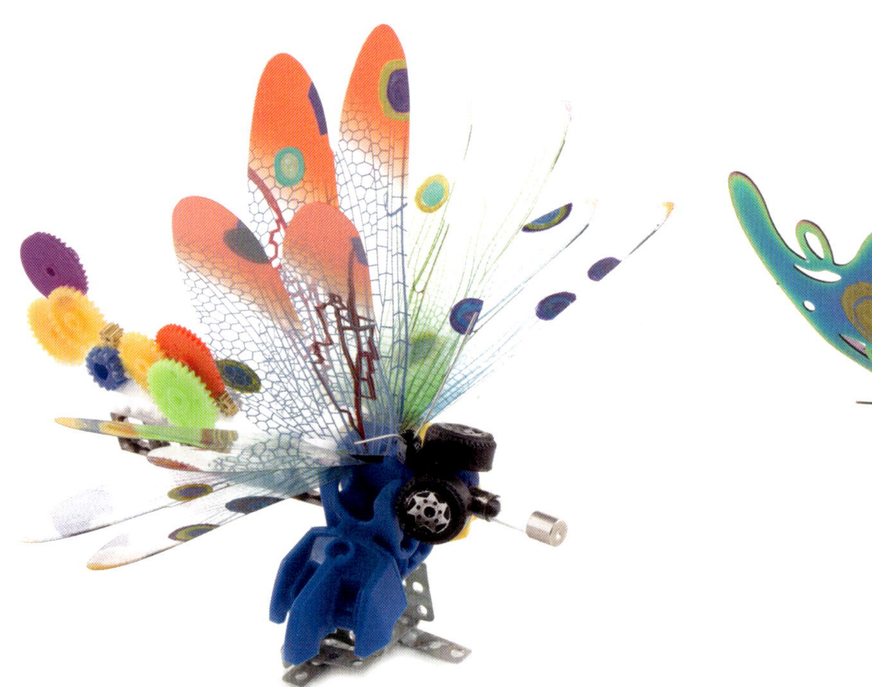

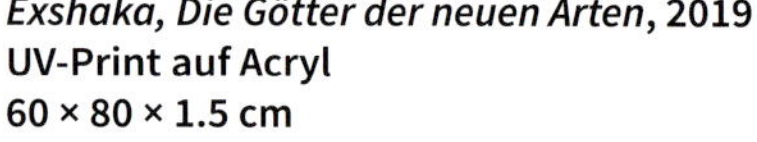

Exshaka, Die Götter der neuen Arten, 2019
UV-Print auf Acryl
60 × 80 × 1.5 cm

Exshaka, The Gods of New Species, 2019
UV print on acrylic
60 × 80 × 1.5 cm

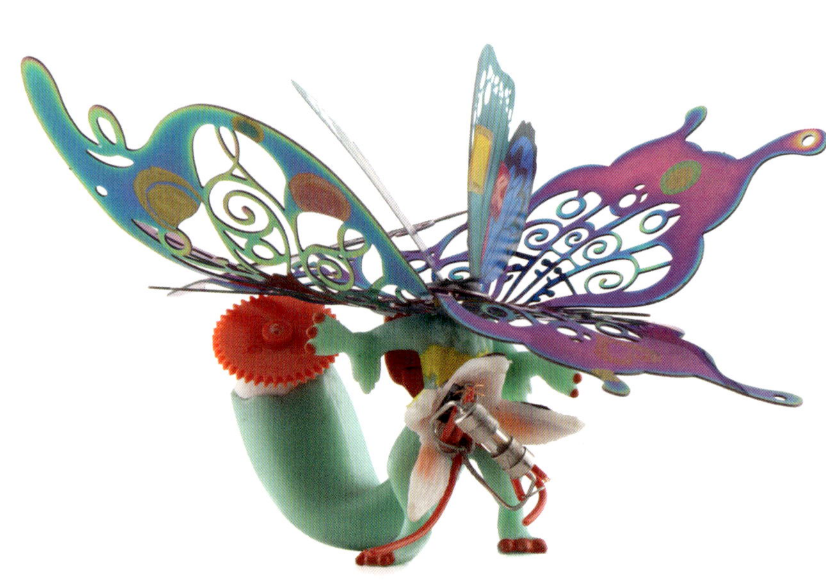

Mandahuhu, Die Götter der neuen Arten, 2019
UV-Print auf Acryl
60 × 80 × 1.5 cm

Mandahuhu, The Gods of New Species, 2019
UV print on acrylic
60 × 80 × 1.5 cm

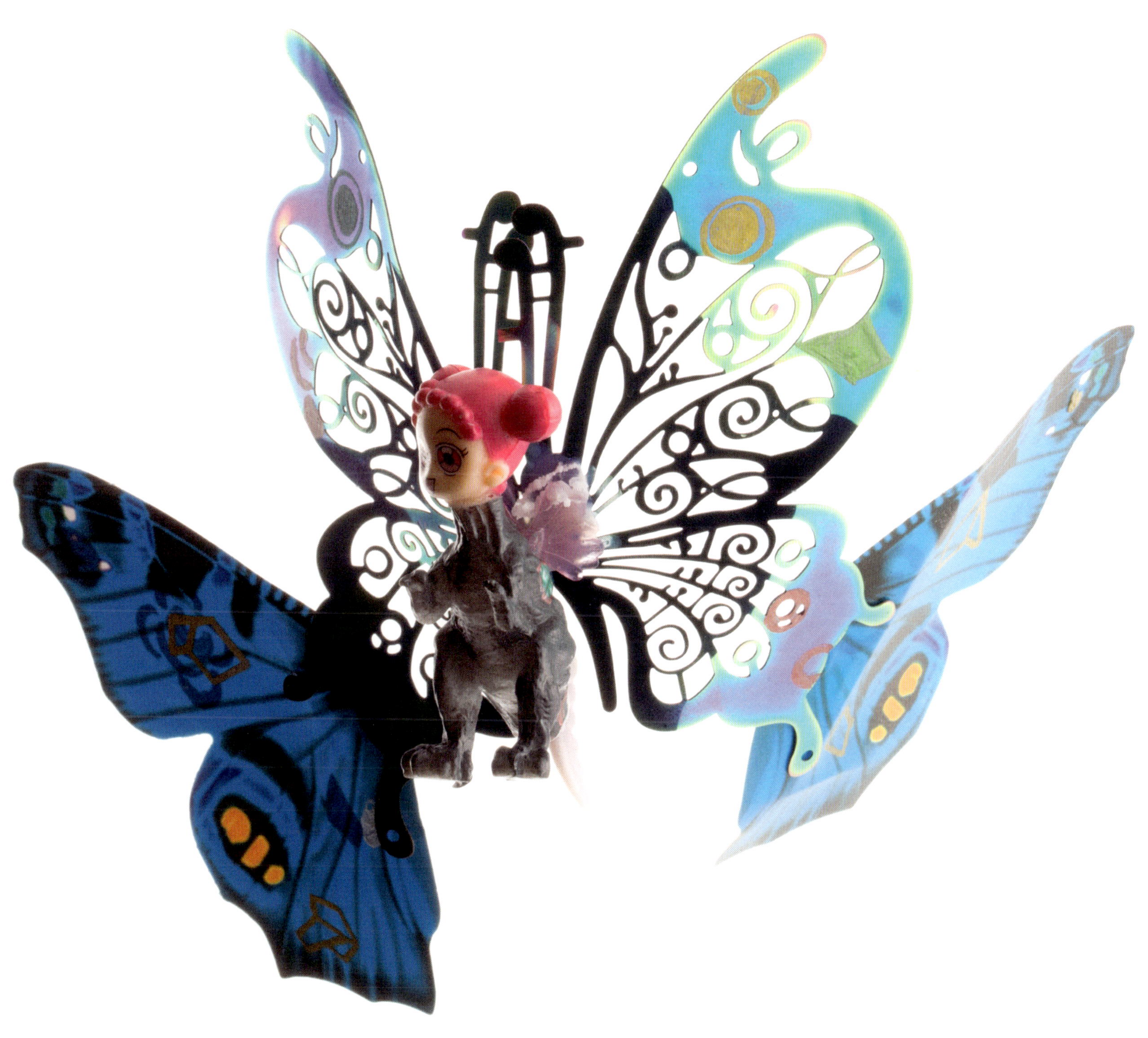

Sicredaq, Die Götter der neuen Arten, 2019
UV-Print auf Acryl
60 × 80 × 1.5 cm

Sicredaq, The Gods of New Species, 2019
UV print on acrylic
60 × 80 × 1.5 cm

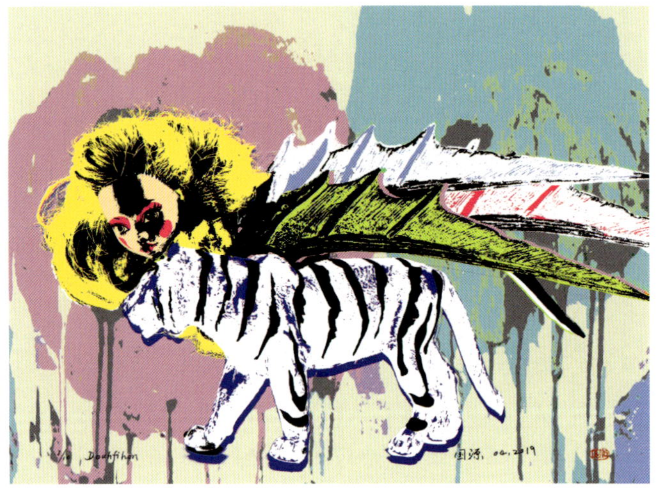

Douhfihon, 2019
Siebdruck
56 × 76 cm

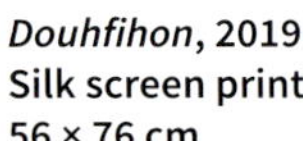

Douhfihon, 2019
Silk screen print
56 × 76 cm

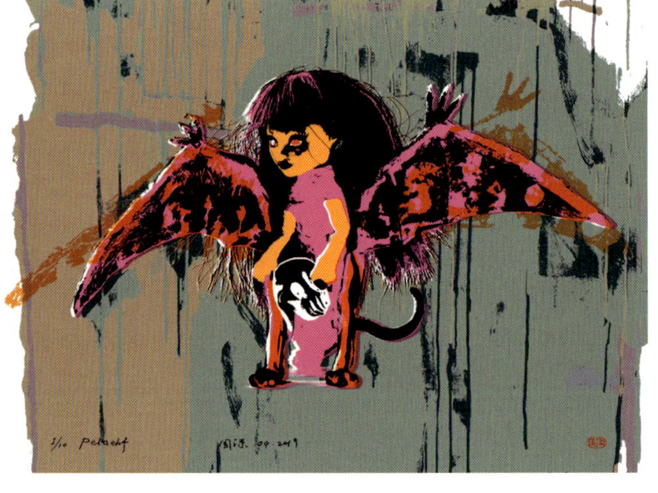

Pelaehf, 2019
Siebdruck
56 × 76 cm

Pelaehf, 2019
Silk screen print
56 × 76 cm

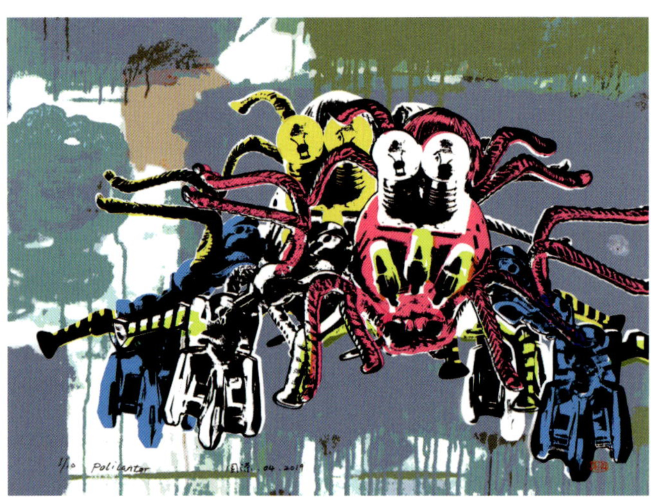

Polilantor, 2019
Siebdruck
56 × 76 cm

Polilantor, 2019
Silk screen print
56 × 76 cm

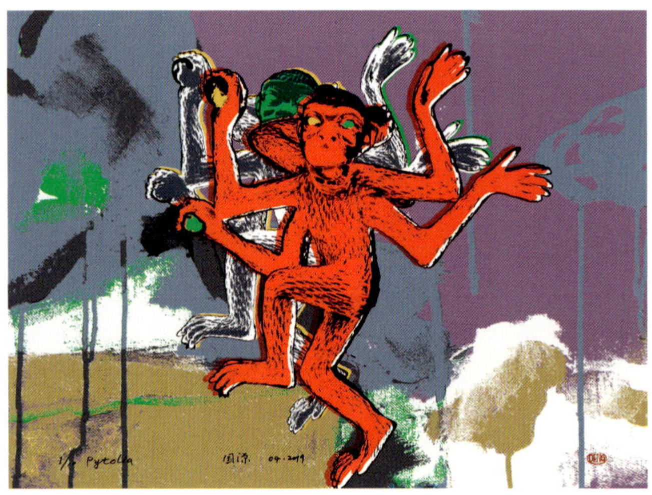

Pytolia, 2019
Siebdruck
56 × 76 cm

Pytolia, 2019
Silk screen print
56 × 76 cm

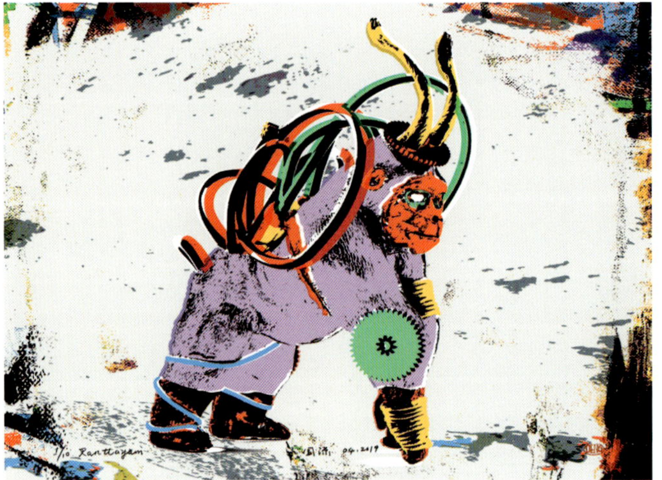

Ranttayam, 2019
Siebdruck
56 × 76 cm

Ranttayam, 2019
Silk screen print
56 × 76 cm

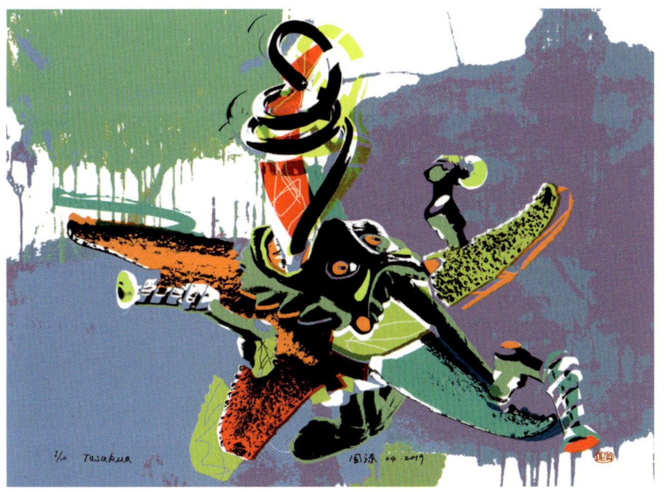

Tasakua, 2019
Siebdruck
56 × 76 cm

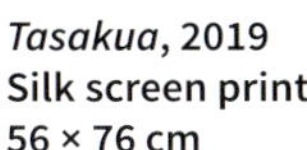

Tasakua, 2019
Silk screen print
56 × 76 cm

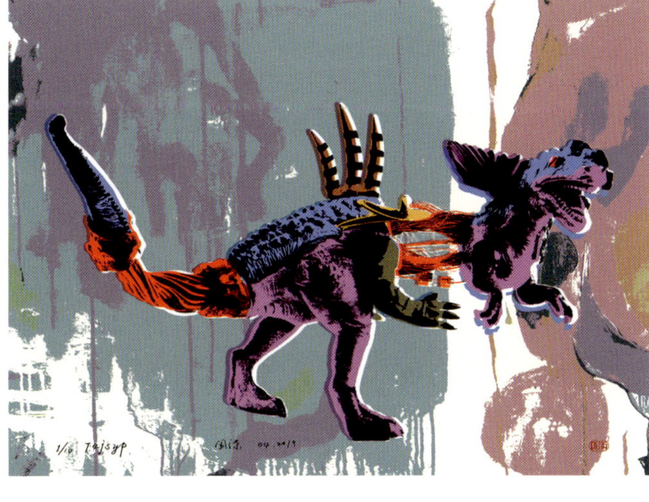

Tejsyp, 2019
Siebdruck
56 × 76 cm

Tejsyp, 2019
Silk screen print
56 × 76 cm

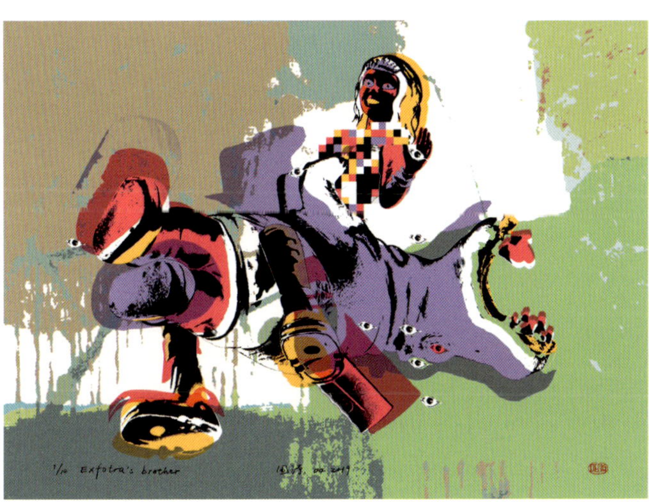

Exfotras Bruder, 2019
Siebdruck
56 × 76 cm

Exfotra's Brother, 2019
Silk screen print
56 × 76 cm

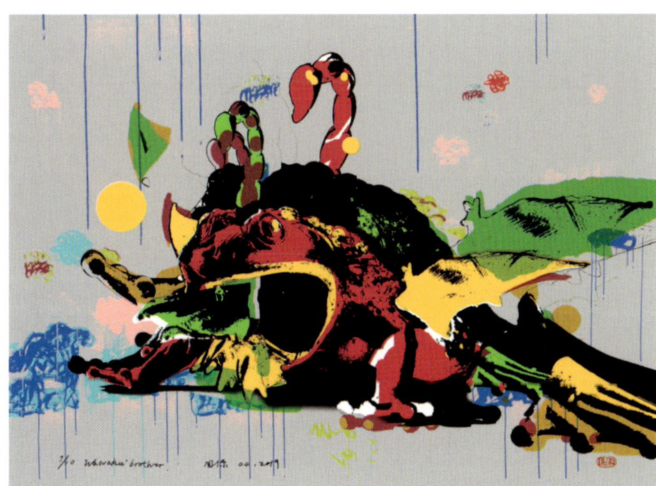

Wawakus Bruder, 2019
Siebdruck
56 × 76 cm

Wawaku's Brother, 2019
Silk screen print
56 × 76 cm

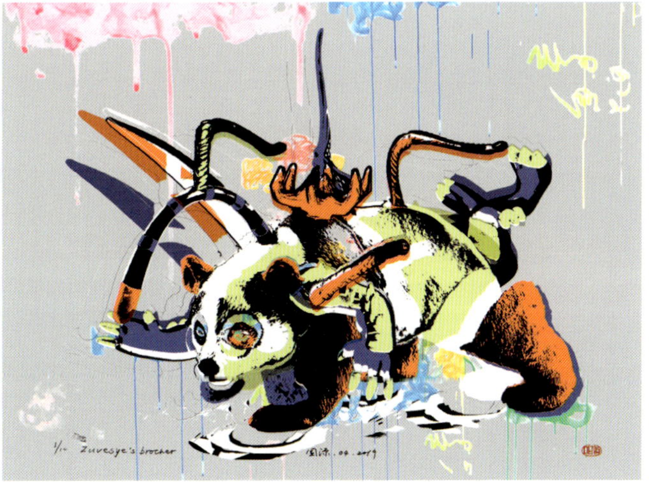

Zuvesyes Bruder, 2019
Siebdruck
56 × 76 cm

Zuvesye's Brother, 2019
Silk screen print
56 × 76 cm

Gemälde

Paintings

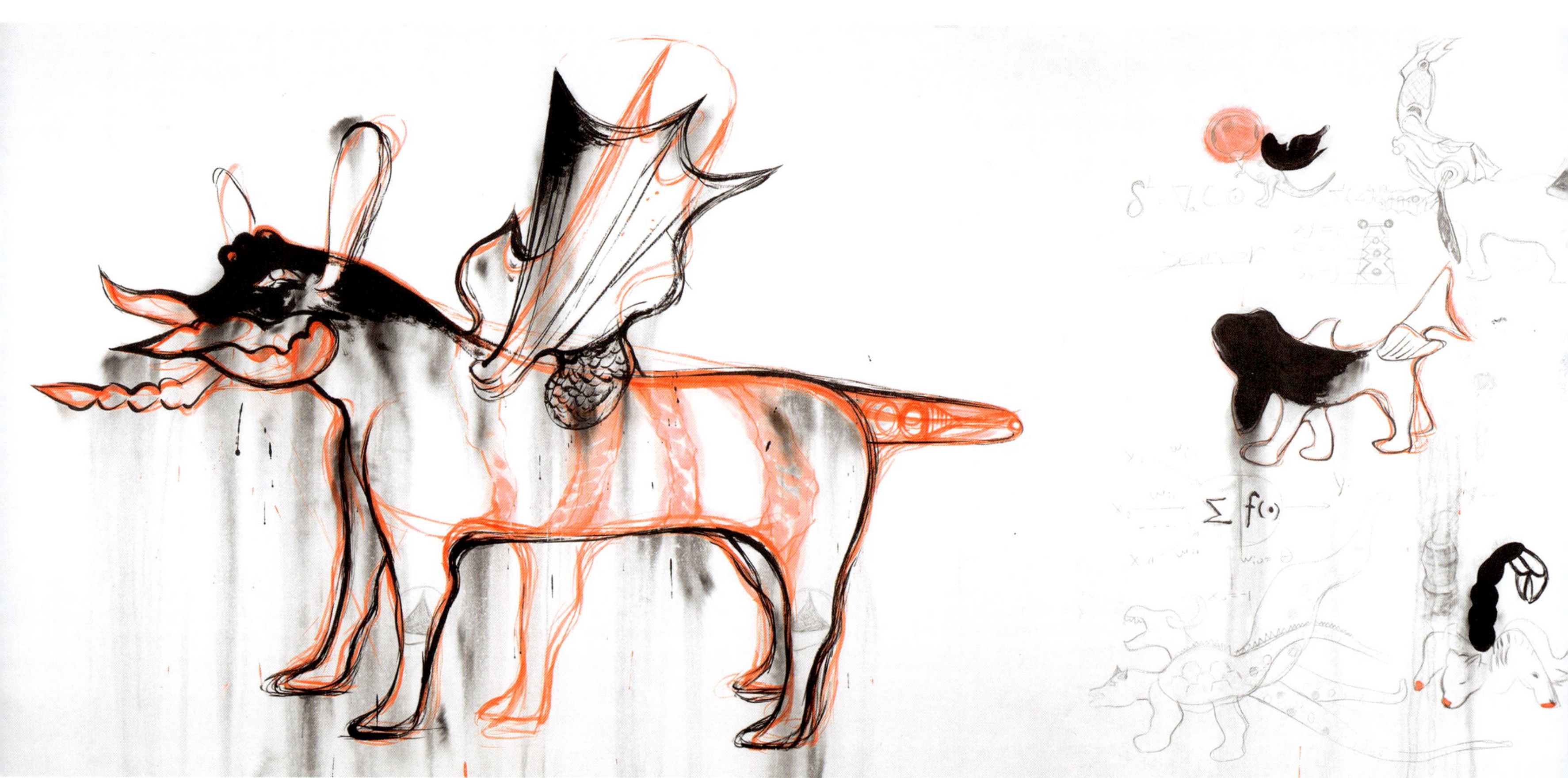

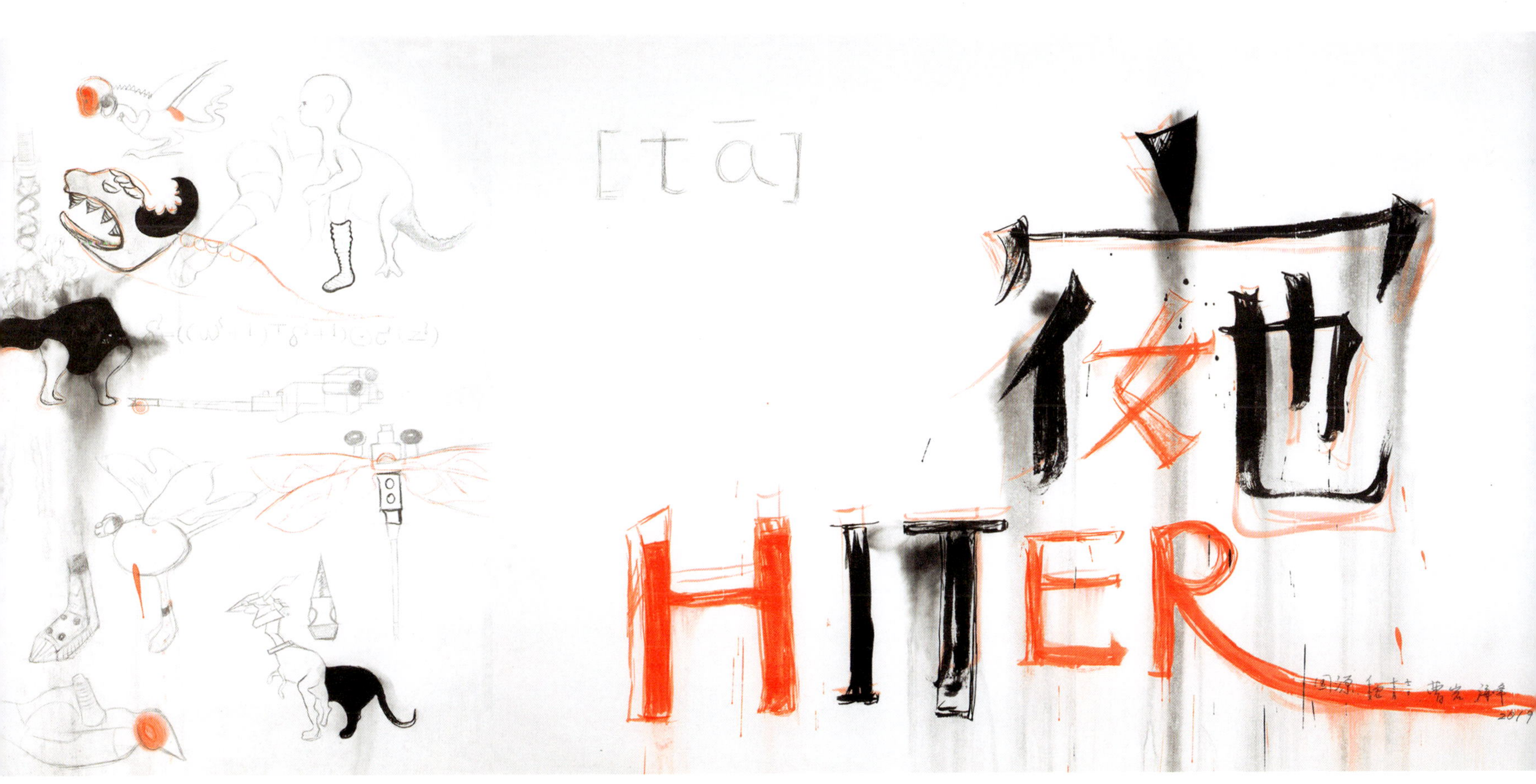

Es Sie Er, 2019
Papier, Tinte, Bleistift
600 × 140 cm

It She He, 2019
Paper, pencil, ink
600 × 140 cm

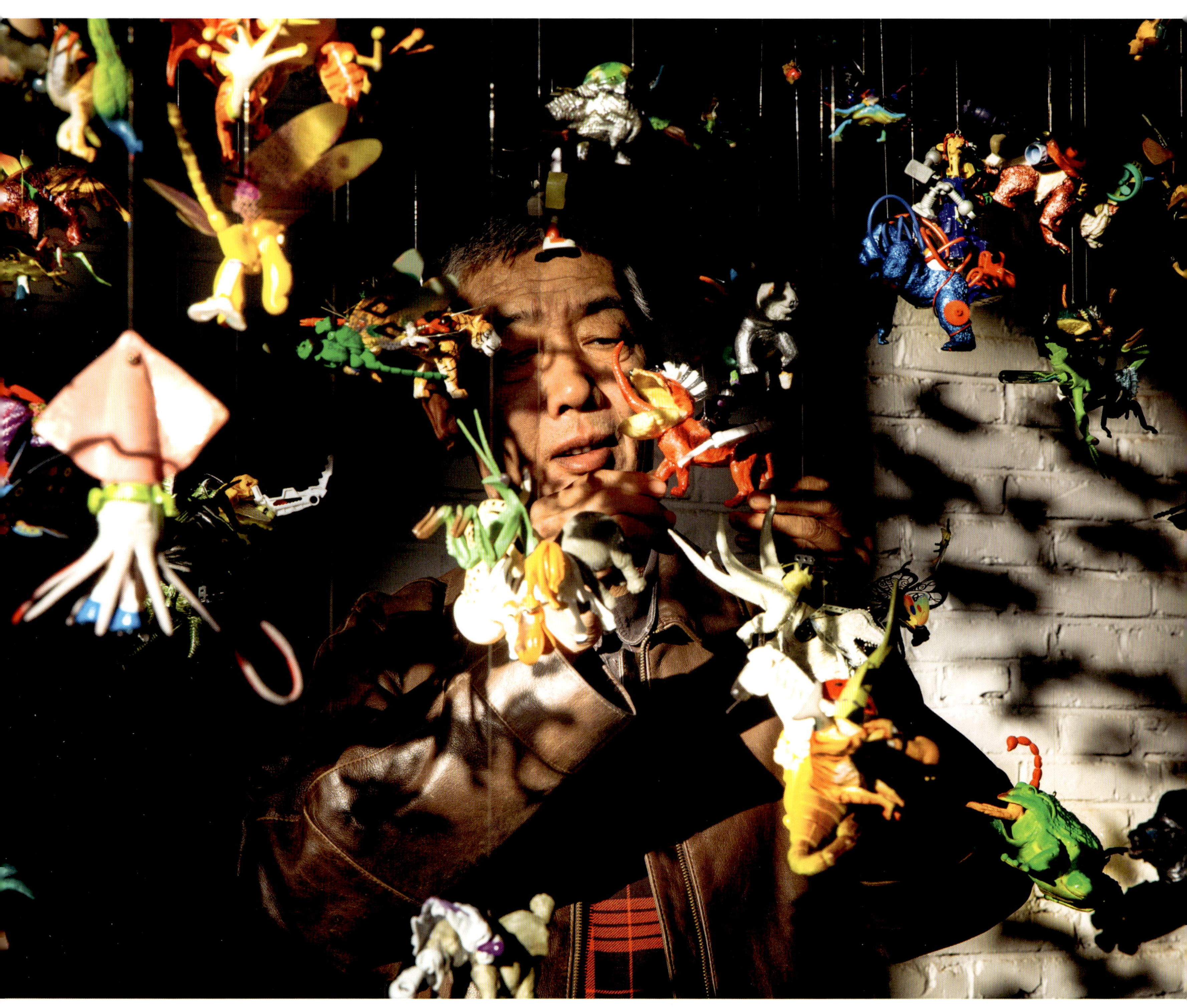

www.dengguoyuan-art.com www.dengguoyuan.org

Biografie

Deng Guoyuan, geboren 1957, lebt und arbeitet in Tianjin, China. Er ist Künstler, Professor und Präsident der Tianjin Academy of Fine Arts, Staatliche Kunstakademie.
Beginnend mit Ölmalerei, erlernt er zudem die klassische chinesische Tuschmalerei. Mitte der 1990er Jahre unternimmt er zahlreiche Reisen und längere Studienaufenthalte in Deutschland. Dort trifft er zahlreiche der aktuellen Künstler, schließt Freundschaft insbesondere mit Jörg Immerndorff und Günther Uecker, die er beide zu Ausstellungen im Kunstmuseum in Tianjin einlädt.
Seit 2000 wendet er sich installativen Arbeiten zu, beginnend mit einer Serie, die er *Noah's Garden* betitelt. Hier entwickelt er Spiegelkabinette und Pflanzenarrangements. In den letzten Jahren auch Einbeziehung von Autoschrott, aus dem er in Anlehnung an die klassische Taihu-Steine neue Skulpturen entwickelt. Klassik und zivilisatorischer Industrieschrott treffen aufeinander.
Zeitlebens engagiert er sich für die Verbesserung der aktuellen Lebensbedingungen, die er in einer überzivilisierten Welt als bedroht sieht. Seine neueste Werkserie thematisiert den gefährlichen Umgang mit Genmanipulationen.

Einzelausstellungen (Auswahl)

2019
Butterflies Conquer the Dinosaurs' Garden, Ludwig Museum, Koblenz, Deutschland.
2017
Entropy Vector Deng Guoyuan Works Exhibition, Art Tianjin, Tianjin, China.
2016
Noah's Garden, Red Brick Art Museum, Beijing, Peking, China.
The Fourth Industrial Revolution, the Power of Transformation, Hauptort von New Champions Annual Meeting of the Summer Davos, Meijiang Convention and Exhibition Center, Tianjin, China.
Lake, Garden – Deng Guoyuan West Taihu Ink Installation Exhibition, Changzhou West Taihu Art Gallery; Liu Haili Xia Yiqiao Art Gallery, Guangzhou, China.
In the Garden – Deng Guoyuan Contemporary Art Tour, Guangzhou 53 Art Gallery, großformatige Installation Kunstausstellung, Guangzhou, China.
2015-2016
In the Garden, Contemporary Art Exhibition of Deng Guoyuan, Lingnan Museum of Fine Art, Dongguan, China.
2011-2012
In the Garden, Wanderausstellung, Samek Art Museum; Bucknell University, Lewisburg, USA; Provenance Center, New London, USA; The Warehouse Museum, Syracuse, USA.
2008
In the Garden, Ludwig Museum, Koblenz, Deutschland.
2007
In the Garden, Museum of Tianjin Academy of Fine Arts, Tianjin, China.
2005
Distanz, Ralf Plein Gallery, Düsseldorf, Deutschland.
Distanz, Grevenbroich Museum, Grevenbroich, Deutschland.
2004
From the Nature in the Metropolis in Rotation, Künstlerverein Malkasten, Düsseldorf, Deutschland.

Biennalen (Auswahl)

2019
Noah's Garden II, NordArt, Hamburg, Deutschland.
2017
China International West Biennale, Inner Mongolia Art Museum, Hohhot, China.
2016
An Atlas of Mirrors, Singapore Art Museum, Singapur.
2015
Kyoto Biennale, Kyoto Art Museum, Kyoto, Japan.

Gruppenausstellungen (Auswahl)

2018
International Abstract Art Exhibition, Jinan Gallery, Xi'an, China.
The Possibility of the Abstract+- Abstract Painting in China, The Original Art Museum Chongqing, Chongqing, China.
The Sun and the Moon, Ausstellung zeitgenössischer chinesischer Kunst, Fondazione Querini Stampalia, Venedig, Italien.
2017
China International West Biennale, Inner Mongolia Art Museum, Hohhot, China.
China Contemporary Art Yearbook, Beijing Minsheng Modern Art Museum, Peking, China.
The Third Experimental Art Literature Exhibition of the Central Academy of Fine Arts Teaching and Learning, Peking, China.
Born in the Garden – Deng Guoyuans Installation, Tianjin International Design Week, Tianjin, China.
2016
An Atlas of Mirrors, Singapore Art Gallery, Singapur.
2015
The 11th China International Gallery Exposition, China National Convention Center, Peking, China.
Beyond Boundary, TEDA Contemporary Art Museum, Tianjin, China.
Quality and Style – Chinese Oil Painter Invitational Exhibition, 1929 Art Space, Shanghai, China.

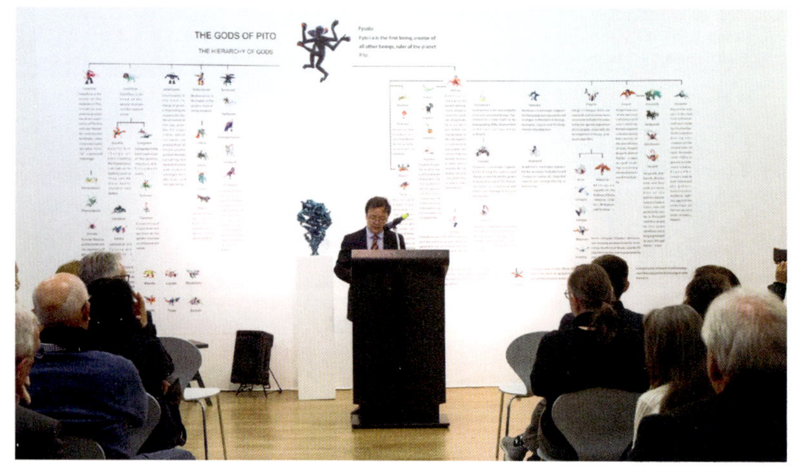
THE GODS OF PITO
THE HIERARCHY OF GODS

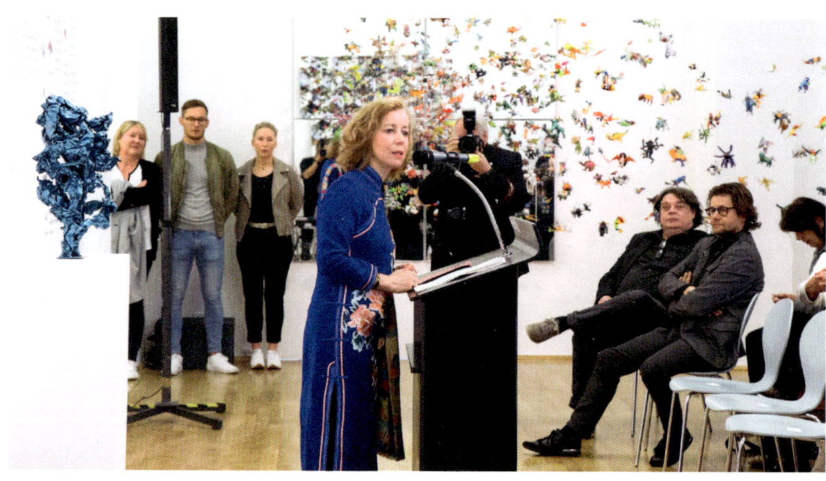

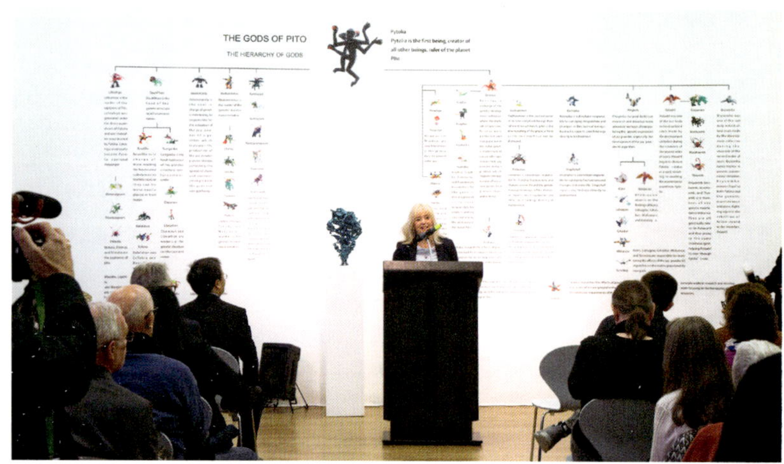
THE GODS OF PITO
THE HIERARCHY OF GODS

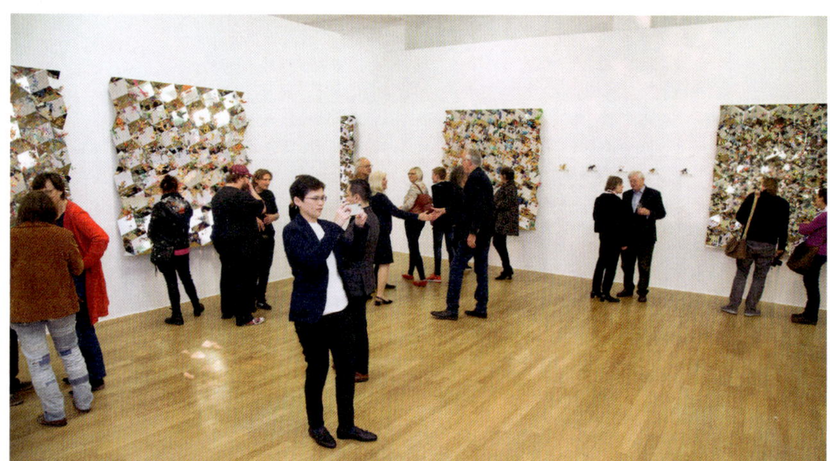

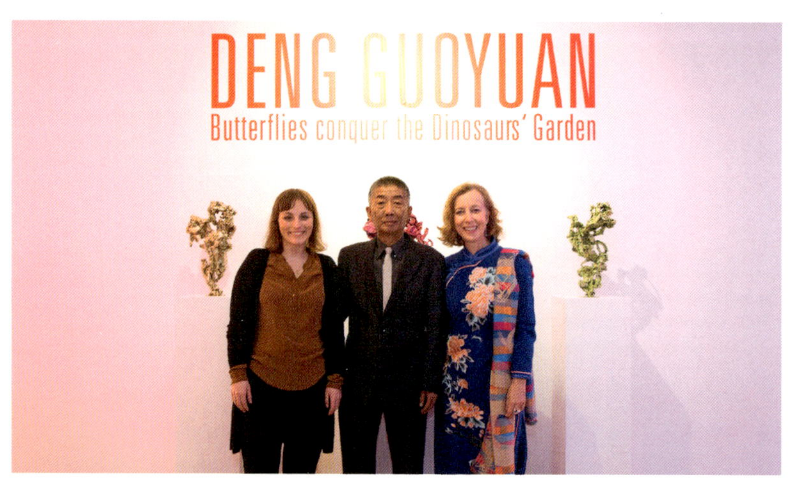
DENG GUOYUAN
Butterflies conquer the Dinosaurs' Garden

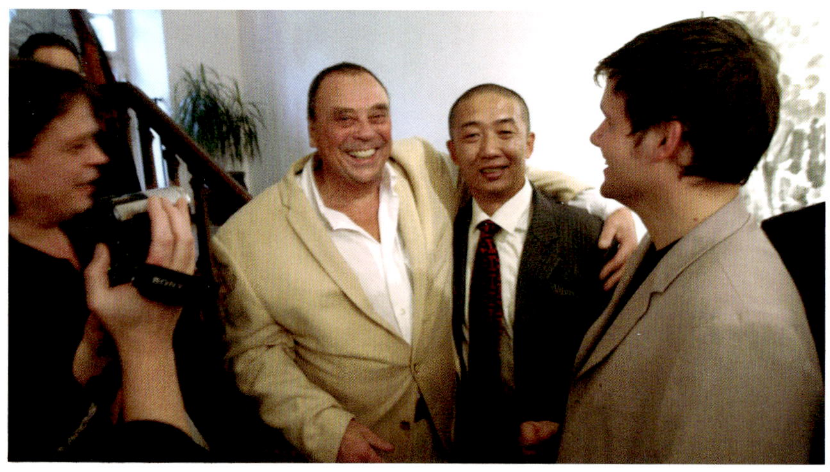

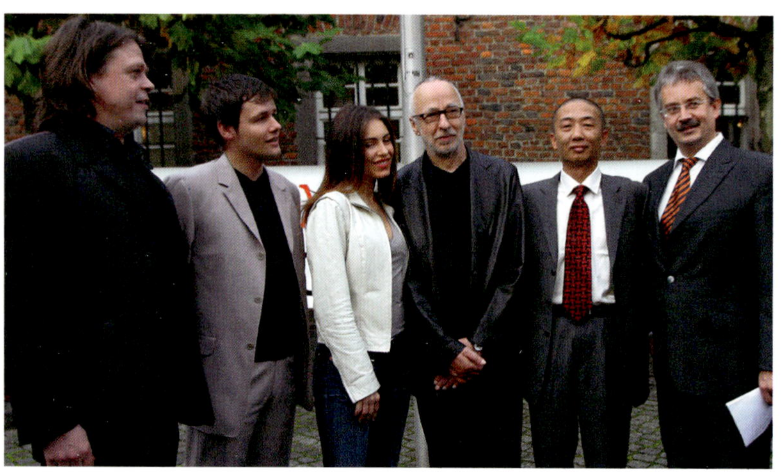

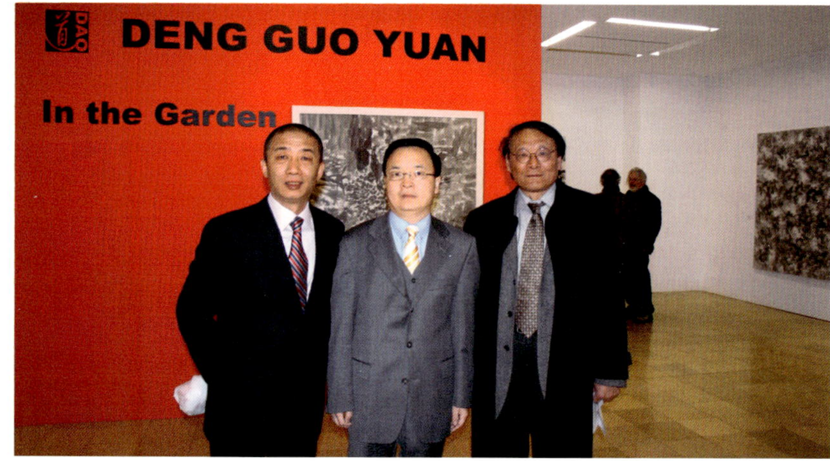
DENG GUO YUAN
In the Garden

Biography

Deng Guoyuan, born in 1957 in Tianjin. He is a famous artist, as well as teaching professor and president of the Tianjin Academy of Fine Arts, State Art Academy. Starting with oil painting, he also learned classical Chinese ink painting. In the mid-1990s he made numerous trips and longer study visits in Germany. There he met many of the current artists, and became friend in particular with Jörg Immerndorff and Günther Uecker, whom he invited both to exhibit at the TAFA Art Museum in Tianjin.

Since 2000 he has turned to installation work, starting with a series he titled *Noah's Garden*. Here he develops mirror cabinets and plant arrangements.

In recent years he started including car scraps, from which he developed new sculptures based on the classic Taihu stones. Classical tradition and Industrial civilization clash each other. Throughout his life, he is committed to improving the current living conditions, which he sees as threatened in an over-civilized world.

His latest work series addresses the dangerous experiments of genetic manipulation.

Solo Exhibitions

2019

"Butterflies Conquer the Dinosaurs' Garden," Ludwig Museum, Koblenz, Germany.

2017

"Entropy Vector Deng Guoyuan Works Exhibition," Art Tianjin, Tianjin, China.

2016

"Noah's Garden," Red Brick Art Museum, Beijing, China.

"The Fourth Industrial Revolution, the Power of Transformation," in the main venue of the New Champions Annual Meeting of the Summer Davos, Meijiang Convention and Exhibition Center, Tianjin, China.

"Lake, Garden – Deng Guoyuan West Taihu Ink Installation Exhibition," Changzhou West Taihu Art Gallery, Liu Haili Xia Yiqiao Art Gallery, Changzhou, China.

"In the Garden – Deng Guoyuan Contemporary Art Tour," Guangzhou 53 Art Gallery, large-scale installation art exhibition, Guangzhou, China.

2015-2016

"In the Garden – Contemporary Art Exhibition of Deng Guoyuan," Lingnan Museum of Fine Art, Dongguan, China.

2011-2012

"In the Garden, Tour Exhibition," Samek Art Museum, Bucknell University, USA; Provenance Center, New London, USA; The Warehouse Museum, Syracuse, USA.

2008

"In the Garden," Ludwig Museum, Koblenz, Germany.

2007

"In the Garden," Museum of Tianjin Academy of Fine Arts, Tianjin, China.

2005

"Distanz," Ralf Plein Gallery, Dusseldorf, Germany.

"Distanz," Grevenbroich Museum, Germany.

2004

"From the Nature in the Metropolis in Rotation," Dusseldorf Kunstlerverein, Malkasten, Germany.

Biennials

2019

"Noah's Garden II – Nord Art," Hamburg, Germany.

2017

"International Abstract Art Exhibition," Jinan Gallery, Xi'an, China.

2016

"An Atlas of Mirrors," Singapore Art Museum, Singapore.

2015

"Kyoto Biennale," Kyoto Art Museum, Japan.

Group Exhibitions

2018

"International Abstract Art Exhibition," Jinan Gallery, Xi'an, China.

"The Possibility of the Abstract+-Abstract Painting in China," The Original Art Museum Chongqing, Chongqing, China.

"The Sun and the Moon," Chinese Contemporary Art Exhibition, Fondazione Querini Stampalia, Venice, Italy.

2017

"China International West Biennale," Inner Mongolia Art Museum, Hohhot, China.

"China Contemporary Art Yearbook," Beijing Minsheng Modern Art Museum, Beijing, China.

"The Third Experimental Art Literature Exhibition of the Central Academy of Fine Arts Teaching and Learning," Beijing, China.

"Born in the Garden – Deng Guoyuan's Installation Art Exhibition," Tianjin international design week, Tianjin, China.

2016

"An Atlas Of Mirrors," Singapore Art Gallery, Singapore.

2015

"The 11th China International Gallery Exposition," China National Convention Center, Beijing, China.

"Beyond Boundary," TEDA Contemporary Art Museum, Tianjin, China.

"Quality and Style – Chinese Oil Painter Invitational Exhibition," 1929 Art Space, Shanghai, China.

Cover
Sterben der Götter, 2019, Detail
Passing of the Gods, 2019, detail

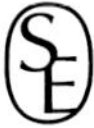

Silvana Editoriale

Direction
Dario Cimorelli

Verlagsleiter / Direction
Dario Cimorelli

Art Director
Giacomo Merli

Redaktionskoordinator / Editorial Coordinator
Sergio Di Stefano

Korrektoren / Copy Editors
Fabiola Beretta
Clia Menici

Layout und Textsatz / Layout
Diego Mantica

Produktionskoordination / Production Coordinator
Antonio Micelli

Redaktionsassistentin / Editorial Assistant
Ondina Granato

Photo Editors
Alessandra Olivari, Silvia Sala

Pressestelle / Press Office
Lidia Masolini, press@silvanaeditoriale.it

Silvana Editoriale S.p.A.
via dei Lavoratori, 78
20092 Cinisello Balsamo, Milano
tel. 02 453 951 01
fax 02 453 951 51
www.silvanaeditoriale.it

Reproduktionen, Druck und Einbindung wurden in Italien ausgeführt
Reproductions, printing and binding in Italy
Gedruckt von / Printed by Grafiche Antiga, Crocetta del Montello (TV)
Fertig gedruckt im Mai 2019
Printed in May 2019